MUNDA–MAGYAR–MAORI

MUNDA–MAGYAR–MAORI

AN INDIAN LINK BETWEEN THE ANTIPODES

NEW TRACKS OF HUNGARIAN ORIG

F.A. Uxbond

GYAN

Published by

Gyan Publishing House
5, Ansari Road
Daryaganj, New Delhi-110002
Phone: 011-47034999, 9811692060
E-mail: books@gyanbooks.com

Distribution Network
gyanbooks.com
India, USA, Canada, UK, Australia, France

ISBN: 978-81-212-0892-5 (HB)

Reprint in India, 2024
First Published, 2006

Printed at: Gyan Press, Delhi.

MundaMagyarMaori an Indian Link Between the Antipodes New Track of Hungarian Origins
Author: F.A. Uxbond

CONTENTS.

PART II.

THE MUNDA, THE LINK BETWEEN MAGYAR AND MAORI.

INTRODUCTION.

General Division.—The Magyar.—The Maori.—Phonetics.—Sources.—The Indian Munda.

General Division. When studying the *Polynesian*, such as the Maori people of New Zealand, we come across certain aspects, which, curiously enough, are suggestive of the Hungarian, or *Magyar*. The apparent points of contact between them are more numerous than one would believe. In any case, they seem worthy of publication, as they may perhaps give an impulse to a thorough scientific investigation of questions, which can only be treated here superficially, that is in their general outlines.

The affair becomes of overwhelming interest, when in research of a link possibly connecting the two antipodal people, we come upon India and its Munda nations. The second, and in this way the more important part of the present study (Chapters X.–XV.) is devoted to this latter. The first part (Chapters I.–IX.) will deal with the enumeration and comparison of some points of contact in religion, culture, social institutions, habits of life, and especially of language, between *Magyar and Maori.*

The Magyar. When in this comparative study the term " Magyar " is used, the inhabitants of the Carpathian basin are meant, who speak the Magyar language (dialects). For the correct pronunciation of the words of this language as quoted here, information may be found in any grammar. However, it may be mentioned that every vowel may be short or long, and that the latter sounds are represented in writing by accents. The written language also includes a certain quantity of double consonants, such as *cs, gy, ly, ny, sz, ty* and *zs*, which are all single sounds.[1] The *s* of Magyar corresponds to the English sh.

[1] Short vowels, long vowels, double consonants of the Magyar language are pronounced approximately as follows :—

Short Vowels.	Long Vowels.
a like the a in " accord "	á like the a in " father "
e ,, ,, e ,, " belt "	é ,, ,, ay ,, " bay "
i ,, ,, i ,, " lift "	í ,, ,, ea ,, " means "
o ,, ,, o ,, " hot "	ó ,, ,, oa ,, " load "
ö ,, ,, u ,, " but "	ő ,, ,, u ,, " burnt "
u ,, ,, u ,, " pull "	ú ,, ,, oo ,, " cool "
ü ,, ,, u ,, French " vu "	ű ,, ,, u ,, " overture "

Double Consonants.

cs like ch in " cherry "	ny ,, n ,, " news "
c (cz) ,, c ,, " cistern "	sz ,, sc ,, " science "
gy ,, j ,, " July "	ty ,, t ,, " tulip "
ly ,, l ,, " volume "	zs ,, s ,, " pleasure "

The Maori.[1] It is only the Polynesian of some of the Pacific Islands who call themselves "Maori", as for instance those of New Zealand, of Rarotonga, Cook Island, etc. (Those of Hawaii sometimes call themselves "Maoli".) Yet the natives of the whole of Polynesia, that is to say of the enormous area embraced by a triangle, the extremities of which are formed by the Sandwich Islands (Hawaii), Easter Island (Rapanui) and New Zealand, belong to the same stock as regards language. The language within this area, spoken in the islands (archipelagos) of Mangarewa (Gambier Islands), Marquesas, Paumotu, Samoa, Tahiti, Tonga, etc., have not more pronounced differences than is usual with dialects of the same speech; and even the ethnographical (anthropological) characteristics of the inhabitants of the various parts are often the same.

Therefore, hereafter, instead of the usual denomination Polynesian, Maori-Polynesian, the expression "Maori" will be used, this as a pure "terminus technicus" for the whole of the Polynesian tribes who speak the same language (dialects), as the natives of New Zealand; a procedure already adopted by some authors.[2] (In this connection however it should be borne in mind, that the Maori of New Zealand have risen to a much higher level of civilization than the inhabitants of the other Pacific Islands; their kinsmen have often been entrusted with high public functions, have entered the liberal professions, have become Members of Parliament, have been given English titles of knighthood, etc., etc.)

Phonetics. When the first missionaries appeared in the South Seas,—the English, in Tahiti, in 1796—the choice of characters was influenced by technical printing limitations.[3] It was then accepted as a rule, that vowels should be written according to *Italian orthography*, and consonants as in English, with the exception of *w*, which was printed, as in Italian, *v*. The French missionaries, who came later, adopted the system of their English predecessors, and this even in the phonetic script of the French sound *ou*, utilizing for it, as well as for the *w*, the Italian orthography.[4]

The right accentuation of vowels,[5] with regard to their short-

[1] This name has various meanings. According to Cowan (P. 12) it means: indigenous, not foreign, native. See also Hoani Nahe: "Maori and Tangata Maori." In *Journ. Pol. Soc.*, 1894. P. 32.

[2] Reclus: *Nouvelle Géographie Universelle.* Vol. XIV. P. 912.—Jaussen: "Dictionnaire de la Langue Maorie, *Dialecte Tahitien.*"

[3] Churchill: *Easter Island.* Chapt. I. (Polynesian Alphabet).

[4] Special attention should be paid to the double consonants *ng* and *wh* used in New Zealand, the former having the sound of the nasal *n* in the French word "encore" and the latter resembling an aspirated w.

[5] Double vowels (ae, iu, etc.) ought to be pronounced always separately.

ness or length, is of the greatest importance in Maori, because the meaning of a word depends on it. Yet the use of phonetic marks for the pronunciation had nevertheless to be abandoned for the following reasons :—

Such marks vary considerably with the authors who make use of them. For instance, some dictionaries indicate the sustaining of a vowel sound by putting a dash above the letter. Others repeat the vowel up to even three times; or they help matters by using various accents (such as á, à, etc.). Further, as the object of this study is by no means a strictly linguistic one, the Maori words quoted (as well as the Munda words), *are intended chiefly to illustrate outstanding aspects.* Thus the phonetic signs will be used extensively for English, French, German, Magyar and Latin words only. (For Munda partially.)

Sources.

Concerning the source of the Maori words, reference will always be made, in brackets, to the island where the words are in use, to the vocabulary to which they belong, and to the name of the author, whose dictionary (or other work) contains the expressions in question.[1] As the greater part of the quotations are of New Zealand origin, in such cases no mention is made of any particular island. Statements of this study drawn from other sources are always indicated in footnotes mentioning the name of the author and the page of his work. The full title of such works will be found in the Bibliography at the end. In case there should be several works by the same author used as sources, the footnotes of course, contain the necessary indications. Words, to which the name of Churchill is added in brackets, are taken from the dictionary of the Rapanui (Easter Island) speech, collected by Hippolyte Roussel,[2] completed and translated into English by Churchill.

At the risk of becoming tedious, sources are quoted as much as possible, because in this way the real purpose of the study may best be served, namely to further future research.

The Indian Munda.

As regards the Indian nations in general, and more especially those which may prove a link between Magyar and Maori, the *Munda*, full information will be found in the second part (Chapters X.–XV.). Here we will only mention, that if a *Santal*, to-day the most numerous of the Munda tribes, is questioned about his name and cast, he usually applies to himself the title "Manjhi", i.e. an important man, a headman.[3] In the same language "ara"

[1] E.g.: "(Samoa, Violette)," meaning that the word quoted is a Samoan and is to be found in Violette's Dictionary.

[2] H. Roussel: *Vocabulaire de la Langue de l'Ile-de-Pâques ou Rapanui.* Published in "Le Museum". Louvain. 1908.

[3] Grierson: *Linguistic Survey of India.* Vol. IV. Part I. Pages 30 and 145.— The Santal "jh" should be pronounced like the Magyar "gy", "dzs"; the letter "h" only showing an aspirated pronunciation of the "j".

denotes : a flock, an army, a crowd, and " ari " : much, many.[1] The noted Hungarian scholar Munkácsi thinks,[2] that the name " Magyar " also " Magyari ",[3] has its origin in the word " *Mansi* " (which is also the folk name of some Siberian peoples).

[1] See Campbell : *Santali-English Dictionary.*
[2] Munkácsi : *Árja és kaukazusi Elemek a finn-magyar Nyelvekben* (Arian and Caucasian Elements in the Finno-Magyar Languages). P. 454.
[3] See more on page 167, foot-note 2.

THE AUTHOR.

PARIS,
June, 1928.

PART I.

MAORI AND MAGYAR.

" As Humboldt somewhere says: 'Surmise, hypothesis, sagacity and divination are the parents of science,' though props to be used sparingly and with judgment."

(Forlong: Short Studies, etc., P. xiv.)

Chapter I.

THE CELESTIAL BODIES.

The Pleiads.—The Milky Way.—Other Stars.—Heaven and Stars in General.—The Moon.—The Sun.

The Pleiads.

There is but little known of the *mythology* of the Magyar; the most important work on it has been written by Kandra.[1] Parts of this subject have also been treated by Kálmány,[2] especially on the basis of linguistic traditions. From these studies we understand that the *Pleiads*, called in Magyar *gönczöl* (also dönczö, dönczöl, dönczör, kincsö; and since the Christian era "St. Peter's star") hold an important position. Kandra deems it very probable that *gönczöl* meant in ancient times the "God of the Magyar", the Patron of the nation.[3] The Maori also consider the *Pleiads* as a sort of astral guardians.[4]

In the popular belief of the Magyar the constellation of the *gönczöl* represents a kind of farm; there is a "threshing floor", a "forest glade", a "chain", "garland", "roof", and a "keeper". But the most important feature is two farm-carts, of which the smaller one, represented by the *Little Bear*, is driven by Christ and the bigger one, the *Great Bear*, by St. Peter. According to a popular legend the load of the latter consists of "loawes, *whale* and scraps of bread". Amongst the Maoris also the duty of supplying food to mankind is entrusted to the *Pleiads*.[5]

Another Magyar legend relates that St. Peter went forth in the cart of the "gönczöl" on a *thieving* expedition.[6] Two stars of the constellation of the *Pleiads* are called in New Zealand "Tupua-nuku" and "Tupua-rangi".[7] "Tupua" means further: to steal (Williams).

Popular names bestowed upon the *Pleiads* by the Magyar are *fias tyúk* or *csirkés tyúk*: hen with chicken.[8] The Maori call them "Ao-kai", and we find in the Marquesas the expression

[1] Kandra: *Magyar Mythologia* (Hungarian Mythology).
[2] Kálmány: *A Csillagok Nyelvhagyományainkban* (The Stars in our Linguistic Traditions).
[3] Kandra. P. 395.
[4] Amongst others by the Waikoto tribe of New Zealand. Cowan. P. 111.
[5] Best. Vol. II. P. 215.
[6] Kálmány: *A Csillagok Nyelvhagyományainkban*. P. 15.
[7] Best. Vol. II. P. 212.
[8] Kálmány (see above). P. 11.

" kai-ata " for " poule sauvage " = wild fowl (Dordillon); in New Zealand " kai-aia " for a bird (Williams); in Samoa " galegale " for " jeune coq qui n'a pas encore toute sa force " = pullet not yet in possession of all its vigour (Violette), and the word " galegaleata " means the appearance of dawn.

As for the seven stars forming the constellation of the *Pleiads*, they were called by the Magyars *hetevény* (seven = hét) also. Concerning this number seven, called by the Maori " whetu ", " hetu ", more will be said on pp. 44 and 55.

It appears that in the ancient chronology of both peoples a certain importance was ascribed to the *Pleiads* with regard to the beginning of the New Year. A Magyar tradition relates that St. Peter on 22nd February drives " his fire-brand into the earth ", whereupon the latter begins to doff its wintry garments [1]; the general Magyar belief is that the " cart of gönczöl " draws the whole earth.[2] For the Maori the *Pleiads* mark the beginning of the New Year.[3]—Hunfalvy suggests in his Ethnography of Hungary that among the ancient Magyar the year must have comprised thirteen months, and the same is said by various writers about the division of the Maori year.[4]

The Milky Way.

Popular Magyar names for the *Milky Way* are, amongst others, *hadak utja* (the highway of armies), *madarak utja* (the track of birds), and *kerek udvar* (the round courtyard, with the idea of a fenced enclosure).[5] Other names are: Isten utja, Isten barázdája, or hajnalhasadék.[6] (God's path, furrow of God, approach of dawn.)

The Maori call the *Milky Way* " ika-roa "[7] in connection with which it should be noted that one of the several meanings of " ika " is: body of men, a troop (Tregear); in Tahiti: birds of the air and fish of the sea.[8] " Roa (loa, noa) " means: long, tall, length, extension. The name of " To-ika-matua-a Tangaroa " is also employed for the *Milky Way*, in which expression " Tangaroa (Tana-roa) " means the " great Tana ", i.e. the deity of this name, and " matua ": the divisions of an army, the main body of an army (Tregear). Finally the appellation " Paeroa o Whanui " is also given to it, where " Whanui " is the star Vega and " paeroa " means: a great fence, " pae " being: to surround with a border (Tregear). This great path of the heavens shows also to the Maori the approach of dawn.[9]

[1] Kandra. P. 208. [2] Ibid. P. 395.
[3] Smith. P. 72. Best. Vol. II. P. 215. [4] Best. Vol. II. P. 186.
[5] Kandra. P. 389.—For the Magyar words " had ", " madár " and " út " see pages 59, 71, 68.
[6] Wiegand: " A magyar csillagos Ég " in the Periodical *Ethnographia*, 1914. P. 271.
[7] Best. Vol. I. P. 389.
[8] Further remarks on the word " ika " on page 103.
[9] Best. Vol. II. P. 213.

Other Stars.

In the Magyar star-legends *Vega* holds the rôle of a *csösz*, or field and crop guardian; thus being brought into direct relation with *agriculture*. As the heliacal rising of that star was awaited by the Maori as a sign of the harvesting season, Best raises the interesting question,[1] whether there exists in any other country a connection between the star *Vega* and agriculture? Its personification as above in Magyar legends seems to supply an affirmative answer.

The Magyar call the constellation of *Orion*: *kaszás* (the mower), or "Szent Ilona pálczája" (St. Helen's stick).[2] By calling *Orion's Belt*, "te Kakau" the Maori recognizes the form of an axe-handle (kakau).[3] In some districts they discover in *Orion* a "tuke": snaring perch, i.e. a stick of some kind.

Sirius, the *sánta Kata* (the lame Catherine) of Magyar, is supposed to move in the wake of the mowers, carrying their food and drink. Curiously enough the Maori call this star "Takunua", in which name "taku" means: slow; "tataku" is: to follow slowly (Tregear).

The planet *Venus* is called by the Magyar among other names *vacsora csillag*[4] (supper star). Its Maori name is "kopu", and this word also means the stomach.

To the *Hyad's* Magyar gave the name of *kikelet hirmondó* (the herald of the Spring); in Maori they are "Mata-kaheru", and "matata" signifies with them a tender growth of plant,[5] "kaheru" an instrument (spade) for tilling the soil (Tregear).

The popular Magyar term for *Aldebaran* is *bujdosók lámpása* (lantern of the exiled wanderer). In Maori this star is "Taumatu-kuku". Curiously enough the word "taumatu" means: an abrupt spur of a mountain.

The constellation of *Altair* is the *tévelygö juhász* (the wobbling shepherd), the Maori calling it "Poutu-to-Rangi", where "poutu (pouturu, poutoti)" signifies: stilts.

A star, probably one of the constellation of the *Archer* has got the popular Magyar name of *kódus* (the beggar), and is believed to be the leader of other stars, "towing them in his train."[6] The Maori call it also "Marere-o-Tonga": the precursor, harbinger of the star *Canopus*. Besides "marere" means: to be given, and "malele" in Hawaii: to call out to one for help (Tregear).

[1] Ibid. Vol. I. P. 133.
[2] Kálmány: *A Csillagok Nyelvhagyományainkban*. P. 21.
[3] Best. Vol. II. P. 214.
[4] Wiegand. In the annex of the Periodical *Ethnographia*, 1914. P. 216.
[5] Maori call "matahi" the first two months of their year.
[6] Kálmány: *A Csillagok*, etc. P. 23.

Heaven and Stars in General.

In ancient times the Magyars called the stars *húgy.* In the Maori language " hui " is: to congregate, to come together, and in the Hawaiian dialect " huihui " means: a bunch, a cluster of anything, *as stars* (Tregear). In Tahiti *Orion's Belt* is called " Huitarava ", and according to Best[1] the expressions of " kahui " and " huihui " are used for constellations in general, just as " Huihui of Matariki " is used for the *Pleiads.*

In the Magyar language *menny* (or menye, ménie, mén, menő-ég) is the word for heaven.[2] In his pursuit of Magyar mythology Kandra was struck by the fact[3] *that no Ural-Altaian language* (not even the supposedly closely related Finn or Vogul) contains a similar expression. Munkácsi presumes[4] an Aryan origin for this word and derives it from the Awesta " mainyu ": spirit, genius, heaven. For the latter ideas the Maori language has the one word " mana "; on the other hand, it possesses the expression " mene " for: to be assembled; in the Marquesas " meni " for: united, jointed; in Mangarewa " mena ": to bend, to bow, and in Tahiti " mene ": round, globular and " menemene ": spherical—all suggestive of the Magyar *menny.*

The Moon.

The popular Magyar belief includes two personifications of *the Moon,* viz. a male and a female, the second of less importance. The Moon is supposed to have a mother and the latter is believed to be an " extremely irritable person ". The Maori-myths, which also include a masculine and a feminine personification of the Moon, relate that he is " ill-treated " by his mother (this being the reason of his waning).[5]

The traditional cult of the Moon is preserved to a large extent even to this day by the Magyar.[6] Their popular belief admits in cases of illness the efficacy of prostration before the Moon and the use of incantations (incantation = ráolvasás). There are many such whose object is the removal of disease by appeal to the Moon.[7] The Maori also with this object invoke one of the personifications of the Moon, " Hine-korako,"[8] and in this connection it may be recalled that the Magyar word *kór* signifies disease.

Magyar popular belief suggests also certain connections between the Moon and agriculture. In the country of Bács for

[1] Best. Vol. II. P. 209.
[2] See Szarvas-Simonyi's *Historical Magyar Dictionary.*
[3] Kandra. P. 67.
[4] Munkácsi: *Árja és kaukázusi Elemek,* etc. P. 462.
[5] Best. Vol. I. P. 110.
[6] Kandra. P. 459.
[7] Further information to be found in Kálamány's *A Hold Nyelvhagyományainkban* (The Moon in our Linguistic Traditions).
[8] Best. Vol. II. Pp. 2 and 45.

instance it is accepted that planting and seeding are not advisable "unless the Moon is under the Earth"; among the Székely's of Zágon it is regarded that "inoculation of trees and seeding of corn" should be done only during the phase of the new Moon, etc., etc.[1]

With the Maori agriculture is closely connected the male personification of the Moon, "the husband of all women in the world." To it is attributed the growth of crops, and some of its phases are reserved for the sowing of certain seeds, especially for the sweet potato, the "kumara" (which should be planted on the night of the 27th to the 28th).[2]

Magyar popular sayings very often address the new Moon as *uj király* (new or young king).[3] The Maori have a similar designation, calling it "Whanau ariki",[4] in which name "ariki" means: king, supreme chief, and "whanau": to be born, or also: to have (Tregear). The Magyar "van" has the same meaning: to have.

The ancient Magyar connected *the corona of the Moon* with a beautiful woman. A Szeged folksong says to this day: "The Moon has a great corona, the handsome maid a world-wide fama." Amongst the Maori the corona of the Moon is personified by a "fair-haired maid", i.e. the above-mentioned "Hine-korako", and a most important position was attributed to her in popular belief.[5]

The Magyar name for the Moon is *hold,* in dialects *hód*; the Maori call it on its 15th day, at the phase of full moon: "hotu". Further the Magyar word for daybreak is *virrad*; in the Maori language by "whiro" is understood that phase of the Moon when the brightness of the new moon is just appearing. In Magyar the word *huny* means amongst other things: disappearance, while the Maori call the total wane of the Moon "huna".[6]

The Sun.

The Sun is in Magyar mythology the son of the first mother, the *bába*.[7] The Maori personification of the Sun, the deity Tane, is the son of the first mother "Papa".[8] An old pagan Magyar hymn to the Sun[9] reads thus: "Thou art the primeval tree of life . . . from which everything springs; by which the night of evil spirits is chased; to which everything in this world returns . . ." The Maori also

[1] Kandra. P. 459.
[2] Best. Vol. I. P. 132.
[3] In the Magyar Language "uj (or uyu, uju)", in Maori "hou" (Williams) means: new; in Rarotonga "ou" (Tregear) is: new, young.
[4] Best. Vol. II. P. 209.
[5] Ibid., Vol. I. P. 70.
[6] Best. Vol. II. P. 181.
[7] Kandra. P. 104.
[8] Best. Vol. I. P. 131.
[9] Published by Kandra. P. 75.

celebrate in their songs the Sun as the representative of every fertilizing power, as the germ of all animal and floral life.

In the creed of both peoples the Sun has daughters. According to old Magyar ideas the " favourite daughter of the Sun " is not so unbearable and red-cheeked as is her mother, but a wonderful, handsome maid, etc. . . ., who " dwells in the garden of dawn " (hajnal).[1]

" Who was this fair Maid "—asks Best[2]—" whose beauty is described by the Maori in such glowing terms, who sprang from the loins of Tane, the Great One ? . . . Hine-titama was she, the Dawn Maid." [3]

The analogies between Magyar and Maori contained in this chapter surely do not lack interest. *It is a question how far these analogies are confined to these two peoples.*

[1] Kandra. P. 70.—Concerning the Magyar word " hajnal " see also Kandra P. 137.
[2] Best. Vol. I. P. 119.
[3] For further reference to the Magyar word for the Sun etc. see page 64.

CHAPTER II.

RELIGION AND RELIGIOUS FIGURES.

THE CREATION.—GIANTS, DWARFS, AND FAIRIES.—IDOLS, HOLY TREES, WATER-VENERATION.—MAGIC AND SUPERSTITION.—SPIRITS AND RELIGIOUS FIGURES.—RITES OF WORSHIP.—PRIESTHOOD.

The Creation.

Although dispersed in various legends, the ancient Magyar idea of the act of Creation is to some extent preserved.[1] Heaven itself was considered as the first creation; from it proceeded air and water, and afterwards the first man. These legends also refer to an Earth Mother; in Kecskemét the custom still exists for sufferers from sore throat to kneel down kissing the soil and exclaiming: "Oh, my dear Earth Mother . . . etc."[2]

According to the Maori-belief, there was in the beginning darkness "po"[3] and void "kore", from whom proceeded the Father Heaven and the Mother Earth, and from them sprang mankind and every earthly creature. This Father of Heaven was personified in the deity "Rangi (Langi)", the Mother of Earth in "Papa". Kandra thinks that the Magyar word *bába* was originally the name of the *first mother* (Nature)[4]; *pokol* signifies in Magyar hell or darkness.

Giants, Dwarfs, Fairies.

Tribal heroes of both of these people became *demigods.* Such a demigod of the ancient Magyar was their legendary giant, the *óriás.*[5] Of the "oro" of the Maori Quatrefages writes[6]: "He is neither a full deity, nor merely a man . . . he was not born a god, he became one later on."

The opposite of the giant is the dwarf, called in Magyar *törpe, topora.*[7] In the Chatham Islands the dwarf is "tupepe" (Tregear); in Tahiti "topaapaa" means: "défiguré, vilain," disfigured, ugly (Jaussen); in the Marquesas "tupoto-io" is "nain", dwarf.

[1] Kálmány: *Világunk Alakuldsai Nyelvhagyományainkban* (The Cosmogony in our Linguistic Traditions).

[2] Kandra. P. 90.

[3] Tregear quotes also the form "papoko".—Churchill (*Easter Island*): "poke," infernal; "pokoga," hell, infernal cave.—P. A. C. (Arorai): "pog," "bog" = "nuit," night.

[4] Kandra. P. 104.

[5] Ipolyi: *Magyar Mythologia* (Hungarian Mythology). Pp. 143 and 313.

[6] De Quatrefages: *La Polynésie.* Pp. 149 and 185.—About "oro" see also page 166, foot-note 8.

[7] Ballagi: *Magyar-Német Szótár* (Magyar-German Dictionary).

A large part of the ancient Magyar religion is filled with legends about *fairies*, from whom, indeed, the very nation itself is supposed to have originated.[1] In the South Sea their importance is equally predominant; the fairies of the dark-haired race of the Maori have slender, but well formed bodies, are of *fair* complexion, possess *light-coloured hair*, hair so abundant as to cover them down to the waist.[2]

The Magyar called their fairies *tündér*, *tünde*. The root *tün* of these words means: disappearance, transfiguration. One of the Maori expressions for fairies is " tini ".[3]

Idols, Holy Trees, Veneration of Water.

The ancient Magyars had no *idols*, but their sacrificial places were decorated by stone columns.[4] Hochstetter, one of the first explorers of New Zealand, characterizes the Maori religion as polytheism without temples and " without definite idols ".[5] Instead of the latter they had stone pillars.[6]

That the ancient Magyars had a mystical veneration for *trees* may be inferred from the fact that even to-day in some houses, especially among the Székely-tribe the " istenfája " (God's tree) is to be found.[7] The veneration of *water* must have been also deeply rooted, because in the XIth century, long after the adoption of Christianity, King St. Ladislas was obliged to forbid most severely to his folk the adoration of fountains.[8] The veneration of trees and water is also one of the well known Maori rites.

Magic and Superstition.

Firm belief in the efficacity of magic formulæ is very characteristic of the old Magyar religion.[9] About the Maori the same may be said. The Magyar have the expression *varás*, *varázs* in connection with sorcery and fortune-telling.[10] In Tahiti " varua " means: " un esprit," a spirit (Jaussen); in Easter Island: a spell (Routledge).

babona is another Magyar expression for superstition and magic, a word to which further reference is made on page 79; *báj*, *bűbáj* means also charm and witchcraft.[11] In New Zealand use is made of the word " pai " (whaka-pai) [12] for: to praise (Williams); in Tahiti the steps leading to the platform of the

[1] Kerékgyártó: *Magyarország Művelődésének Története* (History of Hungarian Culture). P. 425.
[2] Best. Vol. I. P. 168.
[3] " Tini-o-te-Hakaturi," see Best. Vol. I. P. 224.
[4] Kerékgyártó. P. 393.
[5] Hochstetter: *Neu-Seeland.* P. 508.
[6] Best. Vol. I. P. 289.
[7] About the word " fa " see also page 72.
[8] Ipolyi. Pp. 204 and 578.
[9] Kandra. P. 119.
[10] According to Szarvas-Simonyi's *Historical Magyar Dictionary.*
[11] According to the *Magyar Etymological Dictionary.*
[12] About " whaka " see page 40.

sacrificial altar are called " pae " ; in Nukuroa this word means the altar itself (Best), and in the Marquesas the word " paea " has such meanings as " délire, espèce de folie, sorcière qui arrache, qui fait tomber les mauvais dieux, lorsqu'ils ont pris possession de quelqu'un, nom du dieu qui rend les femmes folles, imbécile, folle (se dit des femmes seulement) ", or : kind of folly, sorceress who expels evil spirits in possession of a person, name of a god who causes madness of women, imbecile, mad (used of women only) (Dordillon).[1]

Finally the word *garabonca* was also used by the ancient Magyar to express necromancy and black magic. The " garatai " of the South Seas is quoted by Rivers [2] as one of the words expressing various forms of magic, and in the Marquesas " karahatu " signifies " noir, noirâtre," black, blackish (Dordillon).

Sometimes Magyar and Maori hold the same *superstitions*. For example, the Magyar consider the apparition of an owl as a sign of bad luck ; if a lark rises in the Spring on one's right, it means good luck, if on the left, ill-fortune is to be expected.[3] The Maori have the same beliefs, but the ominous place of the lark is held by a robin.[4]

Spirits and Religious Figures.

A religious figure of the Magyar was the *manó*. According to Munkácsi [5] this term is synonymous with genius, sense, character, and served also to denote a spirit having care of all living creatures, especially mankind. Rather different is the interpretation of the Historical Dictionary of the Magyar Tongue by Szarvas-Simonyi, giving : malus genius, daemon, manducus. The Maori, according to Newman, understand by " manu " a parent god, and Tregear interprets this word by demon, spirit, elf.—(It is somewhat curious that the same word bears two opposite meanings in both languages, each of them being the same in Magyar and in Maori. In the course of this study several examples of similar parallelisms will be quoted.)

To the *fene*, another figure of the Magyar realm of spirits, reference will be made on page 58.

The Magyar ghost *guta* is, according to Kandra,[6] an evil genius, whose breath has a paralysing effect. Szarvas-Simonyi's Dictionary attributes to this word the meaning also of " apoplexia, paralysis ". In New Zealand there is an expression " kuta " for : clog, as old and infirm people on march (Williams) ; in the Marquesas " kote " means " perclus, paralysé ", crippled, paralysed (Dordillon).

[1] The Magyar expression " báj ", meaning charm, is used also of women only.
[2] Rivers : *The History of the Melanesian Society*. Vol. II. P. 463.
[3] Kandra. P. 160.
[4] Best. Vol. I. P. 227.
[5] Munkácsi. P. 457.
[6] Kandra. P. 195.

The mythological figure *lidércz* (lodovércz) of the Magyar, "*unknown to the Finns and other kindred people,*" [1] is generally regarded as a collective term for all the powers of the nether world. Szarvas-Simonyi gives three different explanations for it, viz. "ephialtus, incubus", nightmare; "cacodaemon, lamia", evil genius, villain, and "ignis fatuus", will-o'-the-wisp. The Maori tongue has the expression "rita" [2] for evil spirit (Williams); in Tahiti it has the meaning "spasme, avoir des convulsions", spasm, to have convulsions (Jaussen); and in Samoa "loto" is "cœur, comme siège des affections", the heart, as seat of the affects (Violette).

In Magyar mythology *ukkon* is the progenitor, the forefather.[3] The Maori word "uku" means: ancient times (Williams); in Arorai "ugkwa" is "autrefois, anciennement", once, in ancient times (P. A. C.); in Paumotu "uki" is ancient, a century; further: a generation (Tregear).

Stories are told amongst the Magyars of a *holy sword*, and to this day one may find in the hills or forests of Transylvania swords stuck vertically into the earth.[4] The "Hetaiaha-whaimana" of the Maori was a wooden sword which has accomplished such wonderful deeds, as to have acquired a sanctity and power of its own.[5]

Rites of Worship.

avik is an old Magyar expression for inaugurating and has a further meaning "veterasco", out of date; in its form *avott* it corresponds to "antiquus, priscus, vetustus".[6] In New Zealand "aweko" signifies: knowing, understanding, old, ancient (Tregear); on Tahiti "avea": "example, guide" (Jaussen); in Tonga "avaga": "marriage entre une personne et le diable," marriage between a person and the devil (Miss. Maristes).

Faith is called in Magyar speech *hit*, signifying also oath, act of swearing.[7] The Maori also represent by "hiteki": faith (Tregear), and by "hitihiti" in the Marquesas: "sorte de chant païen," a kind of pagan hymn (Dordillon).

Priesthood.

In both of these nations, Magyar and Maori, the priests were, as in many other countries, scholars, minstrels, jugglers, artists, and teachers. Priesthood was hereditary.[8] The ancient Magyars called their priests: *táltos, tátos*. In the Marquesas "tata-

[1] Kandra. P. 179.
[2] For the frequent interchange of r and l see page 25.
[3] Kandra. P. 94.
[4] Ibid. P. 513.
[5] White: *The Ancient History of the Maori*. Vol. I. P. 48.
[6] According to the *Magyar Etymological Dictionary*.
[7] About the word "hit" see also page 56.
[8] Kerékgyártó. P. 436.

haoho" is "un chirurgien indigène", a native surgeon (Dordillon). In Tonga "talavai" means: "demander un médecin, un remède, expliquer," call for the doctor, ask for remedy, to explain; further "taula" there means a priest, and "talai": to instruct (Miss. Maristes).

Chapter III.

CULT OF ANCESTORS, POETRY, LOVE OF FATHERLAND.

Ancestors.—Genealogies.—Poetry.—The Land of the Forefathers.—Migratory Instinct.

The Ancestors. The origin of the Magyar people is traced back by the old sagas to *Tana* (Thana), the son of Japhet.[1] The son of Tana—no mention is made of his wife—is the giant Nimrod (Nemrut), who went to the country of " Evilat (Eulat) ", where his wife *Ena* (Ene, Eneth) gave birth to two sons " Hunor and Magor ", the supposed ancestors of the Hun and the Magyar.

A Tongan legend describes the origin of the Maori[2] by relating that the great god " Tangaroa (also Tana-roa, Tana-loa, i.e. the 'tall and well built *Tana*') " had two sons; the " white race " descending from one, the Maori from the other. According to New Zealand tradition, the procreator of the first man was the god " *Tane* (*Tana*) "[3]; his wife " *Hina* (Hine) " was the first woman. Tane was protected and instructed by the highest spirit, the Great *Jo* (Ja).[4] The deity Tane, Tana symbolizes also the idea of knowledge,[5] and *tan* is also the Magyar word for knowledge, doctrine. Instead of the malediction " God shall punish him ! " the Magyar peasants of some districts still use the form " May *Dana* punish him ! "[6]

In Mangaia a myth is still current,[7] according to which the personification of the Moon, the god " Rongo " is said to have dark hair and the Sun, the deity Tangaroa (Tana-roa) fair hair, and so we hear there of " the dark haired children of Rongo " and of the " *fair-haired* descendants of Tangaroa ".

Genealogies One is induced to believe that records of genealogies and tribal names were most carefully kept by the old Magyar, because their chronicler *Kézai* writes even as late as in the XIIIth century, that he feels himself excused from enumerating the names of the *108 Magyar tribes*

[1] Jászay: *A Magyar Nemzet Napjai* (Days of the Magyar Nation). P. 17.—See also Kandra. P. 417.

[2] Newman. P. 119.—He relates also another Maori myth according to which there were in all *three races*: the Tangata or Sangata Maori, further the Kanaka Maoli and the " white folk ", whom the Maori were separated even when still in their " old fatherland ".

[3] Ibid. P. 118.

[4] Best. Vol. I. P. 103.

[5] Ibid. P. 72.

[6] *Magyar Etymological Dictionary*.

[7] Best. Vol. I. P. 135.

who immigrated to their present country *because everybody knows them.*[1] The genealogy of the chief *Álmos*, probably born in A.D. 819, father of the first Magyar sovereign *Árpád*, is known up to the present day and—beginning with *Noa*—includes forty-eight names.[2]

One of the most predominant habits of the Maori is the minute preservation of their genealogies. "The Polynesian genealogies and traditions give us as complete information on the Polynesian History, as the Roman Annales with their narratives of legendary and ætologic character on the Oldest History of Rom."[3] The Maori genealogies supply further evidence, that the Maori of all the islands belong to the same stock, because in spite of distances of several thousands of miles the genealogical trees often show the same names at corresponding periods. Naturally it was the genealogy of chiefs which was especially preserved; anybody wishing to attain the dignity of chieftain was expected to be able to enumerate his ancestors, tracing them back at least to twenty generations. There are genealogies existing with more than 100 names. An appendix to Smith's Hawakii contains a Rarotongan genealogy carried to A.D. 1900, and containing ninety-five names. Amongst them the name of *Noa* is to be found in the 79th generation. Supposing we reckon a generation at thirty-four years,[4] the date of existence of the *Noa* of the Magyar and the *Noa* of these Maori would coincide, viz. 790 B.C. A coincidence of this kind is a little curious.

In this connection it may be mentioned that certain New Zealand Maori chieftains still have names resembling those of ancient Magyar leaders, viz. *Kupa, Kewhe*, etc.

Poetry.

Ancestral names and deeds were commemorated by both peoples in poetical form. No doubt, the mere comparison of the characteristics of the poetry of two races—as indeed of many other parallels noted in this study—does not constitute *in any way a scientific proof*. However, when they are as numerous and as interesting as is here the case, they at least deserve mention. And similarly the opinions of various authors on the characteristics of poetic art amongst the ancient Magyar and Maori seem worthy of notice. For instance, Thierry gives the following description[5]: "Among the ancient Magyars everybody was a poet and recited

[1] Kerékgyártó. P. 14.
[2] Jászay. P. 180.
[3] Friderici. "Ein Beitrag zur Kenntniss der Tuamotu-Inseln." In *Mitteilungen des Vereins für Erdkunde zu Leipzig*. 1910. P. 159.
[4] The usual estimate for a generation is thirty years. However, apart from the well-known longevity of the Maori it should be remembered, that in olden days they did not marry before the age of 25. (See Best. Vol. II. P. 450.)
[5] Thierry: *Attila and his Successors*, translated into German by Burckhardt. Vol. I. P. 254.

his own poems or those of others. The songs bequeathed from generation to generation became in a way the annals of the land. Their object was the praise of ancestors and every family had its individual poetical records. Law was sung long before it was written, and later on the songs became an authority for the old customs, political institutions, and civic rights. . . . Song writing was indeed a public institution."

"If figurative language constitutes poetry . . . there was never a people so poetical as the Maori," says Brown.[1] Hochstetter classifies [2] in New Zealand not less than *ten different types* of songs. "Night after night, in the overcrowded wharepuni (school-houses), the interesting ancestral sagas are recited until every person of the community gets familiar with the popular and bush-stories and with the fairy legends of the tribe." [3] Chiefs in particular were expected to show poetical gift,[4] it was part of their duty to recite the whole tradition of the tribe in rhythmical language; Smith tells of a Maori who could recite more than 400 songs and who was familiar with most of the names of the composers and the incidents alluded to in them.[5] Emerson, who has treated the wonderful poetry of Hawaii in a manner as beautiful as it is complete,[6] comes to the following conclusion: "The poetry of ancient Hawaii evinces a deep and genuine love of nature, and a minute, affectionate, and untiring observation of her moods, which it would be hard to find surpassed in any literature. Her poets are never tired of depicting nature; sometimes, indeed, their art seems heaven-born."—When receiving guests—an important ceremony of both peoples [7]—the welcome was often made in poetical language.

Alliterations and parallelisms are said to be special characteristics of ancient Magyar poetry.[8] The same remark applies to the Maori and proofs of this may be found in the beautiful "Song of the Aotea Canoe" published by Cowan,[9] or in some exquisite examples quoted by Emerson. From this collection a poem may be cited, which will surely charm every true lover of poetry.

[1] Brown: *Maori and Polynesian*. P. 89.
[2] Hochstetter: *Neu-Seeland*. P. 508.
[3] Cowan: *The Maoris of New Zealand*. P. 163.
[4] Reischek: *Sterbende Welt*. P. 163.
[5] Smith: *Hawaiki*. P. 16.
[6] Emerson: *Unwritten Literature of Hawaii*. P. 263.
[7] Kerékgyártó. P. 102.—Best. Vol. I. P. 379.
[8] Hunfalvy. P. 256.
[9] Cowan. P. 54.

SONG OF THE TREE-SHELL.[1]

Sung by young girls of Hawaii.

Kahuli aku,	Trill a-far,
Kahuli mai,	Trill a-near,
Kahuli lei ula,	A dainty song-wreath
Lei akolea	Wreath akolea,[2]
Kolea, kolea	Kolea, kolea.[3]
Ki'i ka wai,	Fetch me some dew,
Wai akolea.	Dew from pink akolea.

It would be naturally most interesting if it were possible to discover in Maori poetry any of the special expressions, which lend such a quaint beauty to the popular fairy tales of the Magyar, e.g.: "Merre mégy, hol madár se jár?" = Where are you roaming where not even a bird flies: a reference to the solitude and dreariness of the country.[4] But such researches would exceed the limits set to this study and it may suffice to say that in Maori poems also loneliness is expressed by the absence of birds.[5] Many Magyar proverbs might equally be mentioned as having their counterpart in Maori sayings, as for instance: "My liver is boiling," etc., etc.[6]

The Land of the Forefathers.

Throughout their history the Magyar cherished a special and affectionate interest in the land of their forefathers. Not only in our time, but in medieval days hearts were stirred by it to enterprise and adventure. "No other country of the world can be compared in its beauty to the old fatherland, the *haza* of the Magyar. There the air is more wholesome, the sky more blue, human life much longer, than anywhere else," says their Attila-saga.[7]

In memory of their ancestral home, "the Polynesian have carried with laudable pride and affection, with a strong belief in the sacredness, the beauty, the prolificness of the Fatherland, this great name *Hawa-iki* in their wanderings and applied it to many of their later homes."[8] The Magyar expressions *haza* (fatherland), will be compared later with the Maori "hawaiki"[9]

[1] Shells are used as musical instruments.

[2] "akolea" is a very beautiful and long fern with circinnate tips (like an acacia-tree), with pink blossoms.

[3] "kolea" = the red-breasted plover.

[4] See Solymossy: "Népmeséink keleti Rokonsága" (The Oriental Relationship of our popular Tales) in the Periodical *Akadémiai Értesitő*, 1922. Copies 385–388. P. 13.

[5] White: *The Ancient History of the Maori.* Vol. III. Pp. 13, 27, 158.

[6] Colcott and Havea: *Proverbial Sayings of the Tongans, Honolulu.* 1922.

[7] Thierry. Vol. I. P. 267.

[8] Smith. P. 42.

[9] "Hawaiki" means in New Zealand the country where the Maori came from; in Tahiti "Havaii" is the term for the Universe, also the old capital of Raiatea; in Rarotonga they denote by "Avaiki" the leeward land, in the Marquesas by "Havaiki" the land of the forefathers, in Samoa by "Savaii" or "Savaiki" the main island, where the Maori first settled during their wanderings.

and " hawaii ", as well as the word " honi " (native) with " hono, honu " (pages 53 and 60).

Migratory Instinct.

The migratory instinct must have been extremely developed among the ancient Magyar, for except in their presumed homes, treated in Part II, Chapter XIV of this study, no names have been recorded which would suggest an ancient Magyar settlement until they reached the Danubian land. Even after occupying the Carpathian basin, they still engaged in far-reaching adventures as far distant as Rome or Andalusia.[1] The Maori were in no way less adventurous. This is abundantly proved by their striking expansion all over the Pacific (see Chapter XV), though they were probably never very numerous: numbering 1,300,000 towards the end of the XVIIIth century—nowadays hardly more than 180,000 [2]—their race is undoubtedly scattered over the greatest area of the world.[3]

[1] Gombocz: "A magyar Őshaza és a nemzeti Hagyomány" (The ancient Magyar Home and National Tradition), study published in the periodical *Nyelvtudományi Közlöny* of 1923. P. 30.

[2] The population of Hawaii (natives and half-castes) decreased for instance from 142,000 in 1823 to 40,622 in 1890, or a loss of 75 per cent in sixty-seven years. (See the treatise of A. Marques in the *Journ. Pol. Soc.*, 1893. Pp. 256–258.)

[3] Smith. P. 10. Over an area three times as large as Europe.

Chapter IV.

SOME CUSTOMS AND HABITS.

Birth.—Funeral Obsequies.—Fire and Superstitions Connected with it.—Quack Practices.—Cannibalism.—Matrimony.

Birth. In certain parts of Hungary the Magyar peasantry still practise the superstitious custom of erecting a tent over the bed of *a woman in labour.*[1] According to Maori belief, it is not seemly for a child to enter the world in a house. So they erect a temporary hut for the woman to give birth to her child.[2]

Funeral Obsequies. A number of customs concerning the funeral ceremonies of both these peoples are worth noting; of course they are also to be found amongst other, chiefly Asiatic nations. Magyar and Maori placed their dead, in great state, on a bier, and beside the body all kinds of useful articles were deposited.[3] Sacrifices of human life in honour of the departed were customary amongst both, and suicide of widows was not uncommon.[4] *Burial places* were mostly on hills or in forests and near to a watercourse.[5] In Eger (Erlau), Hungary, niches have been found hewn in the rock and supposed to be the "holy places of ancient Magyar worship and obsequies".[6] The Maori in New Zealand had similar caves. The Magyar called them *kaptár*, and in Maori "kapiti" means: cleft, crevice, shut in by hills, confined (Williams).[7]

Cremation also was practised in both countries, though it was never a universal or even a common custom. The Maori practised it only in districts where no suitable places of concealment for the bones of the dead were available or for such members of their raiding forces, as happened to be killed in enemy territory.[8] About the old Magyars a chronicler relates that in one of their raids (in A.D. 926), they burnt two of their fallen warriors on a pyre near St. Gallen.[9] That cremation existed amongst the

[1] Kandra. P. 292.
[2] Best. Vol. II. P. 6.
[3] Kandra. P. 423.—Best. Vol. II. P. 54.
[4] Kerékgyártó. P. 449.—Kandra. P. 427.—Best. Vol. II. P. 55.
[5] Kerékgyártó. Pp. 563, 567.—Best. Vol. II. P. 64.
[6] Kandra. P. 428.—Best. Vol. II. P. 62.
[7] According to Tregear "kupi" means filled up, and "torero": a cave or a cleft in the mountain into which the bones of the dead were thrown.
[8] Best. Vol. II. Pp. 67, 69.
[9] Kerékgyártó. P. 449.

Magyar in olden times may be inferred from their saying *se híre se hamva,* "no news, no ashes," still used to express: totally disappeared. This term *hír* (or: hér) means not only rumour, shouting, but also fame, reputation. In the Marquesas the word "herohero" (Dordillon) and in Tonga "hili" (Miss. Maristes) are used to express the superlative; "whaka-hirahira" in New Zealand means: extol, to extol oneself (Williams). The Magyar word *hamu, hamv,* a term for ashes, exists in Maori also with the same meaning (Tregear).

In the mourning customs of the ancient Magyar was included self-mutilation by near relatives. According to Best [1] the custom of laceration was practised all over the islands inhabited by the Maori. Another old Magyar custom was a sort of tournament (bajnoki torna), held in honour of the dead. In New Zealand a very strange course of action was sometimes adopted: on the occasion of a death, a party of tribesmen would proceed to the scene of mourning and *attack* the near relatives of the deceased.[2] The ancient Magyar honoured their heroes by a "dance of death"; it occurred even as late as the XVth century.[3] Ceremonial dancing, which entered to a considerable extent into Maori life, was also practised at times of mourning.[4]

The *funeral repast,* a custom common to both people, was called by the Magyar *tor, tori*; in Maori the word "tohi" means: feast with eating (Tregear). In Magyar *tom* is banquet, entertainment (Ballagi); in Tonga we find the expression "taumafa" for: "manger, boire," to eat, to drink (Miss. Maristes); in Samoa the same word means to eat and drink, applied to chiefs only, and in Tahiti "taumaha" is: an offering of food to the gods (Tregear).

Contact with dead bodies was regarded by the Magyar as impure; this impurity had to be expiated by washing and bathing. Similarly the Maori considered persons who had to handle the dead as extremely "tapu", and they had to strip themselves of all clothing and to bathe in water.[5]

The Magyar term *temet* means to bury and *temető*: a cemetery. In Maori there is a word "toma" denoting a burial place (Tregear), and according to Reischek, "temato" means dead. The Maori believed that the souls of the deceased wandered *westward,* in quest of "the old fatherland". Traces of similar recollection of the ancient home may be found in some Magyar countries also, where mourners still, when reciting prayers over a tomb, stand on the east side, in the direction of the old fatherland.

[1] Kandra. P. 427.—Best. Vol. II. P. 55.
[2] Kandra. P. 427.—Best. Vol. II. P. 59.
[3] Kandra. P. 427.
[4] Best. Vol. I. P. 284.
[5] Kandra. P. 429.—Best. Vol. II. P. 69.

Fire and Superstitions connected with it.

Some mystical meanings of fire and its manipulations may also be quoted. In certain Magyar districts "fire-jumping" still survives.[1] The peasants of the village of Balla may be seen on cold evenings running and jumping about, carrying long sticks with wisps of lighted straw, intended to conjure away the frost. The peasants of Ludány do not consider jumping sufficient for the spell; they set light to *twelve* wisps which they proceed to trample down barefooted. The spreading of these embers over cabbage beds is believed to avert the damage done by caterpillars. In the valley of the river Ipoly (County of Hont) there is a superstition, that sick cattle may be cured by driving them through the smoke of a fire kindled by the *rubbing of wood.*

Best relates[2] similar superstitions of the Maori. When frosty weather threatened the crops of a community, firebrands were waved to and fro. "Fire-walking," a general Polynesian ceremony, was observed also in New Zealand. In order to protect the cultivated soil from caterpillars, bright fire was made of burning leaves. Fire kindled by friction is still considered by the Maori as of healing effect. The number twelve also appears from time to time in their sagas. Fire kindling is termed by the Magyars *kotyol* and *palázul.*[3] In New Zealand "katore" means: glimmering, dimly luminous (Williams), and in Samoa the word "palapu": "allumer le four," to kindle the stove (Violette).

Quack Practices.

Both people had magic formulæ by aid of which they hoped to cure certain diseases. The invocation of the Moon, praying to her to "remove" suffering from sick persons, has already been mentioned on page 6. Other spells still in use by Magyar peasants are referred to in a treatise by Dr. Fekete.[4] Best reports a curious habit of the Maori in which sick people were taken to the village latrine, where they had to bite into the "pae-pae", the beam or plank on which persons sat during evacuation. In Magyar-Kanizsa the tradition subsists that in olden days sick persons were cured by besmearing themselves with excrements.[5]

An old Magyar expression for ulcer is *tálé.* In New Zealand "taru" means disease (Williams); in Tahiti: "morve, glaire," mucus, glair (Jaussen); in Samoa "talo" is tubercle (Violette); in the Marquesas "tare" means "espèce de dartre", a kind of skin disease (Dordillon).

[1] Kandra. Pp. 222–228.
[2] Best. Vol. I. Pp. 270, 523. Vol. II. P. 388.
[3] Kandra. P. 133.
[4] Dr. Fekete: "A Gyógytan a régi Magyaroknál" (The medical Knowledge of the ancient Magyar), published in the periodical *Századok*, 1874. P. 380.
[5] Kálmány: "Világunk Alakulásai . . . etc." P. 59.

Cannibalism.

In the course of these considerations the cannibalism cannot be ignored. The first Magyar chronicler, the *Anonymous* of the XIIth century, says[1] about his kinsmen, that "they were originally in their ancient home very gentle people, but had in the course of many wars so much degenerated that they did not shrink even from the depravity of eating human flesh and drinking human blood". The Maori were cannibals up to the XIXth century, yet curiously enough Smith relates,[2] that cannibalism was not an original habit of theirs, but had been adopted later owing to the altered conditions of their life.

Matrimony.

Concerning the relations of the two sexes among the Maori, chiefs had rarely more than one wife,[3] while the licentiousness, which probably stood in a definite relation to the communism[4] of the people, is said to have been more pronounced among the lower strata of the community. In former times intermarriage with other tribes was not frequent. If a man died, his brother could take the widow to wife.[5] The ancient Magyar are said to have been monogamists; women had a high social position. The historian Valentin Kiss records that the brother of a dead husband was expected to marry the widow. Marriage with foreign women did not obtain for very long time.[6]

In spite of the licentiousness alluded to above, there is no trace in the Maori legends and traditions of any violation of woman. Of the Magyar the chronicles of Bonfini and of Münster state, that though extreme cruelty was practised in their raids, yet violation of women was unknown, "not even in the worst exhibition of bloodthirsty frenzy." [7]

[1] Quoted from Kerékgyártó. P. 53.
[2] Smith: *Hawaiki*. Pp. 200, 211.
[3] Keane: *Man Past and Present*.
[4] See also page 95.
[5] Best. Vol. II. Pp. 445, 448.
[6] Kerékgyártó. Pp. 89, 447, 448.
[7] Kerékgyártó. P. 90.

Chapter V.

THE LANGUAGE.

(A) General Remarks.—Phonetics.

General Characteristics of the Maori Language.—Relationship of Maori with Melanesian and Indonesian Languages.—Neither Semitic nor Aryan.—Dissemination of Maori Speech and its Dialects.—Importance of Vowels and their Accentuation.—Phonetic Changes in the Magyar Language.—Consonants as Initial Letters.—Vowels as Terminal Sounds.—Examples showing the Importance of Accentuation.

General Characteristics of the Maori Language.

"Every language is a ruin." Nearly all scholars are of the opinion that the flexionless language of the Maori [1] originates from the repeated intercourse of two peoples, who have failed to master the inflexions of one another's tongues. The following instances are therefore given with the object of inducing a more thorough research into the question *whether possibly Magyar was not one of these languages.*

The great Polynesian linguist *Ray* goes even as far as to compare the development of Maori [2] with the establishment of English as the language of Britain, where, as we know, Celtic, Danish, and Norman came into collision. And other scholars also agree with him. They think that Maori, showing hardly any traces of inflexions, and in which the grammatical relation of words is determined only by their position in a sentence or by auxiliary words and particles, is, as regards its nature, and especially its "perfection", very suggestive of English.[3] On the other hand, we must not leave without mention a quite different opinion. This idea is that of Churchill [4]; he regards Maori as the "most elementary form" of human speech. Perhaps in what follows an answer to this bold suggestion also may be found.

Relationship of Maori with Melanesian and Indonesian Languages.

Above all, special attention should be called to the scientifically established fact, developed by *Schmidt* in his so much appreciated and illuminating work on the Mon-Khmer people, that the Indonesian, Melanesian and Polynesian languages are *all branches of one great family* [5]; an opinion which has since been shared by Ray and many others. (Müller advances the theory

[1] It should be remembered that "Maori" is a term used for the language of the Polynesian in general. See also Introduction, page X.

[2] "The Past, Present and Future Study of the Languages of the Pacific Islander" in *Proceedings* of the Pacific Congress 1924. P. 218.

[3] Brown: *Maori-Polynesian.* P. 82.

[4] Churchill: *Easter Island.* P. 2.

[5] Schmidt: *Die Mon-Khmer Völker.* P. 1.—Also: *Sitzungsberichte der kais. Akademie der Wissenschaften* (Records of Sittings of the Imp. Academy of Sciences). Vol. VI.—See also page 220.

that Polynesian was the first branch to spring from the "common primitive language ",[1] and Churchill, in the course of his studies, is also led [2] to the conclusion that the element common to Melanesian and Polynesian is Polynesian in origin, borrowed by Melanesian through lack of names for new objects, new ideas, or by the influence of some fancy.)

With respect to the connection between *Polynesian and Indonesian,* many writers have long been misled by first appearances. So was Crawfurd, as he found in New Zealand only 85 Indonesian (Malay) expressions in 5,254 Maori words, and in the Marquesas in a total of 6,125 only 74.[3] But *Ray* considers Maori as originating through the superposition of Indonesian on the aboriginal stock. As the Polynesian colonists, who drifted there from or across Indonesia, started from various islands, and at different periods in the development of the Indonesian languages, so we naturally find that the Indonesian elements in Eastern languages—Melanesian and Polynesian—represent sometimes one Indonesian geographical region, sometimes another; or, in other words, the Indonesian element in Maori indicates an earlier or a later stage of phonetics and grammar.

Neither Semitic nor Aryan.

Of course, attempts have not been lacking to discover other relationships. Macdonald for instance tried to establish a relationship with Semitic languages [4]; the famous Bopp,[5] Fornander [6] and others with Aryan. Modern science regards all this as a failure.[7] *Ray even discovered, that the Old-Javanian speech contains many Sanskrit words, whereas, on the other hand, in Maori Old-Javanian expressions are found, but no Sanskrit.* This is all the more important as it enables conclusions concerning the date of the Maori wanderings. (See Chapter XV.) [8]

In the meanwhile more and more students of the Magyar have been led to discover *Aryan elements* in this language; a language supposed till now to belong to the Finn-Ugrian family, or,

[1] *Grundriss der Sprachwissenschaften.* Vol. II, Sect. 2, P. 2.—Most valuable contributions to this question are contained in Ray's *Comparative Study of the Melanesian Island-Languages*, Cambridge, 1927, dealing with no less than 163 Melanesian languages and showing in its grammatical part the leading characteristics, in which they differ widely from those of the Polynesian (Maori) group.

[2] In his *Polynesian Wanderings.*

[3] According to Quatrefages: *Les Polynésiens.* P. 19.

[4] Macdonald: *Oceanic Languages.*

[5] Bopp: *Über die Verwandtschaft der malayisch-polynesischen Sprachen mit den indisch-europäischen.*

[6] Fornander: *The Polynesian Race.* Vol. III.

[7] "Aucune trace de Sanskrit ne se trouve dans les langues polynésiennes" (No trace whatsoever of Sanskrit is to be found in Polynesian languages). Reclus: *Nouvelle Géographie Universelle.* Vol. XIV. P. 925.

[8] See also Labberton: "No relationship between Aryan or Indogerman and the South Sea or Malay-Polynesian Languages." In *Journ. Pol. Soc.* 1924. P. 250.

according to Müller's terminology, to the "Uralian" family of the Siberian languages. Yet it should be borne in mind that many of the "would-be" Sanskrit words are apparently simply derived from *much older Indian languages, which have nothing in common with Sanskrit*,[1] as will be seen in Part II. (Chapters X–XIII).

Dissemination of Maori Speech and its Dialects.

The question whether the languages spoken in Polynesia are really mere dialects of one stock, or whether they represent two or even more independent tongues, is answered by the fact, that the inhabitants of one island can generally easily understand the speech of another some thousands of miles away—so strong is the resemblance in vocabulary and grammar. And this is true not only of islands and archipelagos belonging to Polynesia proper (Chatham, Hawaii, New Zealand, Mangarewa, Marquesas, Easter Island, Paumotu, Rarotonga, Samoa, Tahiti, Tikopia, Tonga, etc.), but also of Polynesian settlements far distant from them, such as those in Mantavai westward of Sumatra, in Nukuoro of the Eastern Carolines, in San Christobal of the Solomon group, in Arorai of the Gilbert Islands, in the Ellice Islands, etc.[2]

The *differences between the various Maori dialects* are chiefly due to the transformation, or even elimination of consonants.[3] Thus the "l" of one island becomes "r" in another, the "s" changes into "h", "t" into "k" and so on. In Paumotu the "r" is suppressed (as in the word of the nutritive plant "taro, talo", which there becomes "tao"); in Mangarewa the "h" disappears, as in "ari" for "hari" = to carry, etc., etc.[4] Incidentally such changes are not uncommon even in the same dialect, as, for instance, in New Zealand; there "m" is often changed into "n" or "ng", "k" into "ng" or "p", "wh" into "h", "r" into "n", etc. Such phonetic rearrangements naturally undergo continual alterations. Thus "k" has replaced "t" in Hawaii only within the last century; and in Samoa the total elimination of the "k" is also of quite recent date and still appears as a hiatus, for instance "fa'a" instead of "faka".

Samoa is said to have been the first settlement of the Maori in the South Seas, from which their language gradually began to

[1] See Munkácsi's work already quoted, and Jacobsohn: *Arier und Ugrofinnen*. —See also Bhandarkar: *Lectures on the Ancient History of India*. P. 26.

[2] A nomenclature of those islands of Melanesia where "Polynesian" is predominant, may be found in Leverd: "Polynesian Linguistics." *Journ. Pol. Soc.* 1922. P. 175.—See further Churchill: *Polynesian Wanderings*. P. 45.

[3] See also Churchill: "Root Reductibility in Polynesian." *Journ. Pol. Soc.* 1906. P. 95.

[4] Comp. with Magyar "hord" = to carry.

spread, and the old "Proto-Samoan" language seems to be the fundamental language of all Maori dialects at present existing. Churchill, for instance, finds in it [1] 18 consonants, whereas modern Samoan has only 9. (Details may be also found in special works, notably in Tregear's book on these subjects.[2])

Importance of Vowels and their Accentuation.

Hardly any other language gives such importance to vowels as does Maori, where they have a special value. All vowels must be either short or long; many diphthongs exist (ae, ai, ao, au, ei, ou, etc.), always pronounced as disyllables, and they undergo like the consonants certain changes, either as a peculiarity of a separate dialect (e.g. in Tongan "e" replaces "a" of all the other dialects), or in any individual island (such as New Zealand, where "a" becomes "e" or "o" and "i" becomes "u").[3] There exist even distinct nuances in the pronunciation of the same vowel. "It is most probable," says Churchill, "that no foreigner has mastered the art of the Samoan vowels. It is as in their music; the intervals, the supertones and the fractions of the tone are developed on a system which we find it impossible to acquire. It establishes a new group of units of vibrations of the vocal cords, for which the fundamental diapason of our own speech is not set in unison." [4] It is quite interesting to compare this statement with those made recently by Hegedüs [5] about the peculiarity of Magyar vowels and their "wonderfully hidden key-board".

As far as *accentuation* of the Maori words is concerned, in Müller's opinion [6] the emphasis should fall on the penultimate syllable; if not, the accent has to be shifted accordingly. As Müller also says that the roots of the Polynesian languages are as a rule bisyllabic,[7] his assertion is not in contradiction with the statements of the New Zealander Williams,[8] who remarks about accentuation: "It may be set down as a general rule, to which there are some exceptions, that Maori words are always accented on the *first syllable*: but compound words which have the bisyllabic root doubled, have a secondary accent on the second portion of the word. The word 'whaka', always on the beginning of compound words, never receives an accentuation." [9]

Churchill makes a comparison between Samoan and English in the *frequency of vowel sounds*, comparing also the consonants,

[1] Churchill: *Easter Island*. P. 15.
[2] *The Maori-Polynesian Comparative Dictionary*.
[3] Williams. P. XII.
[4] Churchill: *Easter Island*. P. 14.
[5] In the Hungarian newspaper *Pesti Hirlap* of July 31st, 1927.—See also Simonyi: *Magyar Nyelvészet* (Magyar Philology). P. 31.
[6] *Grundriss der Sprachwissenschaften*. Vol. II, Sect. 2, P. 10.
[7] With frequent metathesis.—See also Churchill: *Easter Island*. P. 26.
[8] Williams. P. XIII.
[9] About "whaka" see more on page 40.

the "semi-consonants" (l and r) and sibilants (h), etc., using for it a Bible text in both languages. Such comparisons with ancient Magyar texts would be perhaps also curious, but they would exceed the limits of this study and would involve besides a considerable knowledge of phonetics. Still just as a matter of interest we may compare the oldest Magyar literary document, the "funeral oration" (Halotti Beszéd) of the XIIIth century with the above comparison Churchill's. The following table shows approximately the number of some other sounds for 254 vowels in each language :—

	Samoan.	Magyar.	English.
consonants	172	254	462
semi-consonants (l, r)	46	50	97
sibilants (h)	5	7	63
labials (b, p, v, f, m)	38	55	91

As it is known, the accentuation in Magyar also lays on the first syllable. Moreover multi-syllabic words have a secondary accent mostly on the third syllable.[1]

Phonetic Changes in the Magyar Language.

Phonetic changes often occur in Magyar also. The above mentioned general interchange of "r" and "l", that of "p" and "f" (as in Tahiti), of "p" and "m", and of "m", "n" and "ng" (as in New Zealand) is also more or less frequent.[2] (Definite examples of other changes will be referred to later.)

"v" sometimes disappears in both languages. Thus we may find in New Zealand "tapuae" for "tapuwae",[3] just as in the above mentioned Magyar funeral oration "haláláal" stands for the form "halálával". It is probable that the Magyar vowels é, ó, ő were pronounced in olden times as *diphthongs.*[4] Like in the Maori pronunciation, where as we have seen, diphthongs are always dissyllabic, in certain Magyar dialects such separations of sounds exist still to-day,[5] e.g. "keö" instead of kő (= stone),[6] "taul" for tol (= to push),[7] "jau" for jó (= good),[8] etc.

In Maori the vowels o and a are often interchangeable, e.g. "moku" and "maku", for me (Tregear), "noku" and "naku",

[1] Simonyi: *A magyar Nyelv* (The Magyar Language). Vol. II. P. 12.
[2] Ibid. P. 47.
[3] Tregear. P. XVI.
[4] Simonyi: *Magyar Nyelvészet.* P. 23.
[5] Simonyi: *A magyar Nyelv.* Vol. I. P. 207.
[6] According to Tregear "keho" generally means: sandstone; in the Marquesas: basalt, a kind of black marble; in Mangarewa: basaltic stone, hard and cutting; in Hawaii "eho": a pile of stones; in Mangaia "kea": sandstone.
[7] The Maori word "tau" is: to attack (Tregear), "tatau": to draw, or push (Williams), "tautau": to haul (Tregear).
[8] See also page 61.

belonging to me,[1] or in diphthongs, such as "houhou" and "hauhau", cool. According to Szarvas-Simonyi both forms, "houos" and "hauas" snow-capped, were usual in Magyar. *Further the opinion is entertained*[2] *that all the vowels of the old Magyar language were "to a certain degree more closed" than nowadays.*

Very often the Magyar "a" gets changed into "e". Lugossy, the scholar, expressed this strikingly by saying that every "magyar" had a comrade called "megyer".[3] Similar illustrations may be found in Maori, such as "ngenge" and "nganga", weak (Tregear), "tewetewe" and "tawatawa", a mackerel. In Magyar the term "gyenge", "gyönge" means: weak.

The change of the consonant "d" into "z", *unknown in any other "Ugrian" language*, is frequent in Magyar. Thus the word "kéz" (= the hand) came from the old form "kede". In Maori "katau" is the right hand and "katakata" a finger (Tregear); Maori "kata" is the Magyar "kaczag" (= to laugh), "iti" the Magyar "ici" (= tiny), and the form "iti" itself occurred in Magyar.[4]

Consonants as Initials. Simonyi calls special attention to the fact that in no "Ugrian" language, with the exception of Magyar, does any word begin with "f" or "h", and no Turkish word with "l, r and v", or possibly "n". On the other hand, "h, l, r, v" are very often the initial letters of Maori words; in the Marquesas, Samoa, Tahiti, Tonga, etc., "f" is also a frequent initial. Thus we have in Tahiti the words "fa": "tige," stem, trunk, and "fata": "entasser du bois," to pile up wood (Jaussen), the Magyar for wood being also "fa".[5] In the Marquesas "fatu" is the term for "se coaguler, s'épaissir", to coagulate, to thicken (Dordillon), in Tonga it means: congealed (Smith) and in Magyar we find "fagy" for frost and "faggyu" for tallow. In Tahiti further "fau" denotes: "chef, tête, principal," chief, head, principal, "faetoa": "peuple, gens, peuplade," people, nation, tribe (Jaussen). In Magyar we have the expressions "fő, fej" = head, chief, and "faj", "fajta": race, breed. In the Marquesas "faitaa" (Dordillon) and Tonga "feea" (Miss. Maristes) means: "malade," sick, and in Magyar "fáj" is: to ache.

For the Magyar nasal "ny" a counterpart may be found in

[1] See also page 59.
[2] Simonyi: *Magyar Nyelvészet.* P. 22.
[3] Bálint: *A tamul Nyelv a Magyarok Rokona* (The Tamil a Relation of Magyar). P. 218.
[4] Szirmay: *Hungaria in Parabolis.* P. 5.
[5] See also page 72.

the " ng " of New Zealand ; e.g. the word " ngai " according to Tregear " is a word of collection, in some way widening the dual form " and the Magyar " nyáj " means : flock, herd.

It is not impossible that the Magyar " cs " became " k " in New Zealand. Compare " kori ", meaning : to move, to wriggle (Williams) with the Magyar " csór " to turn, to screw, and also " csóvál " : to brandish, to wriggle [1]; further the Maori " koma " : axehead with the Magyar " csomak " : pickaxe, etc. Finally the Maori " w " and " v " suggest a comparison with the Magyar " z " and " sz ".[2]

Simonyi reminds us also of a so far unexplained exception from a general rule, according to which *words of " Ugrian " origin* beginning with " k " change this initial sound into " h ", and he quotes [3] some words which still preserve—as he thinks—the original " k " *only as exceptions*, such as : kar (the arm), kíván (to wish), kúsz (to crawl), etc. Meanwhile we find in New Zealand " kar " as root of the word : to round (Brown), " karapoti " : to surround, as with the coil of a snake, [4] in Easter Island " kara " : a wing (Churchill) ; in New Zealand " kia " : wish, and " kuhu " : to move with violent friction over a rough surface (Tregear).

Vowels as Terminal Sounds.

It is a characteristic of the Maori language that every word ends with a vowel.[5] *Not so long ago this was the rule in Magyar too.*[6] Vowels as terminal sounds are very frequent in the chronicle of " Anonymus " of the XIIIth century, and in ancient Magyar documents, whereas they have quite disappeared in modern speech ; thus Anonymus uses the words *hodu utu* (war path, highway of hosts), the present Magyar form of which is " hadút ". In Tahiti " hotu " denotes : an attack, " hotua " : " force, bravoure," vigour, bravery, " hotui " : " second rang des guerriers," second line of warriors, and " utu " : " voie par terre," land track (Jaussen).

Examples showing the Importance of Accentuation.

Finally an example may be quoted to show how much in Maori the meaning of a word may vary according to its accentuation, i.e. how much the different accents laid upon the same vowel may alter the sense of an expression. For this purpose the current New Zealand expression " para "

[1] See also page 80.

[2] More will be said when treating of the word " Hawaiki " and the Magyar " haza ".

[3] Simonyi : *A magyar Nyelv*. Vol. II. P. 41.

[4] " poti " means : an angle, a corner (Tregear).

[5] Müller (*Grundriss der Sprachwissenschaften*. Vol. II, Sect. 2, P. 9) exposes the view that this strict rule, according to which in each word the terminal sound must be a vowel, is not original, and only appeared after the separation of Polynesian languages from their common stock.

[6] Simonyi : *A magyar Nyelv*. Vol. I. P. 76.

may be quoted, as it suggests quite a series of Magyar synonyms.

Magyar.	Maori.
bara : slough, pool	para : mud
para [1] : fin of a fish	para : a name for fishes
paraj : weeds	para : name of a fern
paraj : cabbage	para : name of a tree, species of cabbage tree
parás, parása : glow, embers	para : turned yellow, sear
parlag : stubble-field	para : to cut down bush, to fell trees
pára : mist	para : dust (Tregear).

If we don't restrict ourselves to the New Zealand language, but take other dialects and compound words into consideration, still further examples may be found, such as :—

balán : white, fair [2]	para : "blanc" white (Marq., Dord.)
parás : soft, mellow	para : to put material in the water to soak (Mang., Treg.)
	mara : prepared by steeping in fresh water (Williams)[3]
	maru : "tendre," mellow (Tahiti, Jaussen)
paraj : excrement	paranga : excrement (Tregear)
pára : (usually in connection with "szegény"): poor devil, sorry jade	parau : slave, slavery (Williams)
parány : smallest unit, atom	parakau : small flounder (Will.)
	maramara : a chip, a splinter, a small piece (Tregear)
parancs : order	poroi : "commander," to order (Tahiti, Jaussen)
part : shore, bank, wharf, pier	paretai : a cliff, a bank of a river (Tregear)
	pari : steep (Newman)
por : dust	para : "poussière, saleté," dust, dirt (Arorai, P. A. C.).

[1] See the word "para" = swimmer (on a fishing net) page 106.
[2] Compare the Magyar word "bálvány" on page 54.
[3] Compare the Magyar word "márt" = to dip.

(*B*) *Grammar*.

GENERAL CHARACTERISTIC OF BOTH LANGUAGES.—MAGYAR SUFFIXES.—THE NOUN AND ITS FORMATION.—FORMATION OF THE PLURAL OF SUBSTANTIVES.—DIMINUTIVES. GENDER OF NOUNS.—DECLENSION, DEFINITE AND INDEFINITE ARTICLE.—THE ADJECTIVE.—COMPARISON OF ADJECTIVES.—PERSONAL PRONOUNS.—THE VERB.—THE FUTURE TENSE AND THE FUNCTION OF "MAJD".—THE QUALIFIED CONDITIONAL. FORMATION OF PASSIVE VERBS, ETC.—ONOMATOPOEIC VERBS.—"WHAKA."—SOME VERBAL SUFFIXES.—INTERJECTIONS AND CONJUNCTIONS.—ADVERBS AND PREPOSITIONS.—"KI."—NUMERALS.—THE NUMBER SEVEN.—THE NUMBER ONE.—THE NUMBER TEN.—SYNTAX.

Before treating this subject it must be emphasized that the present chapter lays no claim to be an exhaustive study; yet this work would be incomplete without some reference, however cursory, to certain grammatical peculiarities. As far as the Magyar language is concerned the choice of instances has been made from the excellent and concise manual of Magyar Grammar by *Simonyi* (Magyar Nyelvészet. Budapest. 1905), occasionally also from his more extensive study of this language (A Magyar Nyelv).

General Characteristic of both Languages.

In the *agglutinative language* of the Magyar the words are chiefly formed by the addition of *suffixes*. Although the Maori do use suffixes, their particles are often placed *before* the nouns or verbs. Thus let us here recall Simonyi's assertion that the *pre- or postposition* of particles is of no importance for the classification of a language. *Szinnyey* further compares the word-formation in Magyar to a "bad mosaic"; the words clearly show the interstices between the small stones and especially how roughly and superficially the suffixes have been inserted.

Magyar Suffixes.

The Magyar suffixes are derived mostly from *nouns*. They require some notice before proceeding to the treatment of other grammatical questions. The Magyar suffix *-féle* comes from the word féle = of this kind (eiusmodi). The Maori "whera" in Samoa "fela", in Hawaii "hela" means: like (Tregear).

The Magyar *-hoz*, *-hez* = to (ad) was in its ancient form in certain dialects *-hon*, e.g. "házhon" = to the house. Maori say "hono" for: to add, to splice, join, unite (Tregear).

In old Magyar words, *h*, *ha*, *he* are used to indicate a wish, a desire, e.g. "gyüh" instead of the present gyüjts (collect it), "meréhe" for meritse (he should draw), "nyóhad" instead of nyujtsd (hand it over). Müller mentions [1] that the prefix "hia" of New Zealand was used to express a desire, as in the word "ohia": to long after (Williams). The same idea is expressed in Magyar by "óhajt" (or ohyt, óhit, áhit).

[1] Müller. Vol. II, Sect. 2, P. 32.

Magyar *-int, -ént* denotes a way, a manner (per), e.g. megint = again, tüstént = immediately, at once. As a verb *int* means: to give a sign, to wink, to warn. The Maori have the words " ina ": for, since, inasmuch as, and " ina ": calling attention, denoting emphatic assent, certainly (Tregear).[1] In Samoa " inati " is " part, portion ", a portion, a share (Violette).

-képt (*kéj-ént*) expresses in Magyar mode, procedure, e.g. páronként (= in pairs), önként (= spontaneously), and is derived from " kéj ", a word meaning originally " the way ".[2] The Maori use " kei " in the sense of: at, on, with, in possession of, denoting quality, state, character.

The Magyar suffix *-kép* (*-képpen*) expresses the manner in which some object is to be effected, and is derived from the noun *kép* (= picture), or in the old language: form. The Maori denote by " kaba " (Tonga): the corners and edges of anything (i.e. its form) (Tregear).

-kor is in Magyar a particle of time, e.g. jókor (= in due time), mikor (= when), öt órakor (= at five o'clock) and is said to come from *kor*: age, time. The Maori call an old man " kara "; in Easter Island they use " koroua " for: old age, worn with age (Churchill); in Tahiti " orua " for: decrepit by age (Tregear), and in Magyar also " koros " means: old, decrepit, worn with age.

A comparative and also restrictive sense is bestowed in Magyar upon nouns by the suffix *-lag, -leg*, e.g. viszonylag (= comparatively), the origin of which is traced back to the word *alak* (= shape). The Magyar verb to form, to fashion, is " alakul ". In Hawaii " ala " is to rise up as a new generation, in Samoa " ala ": to spring from, to arise.

-ság, ség bestows upon adjectives and verbs an idea of condition, e.g.:

éhez = to be hungry, to starve	éhség = starvation
jó = good	jóság = goodness.

According to Simonyi it had originally a notion of time, as it meant: the *day*. In Tahiti[3] adjectives and verbs are changed into nouns by affixing " ra ", and " ra " is also the term for: the day.

The Noun and its Formation.

Maori *suffixes* for the formation of nouns from verbs and adjectives are: nga (ka), anga, hanga, inga, tanga,[4] also: na, tina,[5] and finally: ia. Here are instances of such derivatives:

mahi = to work	mahinga = the work
a = drive, urge, compel	ainga = pressure, hurry, violence
noho = to sit	nohoanga = the seat

[1] Compare also the Maori word " ano ": like, as if, also, not yet.
[2] Simonyi: *Magyar Nyelvészet*. P. 105.
[3] Jaussen. P. 6.
[4] Williams. P. X.
[5] Dordillon. P. 51.

pioi = " frotter ", to rub	pioina = " frottement de deux corps l'un contre l'autre ", friction of two bodies
topa = " tomber ", to fall	topatina = " la chute ", downfall
mate = " mourir ", to die	mateia = " la mort ", death.

Suffixes are added even to nouns ; the new word then has an added notion of time, quality or manner of action.

Magyar language forms from :

tanul = to learn	tanulmány = study
váró = waiting	váromány = heirloom
föl = up	föleny = superiority, etc., etc.

And also from :

harsog = to blare, to resound	harsona = fanfare, trumpet
furuláz = to whistle	furulya = the flute
beteg = sick	betia = disease,[1] etc., etc.

Finally in both languages adjectives may be used as substantives without undergoing any change, e.g. the Magyar fakó (= colourless, faded, also : light bay horse), temetö [2] (= burying, also : the graveyard), etc., etc.

Formation of the Plural of Nouns. There is only one form for the plural in Magyar, the old dual form having disappeared. For its formation either of the suffixes " k " and " i " are used ; or a numeral ; or possibly a noun denoting quantity is prefixed. Such a noun for instance is " raj " (= the swarm). A peculiarity of the Magyar plural is the coupling of " one " and " many ", e.g. " sok egy ember " (literally : many one man), used when speaking of many men in general.

In Maori the plural is formed :

(*a*) by prefixing to the noun another noun expressing quantity, so " rau ", " mau ", etc. [3] ;

(*b*) by using the prefixes " nga, ka " or the particle " i " denoting : in company with (Williams) ;

Also for the already mentioned Magyar peculiarity of coupling " one " and " many " we find an analogy in Maori. There " mau " (or : maha, maua) means : lasting, continuing and " e " is the indefinite article : one. On the other hand " e maha " (literally : continually one) is used to express many.

[1] In the dialect of the Székely tribe. See *Etymological Dictionary*.
[2] For the Maori expression " toma " : graveyard, see remarks on page 20.
[3] " rau " has the same meaning as the Magyar " raj " (= a swarm).

Diminutives. Diminutives in Magyar are formed by adding the suffixes *-ka*, *-ke*, *-ika*, *-ike*; in Maori by adding "iki" or "iti", e.g. "tama (tana, kana)": man, and "tamaiti", tamaiki (also: tamariki): child; or "o": a passage and "oiti": a small passage (Williams).

The Magyar word *kicsi*, *kicsiny*, as well as *pici*, *picin* denotes: small, little, few, trifle; and "iczi, iti" is another form for this idea, suggesting a greater degree of diminutiveness.[1] The Maori have similar words, e.g. in New Zealand "iti": small (Williams); in Tonga "kihii, uhiki": "petit," little, and "ikiiki": "particule," particle (Miss. Maristes); in the Marquesas "iti": "petit," little, "kikino": "petitesse, bassesse," smallness, meanness, and "pikinini", "pikitini": "petit, petite", little (Dordillon); in Easter Island "iti": small, little (Churchill).

Gender of Nouns. Nouns have no gender in either of the languages, and when it is necessary to express gender, a word for it is added to the substantive, for instance in Magyar *kutya* (= dog) and *kan-kutya* (= the male dog). "kane" (kana, tana)[2] is in Maori the term for male also, and in Tonga "gana" is: "homme aimé des femmes," a man beloved by women (Miss. Maristes).[3]

Declension, Definite and Indefinite Article. Declension in Maori may be exemplified by the word "te manu" = the bird. "te" is in the New Zealand dialect ("lo" in Samoan) the definite article, its plural is "e". In Magyar "te" is the personal pronoun of the second person singular. (In Maori also "te" is admissible in the sense of "*you* are the person" (Treg.).)[4]

	Singular:	*Plural*:		
Nom.	te manu	te rau manu	or:	nga (ka) manu
Gen.	no te manu	no te rau manu		no nga (ka) manu
Dat.	ki te manu	ki te rau manu		ki nga (ka) manu
Acc.	te manu	te rau manu		nga (ka) manu.

(*a*) *The Nominative*:

Neither in the Magyar, nor in the Maori declension is there any suffix or prefix to express the nominative. On the other hand most of the dialects (chiefly Samoan or Tongan) use the particle

[1] Szirmay: Hungaria in Parabolis. P. 6.

[2] Smith. P. 144.

[3] Compare the term often used in Magyar "nagy kan" (literally: a great male) to denote a woman hunter.

[4] Of course there is also an idefinite article in Maori (corresponding to the Magyar "e, egy"), e.g. in New Zealand, Hawaii, Tonga: "he," in Samoa: "se," in Tahiti, Marquesas, Mangarewa, Rarotonga: "e."—According to Müller no other Ural-language besides Magyar possesses both a definite and indefinite article.

" o ",[1] if it is emphasis that is desired. The same happens in Magyar, where they use " a ". In Easter Island " " (or " ko ") is even used as a definite article before proper name: a frequent occurrence in Magyar also, as a kind of intensive, e.g. " a Géza", " a Péter ".

(b) The Genitive:

Müller is of opinion that originally the Maori expressed the genitive simply by position, putting the determining noun before its dependant. This was also the case in old Magyar, where they still have expressions such as " úrnap " (literally: Lord-day, i.e. Corpus Christi Day) or " királyfi " (literally: king-son, i.e. the King's son).

Concerning the prefix " no " used for the Maori genitive, it is interesting to note that in ancient Magyar the particle " no " was also used to form genitive.[3]

(c) The Dative:

Maori use the prefix " ki ", Magyars the suffix " k ". According to Müller, when used before Maori proper names *and pronouns*, the " ki " becomes " kia "; in Magyar the dative of the third person of attributive pronouns may assume the form " ne*kie* ", instead of the usual " neki ".

(d) The Accusative:

In Magyar either the suffix " t " is used or the noun remains, as in Maori, in the nominative. E.g. both forms " kezem-et " (= my hand) and " kezem " are equally used.

The Adjective. As we have seen above, in both languages the same noun may be used as a substantive and as an adjective. A further analogy is that adjectives have no gender in either language. Neither is there any plural form unless the adjective stands alone.

Comparison of Adjectives. The comparative degree is formed in Magyar by the suffix *-bb*, e.g. rút (= ugly)—rútabb, puha (= soft)—puhább.[4] In Maori " apo " refers to the idea of " more ", to gather together (Tregear).

Concerning the *superlative*, it is interesting to mention that in certain Magyar dialects the ancient form of *náj* is still in use

[1] Finck: Die samoanische Partikel " o ". *Sitzungsberichte der Akademie der Wissenschaften*. Berlin. LI.

[2] Routledge: *The Mystery of Easter Island*. P. 213.

[3] Simonyi: *A magyar Nyelv*. Vol. I. P. 78.—Traces of this may still be found in certain expressions, such as: " te-n-fejedre," " ö-n-kénye szerint."

[4] The Maori word " puhoi " means: slow, dull (Williams).

instead of the normal superlative prefix *leg-*.[1] In Maori "nai, noi" is = to be elevated, to be high up (Williams); in Samoa "luga" is "sur, en haut, le haut", upon, above, the top (Violette).

If the Maori *duplicate* an adjective (noun) or a verb (either partially or entirely), the result means for the adjective (noun) a diminution of quality and for verbs an increase of intensity of the action, or a reciprocal action, with, in this latter case, a decrease of its intensity, e.g.[2]:

wera = hot	werawera = warm
maro = stiff	maromaro = somewhat stiff;

or, again:

rure = to shake	rurerure = to brandish

Duplication is very common in Magyar also and the results are similar as will appear:

jobban ≐ better	jobban-jobban = by and by better
lassan = slowly	lassan-lassan = pondered
külön = special	külön-külön = separately
néha = sometimes	néha-néha = now and then
már = already	már-már = almost;

and in verbs:

felcsillan = to flash up	fel-felcsillan = to twinkle.

Duplication is indeed very characteristic of both Magyar and Maori. For the sake of euphony it undergoes in Magyar often a small phonetic change, yet it is always the repetition of the same word, e.g. in "tarka-barka" instead of "tarka-tarka" (literally = motley-motley), "ingó-bingó" instead of "ingó-ingó" (literally = swinging - swinging), "mende - monda" (= rumours, gossip), "lim-lom" (= old rubbish), "sürge-fürge" (= very agile, fidgety), etc., etc.

Personal Pronouns.

The personal pronoun of the first person is in Magyar: *én* (ín); its accusative is: *eng*-em, eng-em-et (íng-em-et). Maori, with its "au, ahau, awau", differs widely from it, but we find in the Marquesas for "je", J: "no'u" (Do.) and Maori "anake" means: singly, without others, "anake" (Marquesas, Mangaia) is: only; "enaki" (Moriori): alone; "angaanga": to debate with oneself (Tregear).

The personal pronoun of the second person is in the Magyar language *te*, in New Zealand, "koe", in Tonga "ke". The interchange of "k" and "t" in Maori, as we have already seen, is quite frequent and further that of "t" and "m" is also

[1] Simonyi: *A magyar Nyelv*. Vol. I. P. 119.
[2] Williams. P. VII.

noticeable (New Zealand, Samoa). The use of the Maori "te" in the sense of "*you* are the person" has already been mentioned (page 34).[1] The third person singular in Magyar "ő" is in New Zealand and in the Marquesas "ia", in Tahiti "o, oia" (Tregear), in Easter Island "ia" (Churchill).

In the plural the Maori use also a dual form. Thus in Tongan "ma" means: both of us, he and I. "We without you" is expressed by "mau" (Tonga), "matou" (Tahiti), etc. "We with you" is: "tau" (Tonga), "tatou" (Tahiti). The second person plural in Maori is "mou", "moutolu" (Tonga), "otou, kotou" (Tahiti), "katou" (New Zealand). The third person "ratou" (Tahiti) and "aki-nautolu", "nau" (Tonga). In Magyar, where the dual form has disappeared, the plural is in the first person *mi*, in dialects also "mü, mük". The second person is *ti* (tik), and the third *ők*. Also the dative of the first person of possessive pronouns may be noticed; it is in Magyar "nek-em" and in Maori "naku (noku)" denotes: by me, belonging to me, mine, for me (Tregear).—(The foregoing remarks must be considered only as cursory examples in the important matter of the Maori pronouns. A more exhaustive treatment of the subject is given by Ray.[2])

The Verb.[3] Like Magyar, Maori also makes use of personal pronouns for its conjugation. Thus, for instance, in the verb "tari" = to hold out, to extend, the first person singular of the present tense is: (e) tari (ana) kou (where it should be noted that "ana" shows the present tense, as "ana" means: there; whilst "e", in Tahitian "te", *in Samoan "le"*, corresponds to the auxiliary verb "to be", to the Magyar "lesz").

The present tense of the indicative in both languages is shown as follows:

English.	*Maori.*	*Magyar.* *Definite form:*[4]	*Magyar.* *Indefinite form:*[5]
I am extending (or: holding out)	(e) tari (ana) kou	tárom	tárok
you are extending	(e) tari (ana) koe (toe)	tárod	társz
he is extending	(e) tari (ana) ia	tárja	tár
we are extending	(e) tari (ana) matou	tárjuk	tárunk
you are extending	(e) tari (ana) kotou (totou)	tárjátok	tártok
they are extending	(e) tari (ana) ratou	tárják	tárnak.

[1] Tregear quotes Hawaiian "ko": thine, Tahitian "tou": thine.

[2] Ray: Polynesian Languages of the Santa Cruz Archipelago. A Pileni Grammar. *Journ. Pol. Soc.*, 1920. P. 76.

[3] The Magyar term for verb is "ige". In Samoa "igoa" means: "appeler, être, appelé, nom, titre," to call, to be called, name, title (Violette).

[4] With the third person as object.

[5] Objectless.

Maori form the past tense by affixing to the verb (or verbal adjective) "a", i.e. the past of the auxiliary verb "he, e" (= to be). Thus "fanau" is in the Marquesas to be born and: U fanau *a* te tama ite po = "l'enfant naquit pendant la nuit", the child was born during the night (Dordillon).—The Magyar imperfect tense is in the

Definite form:	*Indefinite form*:
tár-á-m	tár-é-k
tár-á-d	tár-á-l
tár-á	tár-a
tár-ó-k	tár-á-nk
tár-á-tok	tár-á-tok
tár-á-k	tár-á-nak.

It would exceed the limits of this study if the rich and manyfold Maori and Magyar conjugations were treated here in full. However, some remarkable characteristics should be noted, as for instance the conjunctive mood of the above quoted Maori verb "tari" in comparison with that of the Magyar "tár" of the same meaning:

English.	*Maori.*	*Magyar.*	
that I may extend (or:		*Definite*:	*Indefinite*:
hold out)	ia tari kou	tár-ja-m	tár-ja-k
etc., etc.	ia tari koe (toe)	tár-ja-d	tár-j
	ia tari ia	tár-ja	tár-jon
	ia tari matou	tár-ju-k	tár-ju-nk
	ia tari kotou (totou)	tár-já-tok	tár-ja-tok
	ia tari ratou	tár-já-k	tár-ja-nak.

The Future and the Function of majd.

One of the ways of forming the Magyar *future* is the use of the particle *majd* (*maj*) = then, thereupon, soon (mox, statim),[1] suggesting a certain vagueness as to the time of commencement of the action. Maori have also a word "ma" meaning after a future verb: "by," or "for" in the sense of "to be possessed by, to be acted on by" (Williams). So they say for "by whom will we be led?": "ma wai e kane?", and Magyar: "majd vajjon lesz(-e) kalauz?", both expressions being even syntaxically alike. This "ma" of the New Zealand speech appears as "*mai*" *in the older Samoan, Tongan, and Marquesan dialects.* "Used at the beginning of a phrase"—says Dordillon[2]—"it adds a peculiar beauty, which can only be fully appreciated in the spoken language. Used alone it has a depreciatory sense." In Magyar "majd, mai" has also often the meaning: "by, almost."

In the Tonga Islands "mai" serves also "à marquer un désir, un souhait", to express a wish, a desire (Miss. Maristes).

[1] See Szarvas-Simonyi's *Historical Dictionary of the Magyar Language.*
[2] Page 54.

In such cases it must be put *after* the word, e.g. " keina ma ae (moa) ! " = " que ne puis-je manger (une poule) ! ", if only I could eat (a chicken). In Magyar they would say : " ennék majd (egy csirkét) " and here again " majd " would follow the verb.

The Magyar " ma " (= to-day) was originally *a demonstrative pronoun* and probably pronounced as " maj ".[1] In the Marquesas " mai ua " means : " tout à l'heure," presently (Dordillon) ; but used by itself it expresses a desired *acceleration*, e.g. " veve mai " = venez promptement, venez vite ", come at once, come quickly, or " mai a " = " donne donc ", now give it ! The Magyar language expresses the same by a particle denoting time, by " már ", " má ", " mán " (= already),[2] and Magyars would say in cases like the above : " gyere már " (= come along, hurry up !) and " add már " (= give at last).

The Qualifying Conditional, Formation of Passive Verbs, etc.

Magyar conjugation includes a qualified conditional mood, for which the suffix *-na* is used ; thus for the verb *vár* (= to wait) the first person singular of this conditional present tense is e.g. *vár-ná-m,* the second person in plural *vár-ná-tok,* etc. Müller mentions also a " conditional affirmative " in Maori,[3] and shows that the particle " ra, la " is used to form it. Now amongst the numerous phonetical changes in Maori that of " r " into " n " is, as has already been said, very common,[4] for instance :

" raku " into " naku " = to scratch
" wiri " ,, " wini " = to tremble
" ranea " ,, " nanea " = copious.

Magyar and Maori have also *impersonal verbs*. Such a one is the Magyar " villan " (= it is lightning), to which the Maori " e wira ana, e wila ana " corresponds, " ana " denoting, as said already, the transitory state of the verb. A flash of lightning is termed in Magyar " villám " ; in Maori : wira, uira, in Tahiti : uvira, in Hawaii and Samoa : uila.

Onomatopoeic Verbs.

Simonyi devotes special consideration to the onomatopoeic verbs in Magyar and enumerates amongst others the following : durrog (= to crack, to roar), fú (= to blow), morog (= to murmur), nógat (= to urge), óhajt (= to wish, to desire), pattan (= to snap, to crash, to explode), piheg (= to breathe heavily), pihen (= to have a rest). A comparison of supposed Maori synonyms may be added, viz. :

[1] Simonyi : *A magyar Nyelv.* Vol. II. P. 330.
[2] According to Tregear " marie " means : already.
[3] Müller. Vol. II, Sect. 2, P. 33.
[4] Tregear. P. XV.

turituri : étourdissement par le bruit, quel bruit ! = dizziness by noise, what a noise ! (Tahiti, Jaussen).
muraro : murmurer = to murmur (Tahiti, Jaussen).
nonoa : to urge (Tregear).
ohia : to long after (Williams).
patate : to creak, snap, emit a sharp sudden sound (Tregear).
pata : to snap with the finger and thumb upon anything (Tahiti, Tregear).
pihe : song sung over the bodies of the slain (Will.).
piia : être épuisé = to be exhausted (Tahiti, Jaussen).

"whaka."

A very frequent and most characteristic prefix of the Maori language is " whaka", in Rarotonga and Easter Island " aka ", in Tonga " faka ", in Tahiti and in Samoa "fa'a ", in the Marquesas "haka, haa ", in Hawaii "haa ", etc.). When preceding verbs, or even substantives and adjectives, it bestows upon them *a reflexive sense*, denoting that the subject has become the object of its own action ; thus

huti : to hoist	whaka-huti : to drag on
tane (kane) : man	whaka-tane (whaka-kane) : to take courage
ngehe : weak	whaka-ngehe : to be fatigued.

In Magyar there is a particle which has the same effect : " -akod " (-eked), as in

húz : to draw	huz-akod-ik : to take a long time, to hesitate
von : to pull	von-akod-ik : to resist, refuse
mos : to wash	mos-akod-ik : to wash oneself
ver : to hit	ver-eked-ik : to wrestle, fight

and this particle *remains unchanged* throughout the whole conjugation.[1]

May we be allowed to make a few remarks suggested by the " whaka ". In Magyar the word " akad " means : be caught on, to stick fast[2] and derivatives of this verb are : akadozás (= hesitation, stoppage, stammering), akaszt (= to hang), akadály (= obstacle), and perhaps also gát (= dam, weir), with gátol (= to hinder). In Maori we find the words " kati " : to block up (Williams) ; " kati " : to cease (Tregear) ; " aaki " : to be caught or held by a thing (Hawaii, Tregear) ; " kati " : " ferme, être solide, encadré, retenu par, pris, arrêté à, accroché à, embourbé dans," firm, steady, be embodied, withheld by, taken at, to be checked, hooked on, to stick in the mire (Marquesas, Dordillon). In Tongan " kati " means : " ne pouvoir sortir," unable to get out (Miss. Mar.), and concerning

[1] All verbs formed in this way belong to a special group called " ikes igék " (= verbs with " ik "), according to their terminal syllable in the third person singular ; their origin has not yet been entirely traced.

[2] *The Magyar word " fakad " : to dash out (erumpo), to arise (orior), had originally also the same meaning as " akad "* (*Szarvas-Simonyi*).—Concerning " szakad " etc., see also page 65.

"*gata*" *in Samoan*, we understand from Violette that "ajouté au verbe exprime la difficulté", when added to the verb it expresses difficulty.[1]

Tregear finds the origin of "whaka" in the word "hanga": to build.[2] Yet, starting from Magyar, one would be inclined to seek an analogy with the Maori word "kati".

Some Verbal Suffixes.

In the formation of some verbs the particles "ta" and "ti" are used to denote that the "subject has *to accomplish or to endure* the action.[3] In Tahiti "tata" is "a casual prefix answering somewhat to the Maori 'whaka'" (Tregear).—In Magyar we have:

fut (= to run) and futtat (= to make run, let race), vár (= to wait) and várat (= to make wait), ég (= to burn) and éget (= to make burn), etc., etc.

Interjections and Conjunctions.

The following examples represent some exclamations, interjections and conjunctions of both languages, viz.:

MAORI.	MAGYAR.
a (Rarotonga, Treg.): yes!	"a" has sometimes the meaning: yes![4]
anoai (Samoa, Violette): too much, exceedingly; anoano: a great quantity	annyi: exceedingly; a great quantity
ea (Samoa, Violette): that's it!	ez a!, a!: that's it
haere (Williams): come![5]	jere (gyere)!: come!
hea (Will.): what place?	hely: place; hol? (dial.: hó?): where? what place?
heoi, heoi ano (Treg.): is a word denoting sufficiency and completeness, generally with "ano", implying that what follows is the result of what has just been stated; however	héon: a word of the oldest Magyar literary document, the "oratio funebris",[6] and is said to be an expression for: mere, indeed, forsooth
hia (Will.): how many?	hány: how many?
iho (Ngata): implies a direction downwards	ihol!: lo!
ina (Tregear): denoting emphatic assent, certainly, to be sure	isa (Ballagi): yes, indeed, aye!
ina (Samoa, Violette): "de ca que . . .", because that . . .	innét: because that . . .
io (Tonga, Maristes): "oui bien," certainly! all right!	jó!: yes! (expressing assent)

[1] Perhaps a connection might be traced between the Magyar "hagy, hágy, had" (= to abandon, to admit), as well as the Maori "hati": "rompre, se désister de," to break off, to renounce (Marquesas, Dordillon), and "kati": to leave off, to cease, and "whaka-kati": to beg one to desist (Tregear).

[2] The Maori "hanga" may be compared with the Magyar "hány" = to throw, to pile up.

[3] Dordillon. P. 261.

[4] See *Magyar Etymological Dictionary*.

[5] Together with "haere", also "haere mai" is used, being the common expression of welcome.—Compare the Magyar "jere már!" = do come after all!—See also page 39.

[6] See page 27.

MAORI.	MAGYAR.
io[1] (Samoa, Violette): "oui!" sure! well!	jó!: well! all right!
me (Mangarewa, Treg.): which? what? what follows? what then?	mi?: what then?
mea (Treg.): a lapse of time, very soon	mihelyt (myhánt, miáth): very soon
nene (Treg.): a word used to call attention	nini!: see!
ngete (Treg.): to click with the tongue, as to have to urge on a horse	nye te!: an exclamation to urge on a horse
ni (Tonga, Treg.): this, these nei (Tahiti, Treg.): here, in this place nei (Samoa, Treg.): this, spoken of this, now	ni! (itt ni! ez ni! most ni!): here, this, spoken of
noa (Tahiti, Jaussen): "spontanément," spontaneously noa (Tahiti, Tregear): a word of common use noa (Hawaii): to be released from restraint noa (Mangarewa): without ceasing noa (Paumotu): spontaneously	nosza!: now then! go on!
ri (Williams): to scream	rí: to cry in a shrill voice.

Adverbs and Prepositions. We may now compare some Magyar and Maori adverbs and prepositions, taken at random and without special selection.

MAORI.	MAGYAR.
aa (Colenso): through	át: through, across
atu (Ngata): indicates a direction away from speaker	attúl (attól): from, as to leave the object
ei (Tahiti, Jaussen): "pour", for	é (-ért): for[2]
ho (Tregear): "a word expressing the action of giving, presenting, etc. It is very rarely used, except in composition"[3]	-hoz: to, as in "hoz-zá ad" = to add to anything
i (Treg.): during	-ig: to (denoting time and place), till

[1] "io"—"sert aussi de transition et fait ressortir l'opposition de deux pensées, de la conduite de deux personnes; il résume les causes, quand on va en déduire et expliquer les effets; il se met entre l'exposé d'une part et la réplique de l'autre, que fait une seule et même personne," serves also as transition and shows the opposition of two ideas, of the conduct of two persons; sums up the reasons, before the conclusion is drawn or the result is explained; it is placed before the statement and the answer given by one and the same person.—See also Churchill: *Easter Island.* P. 185, under "ae".

[2] Simonyi: *A magyar Nyelv.* Vol. I. P. 208.

[3] Compare with the Magyar "hoz" = to bring, and the above quoted "hozzá-ad" = to add.—See also on page 31 the comparison of the Magyar "-hoz, -hon" and the Maori "hono".

MAORI.	MAGYAR.
maku (Treg.) : for me, myself moku (Williams) : for me magiti (Samoa, Violette) : "rester seul", to remain alone	maga : self, alone
me (Ngata and Treg.) : in addition, with, often to be rendered, by. A further use of this particle is in the future in the sense of "must" or "let"	meg : has many meanings, as : in, again, once more, and, thereto ; set before a verb it widens the sense [1]
mea (Treg.) : because mea (Marques., Dordillon) : "parce que, pour," because, for meia (Tonga, Maristes) : "à cause de", on account of	miá (miatt) : on account of
naku (Treg.) : for me	-nak, -nek : suffix of the dative, nekem : for me
nei (Treg., also in Samoa, Tahiti, Hawaii, Marquesas) : a word denoting near position or some connection with the speaker	ni : suffix of the infinitive mood, in ancient times it was, however, a nominal suffix denoting direction [2]
no (Williams) : at, in, on [3]	-nott [4] : an ancient particle replaced since by -nál, -nél = at, near, on
no (Treg.) : from	nu [5] : still used in the Palócz-dialect instead of : -tól = from
o (Tahiti, Jaussen) : "ici, là," here, there	ott : there
ra (Will.) : by way of, by the top, over	-ra : on, to, over, as in "erre" = hither, "arra" = thither
raro (Marquesas, Tonga), lalo (Samoa, Hawaii) : down, downwards	alól : down, below
to (Tahiti, Jauss.) : "de, du, des," from, of	-tól : from
tua (Will.), tua (Tonga, Treg.) : on the further side, back	-túl : over, yonder
ua (Treg.) : after	után : after

"ki." Special mention should be made of the Magyar *ki.* According to Szarvas-Simonyi it means : who (quis, qui), when (quam), he, she, which, what (pron. rel. quae, quod) and it is also used as an indefinite pronoun. In a more extended sense it denotes besides : out, from (ex, foras, extra) ; further, achievement, perfection ; it is used also for a postposition, and even as a metaphor.[6]

[1] Szarvas-Simonyi's Dictionary.

[2] Simonyi : *A magyar Nyelv.* Vol. II. P. 305 : "bironyi (bironi) megyek" = I am going to the judge.

[3] See "noti" (Treg.) : to draw together with a cord, "noteama" : because.

[4] Simonyi : *A magyar Nyelv.* Vol. II. P. 29 : "Páléknott voltam" = I was at the Pál's.

[5] According to Simonyi they say "kománu jöttem" = I came from my sponsor.

[6] See the saying "kivagyunk most" = now we are cheerful.

Tregear states that the Maori word " ki " also has various significations, and they strongly resemble the Magyar meanings, Tregear quoting: " to, into, towards, against, at, which, for, in quest of, concerning, respecting, in consequence of, by means of, on, in, according to, in the opinion of, in the event of," and finally as a connecting link between action and object.

Numerals.

In Polynesian numeration we may encounter a number of inconsistencies,[1] and in certain islands they employ a binary system, counting in multiples of 20, instead of 10. However, the numerals are, with slight dialectical differences, the same everywhere. Taking the most important numerals, one, seven, and ten, let us begin with *seven*. This number had a sacred significance in Maori life, and the constellation of the Pleiads, consisting of seven stars, was especially holy.[2] Further the number 7 was also used to express a certain degree of superlativeness, of prominence, with special reference to family names [3] (Hue-hitu, Mitie-hitu, etc.). Some authors even see in the 7 canoes of the Saga concerning the first immigration to New Zealand the influence of this fateful number. According to Tregear the general Maori term for seven is " whitu ", in Mangarewa " hitu ", in Rarotonga " itu ", in Samoa and Tonga " fitu ", in the Marquesas " hitu " or " fitu ", in Easter Island " hetu ", in Paumotu " ahito ", in Hawaii " hiku ", in Timur " hetu ".—The Magyar term is *hét*. (In the Finn-Ugrian languages, that is to say in Finn: seitsemän, in Lapp: sietsa, in Suryan: sizin, in Mordwin: sizem, in Ostjak: tlabet, in Vogul: sat.)

The Number Seven.

Magyar sometimes call the *Pleiads hetevény*. The mystical significance bestowed by this people upon the number 7 may be judged by the Saga about the famous " Hetu-Moger " and by the aforesaid division into 7 branches of the immigrating Magyar at the time of the conquest of their present home. The week is also called in Magyar " hét ".

The Number One.

The general expression for one is in Maori " tahi (kahi, tasi) "; but " etahi " and " agatahi " are also used. So we have in Easter Island (Churchill): agatahi = one, e tahi no = unique, e tahi e tahi = simultaneous, and in Tonga [4]: " agataha " = a oneness of disposition, singular (Tregear).

One is in Magyar *egy*. Supposedly in its older form *ed*. (In

[1] Best. Vol. II. P. 175 et seq.

[2] See also page 3.

[3] Tautain: *Notes sur les constructions et monuments des Marquises*. P. 22.

[4] " e " is in Tongan the term for " le, la, un, une, ce, cette, celui-ci, celle-ci ", he, she, one, this, this one. Magyar " e " is this, this one.

Finn: yksi, in Lapp: akte, in Suryan: ötik, in Mordwin: ifkä, in Ostjak: it, in Vogul: akvä, aku.) In both languages, Maori and Magyar, this number bears a certain sanctity.[1]

Of "tahi" it may be said that it means also: together, throughout, altogether (Williams); in Tahiti: "de même, ainsi," also, thus (Jaussen). The Magyar have "tehát (or: tahaag, tahát, haat)", having amongst other meanings: thus, therefore (igitur) and in the speech of ancient times also: "egyszerre" (= at once, at the same time); they said for instance: "Ha ysten volt, haat emberi teste nem lehetett"[2] = In case he was God he could not have *at the same time* a human body.[3]

The Number Ten.

Although the Maori have several terms for "ten", they all begin with "ti", as "tingahuru" in New Zealand, "tirogouru" in Mangarewa, "tino" in Samoa (Tregear), "tinohuu" and "tiokohuu" in the Marquesas (Dordillon). (The two latter ones however only to denote persons, whilst for things "onohuu" or "okohuu" are used.) When enumerating persons from 2 to 9[4] in New Zealand, the prefix "toko" always precedes, but for 10 the prefix "ti" is used.[5] In Magyar ten is: *tiz* (in Finn: kymmenen, in Lapp: lokke, in Suryan: das, in Mordwin: kemen, in Ostjak: jon, in Vogul: lau).

Twenty is in Maori: rua-, lua-, hua-tekau; in Magyar: *húsz*.—A *hundred* is expressed in the South Sea by "rau (lau, kau, hau)", yet the real meaning of the word is: a multiple, a great number (Tregear) and has a similar sense to the Magyar *raj* (= swarm, crowd).—For *one thousand* the Maori use "mano", a word which is said to have meant in ancient times: numberless, countless.[6] Magyar also use the word mennyi! if they wish to express numberless, and *menny, mene* is the term for heaven.[7]

To *express fractions* the Maori make use of the above mentioned term "etahi" (= one). Thus they say in the Marquesas for a quarter: e tahi o te ha, or for the fifth part: etahi o te ima (Dordillon). In Magyar they rely upon the alleged ancient form of one, on the word "ed", using it as a suffix, e.g.

[1] See also Németh in the periodical *Kőrösi Csoma Archivum*, 1922. P. 242.
[2] Szarvas-Simonyi's Dictionary.
[3] See the interesting treatise by Frazer: "The Polynesian Numerals One, Five, Ten," in the *Journal of Polynesian Society*, 1901, No. 42.—The "athi-athi" = single, and "ethu" = one in Aneityum are the same as "tahi, tasi", because it is a peculiarity of this language that in words beginning by a consonant followed by a vowel they interchange, if possible, the two sounds.
[4] About some of these numbers (seven excepted) mention will be made on page 77.
[5] Best. Vol. II. P. 178.
[6] Best. Vol. II. P. 173.
[7] See also page 16.

négy : four
öt : five
hét : seven

negyed : a quarter
ötöd : fifth part
heted : seventh part.

The Syntax.

The syntax of both languages offers also a considerable number of peculiarities worthy of comparison. However interesting they might be, the extent and the purpose of this work do not allow of dealing with them. Valuable information on this syntax may be found amongst other places in Jaussen's work (pp. 35–54). The *structure of the sentences* quoted there often resembles the somewhat peculiar formations in Magyar, as for instance those used by the Székely-people : " te testednek szövétneke mondatik te szemed " (literally = thou of thy body the torch of it is said thou thy eye).

(C) *Examples from the Vocabulary.*

DICTIONARIES.—THE WORD "PO".—THE WORD "WA".—THE WORD "TARA". — COMPARISONS BASED ON TREGEAR'S DICTIONARY. — COMPARISONS BASED UPON OTHER DICTIONARIES. — POSSIBLE RELATIONSHIPS WITH MAGYAR WORDS.—ANIMAL NAMES.—PARTS OF THE BODY. — EXPRESSIONS TAKEN FROM SEXUAL LIFE. — NAMES OF COLOURS.—NUMERALS.—THE MAGYAR ETYMOLOGICAL DICTIONARY.—INDEX OF WORDS.—FINAL REMARKS.

Some examples taken from vocabularies will probably emphasize previous remarks.

Dictionaries. The *dictionaries* from which the words are taken will always be quoted, still for the sake of simplicity only the initials of their authors will be given.

So by Tr. *Tregear*'s "The Maori Comparative Dictionary";

by Wi. *Williams*' "Dictionary of the New-Zealand Language";

by Co. *Colenso's* "Maori-English Lexicon" (an excellent work which unfortunately never got further than the letter A);

by Do. *Dordillon's* "Grammaire et Dictionnaire de la Langue des Iles Marquises";

by Ja. *Jaussen's* "Grammaire et Dictionnaire de la Langue Maorie, Dialecte Tahitien";

by Ma. the "Dictionnaire Toga-Français" edited by the *Maristes Missionaries*;

by Vo. *Violette's* "Dictionnaire Samoa-Français-Anglais";

by Ch. *Churchill's* "Easter Island, The Rapanui Speech, etc.";

by P. A. C. *P. A. C. (Prêtre Mariste)'s* "Vocabulaire Arorai" will be designed.

However certain words have not been taken from dictionaries but from other works about the Maori and their language. In such cases the full name of the author will be given. (For the title of such works see under Bibliography.) For the Magyar words the following dictionaries have served as source, marked also only by their initials:

Ba. *Ballagi's* "Neues vollständiges Ungarisches und Deutsches Wörterbuch".

Et. *Gombocz and Melich's* "Magyar Etymologiai Szótár" (Magyar Etymological Dictionary).

Sz.S. *Szarvas and Simonyi's* "Magyar Nyelvtörténeti Szótár" (Historical Dictionary of the Magyar Language).

If the data drawn from these works result in an awakening of interest, *the chief merit is undoubtedly due to Tregear* and his "Comparative Dictionary", which, to quote his own words, "regarding the Maori speech of New Zealand as but a dialect of the great Polynesian language, has attempted to organize and show in a concise manner the existing related forms common to New Zealand and the Polynesian islands."

The word "po".

To what an extent *comparisons* are made easy by this excellent work, may be judged if we take as a first example of it the Maori word "po" and investigate some of its manifold meanings, both in New Zealand and other island dialects.

po : to become night, to darken into night[1] (1)
place of the spirits (2)
a season (3)
eternity (4)
po (Samoa) : night, to be night (5)
to have war (6)
bo (Tonga) : night (7)
to seize, to catch (8)
fako-bo : murder, murderer, to murder (9)
po (Marquesas) : night (10)
a day of 24 hours (11)
po (Tahiti) : the unknown world of Hades (12)
po (Hawaii) : the place of departed spirits (13)
darkness, to be dark (14)
ignorant, rude, savage, to be uncultivated (15)
unsocial, sour, unfriendly (16)
to overshadow, as the foliage of trees (17)
hoo-po : to assemble thickly together as people; to come in multitudes (18)
to emit an odoriferous smell (19)
to act foolishly; to give without discretion, without intelligence (20)
to absent oneself slily, as in the dark (21)
to be willingly blind or ignorant (22)
po (Mangarewa) : depth, profundity (23)

Magyar words beginning with po (bo) can be quoted of synonymous meanings (see indices).

pokoli sötétség = "darkness of hell" (1)
pokol[3] = hell (2, 12)
pokoli hideg = "cold as in hell" (3)
bogdán (Et.) = sleety, windy weather (3)
boszorkány = witch, spectre (1, 5, 7, 10, 18)
pokol (Sz.S.) = hostile (6)
boru = clouds, gloom, darkness (14)
pór = peasant (15)
pórság (Sz.S.) = peasantry, lower classes, unworthiness (rusticitas, ignobilitas) (15)
bogyán (Et.) = rude (16)
borít (burok) (Et.) = foliage (frons), leafy branch (17)
pologár (Sz.S.) = citizen (civitas) (18)
polos = bug (19)
bódít = benumbed (19)

[1] The indices added to each meaning should facilitate to find quickly the synonyms within the Magyar examples.

[2] For "fako" see "whaka", page 40.

[3] See also page 40. (Mythology).—Comp. Maori "poko" (*Easter Island*, Ch.): infernal: "pokoga": hell; "topa ki te pokoga": go down to hell! "pog," "bog" (Arorai, P.A.C.): night.

bódít (Et.) = to stream (incurro) (18)
bódít (Et.) = stupid, blockheaded (stolidus, delirius, ineptus) (20)
bolyó (Et.) = stupid (20)
bohó = silly, jocular (20)
bosó Dóra (Et.) = crazy, lunatic girl or woman (20)
bóka (Et.) = foolish (20)
potor (Sz.S.) = tramp (erro) (21)
botorkál = to err, to stumble (21)
bogdán (Et.) = to sit up at night, to be awake (22)
bodony (Et.) = hollow trunk (23)

With a less cursory research many other synonyms might be found.

The Word "wa". In the same way many interesting comparisons are offered by the Maori word "wa"[1] and its relations recorded by Tregear.

wa (New Zealand): local extension, distance, definite space, interval, a region (1)
indefinite interval, unenclosed, open country (2)
the time, season, space of time (3)
to be far advanced (4)
wawa: a fence, a palisade[2] (5)
whaka-wa[3]: to charge with crime or wrongdoing; to bring a formal accusation against, to condemn, to inquire into a case (6)
whaka-wawa: to return an accusation with another, to recriminate (7)
to consult together (8)
to dispute noisily, to wrangle (9)
kawawa: the paling of a fence (10)

Extending our investigations from New Zealand to the other insular dialects, the following expressions may be further cited:—

va (Tahiti): space in time, e.g. in "e te va orero reo": it is the time of the speaker (11)
the space between the edges of the layers of thatch in Tahitian houses (12)
vaha: the mouth (13)[4]
tavava: a crack or splitting by the sun (14)
wa (Hawaii): to hit, as a stone hits a mark (15)
a situation without friends or connections (16)
to seek to know, to wish (17)
a space between two points; a definite portion of time (as the life-time of a person) (18)
wawa: the sound or noise of wind or rain, or the agitation of water, unable to speak plainly (19)
a tumult; vain, babbling, foolish talking; noisy on account of great multitudiness, confused noise (20)
waha: the mouth, an opening generally (21)
hoo-wa: to sicken, to make sick (22)

[1] See also Churchill: "Root Reductibility in Polynesian." *Journ. Pol. Soc.* 1926. P. 111.
[2] "wawae" means to part, to separate.
[3] For "whaka" see page 40.
[4] Compare "vae": to share or divide food.

kowa : a vacant space between two things, as the space between the fingers or toes ; a strait, a sound (23)
tauwa : summer.—The Hawaiian year was formerly divided into two " wa ", of which the kau (tau) " wa " was the summer.
vasa (Samoa) : the Ocean, especially the space between two points of a journey (25)
vanu : a valley, a ravine, a chasm (26)
vatele : wide (27)
vateatea : spacious (28)
tavava : to be open as a door (29)
vakai (Tonga) : to discern, to look, to behold (30)

The following Magyar words, set in the same order again as the meanings of the above quoted Maori terms, may have connection with the root " va ".[1] According to Szarvas-Simonyi :

váj = to groove, to excavate (cavo) (1)
vál, választ = to dissolve, to detach (separo, disjungo) (1, 12)
váz = skeleton, framework (1)
vég = end, term, limit, part (1, 4, 18, 25)
tavaly = of the last year (3, 11, 18)
vágás = track, vista in a wood (5)
závár = lock (claustrum), clasp (5)
vád = impeachment, accusation
to accuse (6)
válasz = reply, answer (7)
vaj, vah = somehow or not (o quam), to discuss (8)
káva = hoop, circle (circulus) (10)
kávás = enclosed, set, kerbed as a well (10)
vakít = to blind, to blindfold, to dazzle (14, 30)
való = right, genuine, true, exact (15)
vág = to cut, to beat (15) [2]
vad = wild, to grow savage
vadon = the wilderness (16)
vágy = yearning, to desire (17)
vaczog = chattering of teeth (19)
zsivaj = noise, uproar (20)
vajadalmas = painful (dolorosus), miserable (afflictus) (22)
vajudik = languid (langueo), to be in labour, to have labour-pains (22)
tavasz = spring (23)
táv, távol = remoteness, far off, distant (25, 27)
távolság = distance
vastag = thick, fat (27, 28)

Comparisons like these would perhaps justify a deeper study. Especially the change noticed in Samoan of the sounds " v " and " z " (sz) seems worthy of interest, thus comparing the Magyar " haza " = the fatherland with the Maori " hawaiki ",[3]

[1] According to Simonyi (*A Magyar Nyelv*. Vol. II. P. 267) the suffix -va, -ve, denoting the mood, was in ancient times chiefly used to denote the place ; compare " tár-va " = wide open, with the Samoan " tavava " = to be open as a door.
[2] Compare the Magyar " vagy-vagy " (= either, or) with " vahi " : " qui divise ", the one who divides (Tahiti, Ja.).
[3] See also page 53.

or the Maori "va" with the Magyar "za" (sza) e.g. in the following words :

köz = interval (1, 12, 23, 26)
közel [1] = near (1)
köz = time, lapse of time (3)
község = community (5)
közöl = to communicate (6)
zaj (szaj) = noise (fragor, strepitus) (9)
száj, szá, zaw = mouth, opening (13, 20)
zajos, szajos = noisy, rustling, or bubbling of water (undisonus) (19), etc., etc.

The Word "tara". Following the same system for Magyar words, which, owing to their resemblance and their similar sense, could be compared with Tregear's manifold meanings of the Maori word "tara" (in Samoan: tala, in Hawaiian: kala), we may arrive at such results as [2]:

daru = crane (1)
to carry great horns (2)
greyish white (3)
to be tall and well-built (Et.) (4)
szál = stalk, stem (5)
szálka = splinter, fishbone (6)
száll = to fly, to rise as stars, start up as a song (7)
szarv (szaru) = horn, crescent (8)
szél = brim, corner, edge, end (9)
taraj (tara, taré) = cockscomb, mountain ridge (10)
fringes (11)
lace (12)
head (13)
tarol = to graze, to cut hair (14)

Maori gives (see indexes) :

tara (New Zealand): the name of a bird [3] (1)
tara (Mangarewa): the name of a bird (1)
kala (Hawaii): the name of a bird (1)
tauri: an ornament of feather on a weapon [4] (1)
tauri: anything made of ivory (2, 8)
taurei: white, pale (3)
taueraea (Tahiti): the young, healthy, and vigorous of the people (4)
tara: spines in the dorsal fin of a fish (6)
tara (Mangarewa): a spine (6)
kala (Hawaii): small and sharp like a needle (6)
tara: incantation, to utter the words of a charm (7)
tara: the horns of the moon-crescent (8)

[1] The Magyar "közlet" has the same sense as the word "zavar" = disturbance, chaos.—Compare also the z in "közel" with the v in "távol" = distant.—In Maori "ke" means: different, otherwise.

[2] It should be recalled here, that "d", "sz", "z" of Magyar speech may appear as "t" in Maori, just as the Magyar "cs" as "k".

[3] More about them may be found in Williams: "Maori Bird Names." *Journal Pol. Soc.* 1906. P. 193.

[4] The feathers of the bird "daru" are still to-day a military emblem of the Magyar.

tara (Tahiti) : the horn of any beast (8)
tara (Mangarewa) : a horn (8)
tara : the corner or end of a house (9)
tala (Samoa) : the end of a house in distinction from the sides (9)
kala (Hawaii) : the end of a house in distinction from the sides (9)
tara : a cock's spur (10)
kala (Hawaii) : a cock's spur (10)
tara (Mangarewa) : peaks of mountains (10)
tara (Mangarewa) : the crest of a fish (11)
tara (Tahiti) : a disease of the head (13)
tarotaro : to cut one's hair (14)

Comparisons based on Tregear's Dictionary.

Employing this method, which relies upon the similitudes established by Tregear, we may also try to find Magyar synonyms for other Maori words, such as *ora, taka, whare and rewa.* But once more it cannot be too strongly pointed out that no completeness has been aimed at, but simply an attempt to quote some words susceptible of furnishing a proof for the assertion *how much a thorough comparative study of both languages Magyar and Maori would bring out other and certainly most interesting results.*

See *Tregear* : *ora* (*Somoa, Hawaii* : *olă*) :

MAGYAR :	MAORI :
áld = to bless	ora [1] (Tahiti) : to bless
egészség, elégség = health, welfare, integrity (integritas Sz.S.)	ora : well in health
	ora (Tahiti) : to heal
	ora (Mangarewa) : health
	ola (Samoa) : to recover from illness, to get well
eledel = food	ola (Hawaii) : food
	ora (Mangarewa) : food
eleven = alive, lively	ora (Tahiti) : alive, to live
él (élet, élő, íl, ől) = live, to live on, to enjoy, to use (Sz.S.)	ora : life [2]
	ora (Tahiti) : alive, to live
	ola (Hawaii) : life
	ola (Samoa) : to live
	ora (Mangarewa) : life
illan = to escape, to slip from	ola (Hawaii) : to escape from any danger or threatened calamity
	ora (Mangarewa) : to escape, to save oneself in difficulty

See : *Tregear* : *taka* :

takar = to roll up, to wind (volvo, involvo, Sz.S.)	taka : on all sides, all round
	faka-taka : to twist, to roll
takar = to gather (lego, congero, Sz.S.)	taa (Tahiti) : to be set apart or aside, to remove, as a thing out of place

[1] For the most frequent interchange of "r" and "l" in Maori, see page 25.
[2] According to *Journ. Pol. Soc.*, 1926, P. 335, the word "ira" was so far not recorded by any Maori dictionary and denotes : "life as possessed by mortal beings."

takarít = to clear away	taka (Mangarewa) : to cast away kaa (Hawaii) : to remove, to change one's place
takaró = cover, wrapping	fa'a-ta'a (Tahiti) : the fibres of the cocoa nut husk
takaros = pretty	takataka (Mangarewa) : to be beautiful, well made
tegez = quiver	tea (Tahiti) : an arrow shot from a bow, any piece of wood fastened crossways ; a beam, a rafter, or horizontal stick to fasten an upright piece to
tegez = to gird round (Sz.S.)	taka (Marquesas) : a belt taka (Mangarewa) : to gird
teker = to wind, to twist	whaka-taka : to take a circuitous course
teker = to commit fornication	ta'a (Samoa) : to commit fornication

See *Tregear : whare* (*Hawaii : hale, Tonga : fale*) :

hál = to pass the night, to sleep somewhere	hale (Hawaii) : a dwelling place, mostly for men hale-fea (Hawaii) : the house of separation for the wife during the periods of her infirmity haleone (Hawaii) : a place made by men for a temporary residence
fal = wall	falefale (Tonga) : like or similar to a house, applied to a rock or tree that affords shelter
falu = village	falea (Tonga) : many, plentiful, applied to a place where are many houses.

See *Tregear* : *rewa* [1] (*Hawaii, Samoa* : *lewa*) :

lebeg = to flutter, to waver	rewa
lebeg = to float	lewa (Hawaii) : to float ; the visible heaven
lebeg = to be in suspense	lewa (Hawaii) : to swim in the air as clouds
lebeg = to swing as a pendulum	lewa (Hawaii) : swinging, pendulous, to move backwards and forwards like a hinge
evegő = the air	rewa : the air lewa (Hawaii) : the air, the atmosphere
lé, lév = the juice	rewa : to melt, to become liquid
lézeg, lézeng = to dawdle, to waste time (also : without special attachment)	lewa (Hawaii) : persons without home and local attachment

These similarities might tempt one to establish a connection between the Magyar " haza " (= homeland) and the Maori " hawa,

[1] " whaka-rewa " means : to put afloat. In Magyar " rév " is a term for harbour and " révész " for boatmen.

Hawaiki, Hawaii". Smith states[1] that in the legendary fatherland "Hawaiki-nui" the term "hawa" was used to denote a dwelling-house (like the word "ház" in Magyar). The change of the sound "z" into "w" noticeable in "haza" (still noticeable in Samoan) is not isolated; we may observe it in other Magyar-Maori synonyms too, thus in Magyar hiz (= to grow fat) and in Maori "hivi",[2] in "köz"[3] (= interval) and "kowa", in "tesz" (= to do) and "tivera" (Tahiti, Ja.) "faire avec activité", to do with activity,[4] etc., etc.

Comparisons Based Upon Other Dictionaries. However, in order to widen somewhat the sphere of research it seems to be commendable not to rely only on Tregear's comparisons, where Magyar and Maori words are placed opposite to each other, but to make use also of the *other dictionaries* mentioned at the beginning. The possibility of finding similarities will be thus considerably increased, as the following example will prove:

pure:

bálvány; also: baluuana, baluun, bábány, vávány (Et.) (1) idol	pulotu (Samoa, Tr.): the residence of the gods
	bulotu (Tonga, Tr.): the unseen World
	puleavao (Samoa, Vo.): "pouvoir suprême," omnipotence
	puloa (Tonga, Ma.): "fantôme," spectre, ghost
(2) road-roller (Et.)	purumi (Marqu., Do.): "route, grand chemin uni fait par les hommes," way, road, made by men
	baba (Tonga, Tr.): plain, even as a road much trodden
(3) fins of a fish (Et.)	pala (Tonga, Tr.): fin of a fish[5]
(4) enormous, e.g. "bálvány habok"[6] = very great waves (Sz.S.)	vavea (Tahiti, Ja.): "grande vague," great wave
bálványoz = to adore, to love as an idol	pulupulu (Hawaii, Tr.): cherish
	pure (Marquesas, Do.): "prier," to say prayers
	pure (Tr.): a religious ceremony

ero:

erő; also: ere, erü (Sz.S.) =	
(1) force, power	ere (Tonga, Ma.): "marc," residuum, grounds

[1] Smith: *Hawaiki*.
[2] See also page 74.
[3] See also page 51.
[4] Magyar "tevékeny" = active.
[5] See also under "para" on page 30.
[6] Concerning the Magyar "hab" see also page 59.

(2) virtue, cleverness	erawe (Wi.): "excellent", excellent aravihi (Tahiti, Ja.): "habile," clever [1]
(3) the host (army)	erepuru (Tahiti, Ja.): "mettre en sûreté les restes d'une armée," to bring under cover the rest of an army aro (Tahiti, Ja.): "combattre, faire la guerre," to fight, to carry on war arotahi (Tahiti, Ja.): "combattre en corps," to fight by units

tai:

szajkó = the jay (gracus, graculus)	taiko (Wi.): a bird
táj = country, landscape, surrounding	tai [2] (Marquesas, Tr.): the shore
	tai (Marqu., Do.): "rebord, marge," border, margin
táj = time	tai (Marqu., Tr.): a period of time
tajték = foam, surf	tai (Wi.): the sea, the tide
tajtékkő = pumice-stone	tai (Marqu., Tr.): the sea kai-hulu (Hawaii, Tr.): to be in foam [3]
tutaj = raft	tuto tai (Tahiti, Ja.): "mettre une embarcation en mer" to launch a boat into the sea

whetu:

hetevény = the Pleiads (Sz.S.)	whetu (Tr.), fetu (Samoa, Tr.), hetu (Marqu. Tr.), etu (Mangarewa, Tr.): a star fetu (Marqu., Do.), fetia (Tahiti, Ja.): "étoile," star whiti (Tr.): to shine kowhiti (Tr.), hiti (Tahiti, Mangarewa, Tr.): to rise, to appear as the sun, moon or stars vitu (Motu, Tr.): star hetu (Easter Island, Ch.): star
hét, hete = seven	hetu (Timur, Tr.), whitu (Tr.), fitu (Tonga, Marquesas, Tr.), hitu (Marqu., Do., Mangarewa, Motu, Tr.): seven

[1] In Tahitian "vihivihi" means also: "jet de pierre à la fronde," to fling stones from a sling.

[2] In Maori they denote by "ta": to be oblique, deviate from perpendicular, and "taiuru, taiulu" = to lean, to decline from the perpendicular.

[3] In Magyar "hullám": a wave.

híd, heed (Sz.S.) = bridge	whiti (Tr.): to cross over, to get to the other side of the river whaka-whiti: to convey across faku-hiti (Paumotu, Tr.): to get over hikie (Hawaii, Tr.): a bridge over a stream
hit = faith, oath	hetau: (Marquesas, Do.): " espèce de chant paien," a kind of pagan song [1] hoo-hiki (Hawaii, Tr.): to take an oath, to affirm to be true [2]

Before we treat of the possible relationship between other Magyar and Maori words, let us consider some *beginning with the syllable " ar "*

MAGYAR:	MAORI:
ara (Et.) = near relation, male or female	aro (Tr.): attend to, favour [3] aroha (Tahiti, Ja.): " affection, aimer," affection, to love
arány (erány, irány) = to, in direction of, relating to, in the way of, concerning	ara (Co.): direction of motion ara (Tr.): a road, a path, away arahi: to lead, to conduct ara (Tahiti, Ja.): " route, sentier," way, path aro (Tr.): to have a certain direction; to face, to turn downwards [4]
arat (arató) = to harvest	ara (Tr.): to gather arato (Tahiti, Tr. and Ja.): a person that pulls or drops anything; " trainer, draguer," to drag
arc = face [5]	aro (Wi.): face aro (Tahiti, Ja.): face
ár = the flood; to grow, to raise, to swell	ara (Tr.): to rise to the surface araa (Tahiti, Tr.): to be raised or lightened as a vessel in the water are, ari (Tahiti, Ja.): " vague, flot," wave
ár, áru = price, merchandise, trade; to be sold, valuable	ari (Tahiti, Tr.): the tribute paid to a king or principal chief; the advantages obtained by marriage or otherwise, such as land, property, influence, or government

[1] Also: hitihiti.
[2] See also page 12.
[3] According to Best (Vol. I. P. 363) " kok*ara* " means: mother.
[4] " arra " denotes in Magyar: in direction of.
[5] In the accusative: arc-ot.

ár, árul = to betray, to denounce	araara (Wi.): to talk about, be rumoured
	are te eo (Marquesas, Do.): "bavard qui jase comme une pie," chatterer, who babbles like a magpie
árok = ditch	arohata [1] (Wi.): bridge
	arua (Tahiti, Ja.): "fossé," ditch.

Possible Relationships with Magyar Words.

By further analogies, the Magyar words will be compared not only with consonant or synonymous Maori terms, but also with some supposed *kindred Ugrian or Aryan* (Caucasian) expressions.[2] In this way the following Magyar terms may be examined:

bot, dévaj, ének, fene, fon, hab, hév, hó, hon, húz, ige, jó, kapó, kenyér, kín, kova, léha, magyaráz, mar, mász, mén, metsz, mult, nap, nyúl, szaka, támad, tapad, tart, tető, tol, tör (= to break), tőr (= trap), töródés, törvény, ún, úr, út, vág, vakar, vár, vas, vet.[3]

Here the Maori words, in so far as they are taken from Tregear's dictionary, will always be restricted to one and the same *group of comparisons* made by this author; any exceptions being pointed out in foot-notes. (It may be noted that the pronunciation of the word "tu" was forbidden, *tabu*, in certain Maori dialects,[4] "tua" or "tia" being used instead.)

MAGYAR: **bot** (according to Et. also bath, bat), has, between others, the following meanings: club, stick, bar (clava, baculus, fustis); further: control, custody (tutela).–("patél" means: to beat.)

Munkácsi, amongst other parallels, makes some with the Votjak: bodi, Mordwin: manda, Tcheremiss: panda = stick, and with Sanskrit: math = paddle, stirring pole.

MAORI: patu (Tr.): a weapon, generally a club
patoto: to beat
pato (Best, II. 44): short rod used in fishing
poutoti (Tr.): a stilt
potete (Wi.): a stick used to hold a dog
patu (Tahiti, Tr.): a little wooden mallet
paku (Hawaii, Tr.): to defend, to shield one from harm; partition, wall [5]
batutu (Tonga, Tr.): to beat, to strike repeatedly.

[1] "hát" is a Magyar term for a ridge.

[2] See Budenz': *Magyar-Ugor összehasonlító Szótár* (Magyar-Ugrian Comparative Dictionary), or Munkácsi's repeatedly quoted work *Árja és kaukazusi Elemek*.

[3] The meaning of each of these words will be found when treated in detail.

[4] Jaussen. Pp. 63 and 68.

[5] Magyar "pad" = the bench; Tahiti "patu": a stone wall.—Magyar "páhol, páhul" = to beat, to thrash: Hawaii "pahu": an ancient drum, "pahupahu": to strike; Tonga "bahu": to beat soundly.

dévaj : unruly ; roguish ; cunning, sly ; knavish, extravagant.
Munkácsi makes a parallel with Zend : daeva, Pali : dev = demon, devil, Awesta : daevya = demoniacal, associated with bad spirits, etc.

MAORI : tawai (Tr. and Wi.) : to mock, to jest at, to taunt, jeering.
tawaimanino (Tahiti, Ja.) : smooth, flattering speech
tavia (Samoa, Vo.) : " rodomont," to swagger
tevateva (Samoa, Vo.) : " constamment fâché, dans un état de colère " = to be always angry
teve'e (Marquesas, Do.) : " s'amuser," to amuse oneself.

ének (enök, ynek) : song.
Munkácsi quotes, as well as the Finn : ääne = vox hominis et animalium and the Lapp. : jietna = voice, sound, the Sanskrit : vaha = music.

MAORI : ene (Wi.) : to flatter, to cajole
ho-ene (Hawaii, Tr.) : to sing, to be joyful
ekenaki (Tonga, Ma.) : " accords au dessous du chant," chords below the air.

fene : (feiné, föne, fenye, etc.) is owing to Kandra (P. 194) the term for a virulent, repulsive disease ; it is also the mythological personification of burning without fire, stinging. Sz.S. give the definition : wild, horrible, cruel, hideous.
Budenz suggest a parallel with Finn : peni ; Mordwin : pinä ; Lapp. : piednal = dog, etc.

MAORI : fania (Tonga, Ma.) : " blessé," wounded
fanoa : " une plaie, une saignée," sore, bleeding
fenei (Tahiti, Ja.) : " sale," dirty
fenuu motu : " abandon d'un ami," abandonment of a friend [1]
fene (Marquesas, Do.) : " gâté ; qui a perdu sa vertu," spoiled, the lost virtue
fenei : " rhume, toux," cold, cough.

fon (fan, fony) : to plait, to spin, to twist, *fonál* : thread, rope, string.
Budenz' suggestions are : Finn : puno, Mordwin : puna, Tcheremiss and Votjak. : pun, Lapp : podne = to plait, to spin, etc.

MAORI : hono (Tr.) : to splice, join, unite
hono (Tahiti, Tr.) : to splice a rope
hono (Tahiti, Ja.) : " brasse, joindre, unir," fathom, to join, to unite
hono (Hawaii, Tr.) : to stitch, to sew up, to mend as a garment or net ; stitching, sewing
hona (Mangarewa, Ch.) ; to piece out a substance with another piece of the same material
fono (Tonga, Tr.) : inlaid
fenu (Tonga, Ma.) : " lanières ; torons d'une corde ; bandlettes, bandes," lashes ; strands of a rope ; strings

[1] The Magyar expression "*fenébe ment*" denotes : gone to the devil, lost, forgotten.

fenu (Samoa, Vo.): "unir des choses tressées," to make a join in plaiting
fenuu (Tahiti, Tr.): to twist cords for net-making

hab (haab): waves, flood, billow; to heave.
Budenz' suggestions are: Vogul: kump = wave and the Suryan: gibal = to swim, etc.

MAORI: hapai (Wi.): to lift up, to rise
hapai (Marquesas, Tr.): the heaving of the sea
hopoi (Paumotu, Tr.): to lift up, to raise
hapainga (Tr.): a wawe-sacrifice [1]

had (hod): the host; military force (exercitus); war, fight, duel, battle (bellum, duellum, mars, pugna, proelium).
Budenz' suggestions are: Finn: kunta = complexus, collectio; Esthonian: kond = the entity; Lapp: godde = country; Vogul: kand = people, power; Suryan: kod = with, etc.

MAORI: hoto (Wi.): begin a quarrel, wooden spade, spike
hotu (Tahiti, Ja.): "attaque," attack
hotua: "force, bravoure," power, bravery
hotui: "second rang des guerriers," second row of warriors
hatu (Marqu. D.): "société, assemblement," society, meeting, gathering.

hegy (heegy, hig): mountain, top, point.
Budenz quotes Finn: kärke = cuspis, apex acutus, cacumen arboris and Esthonian: kärg = honeycomb.

MAORI: heie (Tr.): the summit of a mountain
heio: the ridge of a hill
hiku: the top of a leaf, the point
hiku (Marquesas, Do.): "sommet des arbres," the top of the trees
haeroa: high-pitched roof.[2]

hév (hé, héven, heves): warm, hot; *heves*: sudden, hasty, impetuous, raging.
Munkácsi's suggestions are: Tchetchenz: hevgho; Cabard: koabe, Sabzug: fabe = warm; Varkum: ka = summer; Avar: kin = warm, etc.

MAORI: heve (Tahiti, Ja.): "âcre, d'une chaleur cuisante," acrid, burning heat
heva (Easter Island, Ch.): frenzied, delirious
heva (Mangarewa, Tr.): furious
hevaheva: to walk hardily and with proud smartness.

hó (in the accusative: havat): snow.
Munkácsi suggests: Finn: suve; Lapp: sueve = snow; the Sanskrit: him = cold, frost, etc.

[1] See also the Magyar expression "bálvány habok" = monstrous waves, on page 54.—In Tahitian "vavea" (Ja.) means: "grande vague", great wave.
[2] See *Journal Pol. Soc.*, 1926. P. 243.

MAORI : huka (Wi.) : frost, snow, cold
hukapunga : snow [1]
hiona (Tahiti, Ja.) : " neige," snow [2]
hua : " atome, grain, particule," atom, grain, particle
hu (Marquesas, Do.) : " disperser," to scatter
hava (Easter Island, Ch.) : to disperse.

honn, hoon, hón : home, native country (domus, patria) ; *honi* : belonging to one's home (patrius, vernaculus).

Budenz' suggestions are : Vogul : kvol ; Finn : koto ; Esthonian : kodu ; Lapp : kote ; Tcheremiss : kudo ; Mordwin : kut = house, etc.

MAORI : Hono-i-Wairua [3] (Best, I. 66, 320) : meeting place of the spirits
whenua (Tr.) : the Earth ; the whole earth ; a country or district ; the ground, the soil ; the land as opposed to water
honua (Hawaii, Tr.) : a country
henua (Marquesas, Tr.) : a country
honua-ku-i-lalo [4] : the Southern Land
hanua (Motu, Tr.) : a village.

huz : to pull (trahere).

Budenz suggests : Vogul : kas = to pull ; Suryan : kisöd, Ostjak kus = to draw tight, etc.

MAORI : huti, huhuti (Wi.) : hoist, pull out of the ground
hutihuti : rope
huti (Marqu. Do.) : " hisser," to hoist
hutihuti : " arracher les plumes," to pluck feathers
huti (Tahiti, Tr.) : to draw water.

ige (igi) : word, speech, sentence (dictio, logos, lexis, verbum) ; fascination (fascinatio) ; *igéző* : bewitching.
(Budenz and Munkácsi do not mention it.)

MAORI : i (Marquesas, Do.) : " parler," to speak.
iko : " s'entretenir avec quelqu'un," to have a conversation with somebody
igoa (Samoa, Tr.) : name
ioa (Tahiti, Tr.) : name
igoa (Easter Island, Ch.) : name, noun
igoa (Samoa, Vo.) : " titre, s'appeler, être appelé," title, to be called
igoa a po : " mot d'ordre de passe dans la guerre," pass-word in war

[1] " pungapunga " (Tr.) : pollen of the raupo.
[2] Magyar : " hideg " cold, Maori : hotoke (Tr.) : cold.—It should be further noted that " marama " is a general term in the Pacific for the Moon. " zuzmara " (or " mara " itself) is the Magyar expression for : rime, frozen snow.
[3] " wairua " (Wi.) : spirit.
[4] " lalo, alo, raro " (Wi.) : the bottom, the underside ; the North.—Compare the Magyar " al, alól " = under, from below.

igofie: "beau, agréable à l'oeil," beautiful, pleasant to look at.

jó (iov): good, right, well-being; great, much.
Budenz' suggestions are: Vogul: jomas = bonus, dexter; Finn: jumala = deus; Mordwin: jon-die = lightning; Ostjak: jem, umoj = welfare, etc.

MAORI: io (Tr.): power, force, energy, life [1]
ioio (Tahiti, Tr.): handsome, brilliant
io (Tahiti, Ja.): "bon," good
io (Samoa, Vo.): "Ah oui! J'y suis! Je comprends!", yes, well.

kap: to catch, to grasp, to take hold; to receive, to reach, to find; *kapó* = catching.
Budenz' suggestions are: Finn: kaapaa and the Mordwinian: kapede = to lay hold of, etc.

MAORI: kapo (Tr.): to catch at, to snatch
kapo (Marquesas, Do.): "attraper ou recevoir un objet, qui a été lancé à soi," to catch or receive an object thrown at one
apo (Hawaii, Tr.): to catch at as with the hand, to receive, as into the mind
apoapo (Hawaii, Tr.): quick at apprehension
kapo (Tonga, Ma.): "saisir vite, bien comprendre," to catch quickly, to understand well
kabo-ta (Fiji, Tr.): to take hold of a thing with something on the hand that it may not burn, dirty or injure it [2]
kato: (Easter Island, Ch.): to catch
kabouti: (Arorai, P. A. C.): "engouffrer, engloutir," to swallow up, to engulf.

kenyér (kiner): bread, *kenyeres*: pal, companion.
Budenz tries to trace back the word to "kéreg," bark, crust; Munkácsi to derive it from the Caucasian And: ghan, Karata: ghani, Agul: guni and Mingrel: khobali = bread, etc.

MAORI: kinaki: food eaten with other food
inai (Tahiti, Tr.): bread or vegetables to accompany flesh
inai (Hawaii, Tr.): the little delicacies which give relish to food, condiments
inai (Marquesas, Tr.): that which is eaten with something else
kina (Tonga, Ma.): "ce qui accompagne les ignames dans un umu," [3] that what is added to the Yam-roots in the umu.

kín: pain; kínos: painful, difficult (dolorosus); *kínoz*: to torture (vexo, crucio).
Budenz and Munkácsi do not mention this word.

[1] "Io" (Best, I. 233 etc.) is the Supreme Being.
[2] Magyar "kapca" = socks, felt slippers.
[3] "umu" (Wi.) is called the native oven.

MAORI : kino (Tr.) : misfortune, evil, bad
kinonga : evils, troubles
ino (Hawaii, Tr.) : violence, vex, tease
kino (Easter Island, Ch.) : bad, wrong.

kova (koa, koha, kö) : flint-stone, pebble.
Munkácsi's suggestions are : Ingiloj : khuvaj ; Grusi : khua ; Tabassaran : goan ; Abchaz : gyanua = flint-stone, etc.

MAORI : kea (Marquesas, Tr.) : flint-stone
kea (Mangarewa, Tr.) : sand stone
kea (Marquesas, Do.) : " pierre, caillou," stone, gravel
kowha (Wi.) : summer lightning
kowhai (Best, II. 220) : yellow
kowhatu (Tr.) : a stone
kohua (Best, I. 420) : stone boiling.[1]

léha (líha) : thin, scanty, bad (as a stuff) ; empty, lazy, sluggish ; wag, rogue.
Munkácsi compares it amongst others to the Sanskrit : laghu = light, small, weak.

MAORI : rihariha[2] (Wi.) : small, bad
whaka-rihariha : disgusted, disgusting
lihaliha (Hawaii, Tr.) : to be disgusted at immoral conduct
liha (Tonga, Ma.) : " lente," slow

magyaráz (magyeráz) : to explain, expound, interprete (interpretor, perputo, declaro, expono, explano).
(Budenz and Munkácsi do not mention this word.)

MAORI : maka (Hawaii, Tr.) : a guide, a director
makabatu (Marquesas, Do.) : " clairvoyant, pénétrant, prudent, discret, avisé," discerning, penetrating, cautious, discreet, shrewd
mataitai (Tr.) : to satisfy curiosity
metakite : one who foretells the future
whaka-matua : to make known, to teach
whakamaramatia (Best, II. 90) : explain it !
magaro (Easter Island, Ch.) : to pacify, to reconcile
hakamagaro : to soothe, to pacify, to quiet, to appease.

mar : to bite.
Budenz mentions amongst others Finn : murta = to break ; Suryan : murjas = to nibble.

MAORI : maramara (Tr.) : hardy, to itch, quarrel ; to bite
moremore (Easter Island, Ch.) : to divide into bits.

mász : to creep (repo, serto) ; *mászó* : sneaking, crouching (serpens, repens) ; *ki-mász* : to crawl forth ; *le-mász* : to scramble down ; *rá-mász* : to assail.
Budenz quotes amongst others Finn : mata, Esthonian : madu, Lapp : mode = to creep, to crawl, etc.

[1] Magyar " kohó " = furnace, forge.
[2] Comp. " riha" (Wi.) : nit.

MAORI : mate (Wi.) : moving slowly, slack
matike : rise from a recumbent position
matere (Tahiti, Ja.) : " être capable de marcher," to be able to march
matito (Marquesas, Do.) : " marcher très doucement sur la plante des pieds sans faire du bruit," to go very noiselessly on tip-toe
mativo : " se glisser furtivement sans faire du bruit," to slip quickly without making noise
matinu : " ongles, griffes," the nails, claws
masike (Tonga, Ma.) : " se lever tant soit peu ; un peu soulever, faire un mouvement (p.e. pour partir)," hardly to get up ; to rise a little, make a movement (as for going away)
maseasee (Samoa, Vo.) : " glissant," sliding
masii (ditto) : " partir," to leave.

mén, mégy-en, megyen (mön) : to go, to leave space ; to admit.
Budenz' suggestions are : Vogul : min ; Ostjak : man = to go ; Finn : mene ; Lapp : manne ; Mordwin : männe = to free oneself, to get released, etc.

MAORI : mania (Tr.) : sliding readily over another object [1]
maniao (Tahiti, Ja.) : " pied, jambes, ongles," foot, legs, nails
meai (Tonga, Ma.) : " aller," to go
mene : " se retirer (parole souvent deshonnête)," to retire (often an insulting term) [2]
menana : to go [3]
manei (Arorai, P. A. C.) : " introduire, admettre," to introduce, to admit.

metsz (ancient form : met) : to cut, to chop (scindo, seco) ; metszö : (also) dividing (schismaticus).
Budenz quotes amongst other meanings : Finn : mätkää = to knock down, to fling down ; Lapp : mace = confringere baculum ; Suryan : nacki = to slaughter, to kill.

MAORI : motu (Tr.) : a cut
motu (Tahiti, Tr.) : a cut
motu (Marquesas, Tr.) : to cut wood, tear
motu (Marqu., Do.) : " coupé, rompre, casser, interrompre," cut, to break, to smash, to interrupt
motu i te u : " sevrer un enfant," to wean
momotu (Tonga, Tr.) : to sever, separate
mata : " lame d'un instrument tranchant," blade of a cutting instrument
fa a motu (Samoa, Tr.) : to devide in two
motu (Samoa, Vo.) : " être coupé, partagé, en parlant d'un arbre," to be cut or split as wood
motu ese (Vo.) : " être séparé, disjoint," to be separated, divorced
metaro (Arorai, P. A. C.) : " tailler, couper en morceau," to chop, to cut in pieces.

[1] Tregear asserts that there might be an etymological connection between " mania " and " mata ".
[2] In Magyar they say " menj ! " = go away.
[3] In *Journal Pol. Soc.*, 1913. Page 171.

motusi, motusi ese (Vo.): "rompre, briser, séparer violamment," to break, to smash, to split violently
moku (Hawaii, Tr.): to cut as with a sword

múl: to pass by (praetereo), to vanish (evanesco); *mult*: the past; *mulat*: to have a pastime (transigo), to find pleasure (delector), to amuse (recreo), to put an end, to beguile the time (evanescere facio, desinere facio).

Budenz compares with Vogul: muult: to go round; Mordwin: mole = to walk; Ostjak: mugolt = to move in circle, etc.

MAORI: mua: former time, origin; a medium, a mediator
mua (Tahiti, Tr.): previously, in past time
mua (Hawaii, Tr.): previous to
mamua: formerly, previously
mui (Marquesas, Do.); "après, plutard," after, later on
mulimuli (Samoa, Vo.): "le dernier," the last one
mulimuli ane: "ensuite après cela,"[1] afterwards
muliafe: "commettre souvent l'adultère," often to commit adultery
mutu (Wi.): brought to an end abruptly; come or gone without exception
murimuri (Arorai, P. A. C.): "être en retard," to be late.

nap (nop): sun, day.

Budenz tries to trace back the word to Vogul: naj = ignis, nat = lasting very long, and to Ostjak: novi = lux, nyptin = very durable, to last.

MAORI: napoo (Hawaii, Tr.): the setting or going down of the sun; the place where the sun goes down; the rays of the sun reflected on the water[2]
nao (Marquesas, Do.): "se coucher, en parlant des astres;" to lay down when speaking of celestial bodies
napea (Marquesas, Do.): "nom d'une étoile," name of a star
naponapo (Easter Island, Ch.): bright, to shine
na po[3] (Tahiti, Ja.): "hier soir," yesterday evening
a na po: "la nuit prochaine," the coming night.

nyul (nyó): to extend, to touch, *nyujt*: to stretch (protendo, extendo.)

Budenz quotes Vogul: nuns = to stretch; Suryan: nuzöd = to stretch out oneself; Lapp: unofcas = tough, etc.

MAORI: nuku (Tr.): move a wide extent
nuu (Tahiti, Tr.): to slide along, to glide
nuu (Tahiti, Ja.): "glisser," to slide
nulu (Hawaii, Tr.): to rise in the air like smoke
nuiae (Marquesas, Do.): "augmenter progressivement de manière continue," to increase continually[4]
noutua (Samoa, Vo.): "pencher le dos, v.g. en mangeant, en pagayant," to bend down the back, e.g. when eating, when rowing.

[1] In Magyar "multán" means: in the end of . . .

[2] "poko" is: to go out as fire, extinguished; "po": darkness.

[3] Also "i na po".—"po" is also the day of 24 hours, because the natives count day and night.

[4] Maori: "nui" (Wi.): great; "nuiga" (Easter Island, Ch.): greatness. Comp. the Magy. "nagy (also: noyg)" = great.

neua (Tahiti, Ja.): "étendu, lisse, calme,"[1] extended, smooth, calm
hakanui: to grow, to enlarge.[2]

szaka: tract of country (plaga), part (pars, frustrum); *szakajt, szakaszt, szakit*: to tear, to break off (dirumpo, lacero, rumpo); to divide (divido); to knead (subigo).

Budenz quotes Finn: sukuksi = to break into pieces; Ostjak: suk = fragment; Suryan: zugal; Lapp: cuouke = to smash, etc.

MAORI: whaka[3] (Tr.): towards, in the direction of; sometimes used to signify division
whawhaki: to break off, to pluck
faki (Tonga): to pluck, to break off, as bananas or nuts from the bunch
fakifaki (Paumotu): to pluck, to cull
hai (Hawaii): to break open; to separate as the lips about to speak; to crush as a flower[4]
sae (Samoa, Vo.): "déchirer," to tear
saeia: "déchiré," torn
saega: "action d'enlever l'écorce, la peau," to peel, to skin.

tapad: to adhere, to stick; *tapaszt* (tapint): to touch; *tapod*: to tread.

Budenz derives the Ugrian "brethren" words from the verb, tap, tapo = to touch, as in Finn: tapaa = to handle, to find something; Estonian: taba; Lapp: toppe = to seize.

MAORI: tapu (Tr.): to touch
tapa (Brown. P. 129): to macerate
tapi (Tr.): patch or mend
tapasu (Samoa, Vo.): "appliquer un bon soufflet," to apply a good slap in the face.

támad: to arise, to break out (as a storm), to attack; to originate (orior.).

Budenz derives it from the verb "tapo", mentioned before.

MAORI: tamaki: to attack, trouble
tamaki (Tr.): to start involuntarily
tamai (Tahiti, Ja.): "guerre, se quereller," war, to quarrel
tama (Jr.): a son, particularly the eldest son
tama (Marquesas, Do.): "fils, enfant, petit d'un animal," son, child, cub
tamate (Samoa, Vo.): "tuer," to kill.

tart: is a word in Magyar which has besides that of to support (sustineo) many other meanings, e.g.: to contain (contineo), to happen (corripio), to hold (habeo), to last (duro), to prevent from (custodio), to keep (alo), to mean, to believe (puto, censeo), etc., etc.

Budenz quotes Finn: tarma = force, power (vis, robur); Lapp: tarje = be able to (posse); Esthonian: targe = to dare, to endure.

[1] "nyugodt" means in Magyar: calm.
[2] "nyől" is the Magyar term for: to grow.
[3] Samoa: fa'a.
[4] "fel-szakad, fel-fakad" denotes in Magyar: the outlet, evacuation, outburst.

MAORI : taro (Tr.) : to carry
taringa : the circumstance, etc. of carrying·
tatari : to wait, to tarry
taria (tarie) : to be waited for
tali (Samoa) : to wait for ; to answer ; to receive ; to take food, to eat, food given to visitors
faka-tali : to hold out, to extend
tatari (Tahiti) : to wait, to delay
kali (Hawaii) : to wait, to tarry, to stay ; disease, waiting for death ; to be detained ; to hesitate in speaking [1]
tatari (Rarotonga) : to wait
taitai (Marquesas) : a long time, a great while.

tető (teté, tetej) : the top of a body as seen at first sight, e.g. the summit of a mountain ; *tetős* (tetés) : high, tall, heaped ; dignified.

Budenz compares it with Vogul : täj = bough, branch of a tree ; Finn : tähte = star ; Suryan : tidal = to be visible ; Ostjak : tej = the top, etc.

MAORI : teitei (Tr. and Wi.) : high, tall, the summit
tete-i (Samoa, Tr.) : to be rising (of the tide)
teitei (Mangarewa, Tr.) : great, high up ; steep, scarped
aka-tei : to extol, to honour
faka-teitei (Paumotu, Tr.) : to rise, to be heightened
teitei (Tahiti, Tr.) : high, tall, also a large quantity [2]
teitei (Marquesas, Do.) : haut, élevé ; gros, développé = high, lofty, big, expanded.

tol (toly, toj, tul) : to push (trudo) ; *kitol* : to defer, to postpone ; *tolakod* : to trust oneself forward ; *tódolog* : to press forward, to crowd.

Budenz tries to bring this word into connection with *the Magyar* : töm = to stuff, to fill ; with Tcheremiss : tem = implere ; Lapp : tälmo = opprimere, etc.

MAORI : to (Wi.) : drag, haul
to (Tonga, Ma.) : " planter," to plant
to (Samoa, Vo.) : " élever," to lift
tolo (Samoa, Vo.) : " bâton pour remuer les pierres chaudes," stick to shuffle the hot stones
tolo : " ajourner, remettre à un autre jour," to postpone, to adjourn
tolo : " cap, promontoire qui s'avance dans la mer," cap, promontory, advanced into the sea
tulei : " pousser en avant pour faire reculer," to shove, to push
tolo (Tonga, Ma.) : " jeu où on lance une grande boule," a game at which they fling a big ball
tolo aki : " lancer," to fling
toro (Wi.) : thrust or impel endwise
totoro : stretch forth
whaka-toro : push forth
toai, toaki (Marquesas, Do.) : " s'entre-pousser, s'entre-renverser," to push each other, to knock down each other
too (ditto) : " enlever," to lift, to pull up
tovia (ditto) : " soustraction," subtraction.

[1] Magyar : " tartózkodó " : hesitant in speaking.
[2] " tetemes " denotes in Magyar : a considerable amount.

tör : to break, to smash, to pound ; *kitör* : to break out, to burst.
Budenz quotes Vogul : taur ; Finn : särke ; Votjak : ser = to break in pieces ; Mordwin : serede = to be sick, etc.

MAORI : toretore (Tr.) : to split into strips
torere : to rush along precipitatedly
tora (Mangarewa, Tr.) : to be agitated
toli (Tonga, Ma.) : "casser," to break.

tőr : trap, gin, snare.
Munkácsi's suggestions are : Tchagatai and Kirgiz : tor = net ; Tchagatai : töre, tora = snare, springe ; Persian : tor = snaring net, leach ; Mongolian : tokur = network, etc.

MAORI : tari (Tr.) : a noose for catching birds
toro (Tahiti, Tr.) : the name of a fishing net
rua torea (Best, II. 501) [1] : pit traps for rats
torehe : a small, netted, baglike receptacle
toere (Best, II. 417) : hand nets
tururu (Marquesas, Do.) : "espèce de filet," a kind of net.

törödik : to care, to help.
(Not treated by Budenz and Munkácsi.)

MAORI : turu (Tahiti, Tr.) : any support or help, assistance, to prop or render support in any way
turu (Mangarewa, Tr.) : to sustain, to protect, to aid
turu (Paumotu, Tr.) : to support, to sustain
toro (Arorai, P. A. C.) : "serviteur," a servant.

törvény (töruen, teruen, teruin) : law, right ; habit, custom.
Munkácsi quotes amongst others the Sanskrit : dhárman = prop, solid holding, habit.

MAORI : ture (Tr. also on Tahiti, Rarotonga, Marquesas, Paumotu) : law, order, commandment, rule
ture (Marquesas, Do.) : "loi," law
tuutuuni (Tonga, Ma.) : "décret, loi ; fixer, déterminer, ordonner, établir," writ, law ; to fix, to determine, to order, to establish.

ún (unodalom) : to be bored, fed up, wearied ; *untalan* : with frequency.
Munkácsi compares it with Ossiet : omd = vomit ; the Awesta : vam = to spit.

MAORI : unene (Wi.) : to beg with frequency and importunity
unene (Tahiti, Ja.) : "bouffi, gros," puffed up, thick
unahea : "être las de cuire le poisson," to be bored to cook the fish
unaunaa : "grand travail délaissé," some abandoned big work
unu (Marquesas, Do.) : "contrition, être contrit," contrition, to be grieved.

úr : lord, man, husband.
Budenz brings it into relation with Finn : uroho = vir adultus, heros ; Mordwin : uris = hog ; Suryan : verõs = man, husband ; Ostjak : urt, ur = lord, nobleman.—Munkácsi with Sanskrit : ásura = thaumaturgical ; Old-Persian : ahura = lord, the greatest deity, etc.

[1] "rua" (Wi.) denotes : pit, hole.

MAORI : uru (Tahiti, Tr.) : to be inspired as prophet
uru (Tahiti, Ja.) : " être inspiré," to be inspired
urateni : " chef," chief
uru (Tr.) : a deified ancestor of the Polynesian ; the head, the upper end
uru (Mangarewa, Tr.) : an oracle ; to cry out for the presence of a deity ; nature, form, appearance
ururoa : dignity, good qualities, riches
uraki (Moriori, Tr.) : the head
ulu (Tonga, Ma.) : " tête," head
uluaki : " le premier, en tête," the first, ahead.[1]

út (in the accusative : utat) : road ; journey ; method, way ; *utaz* = to travel.
Budenz' suggestions are : Vogul : vuat ; Ostjak : vot = wind, etc.

MAORI : uta (Wi.) : the land, as opposed to the water
uta (Tahiti, Ja.) : " voie (par terre)," road
uta (Marquesas, Do.) : " conduire," to conduct, to guide
utai : " marcher, accompagner," to walk, to accompany
utu (Wi.) : spur of a hill
uka (Hawaii, Tr.) : to make a road.

vág : to cut, to beat ; *vágás* : the cut ; *vágó* : the cutting ; *váj* : to groove, to excavate ; *vájó* : the chisel.
Budenz' suggestions are : Vogul : vuon = to beat, to clap, Finn : vako = the furrow ; Suryan : vundi = to cut ; Ostjak : von = to square, etc.

MAORI : wawae[2] (Wi.) : divide, part, separate
vae (Tahiti, Ja.) : " diviser," to divide
va (Marquesas, Do.) : " couper," to cut
vahi (ditto) : " ouvrir, séparer, fendre en deux, briser en deux, casser," to open, separate, split, break into two pieces, to smash
vahe (Tonga, Ma.) : section
whao (Wi.) : to chisel, to insert
whaowhao : to carve wood
fao (Tahiti, Ja.) : " ciseau," chisel
pao (Marquesas, Do.) : " tailler du bois," to cut wood
vako : " raie, ligne, canelure," stripe, line, fluting.

vakar : to rub, to scratch ; *var, vara* : scab, scurf.
Budenz mentions Mordwin : angirda = to scratch once ; Votjak : ur, Suryan : or, Mordwin : uro = abscess, etc.

MAORI : wakuwaku (Tr.) : to scrape, to remove the epidermis by scraping
waru (Tr.) : to scrape
wharo (Tr.) : to scrape
waruwaru (Tr.) : peeled

vár : to wait, await.
Budenz quotes Vogul : ur = to wait ; Mordwin : varz-a = to inspect, to taste ; Ostjak : uralte = to watch, etc.

[1] " uru " (Wi.) : to arrive at a place : " uru " (Tahiti, Tr.) : to enter as a ship in a harbour.—The Magyar " ér " denotes : to arrive, to reach.
[2] " wa " (Wi.) : interval ; see also page 49.

MAORI : warea (Wi.) : be occupied, be absorbed
vare (Mangarewa, Tr.) : to rest, to remain
vare (Tahiti, Ja.) : "être dupe," to be taken in ; varo : "piège," trap.

vas (vos, vus) : iron.
Budenz tries to explain the word by the Finn : vas-ke = cuprum, aes ; Esthonian : vask ; Livlandian : vask = copper, metal.—Munkácsi (after F. Mátyás) by the Sanskrit : ajas ; Kurd : hasin = iron.

MAORI : whao (Tr.) : an iron tool, a chisel, a nail ; to insert
fao (Samoa, Tr.) : a nail, to nail
veo (Mangarewa, Tr.) : copper or tin
veo (Easter Island) : metal, copper
hao [1] (Hawaii, Tr.) : the name of any hard substance whatever, as iron, or the hoof or horn of a beast.
fao (Paumotu, Tr.) : steel, iron, any metal
fao (Tonga, Tr.) : spikes, nails.

ver : to beat, to hit.
Budenz quotes Suryan : wart = to hit, to tread ; Lapp : verde = to fell trees, etc.

MAORI : wero (Tr.) : to stab.
wewero (Tr.) : to strike with a spear
vero (Easter Island, Ch.) : to lacerate, to transpierce.

vet : to throw, to sow : *vetkezik* : to strip, to disrobe (se devestire).
Budenz quotes Finn. : vältä = vitare, declinare a via ; the Lapp : velte = to fail, etc.

MAORI : veo (Marquesas, Do.) : "lancer," to fling.
vetevete : "délier, détacher," to liberate, to undo.
veti : "ôter l'écorce, l'enveloppe," to take off the bark, the wrapping
veteki (Toga, Ma.) : "disperser," to disperse
veta (Samoa, Vo.) : "s'écailler, en parlant de la peau d'un enfant," to peel off as the skin of a young child
veve (Tahiti, Ja.) : "semeur, semer," the sower, to sow.

Animal Names.

Now, some animal names may be treated in the same way. They are, naturally, only suggestions for further deeper studies. For this purpose the following Magyar nouns will serve as starting points : *bak, béka, boca, héjja, kaba, kuvik, kutya, ló, madár, marha, pók, tehén.*

bak (bok) : buck, jack ; male of animals.
MAORI : Tane-poaka (Tr.) : a furrow-making god
poaka (Tr.) : a pig, a hog
pua'a (Samoa, Tr.) : an animal generally

[1] Rémy in his *Histoire de l'Archipel Hawaiien.* P. 19 mentions that "hao" is also the term for : to plunder, to take away, to lay hold on. He quotes the words of a warrior : "C'est du 'fer', j'irai 'ferrer' le butin, puisque le 'ferrage' est mon métier," this is iron, I am going to "iron" the booty, because fixing the iron is my job.—In Magyar "be-vasalni" means the same, i.e. to exact forcibly.

puaa (Tahiti, Tr.): "perhaps the name will apply to all the larger animals that have hoofs, whether close or not (the term "uri, kuri" may be applied to all other quadrupeds that have claws, except the mouse, rat, etc.)"
puaka (Mangarewa, Tr.): an animal, a beast in general; an injurious expression
puaa (Hawaii, Tr.): a hog, swine; a poetical expression for human beings (as "large white hogs")
kane-puaa[1]: the god of husbandry
buaka-tana (Tonga, Tr.): a boar pig.

béka (bíka): frog (teknös-béka: turtle)[2]; scurfy knot on the knee of the horse; a piece of flesh adhering to the top of the heart (Et.).
Munkácsi compares with Sanskrit: bhêkah.—Christian derives the same word, also from Sanskrit,[3] an origin which is denied by Ray, equally with the comparison with Maori "wheka": cuttlefish.[4]—Fiók considers[5] that the origin of the Sanskrit "bheka" is found in the "Ugrian primitive language".

MAORI: paka (Tr.): scraps
paka (Marquesas, Tr.): crust
paka (Marquesas, Do.): "sec, sans jus, desséché, durci, croute," dry, not luscious, dried up, hardened, crusty
baku (Tonga, Tr.): crust
paa (Tahiti, Ja.): "croute, écailles de la peau," crust, scales
pakaka, pakake (Paumotu, Tr.): hair-seal (according to Tregear "it is included among fish")
pekapeka (Tr.): a bat (Scotophilus tuberculatus)
beka (Fiji, Tr.): the vampire-bat.

boca: a child still hardly able to walk; *boci*: young calf, fawn; pocok: pigmy.[6]

MAORI: potiki (Tr.): youngest child, any infant
potii tarire (Tahiti, Ja.): "bel enfant," pretty child
tagata[7] poto (Easter Island, Ch.): a dwarf
poki (Easter Island, Ch.): child, infant.

héjja (héja, héyja): falcon, hawk.
(No mention made by Budenz and Munkácsi.)

MAORI: huia (Tr.): a hawk; the name of a bird (Heteralocha acutirostris). It is a somewhat rare bird and the tail-feathers are prized as ornaments.
huia (Wi.): a bird (Neomorpha Gouldii).

1. See the Maori "kane" and Magyar "kan" on page 34.
2. The Magyar "teknö" denotes: tub, trough, bowl.
3. Christian: Some Hindustani Cognates of the Maori. *Journ. Pol. Soc.*, 1913, No. 86.
4. Ray, ibid., No. 88.
5. Fiók: "Az Árják és Ugorok Érintkezéseiröl" (The Intercourse of the Aryan and the Ugrian), in Huszka's: *A székely Ház* (The House of the Székler).
6. In Magyar "pocok" denotes also the mouse (field-mouse, water-rat).—In the Maori speech "potipoti" (Wi.) means: shrimp, sandhopper; on the Marquesas (Do.): "espèce de crabe," a sort of crab; on Tahiti (Ja.): "petit, diminué," small, reduced.
7. "tagata": man, mankind.

kaba : a sort of hawk (called also "vércse, kánya"), fluttering and circling specially long before precipitating over the victim.
Budenz and Munkácsi do not mention kaba.
MAORI : kaba (Tonga, Tr.) : to flap the wings
kapapa (Tr.) : to flutter, to flap
kapakapa (Wi.) : palpitate ; flutter, flap
kopea, kopeka (Marquesas, Do.) : "espèce d'hirondelle du pays," a kind of swallow of the country.

kuvik (kivik) : a bird, the night-raven.
(Not treated by Budenz or Munkácsi.)
MAORI : kiwi (Wi.) : apterix, a bird
kiwi (Tr.) : "the night-bird of Tane"
kiwi-karudi (Tr.) : the name of a bird.[1]

kutya (kurja) : dog ("kurja" is more applied to the wolf). "kuri-kutya" = a call for dogs.
Munkácsi quotes Vogul : kūt'aw = small dog ; Votjak : kuca-pi = lap-dog ; Mordwin : kisika = dog ; Hindostani : kutta, etc.
MAORI : kuri (Tr. and Wi.) : a dog
kuri (Rarotonga, Mangarewa, Tr.) : a dog, any quadruped
uri (Tahiti, Ja.) }
kuli (Toga, Ma.) } "chien," dog.

ló (lou, lu, lov, in the plural lov-ak) : horse.
Munkácsi refers to the Vogul : luw ; Ostjak : lou = horse ; Tschetschenz : lū = chamois, gila = horse, in Buduch, Djakh : lak.
MAORI : rou (Wi.) : club-footed
lova : (Tonga, Ma.) : "lieu de la course aux chevaux ou la course même," horse racing-place or the race itself.

madár : bird.
Munkácsi calls special attention to the fact that neither in the Turkish, nor in the Ugrian languages a relationship could be established for this word. He tries to derive it from the Sanskrit "mandra" = sounding sweetly.
MAORI : Tane-mataahi (Best, I. 99) : the deity of birds
mata (Tr.) : the name of a bird
matata : a bird which was offered up by the elder warriors before an engagement
mata kiore : the stitch bird
matuku-hurepo : the name of a bird (the black-backed bittern)
matuku-moana : the name of a bird (the white-fronted heron)
matuku-tai : the blue heron
matuku, matuu : "oiseau de mer," a sea-bird
matuu (Samoa, Vo.) : "grue," crane.

marha : cattle ; wealth, possession ; beast, brute.
ruha-marha : wardrobe (Sz.S.)
marha-erös : very strong
"*nagy marha*" : a great person
"*marha*" : used as an insult for a stupid person

[1] Karuhiruhi (Tr.) : the name of a bird, the shag.—Magyar "karvaly, karuj": falcon, sparrow-hawk. (See also page 88.)

MAORI : marea, mareka (Tr.) : many, multitudinous
mara (Wi.) : term addressed to a man
mara (Marquesas, Do.) : " pour exprimer la jalousie et la piaillerie d'une personne bavarde," an expression for the jealousy and shrieks of a garrulous person
malohi (Tonga, Ma.) : " fort, ferme, puissant," strong, firm, mighty
maroro (Arorai, P. A. C.) " fort, puissant," strong, powerful.

pók : spider.
MAORI : katepo (Hochstetter) : small black spider
katipo (Wi.) : venomous spider
poko (Tr.) : the ant
pukaveevee (Marquesas, Do.) : " araignée, toile d'araignée," spider, cobweb.

tehén (in accusative : tehene-t), teheny, tehin, tejen : cow.
Munkácsi refers to Awesta : daenu = female of animals ; Sanskrit : dhenú = lacteal, etc.
MAORI : tehine (Tr.) : to squeeze out fluid of a female.
teine (Samoa, Vo.) : " fille, personne non mariée, se dit même d'une veuve," girl, unmarried person, applied also to widows.

Parts of the Body.

Let us now compare the names of parts of the body, e.g. *bél, fő, fog, gyomor, has, hát, hiz-ik, láb, nyak, nyál, pocos, púp, rókáz, takony, térd, vér,* just as well as some expressions of the sexual life.

bél : intestine, bowels.
Budenz quotes Finn : väli = locus intermedius, interstitium, quod inter alia est ; Votjak : polin = in, polti = through ; Suryan : pölsen = between, etc.
MAORI : palahi (Hawaii, Tr.) : to discharge liquid matters from the bowels
pera (Tahiti, Ja.) : " ordures, boue," filth, mud
bela (Tonga, Tr.) : purulent
pela (Tonga, Ma.) : " boueux, couler, suppurer," muddy, to flow, to suppurate
pala : " suppuration, pourriture," suppuration, putrefaction
pala (Samoa, Vo.) : " se pourrir, pourriture, maladie des enfants," to rot, putrefaction, illness of children
palasia : " être surchargé de nourriture," to be overfed.

fő (fe, fé, fei, fin, fow, etc.) : chief, head ; life ; human being, person ; cluster, ear, spike ; fountain ; the highest rank, the chieftain, the leader, etc.[1]
A comparison with Maori synonyms will be all the more interesting, as this word can also be compared with the Magyar " fa " : wood, tree.
MAORI : First of all Tregear's comparatives will be treated, viz. :
whau : the name of a shrub, Entelea arborescens, a well-known Polynesian cloth making plant, now extinct in New Zealand

[1] Szarvas-Simonyi refer to no less than twelve groups of meanings for this word.

in Samoan :
fau : the name of a tree (Hibiscus tiliaceus)
fauui : the name of a tree (Frema cannabina)
fauuta : the name of a plant (Masutia australis)

in Tahitian :
fau : the name of a tree ; god, as being head or above ; a king or principal chief was formerly called " fau ", (as being above all others)
faupoo : a hat, cap, or bonnet

in Hawaiian :
hau : the name of a tree or large bush ; anciently the title of the highest rank of chiefs

in Tongan :
fau : the name of a tree ; a turban ; to lead, to teach to work ; very, the sign of superlative degree

in Mangarewan :
hou : the name of a tree ; respect

in Paumotuan :
fau : the hibiscus-tree
hau : to reign, to rule

According to other sources :
fa (Tonga, Ma.) : " espèce d'arbre, pandanus," the pandanus-tree
fana : " mât " mast
fasi : " un morceau de bois," piece of wood
foi : " tête," head
fa'a (Marquesas, Do.) : " pandanus odoratissimus," the Pandanus odoratissimus-tree
fakaha : " sorte d'arbre à pain," a sort of bread-tree
feiau : " espèce de cérémonie pour faire les chefs," [1] a sort of ceremony for the investiture of chieftains
fa (Tahiti, Ja.) : " tige," stub, stem
fau : " chef, tête, principal," chief, head, master
fata : " entasser du bois," to pile up wood
feia : " peuple, gens," [2] people, tribe, race.

fog : tooth ; *fogas* = toothed.
Budenz quotes Vogul : pänk ; Ostjak : penk ; Mordwin : pej ; Suryan : pin ; Finn : pii = tooth.
MAORI : niho (Wi.) : tooth
niho (Tahiti, Ja.) : " dent, corne," tooth, horn
niho (Marquesas, Do.) : " dent," tooth
nifo (Tonga, Ma.) } " dent," tooth
nifo (Samoa, Vo.) }
fai nifo (Samoa, Vo.) : " arracher une ou plusieures dents," to extract one or several teeth [3]
fogifogi : " partie entre la lèvre supérieure et le nez," the part between upper lip and nose
ugi (Arorai, P. A. C.) : " dent," tooth.

gyomor (gyamor, giomra, gumur) : stomach.
Budenz refers to Vogul : namr ; Ostjak : numir = cattle, etc.

[1] " au " means : " respect, considération," respect, consideration.
[2] The Magyar " faj, fajta " terms = race, breed.
[3] Magyar : " fogfájás " = toothache.

MAORI : kome (Wi.) : take food
komiromiro : stomach-ache
ouma (Tahiti, Ja.) : "estomac," stomach
kokoma (Easter Island, Ch.) : bowels, entrails, intestines, rectum.

has : the belly ; *hasas, hasu* = bulgy, pregnant.
Budenz tries to connect it with Vogul : kapsi ; Esthonian : kops = lungs ; Finn ; kupsu = vesica piscium natatoria = swimming bladder of fishes, etc.
MAORI : hawa (Tr.) : the ventral fin of a fish
hawahawa (Marquesas, Do.) : "se coucher sur le ventre," to lie down on the stomach.

hát : back, ridge.
(Budenz and Munkácsi do not mention this word.)
MAORI : hoto, hotu (Easter Island, Ch.) : shoulder
hotoka (Marquesas, Do.) : "nuque," neck.

híz : pinguescere, saginari = to get obese or paunchy.
Budenz quotes Finn : kuut = renes, the loins ; Mordwin : kuja = obese ; Votjak : kvaj = fat and Vogul : kot = to get paunchy, etc.
MAORI : hiva (Tahiti, Ja.) : "abondance," opulence
hivavi (Marquesas, Do.) : très gros," very fat
whiwhi (Wi.) : fat covering the entrails.

láb : foot, pedestal, base ; *lap* : surface, plane ; *lapos* : flat ; *lapát* : shovel.
Budenz quotes Vogul : ba'il, laél = foot ; Ostjak : lakké = the bear's paw, etc.
MAORI ; raparapa (Wi.) : the flat part of the foot
rapa : the flat part of a spade [1]
raparapa (Mangarewa, Tr.) } the blade of a paddle.[2]
rapa (Paumotu, Tr.) }
lapa (Hawaii, Tr.) : a ridge of land between two ravines ; having a flat or square side
lapa (Samoa, Vo.) : "morceau plat des gros arbres à leur pied et qui servent d'arc-boutants," the flat part of the base of big trees serving as their props
lafa (Toga, Ma.) : "plat," flat.

nyak : neck, nape ; *nyakas* : boasting, firm, stubborn.[3]
Budenz derives this word from "to bend", especially from the Vogul : nov = moveri ; Ostjak : nogom = to run ; Suryan : nukledli = to bend.
MAORI : ngaku (Wi.) : bowels, heart
ngaku-nui (Tr.) : hearty, eager
nokunoku (Easter Island, Ch.) : throat.

pocos : ventrus, paunchy.
(Budenz and Munkácsi do not treat this expression.)

[1] Magy. "ásó-lap" = the blade of a shovel.
[2] Magy. "evező-lapát" = blade of an oar ; concerning "evező" see also page 102.
[3] "ngao" (Wi.) : palate ; sprout, shout.

MAORI: potopoto (Samoa, Vo.): "rond, de forme ronde," round, roundish
potopoto (Tonga, Ma.): "rond, circulaire," round, circular
potaa (Tahiti, Ja.): "rond, ovale," round, oval
poitope: "ventre proéminent," a prominent belly
puta (Samoa, Vo.): "gros," fat; estomac," stomach.

púp: hump, bunch, knob; peak, summit.
MAORI: pupaka (Tr.): a knot in wood
pupu (Paumotu, Ch.): to heap
pupupu (Easter Island, Ch.): to agglomerate
bubu (Arorai, P. A. C.): "croître, grandir," to increase
bubuto (Tonga, Tr.): to be bulged out
pupuga (Samoa, Vo.): "grosseurs qui riennent aux aines," knobs at the groins
pupu: "chaînes de roches caverneuses au bord de la mer," chains of rocks with caverns on the coast.

rókáz: to vomit.
Budenz and Munkácsi do not treat this expression.
MAORI: ruaki (Tr.) / ruaki (Rarotonga, Paumotu, Tr.) / ruai (Tahiti, Ja.) } to vomit.

szem (zeem, zöm, szöm): eye; ring; grain, granule; bud; point; mesh of a net.
Budenz refers to Vogul: säm; Mordwin: selmä; Finn: silma = eye.
MAORI: samaivao (Samoa, Vo.): "pigeon borgne pris dans les bois," a pigeon caught from the bush having an eye blind
somoa: "avoir les yeux collés," to have the eyes agglutinated
somosomo: "petit rejeton," a small sprout
sumu: "constellation d'étoiles," a cluster of stars.[1]

takony: glanders, phlegm (especially the one from the nose). "taknyosok" is a term for persons (mainly children) who are still irresponsible.
Budenz and Munkácsi do not quote comparatives for this word.
MAORI: tako (Wi.): palate, gums
takurutu: feeble, sluggish. "Kia ata haere tatou i nga takurutu" = let us go slowly with regard to the feeble ones
tokai (Marquesas, Do.): "lie," phlegm, spittle
tokoai: "malpropre, tout couvert de saleté," dirty, entirely soiled

[1] The most usual expression for "eye" throughout the Pacific—and even beyond, through the Malay Archipelago and the Malacca Straits—up to some tribes on the Ganges—is "mata", "meta". (In Hawaii: "maka"; Lifu: "mek"; Murua, Kibiri: "magi," Kisa: "makan," etc.) Like the Magyar "szem" it has (Tr.), besides the meanings of eye, face, those of grain, granule; bud; point; mesh of a net. Further significations are: the sharp edge of a tool; the foreskin of males cut off in circumcision (Hawaii); a person beloved, courted, etc.

We find in Magyar: "mag": grain, granule; germ, bud; "mátka," "maca" are synonyms of beloved; "matat" (Ba.) is: to search; "mátoha": a spectre, an apparition; "motoz": to search; "met," "metél": to cut, and "mét-háló" is the name for a kind of fishing net.

térd : knee.
No comparatives with Budenz and Munkácsi.
MAORI : turi (Tr.) : the knee
turi (Tahiti, Tr.) : knee
turi (Mangarewa, Tr.) : knee
turida (Brumes Island, Tr.) : knee.

vér (vyér, vir) : blood.
Budenz refers to Vogul : vur ; Lapp : varra ; Mordwin : ver ; Finn : vere ; Suryan : vir = blood.
MAORI : ware (Wi.) : viscous fluid ; spittle ; exudation of trees
vari (Tahiti, Ja.) : " sang, tiré ou écoulé," drained or flowing blood, blood, outside of bodies
evaria (Arorai, P. A. C.) : " saigner," to bleed.

Expressions taken from the Sexual Life.

In connection with the parts of the body treated above, some expressions for genital organs or taken from the sexual life may be also compared. For the Magyar terms as : here (= testicle), makk (= glans), mony (= penis), ondó (= semen), pina (= vagina), we may find in the Polynesian languages the following counterparts :

hore (Easter Island, Ch.) : to castrate
raho (hora ?) (Wi.) : testicles [1]
mokiki (Tr.) : membrum virile, erection of the penis
makewa (Newman, 220) : a Maori epithet for linga
monga (Tr.) : see " mokiki "
oni, one (Tahiti, Ja.) : " mâle," male
puna (Tr.) : spring ; prolific as a female ; a man with two wives
puna (Samoa, Vo.) : " source, saut," a spring
puna-toto (Samoa, Tr.) : menorrhagia [2]
pinaki (Marquesas, Do.) : syphilis.

The Magyar expressions referring to the sexual intercourse itself, as : herél, hergel (= to have sexual intercourse),[3] hím (= male), ivás, ivar, ivadék (= spawning, genital, family), teker, tikerél, tosz (= to have sexual intercourse), and those in connection with pregnancy, viz. : havadzás (= menstruation), teher (= pregnancy) permit a juxtaposition to following Maori terms :

hari (Tr.) : sexual intercourse
here (Paumotu, Tr.) : to love
hema (Tr.) : procreative power
himu (Tr.) : a man
Hina-te-*iwaiwa* = one of the many personifications of the goddess Hina,[4] relating to procreation
ivi (Easter Island, Ch.) : parent, family, ancestry
teke (Tr.) [5] : sexual intercourse
tiki = an amulet, representing the embryo, meant to assure fecundity.[6] The god " tiki " was also a personification of the phallus (Best)

[1] " here " (Wi.) : cherries.
[2] " toto " (Samoa, Vo.) : " saigner," to bleed.
[3] Munkácsi : A magyar népies Halászat, etc. (The Hungarian popular Fishing, etc.) P. 6.
[4] See also " Hina-te-korako," page 6.
[5] See also page 53.
[6] See also page 93.

hawa (Marquesas, Tr.): dirty
hawahawa (Hawaii, Tr.): dirty, especially with such dirt as sticks to one
tahawahawa (Tahiti, Ja.): "être souillé," to be soiled
tahe (Tr.): the menses, the monthly course of women; abortion
tahe (Mangarewa, Tr.): the menstrual flow of females.

To this group of notions belong also *the Magyar words fajit, fajul* = degenerare, degenero = to degenerate, to deteriorate, *fajtalan*: lascivus = lascivious, *fajzás, fajzat* = parturition, offspring, *fajtalankodik* = to commit an incest, and may be set against with following Maori terms:

fai (Samoa, Vo.): "commettre un inceste," to commit incest
faivale: "commettre l'inceste ou un autre crime énorme," to commit incest or another ghastly crime
faitaa: "forniquer," to fornicate
faitagata (Tonga, Ma.): "courir les hommes," mad after men
faiere (Tahiti, Ja.): "accouché, gésine," to be delivered, childbed.

Names of Colours. Some Maori expressions for colours may be also compared with Magyar correlatives.

MAGY.: *vörös, veres*: red.—Budenz derives the word from "vér" = blood.
MAORI: whero (Wi.): red, reddish brown
wera: heated
vera (Easter Island, Ch.): fire
vera (Tahiti, Ja.): "incendie," great fire
MAGY.: *mura* (Ba.): carrot.
MAORI: mura (Tr.): glowing redly; a flame to show a brilliant colour
MAGY.: *kova*: flint stone, yellow pebble.[1]
MAORI: kowhai (Best, II. 220): yellow
MAGY.: *póka*: light brown.[2]
MAORI: paka (Best, II. 220): light brown
MAGY.: *kék, kik*: blue; kék (kik) ég = blue sky.
MAORI: kikorangi (Best, II. 220): the blue sky[3]
MAGY.: *fekete*: black.
MAORI: wheko (Tr.): become black
wheke (Wi.): squid, octopus
feke (Marqu., Do.): "poulpe," octopus
pikeekee, pikerekere: "noir, sombre, obscure," black, dark, obscure.

Further Numerals. Some Maori and Magyar numerals, viz. one, seven, ten, etc. have already been dealt with in Chapter V (B), Grammar, and there some analogies have been established. All the following reflexions about other numerals *are of a far more hypothetical nature.* Nevertheless these somewhat fantastic deductions may be advanced for what they are worth.

Three is in Maori: toru (oru, tolu, kolu, tou; in Timor: tolo).
h and t are, according to Tregear, very often interchanged in New Zealand. So they have "tangoro" for "hangoro" (= loose),

[1] See also page 62.
[2] Magy. "póka-képü" (Ba.) = light brown skinned in the face.
[3] "rangi" (Wi.) denotes: sky.

"tapi" for "hapi" (= oven of the natives), "tikaro" for "hikaro" (= to cut steps), etc.

In Magyar three is = három, hormu, Sz.S. (Finn: kolme; Lapp: kolma; Suryanian: kuim; Mordwinian: kilma; Ostjak: kudlem; Vogul: korom).

Another expression for three is in Maori: "tengi" (Tr.). In Samoa and Tonga "tega" (Tr.) means the upper part of the arm and the arm consists of *three* joints. It may be noted here that human figures in Maori carvings very often have no arms, but *three fingers* instead.[1]

In Magyar "tenyér", or "terenye" is the palm, i.e. the *third* part of an arm bearing three joints.

Five is in Maori: rima (lima, nima, ima).

In Tahitian (Ja.) it denotes also: "main, doigt," hand, finger, and "airuma" (composed of "kai" = food and "rima" = finger): "manger salement, impoliment," to eat ill-behaved, improperly (this being the case if the entire hand, *all the five fingers*, are used for the purpose).

Another Maori term for five is "pae" (Tahiti, Ja.), the roots of which are "pá": "donner", to give, and "e": "faim," hunger.[2]

In Magyar five is: "öt" (Finn: vusi; Lapp: vita; Suryan: vit; Mordwin: vete; Ostjak: vet; Vogul: āt) and the word "ét" means food.

The Magyar Etymological Dictionary.[3] The "Lexicon Critico-Etymologicum Linguae Hungaricae" by *Gombocz* and *Melich*, edited by the Hungarian Academy of Sciences, a complete work of highest scientifical standard, begun in 1914 and at present carried up to the word "dunnyog", often contains the remark, that the *origin of the expressions treated is either unknown or untraceable in a reliable manner.*

An attempt will now be made here to trace such terms to the Maori language.

For instance:—

ágaga: of tall and lean figure
MAORI: angoa (Tr.): thin, lean, wasten
agoago (Paumotu, Tr.): light, slender, elegant

ajnároz (ajnárol): to care
MAORI: anai (Tahiti, Ja.): "soin," care

ájó: a crescent-like mark on the ears of cattle
MAORI: aio (Wi.): the moon on the eighth day

[1] Hamilton: "Notes on a carved Maori Burial-Chest found near Hokianga." In *Bulletin No. 3 of the Dominion Museum*. P. 110.

[2] See also page 96. Besides they have "eeva" (Samoa, Vo.): "faim," hunger; "eto": "gouter en léchant," to try by licking; "ete" (New Zealand, Wi.): thicken in cooking.—Comp. Magy. "ét-vágy" = "appetite," hunger.—Note also the Maori term "nima pai" (Tonga, Ma.): "main crochue," bent fingers.

[3] *Magyar Etymologiai Szótár.*

ápró : haystack
MAORI : apoapo (Wi.) : put into a heap

átán (atány) : tamarisk, black ring
MAORI : ate (Wi.) : totara wood of dark colour

ava : an archaic form for al = under, below
MAORI : ava (Newman, P. 22) : away, off, down

avik : to become obsolete
MAORI : aweko (Wi.) : old, ancient

babona (bobona) : superstition, sorcery
MAORI : papo (Marquesas, Do.) : " chant à la naissance d'un chef," song sung on the birthday of a chief
popoa (Tr.) : sacred food eaten in religious ceremonies
ponoi (Tonga, Ma.) : " un mot qu'il ne faut pas dire, parcequ'il a un sens mauvais," a word forbidden to spell because it has a bad meaning

baj : disease, sickness
MAORI : paipai (Tr.) ; a contagious disease

bákány : lively as a child
MAORI : whaka-pakanga (Wi.) : youngest in the family or youngest brother

bákány : a bird, the ordinary starling
MAORI : pakahaa (Tr.) : name of a bird (puffinus gavia)

bán : pain ; to be afraid, to regret ; grief
MAORI : panapana (Tr.) : to waver, quiver
pani, papani (Wi.) : orphan, widow
panoonoo (Tahiti, Ja.) : " anxiété," grief

banya (bánya) : genitals of a woman ; a hag
MAORI : pania (Mangarewa, Tr.) : a wife by second marriage, the first wife being alive

barázs : to rake the surface of the earth ; to take off the top layer or the loam of it ; *barizsol* : to scrape
MAORI : pariri (Tr.) : a piece of land from which the trees have been cleared, but on which the second growth is again springing up
pari (Tahiti, Ja.) : " équarir," to square, to cut up

bikos : hungry (?)
MAORI : pikoko (Tr.) : hungry

bőke : crooked, curved
MAORI : piki (Wi.) : closely curling
piko (Wi.) : bent, curved

borit (burit, buruhatok) : cover (contego). To this word are related :
MAORI : pulupulu : to cover the body with a cloth
puru (Tahiti) : the husk of the cocoa-nut shell
pulu (Hawaii) : deceitful [1] ; to brood over as a hen over her chickens
bulon (Tonga) : a veil, to veil or cover the face
purupuru (Arorai, P. A. C.) : " fourrure, poil des animaux," fur, hair of animals

buja (bua-ság) : voluptuous, lewd ; to fornicate ; richly abundant
MAORI : puapua (Tr.) : mons veneris
mapua : bearing abundance of fruit
puapua (Hawaii, Tr.) : to be glorious, to be beautiful
fua (Tonga, Tr.) : to bear fruit
pua (Marquesas, Do.) : " fleurir, écumer," to flourish, to foam

buti : axe, hatchet
MAORI : patiti (Best, II. 253) : tomahawk
butu (Arorai, P. A. C.) : " lame, arme," blade, weapon

csór : nuevo, agito = to wriggle, to swing ; *csóringál* : to pile the corn
MAORI : kori (Wi.) : move, wriggle ; bestir oneself

dal (dalevező) : scalmus, rowlocks
MAORI : taloa (Samoa, Vo.) : " gabord d'un canot," the garboard of a canoe
tarau (Wi.) : paddle sideways

Index of Words. For the task of investigations the above examples taken from their vocabulary should be completed by a *list of Magyar words* with Maori synonyms affixed to each of them. (Mostly taken from Tregear's dictionary.) They are mentioned *without any attempt at close examination, but simply for the purpose of supplying further material.* Perhaps in some of these cases a nearer connection may be found later on.

MAGYAR : *ad* (to give) and MAORI : *ata* ; *ág* (branch) and *aka* ; *akna* (shaft, hollow)—*ana* ; *apród* (page, squire)—*apuru* ; *ármány* (intrigue, malice)—*arumaruma* (Ja.) : *atya* (father, god)—*atua* ; *avar* (meagre grass, heath)—*avera* ; *avat* (to contract) and *ava*.

balga (silly, crazy)—*palaka* ; *beteg* (sick)—*peto* (also : *heto*) ; *betüz* (to decipher)—*patai* ; *boka* (ankle)—*pona* ; *boru* (dark clouds)—*poruru* ; *bosszankod-ik* (to be angry)—*pasipasi* (Vo.) ; *bú* (grief)—*pouri* ; *buta* (stupid)—*potete*.

csalit (grove, shrubs)—*korito* ; *csepp* (drop)—*kopa* ; *csiga* (snail)—*kiko* ; *csillag* (star)—*kiwa* ; *csorog* (to leak, to flow)—*korote* ; *csoria* (a sort of sea-bird)—*korora* ; *csóva* (whisk, bundle)—*kovee* (Do.) ; *csunya* (ugly)—*kuna* (also : *kumu*) ; *csúszó* (crawling)—*kutu*.

dal (song)—*tau* (Best, Vol. II, P. 144) ; *dalol* (to sing)—*taalili* (Vo.) ; *derül* (to become clear)—*teretere* ; *donga* (stave)—*tonga* ; *dörög* (to thunder)—*tiri*.

[1] Comp. the Magy. " burkoltan mondani " = to say something in covert words, to hint at a thing.

ég (to burn)—*iki*; *egyenget* (to smooth, to level)—*whaka-ene*; *ekecsel* (to dally)—*eka* (Do.); *enyh* (shady, fresh, mild)—*enene*; *eped* (to yearn)—*epa*; *esd* (to implore)—*eke*.

fal (to eat greedily)—*foloo* (Vo.); *fakó* (fallow, cream coloured horse)—*rako*; *fej* (to milk)—*pae*; *félő* (fearful)—*feuu*; *fenyő* (pine)—*faniu* (Ja.); *fen*, *el-fen* (to steal)—*whenako*; *fenék* (bottom)—*whenua*; *fogadalom* (oath)—*fuakava* (Ma.); "*fogja*" (got hold of it, holding)—*fogia* (Ma.); *fú* (to blow, as wind)—*pu*; *fúr* (to bore)—*furi* (Journ. Pol. Soc., 1913, p. 89); *fut* (to run, to flit)—*rutu*; *fül* (ear)—*whera*.

gere (lance, dart)—*mere*; *gerjed* (to inflame)—*keriti* (Easter Island, Ch.); *gulya* (cattle, cow)—*kuli*; *gyalul* (to plane)—*kalu*.

hahota (loud laughter)—*hohe*; *haj*, *haja* ("*eheu!*"—jubilation)—*hau* (Do.); *hajnal* (dawn)—*hana* (Paumotu); *hála* (gratitude)—*hao*; *hamis* (perfidious, false)—*hamaau*; *hám* (bark, shell)—*hamore*; *hány* (to throw)—*hani* (Best, II. 247); *hara* (mattress)—*haronga*; *harag* (anger)—*huru*; *Hári* (a legendary family-name)—*Hari* (see Best, II. p. 151); *harmat* (dew)—*haumaki*; *henye* (idle)—*hianga*; *hiba* (mistake, fault, lack)—*hipa*; *higit* (to dilute)—*huiga* (Ma.); *higy* (ear-ring)—*hui*; *hiú* (empty, vain)—*heu*; *hív* (to call, to name)—*hiwa*; *hónalj* (armpit)—*honoai*; *hórihorgas* (very tall and lengthy)—*harahara*; *horkol* (to snore)—*ooro* (Ja.); *hugy* (urine)—*huaki*.

ibrik (ewer)—*ipu*; *ideges* (nervous)—*eteete* (Easter Island); *idegen* (foreign)—*etua* (Easter Island); *igér* (to promise)—*uga* (Vo.); *ihl* (to imbue, to inspire, to insinuate)—*iho*; *ijedt* (to be frightened)—*ihi* (see also: *wehi*); *ingó* (wavering)—*ingo*; *irha* (skin, leather)—*iri*; *ital* (drink)—*ita* (Mangarewa); *itél* (to judge, to form an opinion, to criticize)—*ite*; *izé* (a word of confusion which may denote anything)—*iku*.

kába (foolish)—*kapo*; *kacsa* (duck)—*kaka*; *kád* (receptacle)—*kete*; *kajtár* (voracious)—*kai*; *káka* (reed)—*kaka*; *kalák* (a premium for a disclosed theft)—*kaia*; *kaláka* (meeting for mutual execution of a work)—*kara*; *kalauz* (guide)—*kairahi*; *kanót* (fuse)—*kaunoti*; *kápa* (bridge of saddle)—*kapa* (Ma.); *kapál* (to hack)—*kabokabo* (Tonga); *karicsál* (to chatter)—*kariei* (Smith, p. 138); *karó* (pile)—*karo*; *katona* (soldier)—*ka-tane* (Mangarewa); *kedv* (pleasure)—*kea*; *keh* (cough)—*ke*; *kel* (to raise)—*keu*; *ken* (to wipe, to smear)—*kani*; *kén* (sulphur)—*kenokeno*; *kép* (image)—*kopare*; *kerecsel* (a legendary bird)—*karae* (Wi.) and *karaharatua* (Do.); *kevés* (light)—*kawe*; *kiadós* (abundant, compact)—*kiato*; *kiált* (to shout)—*ke*; *kigyó* (serpent)—*kioe* (Do.); *kobak* (gourd-bottle)—*kopako*; *kocér* (wooden knife)—*ko* (Best, II. 369); *kokál* (to trash)—*kokoti*; *kokojcza* (whortleberry)—*kokaha* (Best, II. 45); *koma* (an expression of friendship, employed but to denote men)—*koona* (Marquesas); *könyök* (elbow)—*koko* (Tonga); *kopács* (green bark)—*kopaki*; *kopár* (barren)—*kopa*; *kopasz* (bold)—*kopakopa*; *kópé* (wag, rogue)—*kopeka*; *koporsó* (coffin)—*koporo*; *korom* (soot)—*kauruki*; *koros* (aged)—*koro*; *kotárka* (verandah)—*kotare*; "*kotkodács*" (cackling of hens)—*kotoko* (Ma.); *köd* (fog)—*kou*; *követ* (to follow)—*koa* (Ch.); *kuka* (dumb)—*ku*; *köszön* (to thank)—*kaoha* (Do.); *kumak* (a great lump)—*kumi* (Best, II. 191); *kupa* (the mark on the teeth of horses)—*kupa*; *kupa* (bowl)—*kapu* (Mangarewa); *kusza* (confused, intricate)—*kasigu*.

lak (dwelling)—*lala*; *lanyha* (slack)—*langa*; *lány* (girl)—*langi*; *lapátolt* (levelled)—*lapatai* (Vo.); *légy* (fly)—*lago* (Vo.); *levent* (at once, instantly, illico ?)—*rewa*; *levente* (hero, warrior)—*lave* (Vo.); *lobb* (to swim)—*lofia* (Vo.); *lóg* (to hang)—*logo*.

magos (elevated)—*mauga* (Vo.); *mámor* (intoxication)—*mamoa*; *már jó* (it is still good)—*marie*; *más* (the wrong)—*masei*; *másik* (the other one)—*matikao* (Do.); *maszat* (poisonous food, putrefaction)—*masai*; *mátka* (bride)—*matau*; *meleg* (warm)—*mulu* (Vo.); *merev* (rigid, stiff) —*maro*; *méz* (honey)—*miti*; *mohoz* (to calk)—*mohuta* (Best, II. 546); *móka* (joke)—*poka*; *mókus* (squirrel)—*moko*; *monyoró* (hazel-bush)—*monoa*; *morágy* (a species of trees)—*more*.

nagy (big, great)—*naunau* (Vo.); *nadály* (leech)—*ngata*; *nátha* (coryza)—*naehapu* (Do.); *néhai* (late, old)—*nehe*; *néne* (aunt)—*keke*; *nevet* (to laugh)—*nenea* (Vo.); *név* (name)—*nei*; *ni* (now)—*nei* (Vo.); *nő* (to grow)—*nui* (Vo.); *nyafog* (to growl)—*ngangara*; *nyár* (summer) —*ngarehe*; *nyárfa* (poplar)—*ngarehe*; *nyíl* (to appear)—*ngia*; *nyit* (to open)—*nii* (Ch.); *nyom* (track)—*ngao* (Best, II. 579); *nyű* (mite, worm) —*ngungu*.

óhaj (wish)—*ohia*; *ok* (reason)—*uiga* (Vo.); *ón* (tin, lead)—*one*; *ont* (to spill, to shed)—*oni*; *ont* (cub)—*ono*; *orom* (top of a mountain, peak)—*oro* (Smith, Hawaiki, p. 55); *orsó* (spindle)—*ore* (Best, II. 197).

pad (bench)—*pae*; *pajta* (granary)—*paito*; *pajtás* (pal)—*paitau* (Journ. Pol. Soc., 1913, p. 89); *pányva* (lasso)—*panga*; *para* (cork tree)—*pura* (Best, II. 369); *pataró* (impotent)—*patari*; *pép* (mash)—*pepe*; *pepecsel* (toying, to dally)—*pepee*; *pereg* (to roll)—*viri* (Ch.); *pihe* (down)—*pihenehu*; *pihen* (to rest)—*pihe* (Best, II. 60); *pille* (butterfly)—*piri*; *piszkos* (dirty)—*pisia* (Vo.); *pitvar* (front corridor)—*pito* (Best, II. 11); *pityóka* (potato)—*pitau* (Best, II. 372); *ponc* (hieroglyph)—*pokai* (Best, II. 201); *pogány* (alien, heathen)—*pakanga*; *pogony* (preserve, earth-vault)—*pokonao*; *pohár* (a vessel)—*poha*; *póka* (swaddling)—*pona-pona*; *poklos* (leprous)—*poka* (Mangarewa); *poré* (band, much liberty)—*poria*; *puffadt* (flatulent, swollen)—*pufa* (Tahiti); *puha* (soft)—*puhoi*; *pukkan* (to snap)—*pukaea*; *pulyka* (turkey)—*poua* (Best, II. 487); *pub-denevér* (bat)—*pupura*; *púp* (*hump*)—*pupu*; *puszta* (clean)—*puata-ata*; *putri* (earth-hut)—*puta*; *puttony* (coop)—*putea*.

rab (slave)—*ropa*; *rángat* (to drag)—*ranga*; *ráró* (black as raven)—*raro*; *rásza* (slip for planting)—*rata* (Best, II. 458); *ravasz* (sly)—*ravai* (Tahiti); *reng* (pending, to float)—*ranga*; *répa* (beet)—*repe*; *részeg* (intoxicated)—*rearea* (Ja.); *rév* (ford)—*rewa* (Mangarewa); *rigó* (thrush) —*riroriro*; *ringat* (to rock in the arms)—*ringa*; *ripacs* (scarred)—*ripa*; *róka* (fox)—*rakaraka*; *róna* (plain)—*ronaki*.

síkos (slippery)—*sikitia*; *songata* (sprout, scion, proles ?)—*sangata*; *süv* (brother-in-law)—*kuwha*; *szalad* (to run)—*sali* (Samoa); *szaporod-ik* (to procreate)—*taparu*; *szár* (stem)—*saro*; *szekér* (cart)—*wheke*; *szel* (to cut)—*sele*; *szeles* (careless)—*sela* (Vo.); *szél* (brim)—*sila* (Vo.); *szél* (wind)—*sulu* (Vo.); *szeret* (to love)—*solu* (Vo.); *szín* (shine)—*sina*; *szín* (pretext)—*sinoi* (Vo.); *szita* (sieve)—*hitari*; *szomogyos* (bitter, dry)—*soma*; *szomorú* (sad)—*soo* (Vo.); *szöcske* (locust)—*se*.

"*tagadom*" ("I deny it")—*tage* (Ma.); *tág* (wide, loose)—*taga* (Vo.); *talán* (perhaps)—*talaiha* (Ma.); *találgat* (to guess, to try)—*talatagata* (Ma.); *talp* (sole of the foot)—*taputapu* (Ma.); *támaszték* (prop)—*tamaeke* (Best, II. 488); *tanu* (witness)—*tonu*; *tányér* (plate)—*tanoa*; *tapló* (fuze)—*tapi*; *tarló* (stubble-field)—*taru*; *tart* (to last)—*turu*; *taszít* (to push)—*tasitasi* (Vo.); *tat* (stern)—*tuta*; *tótat* (syllable)—*tatau*; *tavar*, *tár* (load)—*tawari*; *tavasz* (Spring)—*tau*; *tekint* (to regard)—*tiketike*; *tele* (full)—*tele* (Samoa); *telek* (ground, premises)—*tele*; *terel* (to guide)—*tere*; *terem* (to grow)—*teremu* (Best, II. 382); *tesz* (to do)—*tewha* (Best, II. 146); *tibáz* (to dishevel)—*tipi*; *tikkadt* (exhausted, starving)—*tikaka*; *tilim* (silence)—*tiwha* (Best, II. 287); *tilos* (forbidden)—

tilo tilo i tua (Vo.); *tinó* (young bull)—*tino-ariki*; *tipor* (to trample down)—*tipi* (Best, II. 255); *tiszta* (pure, clear)—*tasilo* (Ma.); *titok* (secret)—*titei*; *tolvaj* (thief)—*tolovaia* (Ma.); *tömött* (crammed)—*tumu* (Vo.); *topa* (twisted ankle)—*tapoa*; *torony* (tower)—*taranga*; "*tott*" ("I say!", *inquam*)—*toto*; *túlmén* (to trespass)—*tulimanu* (Ma.); *tunya* (idle, lazy)—*tunga, tunewa*; *túr* (to dig out)—*turaha*; *turó* (curd)—*tuturu*; *tűz* (fire)—*tutui*; *tyúk* (hen)—*tiutiu*.

unoka (grandchild)—*uniki*; *unszol* (to urge, to incite)—*usuisui* (Vo.); *ugat* (to bark)—*ou* (Vo.); *ujjong* (to exult)—*uio* (Vo.); *utálatos* (disgusting)—*utafanua* (Vo.); *utolsó* (last)—*iutagata* (Vo.).

vadon (wilderness)—*wao*; *vagyok* ("I am")—*wai* (Best, I. 138); *vágy* (desire)—*vago* (Ma.); *vahorász* (to practise withcraft)—*wahinoe*; *vak* (blind)—*vakai* (Ma.); *vakkant* (to yelp)—*whakaau* (Journ. Pol. Soc., 1926, p. 156); *valag* (central parts of the body)—*vala* (Ma.); *vall* (to confess, to pretend)—*wha*; *válúz* (to groove)—*waro*; *várna* (caste)—*whanau*; *vége* (end)—*waenge*; *vesz* (to take away)—*wehe*; *veszeked* (to quarrel)—*vesivesi* (Vo.); *világ* (light)—*vela*; *vín, vén* (old, aged)—*wini*; *visz* (to carry)—*widia* (Arorai, P. A. C.); *vív* (to fence, to fight)—*winiwini*.

zabál (to feast, to glut)—*savala* (Vo.).

Final Remarks. The linguistic part thus brought to an end, has perhaps proved very lengthy. However a study based in particular upon phonetic laws would be a difficult task even for persons with expert phonetic training, in view of the great decay of Maori idiom. There was no other solution but to choose in great numbers such words, as in each language have *several distinct meanings* and thus compare them.

One of the results of this investigation may be to bring us nearer to the acceptation or rejection of the theory of Churchill and others, quoted at the beginning of this chapter (A), that Maori is a *primitive language*. In Churchill's own words: "Polynesian is the most elemental type of human speech . . . As the placing of the Sanskrit within the reach of investigators created the science of comparative philology, even so I indulge myself in the reverent aspirations that the presentation of these data for a widely extended speech of the isolating type will carry our students very close to the origin of the human utterance of deas, so close that philology may then be justified in calling upon pschology to explain the process whereby the primitive man has learned to differentiate his animal cry into thought-directed speech."[1]

On the other side notable scholars, including Ray, perhaps the most distinguished authority on Polynesian linguistic matters, are, as we have said,[2] of an absolutely contrary opinion: for them, *Maori is a decayed form of another language*. The reader can easily judge for himself, which of these conflicting theories is the right one.

[1] Churchill, Easter Island. P. 10. [2] See page 23.

CHAPTER VI.

GEOGRAPHICAL CONNECTIONS.

The comparison of geographical denominations as a rule supplies only very unreliable results.

In our case, however, the isolation of the Maori up to the XVIIIth century has to be taken into account, as also the fact that the Magyar, when they occupied their present home, found a completely devastated country, almost totally devoid of habitations.[1] Ptolemaeus enumerates as late as about A.D. 150 many towns and settlements in the eastern part of the present Hungary; at the end of the Magyar immigration, in the IXth century, the names of these places had already disappeared, as also the names of the rivers, to which reference is made in other writers of the VIIth century (e.g. Dricca, Gilpit, Arine, Miliare), and this though as a rule river names are more lasting than those of mere habitations.

It is therefore probable that for both, Magyar and Maori, the naming of their settlements was free from any foreign influence. Similarities between them thus deserve consideration.

Consulting an index of New Zealand places [2] or any reliable atlas,[3] one may find at once quite a large number of geographical names, for which analogies may easily be found in present (or former) Hungarian territories [4] inhabited by Magyar. Some examples selected at random may illustrate this assertion:

MAORI (NEW ZEALAND):	MAGYAR:	
Kaawa	Káva	(County Komárom)
	Káva	(„ Pest)
	Gáva	(„ Szabolcs)
	Kávásd	(„ Bihar and Zala)
Karaka	Karakó	(„ Vas and Veszprém)
Mere-Mere	Mere	(„ Hont)
	Méra	(„ Abauj and Kolozs)
Paka	Paka	(„ Pozsony)
	Baka	(„ „)
	Páka	(„ Pest and Zala)
Pari-Pari	Pari	(„ Tolna)
	Bári	(„ Zemplén)
Tahi	Tahi	(„ Pest)
Tura	Tura	(„ „)
Waiau	Vaja	(„ Maros-Torda, Szavolcs and Szilágy)
	Vajka	(„ Tolna)
	Vajta	(„ Fejér),

[1] Karácsonyi: *A magyar Nemzet Östörténete 896-ig* (The primeval History of the Magyar Nation up to A.D. 896). P. 92.

[2] *Every Place in New Zealand.*—The New Zealand Index.

[3] Andree's Handatlas, 8th Edition.

[4] Jekelfalussy: *A magyar szent Korona Országainak Helységnévtára* (Index of the Settlements of the Holy Crown of Hungary).

and many New Zealand names beginning by Puta (Puto) may be compared with the frequent Magyar names for settlements beginning with Bod or Bud.[1]

But it would lead us too far were we to make an exhaustive investigation into these analogies. As a matter of interest however some other Maori place names may be quoted here, possessing a certain Magyar timbre, as for instance in the Tongan Islands: Ata, Atata, Ava, Bea, Euka, Hobonga, Honga, Kallau, Kapa, Mua, Tau, Toku etc., in the Paumotu Archipelago: Anaa, Apataki, Hereheretue, Makemo, Mehetia, Tatakoto etc., and again in New Zealand: Akato, Harihari, Kamo, Karia, Mohaka, Mako, Okau, Papa, Para, Patea, Parakau, Tarara, Tata, Werita etc., etc.

[1] See also pages 116 and 183.

CHAPTER VII.

ORNAMENTS.

DECORATION OF DOORS.—ORNAMENTAL MOTIFS.—ZIGZAG MOTIFS AND SPIRALS.—ROSETTES.—FOURFOLD DIVISION.—" KORO " AND " TURUL ".

Art is considered to be one of the most important characteristics of a people ; no external distinguishing feature of a race is more enduring than its decorative art. The Székely tribe [1] of the old Magyar and the Maori are alike in their predilection for rich decorations on their doors. In Magyar they call the upper part of the lintel *pártázat* ; further *párta* is the term for the decorative headgear of girls. In Maori " paratu " means high up (Tregear), and according to Cowan,[2] the carved portion of the massive ridge-pole in the porch is called " parata ".

Decoration of Doors.

Both Magyars and Maori placed special idols on their doors [3] ; in Magyar they were called *kapu-bálvány*, a word composed of *kapu* (= door) and *bálvány* (= idol).[4] In Maori " kapu " denotes : entrance, door. Ornamental motifs of ancient Magyar (Székely) doors [5] apparently reappear in various Maori decorative elements, as for instance in the artistic tattooing on the forehead and chin of a chief, as reproduced in Reischek's book about New Zealand.[6]

Ornamental Motifs.

This resemblance is also exemplified in certain Magyar ornamental motifs described in Huszka's work on this subject.[7] Or they are to be seen on relics of ancient Magyar tombs,[8] which may be compared with the carving representing a lizard on a wooden

[1] More about the Székely's in the Periodical *Kőrösi Csoma Archivum.* 1921. P. 172.

[2] Cowan : *The Maori of New Zealand.* P. 160.

[3] See Best : " Maori Storehouses and kindred Structures," in *Bulletin* 8 *of the Dominion Museum, N.Z.*

[4] About " kapubálvány " see further *Kőrösi Csoma Archivum.* P. 155 ; and about " bálvány " on page 154.

[5] Huszka : *A székely Ház* (The Székely House). Plate X.

[6] *Sterbende Welt.* P. 128.—See also Te Rangi Hiora : "Aututaki Moko. Some tattoo-patterns from Aututaki." In *Bulletin 3 of the Dominion Museum.* P. 96.—Material for interesting comparisons is offered also by Kuper : "Tapitapi, or the Tattooing of Females on Santa Anna and Santa Catarina." *Journ. Pol. Soc.* 1926. P. 1.

[7] Huszka : *Magyar Ornamentika* (Magyar Ornaments). Plate XIV ; Fig. 22.

[8] Hampel : *Altertümer des frühen Mittelalters in Ungarn* (Early medieval Antiquities of Hungary). Vol. III, Plate 476. Tomb 58.

coffin in New Zealand, as shown in Best's study.[1] The rich Polynesian collection of the Vienna Natural History Museum contains a very interesting *warrior's belt*, made of bast and coming from the Tonga Islands; its looplike ornaments resemble the still existing trimmings on Magyar uniforms. The latter are called *vitézkötés* (literally = a hero's sash, from "vitéz" = hero), and the above-mentioned loin-girdle of Maori warriors is considered by them as a god-given talisman for their battles.[2] Moreover the word "whitiki" denotes: belt, girdle (Wi.). In the Marquesas "fitiee" means: "actif, vif, vigoureux, plein d'ardeur, courageux," active, lively, strong, full of go, courageous (Do.) and in Samoa "fitia" is: "être agité par le désir de faire la guerre," to be excited by a desire for war (Vi.).

Zigzag Motifs, Spirals.

The very developed Maori ornaments show[3] two predominant motifs: the rectilinear zigzags or triangles in characteristic sequence, and the much intertwined, curvilinear motifs expressed by very artistic spirals, and especially *double-spirals*. The latter however are to be found only in New Zealand.[4] Similar spirals are used for the decorations of some ancient Magyar goblets.[5] In Hampel's above quoted work we find about certain tomb relics, especially about those with double spirals, his remark, that "they are inexplicable".[6]

The rectilinear zigzag ornaments of ancient Magyar tomb relics[7] and the decorations on the lintels of the Székely doors, or on the gables of their roofs,[8] offer a great resemblance to designs on flutes of the Marquesas or on whalebones of Tahiti etc., as exhibited in the Natural History Museum of Vienna.[9]

Rosettes. The Fourfold Division.

This museum contains also[10] neck and chest ornaments from the Tonga Archipelago, showing rosettes as they are still worn to-day as a characteristic decorative element of Magyar national dress. Rosettes found in tombs of

[1] Best. Vol. I. P. 277, and by the same author: "Māori Agriculture." In *Bulletin* No. 9 *of the Dominion Museum*.
[2] Newman. P. 283.
[3] See also Brown: *Peoples and Problems of the Pacific*. Vol. I. P. 163.
[4] See also Skinner: "The Origin and Relationship of Maori Material Culture and Decorative Art." *Journ. Pol. Soc.* 1924. P. 243.
[5] See Huszka: *Magyar Ornamentika*. P. 14.
[6] Vol. I. P. 536.—See also Vol. III: Plate 477, Figs. 1*a* and 1*b*, and Plate 38, Fig. 2, etc.—Single spirals on Plate 480, Figs. 15–19 etc.; intertwined ornaments on Plate 489, Tomb 312, Figs. 1 and 2; all recalling New Zealand motifs.—A very interesting decoration also appears in the *Journ. Pol. Soc.* 1926. P. 261.
[7] Hampel. Vol. III. Plate 390, Fig. 11 etc.
[8] Huszka: *A székely Ház*.
[9] Room XVII. Showcases 95 and 44.
[10] Room XVII. Showcase 40.

ancient Magyar warriors show, with few exceptions, a *fourfold division.*[1] This fourfold division also often occurs in Maori ornaments, especially in their tattooing, which in its original form consisted simply of *four lines*. Another characteristic fourfold division is shown by the so-called "kaka-rings" of the Maori. When fettering the sacred bird, the "kaka" (= cuckoo), the Maori always used a *special ring*. Made most artistically of bone or greenstone, and wonderfully polished, this ring was very often worn as a talisman, in the form of ear-rings, etc.[2] The most remarkable feature of these rings consisted of *four legs, each of three sharp points*, fixed on the circumference at the extremities of two diameters intersecting at right angles. Later on, the three sharp edges were conscientiously reproduced even on rings, which were too small for fettering.

Similar rings may be seen amongst the ancient Magyar tomb-relics in the Vienna Natural History Museum.[3] Likewise an ornamental ring illustrated in Hampel's work,[4] shows the central cross and the four legs with their three sharp points. But in this case the points are found on the inner side of the circumference.[5]

"Koro" and "Turul".

The Viennese collection contains also the plaster copy of a Maori relic from New Zealand, a bird made of dark green serpentine, which they brought thither from their "old fatherland", and which they took with them in their wanderings. The name of this bird, much venerated as the personification of the fortune of war, was "koro" and it resembles a sparrow-hawk.[6] A similar emblem of war was venerated by the Magyar also. *Their bird*, as may be seen in the coats of arms of their ancient leaders (vezérek), is described as looking "more like a raven than an eagle".[7] Its name was *turul*. The Magyar historian *Szabó* however asserts that no bird of the name *turul* ever existed and that the origin of this word is due to a clerical error commonly occurring when copying old chronicles. He thinks that originally the name sounded *karoly* (also: karvoly, karvaó, karuj, kara) and meant a hawk (falconisus).[8] In the decoration of an old

[1] Huszka: *Magyar Ornamentika*. P. 5.
[2] Newman. P. 281.
[3] Room XIII. Showcase 28.
[4] Vol. III. Plate 502. Figs. 2*a*, 2*b*.
[5] According to Ipolyi: *Magyar Mythologia*. P. 319, the cuckoo was one of the main figures of Magyar mythology.
[6] Reischek. P. 154.
[7] Ipolyi. P. 240.
[8] Munkácsi: *Árja és kaukazusi Elemek a finn-magyar Nyelvekben* (Aryan and Caucasian Elements in the Finn-Magyar Languages). P. 313.

Magyar cap peak (tomb relic) a hawk is represented as tearing out the vitals of a fish.[1]

Finally it should be noted, with respect to ornaments and carvings, that in Magyar *ró* means : to notch, to indent (incido), and *ir* : to write, to draw ; further *iró* : the writer and *irogat* : to write occasionally. In New Zealand they say " ro " : in, into, " whaka-iro " is : to carve, carved, ornamental, tattooing ; in Mangarewa " iroga " denotes : a mark, a sign, to mark (Tr.) ; in Samoa " faa-ilo " : to mark ; in Tonga " iro " is : knowledge, understanding.

[1] Hampel. Vol. I. P. 276.

CHAPTER VIII.

PHYSICAL FEATURES. CLOTHING AND PERSONAL ORNAMENTS. WEAPONS.

FACIAL AND CRANIAL CONSTRUCTION.—ANTHROPOLOGICAL RACE-STRUCTURE, OF THE MAORI.—BEARD AND HAIR. COIFFURE.—JEWELRY.—CLOTHING.—WEAPONS.—DOMESTIC LIFE.—MUSIC AND DANCE.—RIDING.

Facial and Cranial Construction.

With respect to the physical characteristics of the ancient Magyar at the time of their immigration into the Danube basin (in or before the IXth century), especially concerning their cranial and racial features, scientific researches have recently been made by *Bartucz.*[1] He resumes the results as follows: "A people of mostly Caucaso-Mongolian racial type was grafted upon another people, which, although chiefly of Eastern Baltic origin, yet contained also Mongolian, Rhjaesan and Mediterranean racial elements." From this mixture issued the ancient Magyar, in whom however "the Caucaso-Mongolian element upheld its predominance". For further details and writings reference may be made to the above mentioned recent researches. Here we shall restrict ourselves to the remark that approximately 40 to 45% of the Magyar skulls examined showed "Mongolian characteristics". The so far established average indices for the length and breadth in old Magyar skulls are, for men 82·3 and for women 80·6; that of the nasal indices 47·1 and 50·8 respectively. According to Kollmann the facial indices show 89·6 and 84·2. The average height of men (taken from 25 skeletons) was proved to be 163·70 cm., that of women (taken from 31 skeletons) 152·88 cm. (To-day the corresponding average measurements for skulls are respectively 85 and 84·9, and the stature 167·60 and 154·00.)

Ruggiera writes [2] as follows about the ancient Magyar skulls: "I have seen the skulls of ancient Magyar as found in dozens at the Anthropological Museum in Budapest, and scarcely any of these represented the characteristic large type of Asiatics of the Central Ranges. I do not assert that none of them came from there, but they were far less in numbers than anybody would believe . . ." And Bartucz lays stress upon the fact

[1] Bartucz: *Honfoglaláskori Magyar Koponyák* (Magyar Skulls of the Time of the Home-Conquest).

[2] Ruggiera: *Homo Sapiens*, Vienna. 1913. P. 117.

that as regards indices of length and breadth, the ancient Magyar "*differed remarkably in cranial type* from their nearest linguistic relatives, the Ostjak and the Vogul".—The ancient Magyar chieftains, Álmos Taksony, etc., are described as very tall men, with dark eyes and black hair.

About the Maori the well-known anthropologist Luschan [1] says: "Many Polynesian might be easily taken for full-blooded European." In the vast majority they are well-built and intelligent creatures. About the natives of New Zealand, those who know them best tell us that a stalwart physique and a high order of intelligence are their leading features. All scholars dwell upon the remarkably proportioned, well-built, and tall figures of the natives of New Zealand, Tonga (where they are said to possess the finest physique),[2] Tahiti, Hawaii and Samoa.[3] About the women of the Marquesas Islands, where the race has preserved the most its purity, we are told that "they are not darker than South-Europeans", and that they very often show a profile and physique quite equal to the antique and are "of unrivalled beauty".[4]

Anthropological Race Structure of the Maori.

Quatrefages and other ethnologists established the existence of a primitive—more or less pure—*white element* in Polynesia.[5] Old sailors, such as Quiros in 1606 and Wallis in 1767 found in Tahiti, Mendoza and Mindana in 1560 in the Solomon Islands, especially amongst chieftains, red-haired or even fair-haired men; Roggeween in 1772 on occasion of the discovery of Easter Island, also natives who were quite white.[6]

Sullivan [7] has established in the anthropological race structure of the natives of Polynesia two main elements, viz. one of a people of tall figure, average height of 171 cm. and a cranial index in length and breadth of 77 to 78, and another element of smaller stature and an index of 81 to 82, the latter very likely belonging to a later immigration. *The Melanesian (Negrito-) element is comparatively insignificant.*

In view of anthropological researches of the Maori scholar Te Rangi Hiroa (Buck) [8] in New Zealand, of I. F. G. Stokes and

[1] "Dr. Felix von Luschan and Polynesian Origins" in *Journ. Pol. Soc.* 1924. P. 78.

[2] See amongst others, Best. Vol. I. P. 1.

[3] Reischek. P. 152; Cowan. P. 37.

[4] Caillot: *Les Polynésiens orientaux.* P. 8.

[5] Quatrefages: *La Polynésie.*

[6] See also "Blondism" in Brown: *Peoples and Problems of the Pacific.* Vol. II. P. 159.

[7] Sullivan calls also attention to the fact that we may find on Tonga, Samoa, Tahiti, and their neighbouring islands, further on Hawaii and partly even on the Marquesas *artificially shortened skulls.* He thinks it is a question whether we have to deal with a distinct type of men. Artificially shortened skulls had been also found in ancient Magyar tombs.

[8] To Rangi Hiroa: Maori Stomatology. *Journ. Pol. Soc.* 1922. P. 31.

R. F. Aitken in Easter Island, of E. S. Handy and Ralph Luiton in the Marquesas, as well as of his own researches in Samoa [1] and in Tonga,[2] Sullivan expresses the opinion [3] that at the present time it is impossible to determine the exact place of the Maori in the human family. The available data seem to indicate that *the Polynesian is a type intermediate between Caucasian and Mongol.* "At present"—he says—"I am inclined to believe that they are an offshoot from the primitive Mongoloid stem close to where the Caucasian stock arose. Individually they may be regarded as a somewhat unsuccessful attempt of Nature to produce a Caucasian type. That they are closely related to the Caucasian stock, there can be no doubt. Some such type as this must have given rise to the Caucasian stock. Descendants of this or closely related stocks pass for Caucasians in Europe to-day."

Based upon *measurements* made on living natives, Sullivan establishes for the Samoan an average index of length and breadth (head-index) of 81·3 for men and of 80·8 for women; he determines the nasal height at 59·8 and 54·3 respectively, the nasal breadth at 43·8 and 41·2, the nasal index at 73·6 and 76·3, the anatomical facial index at 89·9 and 89·8 and the height of stature at 171·7 and 161·2. As a conclusion he finds of a total of 23 different racial affinities 11 to be Mongoloid, 5 European, 5 Mongoloid-European and 2 of Mongoloid-Negroid character.

The "Mongolian Spot" (Mongol Fleck), a patch of pigmented skin which is frequently found on Mongol children near the base of the spinal column, and which has been noticed, e.g. on Maori of Tahiti, was observed by *Sperck* also in Vienna, but only in children one of whose parents was a Magyar.[4]

Beard and Hair. Coiffure.

The Magyar call the back of the head, amongst other names, *kobák*. The Maori express it be "kopako" (Tr.). The *cutting of the hair* had a religious significance among the ancient Magyar; thus we read in old chronicles about Vata, the leader of a revolt against Christianity in the XIth century, that as a symbol of his rebellion he cut off his hair "according to pagan custom", keeping however three tufts. The operation of shearing is expressed in Magyar by *tarol*,[5] hair-cutting by *haj-vágás*, the word *haj* denoting the hair. A tuft of hair is called *kók*.

The act of hair-cutting is also a very important ritual function among the Maori of high rank.[6] "tarotaro" is: to cut one's

[1] Sullivan: "Contribution to Samoan Stomatology." In *Memoirs of the Bernice Puahi Bishop Museum.*

[2] Sullivan. Ibid.

[3] In *Journ. Pol. Soc.* 1922. P. 37.

[4] See Ruggles: "Mendelian Heredity and Racial Differences." In *Journ. Roy. Anthropological Inst.* 1925. P. 478.

[5] According to Szarvas-Simonyi.—The Maori express by "koukou" a mode of wearing the hair (Wi.); "kaka" is: a single hair (Tr.).

[6] Best. Vol. II. P. 533.

nair; "iha" denotes the hair and "whaka-iha": hair-cutting (Tr.), in which last word "whaka" means the cutting itself. In Easter Island "hau" is a term for headgear (Routledge) and in the Marquesas "pae hauaui": "chapeau," hat (Do.); "hao" in Tahiti: "arranger les cheveux," dress the hair.[1]

A short glance at the portraits of Maori chiefs may convince anybody of their well developed moustaches and exuberant growth of beards. *Nagy*, in his history of Hungarian dress[2] draws attention that "in opposition to the sparse moustache and beard of the Mongolian type", the Magyar show more the "Irano-Caucasian character" with its wealth of hair.

Heron feathers and heron tufts, worn as decorations on headgear, have still to-day a certain martial significance for the Magyar and form part of the outfit of their national gala-costumes. In the Marquesas the red heron is venerated as the god of war.[3]

Facial tattooing, a general habit of the Maori, is said to have been practised also by the ancient Magyar.[4]

Jewelry. Ear-rings found in old Magyar tombs, as reproduced by Hampel,[5] show a certain resemblance to Maori pendants illustrated in Best's work.[6] Amongst others mention may be made of a whalebone set in a frame and found in an ancient Magyar tomb, about which Hampel expressed the opinion that it was probably an object of superstitious veneration.[7] Shark-teeth as ear-pendants were used by the Maori and some of them (Lamna cornubia) were highly prized.[8]

It was a custom of the ancient Magyar for the bride and bridegroom to wear small idols on their necks.[9] It is also a characteristic habit of the Maori to wear on the neck their small idol, the "tiki", symbol of fecundity.[10]

Clothing. It is remarkable that the clothing of ancient Magyar was not designed for protection against cold weather. The chronicler Reginus tells us on this subject that: "Lanae his usu ac vestium ignotus; *et quanquam continuis frigoribus afficiuntur,* pellibus tantum perinis ac murinis induuntur."[11] (= The use of wool for clothing was unknown to them; and though they suffered very much from the continuous cold, they wore nothing but skins of slaughtered animals and martens.) We understand from Nagy,[12] that old picture-chronicles portray the Magyar always wearing high

[1] The hair of the Maori is always smooth or wavy, never curled or woolly.
[2] Nagy: *A magyar Viseletek Története.* P. 19.
[3] Newman. P. 246.
[4] Jászay: *A magyar Nemzet Napjai.* P. 140.
[5] Hampel. Vol. I. P. 455: Fig. 1419. P. 459: Fig. 1448 etc.
[6] Best. Vol. II. P. 538.
[7] Hampel. Vol. I. P. 72.
[8] Best. Vol. II. P. 537.
[9] Kerékgyártó. P. 446.
[10] Best. Vol. I. P. 141.—Compare also the Magyar term "tikerél" on page 76.
[11] Katona: *Historia critica primorum Hungariae Ducum.* P. 32.
[12] Nagy. P. 24.

pointed caps, which, in contrast to the dress of other peoples, are made of *white furs*. In Best's repeatedly quoted work we find illustrations [1] of Maori chieftain caps, also showing pointed forms and made of white furs (dogskins), though this material was often difficult to obtain.

In his excellent work about old Magyar costumes Nagy mentions [2] the sleeveless wrapper reaching only to the knees as a characteristic garment of " Magyars and Petchenegs, whilst other races living with them never wore it ". It is most interesting to note that such clothes are customary among the Maori in New Zealand.[3]

One of the oldest Magyar terms for clothing in general is *mez*, and *meztelen, mezítlen* means : naked. In Samoa " masei " is : " être non couvert, à nu (en parlant du corps)," i.e. naked (Vo.). Another Magyar expression for garments and clothing is *ruha* and it also means : a piece of stuff (Ba.). It may be found in Maori too and used in the sense of : worn out, as of a *garment* (Tr.). To this word " ruha " corresponds in Samoan " lufa " ; this latter word denotes : " large ' siapo ' noir " a big black " siapo " (Vo.), i.e. the material used by the natives for making clothes. The old Magyar term *páj, pája* meant perhaps : pannus (Sz.S.) = web, fabric ; it carries at any rate the notion of a material used for making clothes. It is noteworthy that in New Zealand " pae " (Tr.), as in the case of " ruha ", does not mean the garment itself, but the wear and tear of it (worn out). " paeparoa " [4] is : a mat having a broad ornamental border.

The cloak, an overall, is generally called in Magyar *kabát*. The Maori have the terms : kopaki = wrap, envelop (Wi.) ; kapoi : " envelopper ", to wrap in (Marqu., Do.) ; kapui : " envelopper, entourer," to wrap, to envelop ; kapa i kofu : " bord de l'habit, de la robe," the seam of garments (Tonga, Ma.)—*guba* is a Magyar upper garment made of *black leather* and worn over the shoulders. The Maori wear a " kupara " : dogskin mat, *black* throughout (Wi.). The Magyar term *kaczagány* is applied to a cloak without sleeves, reaching down to the knees ; *kecse* is the cloak of the soldiers. The Maori have the word " kaka " : a garment (Wi.) ; " kakahu " : the superior garment (Best). A short Magyar jerkin is called *bekecs* ; the Etymological Dictionary remarks that no acceptable explanation can be found for the origin of this word. Yet the Maori have " pekere " : a small garment for the shoulders, a cape (Wi.) ; " peke " : the upper arm ; and " pekekahu " : " habit trop court," a garment too short (Marqu., Do.).

aba is said to have been a sort of felt of the Magyar.[5]

[1] Best. Vol. II. P. 508.
[2] Nagy. P. 25.
[3] Best. Vol. II. P. 504.
[4] " roa, loa " means : great, large.
[5] See Nagy. P. 42.

In New Zealand they call "apa": the fold of a garment (Wi.), in Marquesas "apana": "pièce d'étoffe à rapiècer," a piece of material for mending (Do.) and in Samoa "apapalagi": "indiennes étrangères," foreign calico or chintz (Vo.).

tű denotes in Magyar needle, *tűz*: to sew, to stitch, to pin. In Maori "tui" means: to pierce, to penetrate (Tr.); "titi": to stick in; "tui": "coudre, enfiler," to sew, to thread (Marques., Do.); "tui": "coudre, percer," to sew to stitch (Tahiti, Ja.), and "tuioti": "transpercer," to broach (Samoa, Vo.). In New Zealand the upper fastening of cloaks was sometimes affected by means of a curved cloak-pin, called "autui".[1]

The Magyar speech possesses an expression *tulkó* for denoting: *a belt, a girdle* (Ba.), and *tatu* is: the armadillo. Maori use for belts amongst other terms "tu" and "tatua".[2]

Weapons. Like the terms for clothing those for ancient weapons offer in both languages certain resemblance and thus means for comparisons. Let us consider the following:

The arrow of the ancient Magyar was called *nyíl* (sagitta, telum, jaculum). In New Zealand they understand by "niu": a means of divination[3] by throwing *small sticks*, the sticks so thrown; by "niti": a dart, to throw the dart in a game (Tr.).—In Magyar *lő* means: to shoot, to fling and in Maori they have "li": "jeter, lancer," to throw, to fling (Tonga, Ma.); "lia-liai": "s'apprêter à lancer," to make ready to throw (Samoa, Vo.).—*tegez* is the Magyar quiver; more is said about this word on page 53.

Magyar denote by *taják* the upright part of ears of corn (Ba.); "taiaha" is one of the Maori terms for spear.[4] The Magyar *kopja* is: a lance, usually fitted with a small flag. The Maori have also a sort of lance called "kopeo".[5] "To beat, to thrash" Magyar express by *huall* (Ba.); "huata" in Maori is a spear.[6] Another Magyar expression for thrashing is *patyókál*, and *patél* (Ba.) is to beat out. The Maori say "patu" for: to strike, beat, thrash (Wi.).

Domestic Life. In ancient times the Magyar lived a kind of communistic life. The Greek emperor Constantinos Porphyrogenetos refers to it in these words: "Each tribe has its chief, but the tribesmen are not his subjects."[7] And their chronicler Anonymus mentions the ancestral law by which "no one could be excluded from what was won by common effort".[8]

[1] See Best. Vol. II. P. 505.—Compare the Magyar "hajtű" = pin for fastening the hair or hats of women.
[2] See Best. Vol. II. P. 229.
[3] Compare the Magyar "nyilatkozás" = revelation.
[4] See Best. Vol. II. P. 242.
[5] Ibid. P. 241.
[6] See Best. Vol. II. P. 240.
[7] Hunfalvy. P. 217.
[8] Kerékgyártó. P. 267.

Keane writes: "The Polynesians are largely communistic, probably more so than the Melanesians and afford one of the best examples of communism in property with which we are acquainted." [1]—This communism has found its expression in various ways and amongst them in the cultivation of the soil. Concerning the latter, *eke* is the Magyar word for plough. In Tongan "ekei" means: "remuer, agiter tout dépôt dans un liquide avec ou sans instruments," to move or to stir up the deposits of a liquid with or without an instrument, and in Easter Island "ekaeka" means: to blend, to mingle, to mix (Ch.). The Magyar terms: *páhó* (= storeroom), *rakás* (= pile, stack), *gát* (=dam, weir),[2] *tanya* (= farm) seem to have their counterparts in the Maori words "paho": magazine (Tr.), "roku": to draw together, to gather, to pucker, "kati": to block up, to close against anyone, "gata": to set bounds or landmarks, to restrict (Tonga, Tr.), and "kato": a wall of stone-like dyke (Mangarewa, Ch.). (Analogies for the word *tanya* will be dealt with on page 103, foot-note 3.)

An oven is called in Magyar *kohó*, roasting: *pirit*, a glow: *parázs*,[3] ashes: *hamu*, to burn: *ég*, *ig*. The Maori have the expressions (Tr.) "kohua": oven, "pira": roast, "hamu": to gleam, "iki (on Hawaii: ii)": to burn.

éh is the Magyar term for hunger and *étel* for food; *enni* is to eat. On Tahiti "o'é" means: famine,[4] and in New Zealand "ete": thicken in cooking (Wi.); "ai" on Samoa (Vo.): to eat and "aina": eatable, as well as eaten.—"kai" is a general expression in the South Seas for food, and *kajgonya* is a Magyar dialect-term for dish of eggs (Ba.); *kajtár*: is voracious (Ba.).

Music and Dance.

The slow, solemn and dignified character of some Magyar dances finds also its counterpart in those of the Maori. According to Brown,[5] in Polynesian dancing the body generally suffers no displacement from the same spot; the feet are only occasionally moved and then only for forward and backward steps, as before a shrine or in the noisy stamping of the war-dance.

ének denotes in Magyar: song, *hang* is: voice, sound. In New Zealand "ene" means: to be joyful, to sing, and "hangu": to be silent, dumb (Tr.).[6] The violin is called by the Magyar *hegedü* (= cithara, lyra, pandura, fides, tetrachordum), whilst in Maori "heke" denotes: rope, and "toe": division (Wi.).

[1] Keane. P. 554.
[2] The Magyar "gát-ol" means: to hinder, to restrain.
[3] Concerning "parás" see page 30.
[4] Calderon (Tihoti): *Tahiti*. P. 134.
[5] Brown. P. 203.—More about Maori dancing and music—the latter showing also some strange syncopations—may be found in Emerson's *Unwritten literature of Hawaii* (The sacred Songs of the Hula). Pp. 138–175.
[6] "u" means: to be fixed (Wi.).

Riding From time immemorial the Magyar were considered to be horsemen. The Maori, although having primitively no horses in their islands, seem nevertheless to have had some knowledge of riding. New Zealand traditions tell that the ancestors used to ride in "Hawaiki" on big four-footed animals [1]; on some old Maori stone-carvings horselike quadrupeds are quite distinguishable.[2] Also certain habits of Maori mothers in their treatment of the legs of their babies is suggestive of an equestrian ancestry.[3]

[1] Newman. P. 280.
[2] Ibid. P. 160.
[3] Brown. P. 74.

CHAPTER IX.

ABOUT WATERS AND FISHING.

IMPORTANCE OF FISHING AMONGST BOTH PEOPLES.—STAGNANT WATERS.—FLOWING WATERS.—CONVEYANCE BY WATER.—BODILY STRUCTURE OF THE FISH.—NAMES OF FISHES.—FISHING IMPLEMENTS.

Importance of Fishing with both Peoples.

The Magyar speech is remarkably rich in expressions referring to fishing. This fact is corroborated by *Herman*,[1] who studied the traditional implements and the documents relating to them, and also by *Munkácsi*, who classified its terminology.[2] The latter holds the view that *the Magyar undoubtedly must have originally come from an ancient home where fish was abundant.*[3] To this very day fish is often the chief dish at peasant wedding-banquets.[4] These statements are of special interest if we bear in mind the Maori tradition according to which they are said to have *learnt the making of fishing-nets from a light-skinned people*, encountered by their ancestors in far lands.[5]

Fishing plays a large rôle in old Magyar cosmogony. Its teaching is that the earth rests on " the back of fishes ", especially of *whales*. (And these live, we know, in the high seas and are not to be seen in any inland waters.) The popular belief is still held in Temesköz-Lőrinczfalva to-day that the Universe is supported by three whales. In Magyar-Szt. Mihály and in other places the number of whales is four. They are said to turn over every third year and to make the whole earth tremble.[6] If at any time they were to die, the world would cease to exist : such is the legend in Felsőbánya.[7] According to certain Maori traditions also, the earth is represented as swimming.[8] So they regard

[1] O. Herman : *A magyar Halászat Könyve* (Manual of Magyar Fishing).

[2] B. Munkácsi : *A magyar népies Halászat Műnyelve* (Terminology of Popular Magyar Fishing).

[3] In *Keleti Szemle* of 1905. Vol. VI. P. 195.—See also Herman : Az Ősfoglalkozások Kérdése (The Question of primitive Occupations) ; in *Budapesti Szemle*, 1897. P. 413.

[4] Kandra. P. 448.

[5] Best. Vol. I. P. 219.

[6] Kálmány : *Világunk Alakulásai*, etc. P. 9.

[7] Kandra. P. 39.

[8] Newman. P. 24.

their islands as so many fish, hooked and brought to the surface by their gods and demigods (Maui, etc.) from the depths of the Ocean.[1]

Stagnant Waters.

Nowadays the usual Magyar term for water (also juice) is: *víz, veez.* A less usual Maori expression for it is "wee"[2] (Tr.), the common one being "wai" (Wi.). Maori "waiu" (Wi.) denotes: milk[3]; in Samoa "vaivai" (Tr.) means: to be thin and watery as gruel, and *vaj* is in Magyar: butter.[4]

in means in Magyar: to drink; the general expression in Maori is "inu".

kut is the Magyar well, fountain. In Maori "kutai" (Marquesas, Do.) means: "plein d'eau, très humide," full of water, very wet; "kutokuto" (Easter Island, Ch.) is: foam, bubbles, to strangle with water.

A swamp is denoted in Magyar by *mocsár*, a lake, a swamp, also the stagnant water of the seas by *morotva* and the verb to wash by *mos, musia.* The Maori signify by "makao, makoa" (Tr.): at the lowest ebb, by "moana" (Ch.): salt water, deep sea, by "mote" (Wi.): water.[5] In Arorai "marava" (P. A. C.) is: "haute mer," the high sea.

tó is the Magyar term for lake, sea.[6] In Maori "to" (Wi.) means: calm, "roto" (Tr.): a pond, a lake, a lagoon; it appears in Hawaii as "loko", in Tonga as "loto" (Tr.), in Tahati as "roto" (Ja.), in the Marquesas as "oto" (Do.).

The Magyar *tenger*[7] means: the sea, and *tengeri*: sea-like, plentiful, many, highest (summus), as in "the supreme wisdom of God". The Maori deity Tanga-Roa, Tana-Roa, the "great" Tanga (Tana), is their "*Lord of the Ocean*". This Tanga is said by Forlong[8] to be the "Ta, Tan, Ten"[9] of the Mongolian God Ten-gri, who was, long before, a God Ding-er, Tenger of the Sumers, from the root Ding: to create.[10] Further, "tangere" (Tr.) means: "bottom of deep water."[11]

[1] Best. Vol. I. P. 144, etc.

[2] In Nengone, Duraru, Murare, Tanna it is "wi".—See Churchill: *Polynesian Wanderings.* P. 340.

[3] "u" denotes in Maori: the chest.

[4] In Samoan "vau" (Vo.): "mêler, démêler en pétrissant," to mix kneading.

[5] In Tahitian "ma" (Ja.) means the same as "lavé", washed.

[6] In accusative: "tav-at."

[7] This word apparently does not exist in any "Ugrian" language. See Kandra. P. 11.

[8] Forlong: *Short Studies in comparative Religions.* P. 282.

[9] See Magyar "*Isten*" = God.

[10] Tonga-Nui (Tanga-Roa's grandson) was also a Maori *marine deity.*

[11] Newman mentions (page 104) the so-called "Tenggerese" tribe of Java, a people quite different from the surrounding Javanese and "who some writers show are much like Maoris". In Magyar "tengerész" is: the seaman.

Flowing Waters.

Concerning the expressions for flowing waters reference may be made first of all to the word *ár* (= the flood), already alluded to on page 56. Of other terms we may mention :

hullám = wave	huri : to overflow[1] fuli (Samoa, Tr.) : to roll along fulafula (Samoa, Vo.) : " gonflements, endroits gonflés du corps," swelling, swollen parts of a body huli (Hawaii, Tr.) : to turn generally in any way, to turn over and about[2] uri (Rarotonga, Tr.) : to roll over uriia (ditto) : a cyclone huriavero (Tahiti, Tr.) : to be overturned by a storm huhuri (Easter Island, Ch.) : rolling, to water, to wet
jó (iou) = river[3]	ia (Tr.) : a current, stream iu (Marqu., Do.) : " eau de mer, qui entre dans une embarcation voie d'eau," sea-water penetrating into a boat, waterway
patak, pataka = rivulet, brook, creek	pata (Wi.) : drop of water pata (Marqu., Do.) : " goutte d'eau," water-drop patana (Tr.) : brook, silt, rivulet

The following Magyar words are also connected with the notion of flowing waters : *ágy, hid, mály, part, ragol, rév, úsz.*

ágy (e.g. folyó-ágy) = bed of a river	aga (Tonga, Ma.) : " place, endroit où une chose se met, se fait, se passe ; il se met alors à la fin du mot," a place, where something is done or something happens ; in this case it is affixed to the word
hid = bridge	see page 56
mál = according to Szarvas-Simonyi the sense of this word is not reliably ascertained and may denote " river's banks "	ma (Wi.) : brook, watercourse, ditch ; branch of a tree, dredge mara (Wi.) : a plot of ground under cultivation

[1] Magy. " hull " means also : to fall.
[2] " hu " is in Maori also : to bubble up.
[3] Appears often as terminal syllable in Magyar river-names, e.g. Berettyó, Héjő, Sajó, Somlyó, Tápió, etc.—In the same way the terminal syllable " va " (comp. Maori : wai) may be found in river names, as Zagyva, Boldva.

just as well as the "slope of a mountain" in connection with wine-growing [1]

mala (Samoa, Tr.): a new plantation
mala (Hawaii, Tr.): a field
malae (Tonga, Tr.): cleared of weeds
malao (Tonga, Ma.): "place à découvert où se réunit le peuple," an open space for meetings

part = shore [2]

pari (Tahiti, Tr.): the rocks or perpendicular cliffs by the sea-side
pari (Tahiti, Ja.): "rocs à pic sur la mer," steep rocks on sea-shore
pali (Hawaii, Tr.): the side of a steep ravine, a steep hill

rév = a ferry, harbour, port

rewa (Wi.): to be elevated, high up
whaka-rewa: to put afloat
aka-rewa (Mangarewa, Tr.): to transport, to carry from one to another, or from place to place
revata (Fiji): to lie to, as a canoe

úsz = to swim

u (Wi.): to reach the land, arrive by water
uta (Tr.): to be carried or conveyed by water
au (ditto): "nager," to swim
uta (Mangarewa, Tr.): to carry by sea to land or by sea to another country
usi (Samoa, Vo.): "fondre à la chaleur," to melt in the heat
usiusi (ditto): "poisson," fish
uaua, uoua (Arorai, P. A. C.): "nager," to swim.

Conveyance by Water.

For the various notions in connection with conveyance by water, the Magyars have, among others, the following expressions: *alj, evező, hajó, manga, vitorla.*

alj, alia = the lower part, the bottom of something (e.g. of a boat)

alia = was the name of double-canoes of Samoa, on which a platform was built and usually a house erected [3]

dal

see page 80

[1] See also page 119, foot-note 2.
[2] See also page 30.
[3] Smith: *Hawaiki.* P. 180.—See also page 176, foot-note 8.

evez, ouez = to row, to scull	ue (Wi.): to move a canoe with a paddle worked against the side ue (Tr.): to scull, to steer with a paddle hoewai: a broad form of paddle [1]
hajó = ship, boat	uruao = the legendary ship first built by the ancestors of the Maori [2] ao (Marquesas, Do.): "aller par mer en embarcation," to go by sea in a small craft hai o (Tahiti, Ja.): "remplir de viatique, provisions," to load with provisions and food
manga = row	manga (Tr.) [3]: the branch of a tree, brook, watercourse mangaingai: slow, moving heavily [4]
vitorla = sail	viti: to coil up, to curl up la: a sail. (Tr.)

Bodily Structure of the Fish.

Before considering the name of various species of fishes, some terms of both languages for fish in general and for their parts should be quoted. Starting from the Magyar expressions of: *hal, hólyag, ikra, kopoltyú, para, pikkely,* we may arrive at:

hal = fish	halo (Hawaii, Tr.), the motions of the fins in swimming, to spread out the hands as in the act of swimming hai (Marquesas, Do.): "raie," ray haoa (ditto): "gros poisson," big fish alogo (Samoa, Vo.): "poisson," fish
hólyag, hupolyag = swimming bladder of fishes	hopu (Tr.): to be swollen like a blister hopupu (Hawaii, Tr.): to be filled or puffed up with wind, a bladder or the bowels

[1] *Journ. Pol. Soc.* 1926. P. 244.
[2] Smith: *Hawaiki.* P. 115.—Concerning "uru" see also pages 67 and 179.
[3] See also page 100.
[4] Comp. the Magyar "manga, mankó" = props.—In the Marquesas "manana" (Do.) means: "qui se divise en deux embranchements," what is divided in two parts.

ikra = roe, spawn [1]	ika [2] (Tr.) : the general name of all fish ika (Tonga, Marquesas, Mangarewa) ; ia (Samoa, Tahiti, Hawaii) ; ikatu (Mangarewa, Tr.) : fish which go in shoals to deposit spawn inaa (Tahiti, Ja.) : "frai de poisson," spawn, fry taunga ika (Best, II. P. 402) [3] : fishing ground ia (Samoa, Vo.) : "nom générique de poisson, excepté la bonite et les coquillages," general term for fishes, excepting tunnies and shellfish
kopoltyú, kopotó, koppantyú = gill	koputa (Tr.) : blistered koputaputa : the fish-bladder koopu (Marques., Do.) : "ampoule, enflé, gonflé," bladder, puffed, swollen kapoga (Tonga, Ma.) : "nageoire de dessus, le dos de poissons," upper fins, the back of a fish
para = fin	see page 29
pikkely = scale. — Munkácsi calls special attention to the "peculiarity" that there is no term of Magyar origin either for this important word or for "ikra" (= spawn), i.e. *the Magyar term is quite different from those of its "relations" of the Ugrian languages.* [4]	piki (Tr.) : a plume, a feather biki (Tonga, Tr.) : to stick to, adhere, adhesive piki (Tonga, Ma.) : "être collé à," to stick at pikohe (Marque., Do.) : "mollasse (en parlant des crustacés dépouillés de leur test)," soft, speaking of crustaceans taken off the shell pikahehaa : "tomber par écailles," falling by scales.

Names of Fishes.

When dealing with denominations for the various sorts of fishes we are undertaking an especially hard task, but very interesting conclusions may thus be arrived at in connection with the wanderings of both nations. Unfortunately material actually at hand is insufficient for such a purpose, and besides the rather limited scope of this study does not allow of a thorough investigation.

[1] In Magyar "rak" denotes : to pile up, to lay.
[2] See also page 4 (Celestial Bodies).
[3] The Magyar term "tanya" has various meanings, viz. : place for fishing, lake, stopping place, farm. According to Munkácsi (P. 74) the Magyar fishermen denote by it that spot of the river where they stretch their nets.—In Maori we have the expression "taunga" (Tr.) : shoal of fish, a haul of fish, a place of alighting, a bond of connection between families, to become at home in a place, domesticated, resting place.
[4] Munkácsi. P. 6.

Still if examples of comparisons are adduced here, the object is to stimulate scientific researches in this field, because even a superficial glance at such Magyar words as: *ingola*, *karda*, *keszeg*, *ol*, *ponty*, etc., may convince anyone that these are perhaps not simply cases of fortuitous consonance, but of real analogies, as they cover in both languages expressions for *the same species of fish*.

MAGYAR[1]:	MAORI:
dévér = abramis brama	tewetewe (Wi.): a fish like a mackerel
ingola = a sort of eel, petromyzon fluviatilis	ingoingo (Wi.): young eel
karakatna = diving bird, colymbus	karakahia (Wi.): a bird, the white duck (nyroca australis) karokara (Marques., Do.): "espèce d'oiseau," a sort of bird
karda = sword fish, peletus cultratus	karehu (Wi.): spade
keszeg = generally any whiting	kehe (Tr.): the name of a fish[2]
kolsz, kocz = aspro	korokoro (Wi.): lamprey koroama: a small fish
macza = acernia cernua	matarehe: a kind of eel mataeleele (Samoa, Vo.): "poisson," fish
mény-hal = lota vulgaris	manihira: a small fish
ol = petromyzon fluviatilis	oreaa: a kind of eel
peleh-hal = fish used as bait	pelupelu: "nom d'un poisson parfois mortellement vénéneux," name of an occasionally deadly poisonous fish pela (Samoa, Vo.): "nom d'un poisson," name of a fish
porhó = acernia cernua	porohe: a fish
tat-hal = tinca vulgaris	tataahae (Marqu., Do.): "espèce de poisson," a sort of fish
tok = accipenser schypa	toke: the name of a fish toke (Tonga, Ma.): "anguille de mer," sea-eel
tomolykó = a sort of whitebait, squalius dobula, leuciscus rutilus	tamure: pagrus unicolor, a fish
varsinta = aspro	wariwari: garfish

Fishing Implements.

Even richer results may be obtained by investigations into the terminology of fishing tackle, where the excellent studies of Herman and Munkácsi on one side, and of Best and Hamilton[3]

[1] Terms taken from Munkácsi: *A magyar népies Halászat Műnyelve.*
[2] "koho" means in Maori: very clear.
[3] Hamilton: *Fishing and Sea-Food of the Ancient Maori.*

on the other, supply abundant material for research. Some examples taken at random follow.

ág = fishing rod

okooko (Best, Vol. II. P. 419): a wooden fish-hook
agasala: "pêcheur," fisher
akarau (Easter Island, Ch.): to bite at the hook

apacs = swimmer of a net

apaapa (Marqu., Do.): "ailes ou côtes du filet," wings of the side of nets
apai (Mangarewa, Tr.): to carry
apaga: a bundle
apatari (Wi.): to carry

boné, poné = the string of a certain net (of the so-called "kecze")

pona (Wi.): a cord, a string of fish
pona (Mangarewa, Tr.): to knot, to unit the two ends of a chain

cége = an expression used in fishing by a barring process. The real sense of the word could not be quite established by Munkácsi (P. 45); he thinks that it may denote the barricade itself used by this method

tekei (Tonga, Ma.): "pousser, repousser, chasser, rejeter, refouler," to push, to reject, to drive, to throw back, to jam
segi (Samoa, Vo.): "prendre, saisir," to take, to seize

csorpák = a tight network fastened on the fork-shaped end of a rod

korapa (Best, II. 405)[1]: a scoop or landing net

háló = net in general

hao (Tr.): to draw round, as to *encompass fish*; a basket in which cockles are collected; a prayer and ceremonies formerly used at the dedication of a new house or canoe[2]
hao (Wi.): to catch in a *net*, capture a fortress
hao (Tahiti, Ja.): to encircle as fishermen in bringing both ends of a *fishing net* together
hao (Marquesas, Do.): "cerner, entourer," to surround, to encompass
hao (Hawaii, Tr.): to collect together, to put less things in a greater

káta = the sack in the centre of the net

kete (Best, II. 404): the belly or the middle part of the net, "kaharoa"[3] (a large seine or drag net)

[1] Small hand-nets as they are shown in Best's work (Vol. II. P. 413) may still be seen to-day with Magyar fishermen on the Danube or on the Tisza.
[2] In Magyar "hála" means: thanksgiving, gratitude.
[3] In Magyar "kecze" is a term for big ground-nets.

káva = the transverse hoops of a hand-net (as "csorpák") for stretching it [1]	kawai (Tr.): the loops or handles of a basket kawei (Tonga, Tr.): the hangers of basket-tops kavakava (Easter Island, Ch.): rib
korcz = cross-beam on the wicker-work	koraparapa (Tr.): cross-grained, twisted korapa (Best, II. 441): a net-trap
kótis = parts of the net-frame (the lead-rings of the "ín")	kotinga (Rarotonga, Tr.): a border, an edge
kotrácza = the inner part, the bottom of a net, where the fish arrives after having passed the outer court	korotete (Best, II. 437): a corf, a fish-trap with a small net fastened to the inner end, preventing escape; the other end is the "kotore"
kötél = rope, cord, line	kotui (Tr.): cord, rope, line kota (Best, I. 233): rope
matring = skein	matala (Tonga, Ma.): "détaché," detached matala: "non roulé, non lié," unrolled, not fastened [2]
para [3] = a piece of wood fastened over the net in order to keep it swimming	para (Mangarewa, Tr.): to put material in the water to soak palepale (Tonga, Ma.): "toutes espèces de planches ou de claie suspendue," all sort of planks or suspended hurdles
pekle = the thin thread on which the hook is fastened	pekapeka (Best, II. 421): a spreader for hooks
szák = a small net	takeke (Wi.): a net name saa (Samoa, Vo.): "court," short
szigony = fish-spear, barb, harpoon, also the simple angling hook	tito (Best, II. 421) [4]: barb or point of a hook tito (Marqu., Do.): "becqueter, mordre à l'hameçon," to snap at a bait sega (Samoa, Vo.): "queue d'un da," end of an angling rod for flying fishes
ták = annex, supplement, patch	taka: a twine used to secure hook to a line

[1] "káva" of a well means its border or curb.—Concerning Magyar "kut" see also page 99.

[2] Magyar "motol" to roll, to coil up or down.

[3] See also page 29.

[4] In Maori "titi" (Wi.) means: stick in, peg, pin, nail.—See also Magyar "tű" = needle, pin, on page 95.

tőr = a fishing trap	torehe: small netted bag-like receptacles [1] toere (Best, II. 417): hand net
varsa = weir-basket for fishing or lobster-catching (Ba.) [2]	wharua (Best, II. 437): the form of eel-pot, having an entrance at each end
vető = in the region of the Balaton-Lake has the same meaning as "tanya", i.e. favourable place for fishing	wetoki (Wi.): to swim in shoals.

[1] See also at "tőr" on page 67.

[2] The drawing of a "varsa" in Herman's work, P. 159, shows the analogous construction as the lamprey-weir of the Maori illustrated in Best. Vol. II. P. 445.

PART II.

THE MUNDA, THE LINK BETWEEN MAGYAR AND MAORI

We simple ones love justice and resist coercion ;
But will fly our beloved land to live in peace.

Great crimes are unknown amongst us ;
And we have no laws relating unto criminals.

Of hard and uncharitable men we know many,
They will be sufferers both now and hereafter ;
Also they who try to make money of the stranger,
And feel no pain in the distress of another.

Man must live chastely and be the husband of one
wife ;
Content with what heaven bestows, and loving all.

" Gleanings from Turanian or Pre-Aryan Indians, from Sontâls of Southern Bengal Hilly Tracts, a Race of great Antiquity."—Forlong.

CHAPTER X.

A GLANCE AT PRE-ARYAN INDIA.

PRE-ARYAN CULTURE OF INDIA.—CHARACTERISTICS OF THE PRE-ARYAN POPULATION.—THE MUNDA TRIBES.—THE DRAVIDA TRIBES.—RELATIONS BETWEEN MUNDA AND DRAVIDA.—WANDERINGS OF THE ARYA.—ARYA'S RISE TO POWER.—THE "BUD" RELIGION.—PRE-ARYAN COMMERCE.

This second part may possibly render more plausible the former part with its unexpected interesting analogies between Maori and Magyar. Thus the contradictions between the generally accepted scientific views of to-day and the inferences advanced here may be to a great extent resolved. But for this purpose we must transfer our "scene of operations" to the *South-Asian Continent,* and especially to *India,* this melting pot of ancient races. And then we shall also discover *the real family* of the, supposed Finno-Ugrian (Uralian), *Magyar language.*

Pre-Aryan Culture of India.

What must be first noted, is the deeply-rooted error of people with average but not specialized knowledge, accepted because of the support of the earliest Hindu literature, that in remote times India was a totally uncultured country and that the *Aryan immigration was solely responsible* for its civilization, including its highly developed language, *Sanskrit.* Recent researches reveal quite different facts.[1] They have exploded the tradition that the Arya had overrun not only the whole country watered by the Ganges, but also a considerable area of the Eastern and Western coasts of India, the *aboriginal* inhabitants having been either driven into the mountains or reduced to semi-slavery.

The immigration of the Arya, probably due to the growing aridity of their settlements on the banks of the Oxus, is supposed to have begun approximately in 2000 B.C.[2]; but long before this, up to forty centuries B.C., there already existed an intensive sea-

[1] ". . . totally at variance with the actual fact," says Hewitt in his "Notes on the Early History of Northern India." *Journ. As. Soc.*, 1888. P. 321.—See also: Viswanatha: *Racial Synthesis in Hindu Culture,* a most excellent work.

[2] This exodus from the Oxus was not directed exclusively to India, but also through Media to Persia. See Kennedy: "The Aryan Invasion of Northern India." *Journ. Asiat. Soc.*, 1919. P. 495.—See further Wilson: *The Persian Gulf.* P. 28.

trade between ports on the West Coast of India and the lands of *Akkad and Sumer*, the precursors of the Assyrian Empire. At that time the early builders of *Ur* must have brought their teak-wood from the Malabar Coast of India, as it is only there that this wood grows sufficiently near to the sea. Hewitt tries to prove [1] that as early as 6000 B.C., in Proto-Chaldean times, and long before there were any Semites or sun-worshippers in Assyria, the inhabitants not only sailed to and traded with India, but permanently settled there. At any rate there is no doubt that objects have been found identical in shape and bearing the same signs and figures, both in Kish (in Mesopotamia), in Susa and in Northern India. These belong to the historical period of 3000 B.C. Recent excavations have proved the existence of *entire cities* of this epoch, e.g. Harappa (in the Punjab) and Mohen-jo-Daro (in Sind). Nothing so far discovered affords any indication that the builders of these prehistoric places were the Rigvedic Arya.[2] [3] On the contrary, in several passages of the Rigveda we hear of the strongbuilt cities of the *aborigines*.[4]

Thus the question arises—*who lived in India before the advent of the Arya, i.e. the Hindu* ?

Characteristics of the Pre-Aryan Population.

In addition to primitive and uncivilized neolithic inhabitants, there existed *two civilized races*, of whom both had immigrated. The representatives of the one race are described as gregarious, excitable, turbulent when roused, but generally peaceable and good-humoured. Brave, adventurous, witty, very fond of amusement, not given to work more than necessary, they were as a rule very careless of the future.[5] They began by clearing the forests and tilling the land. The centre of union in their tribal life was the priest. And it is to these alone that are attributable the earliest forms of social institutions, which formed the framework of the government of the country.[6] Various generic names were bestowed upon them; thus they were called *Kol's, Kolarians*, a name derived from the "Kol"-language spoken by a great part of them [7]; they were also called *Munda*, and this is the name

[1] *Journ. As. Soc.*, 1888. Pp. 204, 337.—1889. P. 305.

[2] Ramaprasad Chanda: "The Indus Valley in the Vedic Period," in No. 31 of the *Memoirs of the Archæological Survey of India*. P. 4.

[3] Waddell in *The Indo-Sumerian Seals* thinks that Harappa was built by the Sumerians, but that the latter were "Vedic-Aryans." (P. 3.)—Viswanatha, P. 28, shares not these views; according to him these discoveries tend to show features of both cultures—Arya and Dravida (Munda).

[4] Roy: *The Mundas and their Country*. P. 56.—See also Viswanatha, P. 37.

[5] Hewitt: *Journ. As. Soc.*, 1888. P. 330.

[6] Ibid. P. 328.

[7] Prior to the Aryan conquest of the Gangetic provinces "Kol" was the predominant language of that part of India.

we shall use for them, as a technical term, in the course of this study.[1]

The other race was composed of thrifty, even avaricious people. Patient and laborious, indomitably obstinate in all their undertakings, they were careful to see that they got all possible profit out of their actions. Silent, undemonstrative, except when strongly moved, they were somewhat slow of apprehension, this not from want of intellect, but from a determination to see all sides of a subject and know it thoroughly in all its phases. Thoughtful of the future they laid great stress upon the education of their children and upon the preservation of strict discipline. As an eminently practical race they believed in the necessity of strong central government. Their discipline permitted the amalgamation of *originally Munda-created communities* into greater units. Unlike the latter they brought large herds of cattle with them. They are known under the generic name of "*Dravida*", a word derived from the Sanskrit "damila" (tamul) = southern people. As in the case of the name "Munda", the expression "Dravida" is also a collective name, applied originally only to a branch of the race, but subsequently extended to the whole.

The Munda Tribes.

The Munda belonged to the Southern group of the *Mongolian race*, whose home was probably situated in N.W. China.[2] They came into India partly from Tibet down the valley of the Brahmaputra, partly through Burmah, by the rivers Mekong, Salween and Irawaddy. Apart from these valleys, except for a few difficult and lonely mountain-paths, the only access to India is in the North-West and West. The Dravida are presumed to have followed these latter tracks, and at repeated times; perhaps viâ Afghanistan and the Khyber Pass, perhaps across Baluchistan (the Bolan Pass, etc.). This second route is the more probable one, because there still exists to-day an isolated Dravida district in the South of Baluchistan.[3] Whether the Dravida are ultimately to be traced to a Central Asian or to a Western Asian origin, cannot at present be decided with absolute certainty. But the latter hypothesis receives very strong support

[1] Chatterji, in his "The Study of Kol", *Calcutta Review*, 1923, P. 451, gives very valuable reasons for the preference of the term "Kol" to any other. If here, nevertheless, the term "Munda" was chosen, the reason is that their speech is treated by the English *Linguistic Survey of India* as those of the "Munda", i.e. as Munda languages.—About one other name, covering once all the Kol tribes, the name *Savara*, more will be said on page 125.

[2] Rapson in Chapter II of *The Cambridge History of India*. Vol. I. P. 39.

[3] It is the district where the Brahui language is spoken. See Trump: *Grammatische Untersuchungen der Brahui Sprache* (Grammatical Researches concerning the Brahui Language).

from the undoubted similarity of the Sumerian and Dravidian ethnic types.[1]

It would lead us of course too far if we were to embrace in our considerations the lands of Sumer and Akkad also; however two points of importance deserve to be dealt with. In contrast to the Munda, who worshipped the Mother Earth, the Dravida

The Dravida Tribes.

were Moon-worshippers, and later on became adorers of snakes and of the phallus, as the visible sign of generative power. With the Munda, until they were converted also to the veneration of snakes and of the phallus, the trees and the local deities supposed to dwell in the neighbouring forests were their familiar objects of daily worship; and next, the great Earth Spirit, Mother Earth.[2] Now, Moon-worship was abandoned in Sumer as early as 4700 B.C., i.e. long before Ur-Bagas, the first known king of Babylonia, laid the foundations of the town of Ur,[3] a fact from which certain chronological conclusions may be drawn.

Coming to the second point of interest, the people of *Akkad* and *Sumer* were, according to Kennedy,[4] "*Turkish or Uralo-Altaian*" races. Hewitt, going even further, declares the Akkad language to belong to the Ugro-Finn family.[5] In any case, it is for some scholars a historical fact that there was a descent of "Turano-Scythian" populations into the region north of the Persian Gulf, carrying with them their language, religious beliefs, legends and traditions, and that this was probably due to unfavourable climatic changes in their original home.[6]

Relations between Munda and Dravida.

Harmonious intercourse was characteristic of the relations between Munda and Dravida; the former who came first, always extended a hearty welcome to the Dravida latecomers. They, in their advance through India, did not move forward, like the Munda, in small parties, scattering through the forest clearings, but proceeded in large bodies, like an army.[7] The Dravida chose good land for themselves, but in other respects *they treated the Munda as equals,* leaving them in undisturbed possession of lands they did not want themselves; there was plenty of room for both. Further amalgamation between the two races was easy, as there was no racial intolerance to separate

[1] Some scholars, like Hall (*The Ancient History of the Near East.* Pp. 173) hold the opposite view, viz. that the Sumer came into Western Asia from India.

[2] Hewitt. *Journ. As. Soc.*, 1889. P. 188.

[3] Ibid. P. 325.

[4] Kennedy. P. 497. He writes also: "I have studied their history with great care, and I have found that they have no creative genius whatever: they preserve or destroy, but they do not invent."

[5] Hewitt. *Journ. As. Soc.*, 1890. P. 476.

[6] Terrien de Lacouperie: "The Origin of the Babylonian Characters from the Persian Gulf." *Journ. As. Soc.*, 1888. P. 316.

[7] Hewitt. Vol. I. P. 331.

them. On the one side there was practical good sense, and on the other the friendly welcome always given by Munda tribes to peaceable strangers.[1] In many districts, especially in border tracts, *the two races have completely blended* and have formed new tribes; in many places it is only the Munda speech which indicates the original dweller. In any case the Dravida land-organization can only have been based upon a Munda division of the country into villages and provinces, for these divisions are found later on even in parts of the country, where there are no traces whatever of Dravida or Arya rule.[2] When speaking of the Indian predecessors of the Arya and when reference is chiefly made *to Dravida and very seldom to Munda*: the reason lies in the facts we have just adduced. It is only the most recent researches which have thrown clearer light upon the real past of India and on the situation existing there at the time of the Aryan immigration.

Wanderings of the Arya.

Concerning the primitive homes of the Arya many theories are advanced; one of the latest is due to Giles and suggests[3] that they originally dwelt in *Central Europe*, possibly in a region enclosed by the Carpathian Range, the Balkans, the Alps, the Bohemian Forest and the "Erzgebirge".[4] From there they dispersed in all directions. One portion may have left the regions of the Danube not earlier than 2500 B.C., their route leading probably along the Southern coasts of the Black Sea, further across the mountains between the Van- and Urmia-lake, south of the Caspian Sea to the Oxus, and finally through Herat to India.[5] As already mentioned above, the Arya appeared on the frontiers of India about 2000 B.C. Kennedy thinks they may have *numbered three-quarters of a million.*[6] The Aryanization of India began in the Punjab approximately in 1600 B.C.; later on Northern and Central Rajputana were colonized, afterwards the Gangetic Doab, Oudh and Behar. It was completed in all its main outlines before 600 B.C.[7]

Arya's rise to Power.

The literary documents of the Arya, especially the collections of their religious hymns (Vedas), the first of which is believed by *Max Müller* to date from about 1200 B.C.,[8] and especially their well-known epics, describe the Aryan invasion

[1] Hewitt. *Journ. As. Soc.*, 1890. P. 462.
[2] Ibid. P. 461.
[3] Giles: The Aryans, in Chapter III of Rapson's *The Cambridge History of India*. He suggests "wiro" as collective name for the Indo-German languages, because this is the term for "men" in most of them. P. 66.
[4] See also Kean. P. 503 (Indo-European Cradles).
[5] Giles in Rapson's *Cambridge History of India*. Vol. I. P. 70.
[6] Kennedy. P. 521.
[7] Ibid. P. 506.
[8] See also foot-note 4 on page 175.

of India as a campaign with victories and complete overwhelming of their "wild and uncivilized" adversaries. ("Arya" in Sanskrit, "Airya" in Zend, means: of good family, noble, and was an epithet applied by the composers of the Vedic hymns to distinguish their own stock from that of the earlier inhabitants.)[1] The real facts are quite otherwise.[2] The Arya reached supreme power not only by wars, nor by their numbers, etc., but perhaps chiefly by their diplomatic and political ability, by their readiness of resource, by the religious reverence inspired by their missionaries and by alliances and marriages with ruling races.[3] They secured their ascendancy in no slight degree by abating their pride of race and submitting to intermarriages with the natives of the country, and by tolerating if not accepting their religion. But their language, being the language of the leaders, became that of the people. The Rigveda, the Zendavesta are not religious books of an isolated race or sect; they are the outcome of the religious records *of the successive races* who ruled India and Iran from the first dawn of civilization.[4]

This leading position of the Arya was due mainly to the great moral and political influence, the excellent organization, the self-denying earnestness, perseverance and tact of their *Brahmins*.[5] The Brahmin ascetics entered the country first; they gained a reputation for sanctity, established schools or secured the direction of the training of the children, just as do the Missionaries of present times. They were followed by the Arya cattle-herdsmen, and so they gradually settled in the new land.[6]

The "Bud" Religion.

The religion found in India by the invading Arya, was characterized by the *worship of the phallus*, as the symbol of generative power; as also by that of the snake, with the same significance. This religion prevailed for a very long time in certain parts of India, and even to this day it finds some adherents.[7] This religion of the "Bud" or "Bod", a term which has been traced back to the word "pu": cause to breath, to create,[8] has of course nothing common with the widespread *religion of Buddhism*.

[1] Berriedale Keith: "The Age of the Rigveda," in Chapter IV of Rapson's *Cambridge History of India*. Vol. I. P. 78.

[2] For the relations between the Arya and the non-Arya see in particular Viswanatha's *Racial Synthesis in Hindu Culture*, especially its Part III. He suggests also another cradle-land for the Arya than Giles.

[3] Hewitt: *Journ. As. Soc.*, 1890. P. 322.

[4] Hewitt: *Journ. As. Soc.*, 1889. P. 334.

[5] Ibid. P. 188.

[6] Ibid. P. 310.

[7] It was introduced by a second wave of Dravida invaders, arriving much later than the first (who worshipped the great Mother Earth and the Moon-goddess). They brought the snake-adoration from Sumer, of which Ea and Hea, the snake-god was the reputed creator and ancestor. (Hewitt, *Journ. As. Soc.*, 1890. P. 331.)

[8] Compare the Magyar "fú": to blow.

(The old god, nevertheless, no doubt, greatly facilitated the progress and popularity of the new saint amidst all Turanian populations, where these were devoid of any etymological knowledge except that which appealed to their uneducated ears and fancies.[1])

The symbols of the Bud were stones and even sometimes mountain peaks of a certain configuration, and the name itself was extended to many localities. In villages of Southern and Central India, in Further India, and occasionally in Upper and Himalayan India, there were and still are many holy "Bud"-stones, called "Bud-a-Kal".[2] The holy mountain, the "Bud-ar" (also: Arbuda) is dome-shaped. Forlong gives[3] the characteristic of the site of such Bud-ar's in the following description of a famous place of pilgrimage in Siam: "A high, picturesque, strongly marked conical limestone hill, rising abruptly at the edge of a great forest which here ends on the bifurcation of two branches of a river. Topographically such sites are selected as the bifurcation is a yonish one."

Pre-Aryan Commerce.

There can be no doubt that the Arya on their arrival in India found a flourishing civilization, with occasional large cities. By means of these cities, the Munda and Dravida populations maintained long before the advent of the Arya *a flourishing inland and foreign trade*; and such a trade could only have been commenced and maintained by races possessing considerable culture.[4] Phoenician travellers along the Arabian coasts to India mention as far back as 1050 B.C. the ports of Karteia and Tsor, the present Kuryat and Sur, regions where no Arya could have dwelt in those times. Also the Greeks possessed[5] the Dravida (Tamil) term for rice (which has no connection with the equivalent Sanskrit term for it) *before* 300 B.C.; thus when this word found its way westward, the Indian ports must have been inhabited by a people speaking Dravida and not Arya. The wealth in land and cows, gold and jewels that the non-Aryan people possessed is frequently referred to in the Rigveda,[6] and the first two Jataka-stories of it, amongst the oldest of the collection, tell of *caravans of five hundred bullock wagons*, which merchants used to send to and fro between Benares and the sea coast, and the difficulties of passing through the desert.

[1] See Forlong: *Short Studies in the Science of comparative Religions*. P. 104
[2] Ibid. P. 75.
[3] Ibid. P. 79.
[4] Hewitt: *Journ. As. Soc.*, 1889. P. 199.
[5] Hewitt: *Journ. As. Soc.*, 1889. P. 205.
[6] Viswanatha: *Racial Synthesis*. P. 38.

CHAPTER XI.

SOME INDIAN TRIBES.

INDIAN TRIBES IN GENERAL.—THE MALA.—THE TAKKA.—THE MADRA.—THE KURU AND THE MATSYA.—HABITS OF SOME MUNDA AND DRAVIDA TRIBES.—THE SANTAL.—SOUTH INDIAN TRIBES.—EMIGRATIONS FROM INDIA.—FURTHER INDIA.—EXTENSION OF WANDERINGS.

The aim of this chapter is to give a short review of such Indian tribes, especially some of the most ancient, who seem to deserve mention here, if it must be only just a glance.

Indian Tribes in General. As the present population of India represents the flotsam and jetsam collected from many streams of ethnical movements, any attempt to sort out the existing races into a set of pigeon-holes, each representing a defined type of race, is impossible in the present state of our knowledge.[1] To begin with, such a task would be extremely difficult if only owing to the great number of peoples and tribes involved. Already in about 500 B.C. Herodotus [2] reports that the Indian are by far *the most numerous* of all the peoples whom he knows. "There are many nations of Indians, differing from one another in tongue; some of them are roving tribes, some of them settled, some dwelling in the river-swamps and living on raw fish, which they catch from boats made of reeds . . ."

Recent scholars, especially the English and the Indian, may therefore be greatly congratulated on the light they have succeeded in throwing on this "jungle". Their researches allow us to trace back, to identify and to locate certain Indian tribes as far back as 1000 B.C.; chiefly in connection with those tribes which took part in the "Battle of ten Kings", as described in the old Indian literature (Rigveda).[3] This is interesting if only for the fact that many of these very tribes, whom we can locate at such an early date *in the North Western corner of India*, are found later in quite different regions, as far away as the South Eastern end of the Peninsula, or even across the Sea.

The Mala. First of all the tribe of the *Mala* deserves attention. This people, known also in ancient Indian History as *Mugh, Mund, Magh, Mon, Man, Kol, Kasi*, etc.,

[1] W. Crooke, quoted by Keane in *Man, Past and Present*. P. 548.
[2] Lib. III, 98–101.
[3] Keith. In Chapter IV of Rapson's *Cambridge History of India*. Vol. I. P. 81.

belongs to an early influx of the Southern, i.e. longheaded Mongols,[1] *and thus to the Munda race mentioned in the previous chapter.* Issuing from the "mountains", the Hima-Malas or Himalayas, their name is said to be derived from this word.[2] A large body of Malas entered India through the high passes of the principal rivers of the old "Kosala", the present Oudh, such as the rivers Sarayu[3] (to-day Ghagra), Iravati (to-day Rapti) and others. Their religious cult was markedly arboreal, their gods were the spirits of the groves, forests and jungles. Repeatedly, when traversing the thickness of an apparently untrodden jungle, one's eyes suddenly light upon a clearing of bright green sward, with an accompanying clump of trees, dedicated to the spirits of the woods, hills and streams; and possibly on some huge, grotesque figure.

We find the Mala in the North as neighbours of other great nations, of the *Madra* and *Takka*, of whom mention will be made later on. The Mala are often confederated with these as well as with other tribes.[4] When in 510 B.C. the armies of the Persian king Darius I seized the Punjab, these mountaineers were already acquainted with river navigation. It was the Mala mariners who helped the Persian admiral Scylax and two centuries afterwards enabled Alexander's Greek army to embark on the *Indus*. At this time we see them already in more southerly homes, between the rivers Chenab and Ravi. Curtius[5] describes them as "validissimae Indorum gentes", the most gallant people of India, and from them Alexander the Great receives his severe wound. Whether all the Mala met with later in Central and South India came from this North Western region, or whether *an immigration took place from North Eastern India*, cannot be ascertained at present. At any rate the rich Doab between the rivers Godavary and Krishna was ruled long before our times by Naga-Malas, i.e. serpent-worshipper Malas, whose capital was Mallanga (probably Mal-linga). Similarly in the time of the emperor Açoka, about 242 B.C., the people of Nar-bada, the present Nerbuda, were known as Munds or Mala.

The Mala, as also the Madra, on their way from the North West of India, settled subsequently in the Saurrashta seaboard of the Gujerat, at the *mouth of the Indus*. Which of these two peoples were the first to settle there is not known, but certain authorities regard the precedence of the Madra as more probable.

[1] In contrast with the Northern Mongols, whose chief characteristic is considered by Ujfalvy to reside in their short heads. (See Keane. P. 166.)

[2] Forlong, p. 113, gives the following etymological definitions: "hima" means snow; "mala," "male" are common widespread words for hill through India, "alya" is place or abode.—Magyar "zimankó" denotes: sleety or snowy weather.—Concerning Magyar "mál" and "alj" see also pages 100 and 102.

[3] Compare "yu" in Magyar river names; page 100.

[4] Ibid. Pp. 115, 116.

[5] Lib. IX. Cap. 4.

The roving Mala found at last their true vocation on the great inland seas and later on the Ocean, finally annexing as their own all the 500 miles of the Western Indian littoral. From the West (the Malabar Coast), as well as from the East (the Coromandel Coast) the Turanian colonies of the *Munda* Mala pushed seawards and landwards; and from that time onwards their history and general character partake of that of the Pelasgi, the Phoenician and Venetian. Many of the Mala clung ever since to a seafaring life; their coast tribes of East India as well as the "Malay" of Further India. From the time they reached the Ocean they considered it as their domain, and their colonies extended as far as Madagascar, or even the Cape of Good Hope. For two thousand years and more they were the carriers of nations, especially in the Eastern Seas. Summing up, *the Mala are one of the greatest races of History*, and the exploits of these mountaineers of bygone times as bold navigators may certainly compare favourably with those of the Normans and Vikings. Some authors even consider them to have been the now extinct Maya people of Central America.[1]

The Takka.

A neighbouring people and very often allied to the Mala were the Dravidian *Takka*, Taka, or Tak's, Taksha's. In connection with our present subject they possess a special interest, seeing that *certain authorities uphold their Finn relationship* and also assert that they were the people of *Magog* of ancient traditions.[2] The interesting fact may be here noted that the Maori of the Marquesas, who alone kept records of a national name, call themselves "Take".[3] The religion of these Indian Takka, calling themselves "Children of the great Mother Earth", is, apart from snake-worship, very much connected with the *Pleiads* and the number seven.[4] Amongst these people all males of a certain age were obliged to be solemnly consecrated to God's service and *to have their hair cut* as a part of the ceremony.[5] They seem, before they entered India, to have passed beyond the early stage of savagery and to have been those "Sons of the Mountains", who as Arabian writers state, used to eat the raw flesh of their victims and drink their blood.[6] According to Hewitt, the cattle-herding folk of the Takka probably came with their flocks from the

[1] So Professor Cyrus Thomas of the Bureau of Ethnology in Washington tries to establish a relationship between the Maya of Mexico and the Malay (*Journ. of Pol. Soc.*, 1898. P. 89).—See also Tregear: "Notes on Maya and Malay." ibid. P. 101.

[2] Hewitt: *The Ruling Races of prehistoric Times*. Vol. I. P. 620 and seq.

[3] Tregear: *Comparative Dictionary*. P. 58.—Also Smith: *Hawaiki*. P. 79.

[4] Hewitt: *The Ruling Races*. P. 616 and seq.

[5] Ibid. P. 279.

[6] Ibid. P. 197.

South Western borders of the Caspian Sea viâ Herat to India.[1] At the time of the "Battle of Ten Kings" recorded by the Vedas, i.e. thousand years before the beginning of our era, the Takka are to be found along the upper course of the Indus and eastwards of it, in the southern part of the present Hazara-district [2] and on the banks of the Chenab. There, not very far from the present town of Rawalpindi was situated their capital Takka-sila (the rock of the Takka),[3] the Taxila of Greek historians.[4]

Taxila, and with it the Takka nation, belonged for a while to the *Persian Empire*, probably from 518 B.C. onwards.[5] Under its ruler, the king "Taxiles" of the Greek historians, and under his son Omphis (Amphi),[6] this city rises to a certain importance during Alexander the Great's campaign (327 B.C.). Later the Takka emigrated. This emigration may already have begun partly as early as the fifth century B.C.; obstinate snake-worshippers and ophiolatrous lingaites as they were, this people was evidently disturbed by the increasing Buddhism. They moved in two bodies, eastwards and westwards. The latter body is said to have arrived as far as the East coast of South India, where the Takka appear under the name "Chola", also "Chalu, Chalukia",[7] their land being called in the edicts of the emperor Açoka "Chola Mandala" (the land of the Chola), the present coast of Coromandel. The eastward group soon found a new home on the banks of the Bias and Sutlej, and their descendants are considered to be the *Sikhs*, the tallest and most handsome men of India, renowned for their bravery and fighting spirit.

In dealing with the Takka, Taksha, some difficulty may arise from the fact, that Taksha means an artificer in general [8] (from "Tak", a snake, clever). So Forlong tells us of Taksha Malas "who left North Western India after Alexander's invasion" (P. 86), and then he speaks of "Taxila Malas" who left the Gujerat coast in A.D. 322 or earlier (P. 98) and are at present the inhabitants of the islands of the Makkasar-Straats.—Also the

[1] The Takka appear also under the name "Tugras, Trigartas", etc. in the ancient literature of India, then as "Shiva", a generic name for all the cattle-herding people of the Rigveda.

[2] The Munda word "hasa" means: earth, soil, land (Campbell: *Santali-English Dictionary*).—See also the Magyar "haza" (= homeland) and Maori "hawa", page 53.

[3] Compare the Magyar words "szikla" (= rock), "szilárd" (= solid, hard), and the Maori "tiro" (Wi.): survey, view; "telea" (Tonga, Ma.): "rocher, terrain taillé," rock, cleft ground; "silafaga" (Samoa, Vo.)": "point de vue, endroit bien découvert," sight, view, prospect.—See also Marshall: *A Guide to Taxila.*

[4] Rhys Davids in Chapter VIII of Rapson's *Cambridge History of India.* Vol. I. P. 214.

[5] Jackson, ibid., in Chapter XIV. Vol. I. Pp. 334, 338.

[6] A grandchild of the Magyar prince Árpád was called Taxis; a Magyar prince: Taksony. See Kerékgyártó. P. 172.

[7] "Csalló" is a Magyar proper name for localities, families, and rivers (Et.).

[8] Compare Magyar "takács": linteo, textor = spinner, weaver, and "ács": artifex, faber = artisan, carpenter.

Gonds of Further India, a Mon race, are said to be related to the Takka.[1]

The Madra.

Simultaneously with the Takka, or even before, another and cognate non-Arya people, the *Madra*, appear in North West India. According to the Indian author Hemachandra of the XIth century, *the Madra were simply a branch or subdivision of the Takka.*[2] This very ancient and important people, also snake worshippers, dwelt long before Aryan times in the Doabs of the Bias and Chenab, a region to this day called "Madradesh". Their capital Sakala or Sangala, the "city of the united tribes" (sanga), was situated on the river Ayak, between Chenab and Ravi.[3] This town is mentioned in Indian literature as early as 600 B.C. The Madra took part in the fights against Alexander the Great as allies of the Pura or Paurava, the king of whom was "Porus" (the Pura) of Greek history.[4] Later on they moved on along the mouth of the Indus and beyond, and they gave their name to many towns, rivers and shrines in India, first of all to Mathura in the Vindhya Mountains, to Madura and Madrapatam. Their name Mad-rah is said to be derived from "madhu": an intoxicating drink, apparently used, as Hewitt tells us, *by Finns* to inspire magicians.[5]

The Kuru and the Matsya.

The Madra were at one time allied also to other nations, for instance to the great tribe of the Kuru.[6] This people who was also known as Kaur, Kurmi, Kauraya, originally lived in the North, beyond the Himalaya. Afterwards the Kuru dwelt about 60 miles north of the present Delhi,[7] where their chief town was Nagapura,[8] and then migrated to the present Hazara district, to Hastinagur, on the banks of the Ambi. With regard to the Takka they stood in a condition of tribal confederation, known as the "Vaikarna".

Of the many tribes closely allied to the Kuru, the *Matsya* may be mentioned. We know that they lived on the Upper Indus and that next to cattle raising their chief occupation was

[1] Hewitt: *The Ruling Races*. Vol. I. P. 113.

[2] These Madra ruled with the Gandhari the Northern Punjab. But the latter, who are said to be identical with the Partha (Parthians ?), are already found in 509 B.C. more to the South, near the present Multan. The Madra also wandered southwards and lived for a certain time *in the delta of the Indus* (see page 119). Hewitt: *Journ. As. Soc.*, 1889. Pp. 195, 240.

[3] Rapson. In Chapt. XXII of his *Cambr. Hist. of India*. Vol. I. P. 549.

[4] Keith. In Chapt. IV of Rapson's *Cambr. Hist. of India*. Vol. I. P. 83.

[5] In Maori "matorutoru" (Tr.) means: benumbed.—See also page 183.

[6] Keith. In Chapt. IV and Hopkins in Chapt. XI of Rapson's *Cambr. Hist. of India*. Vol. I. Pp. 83 and 274.

[7] Hopkins, ibid. P. 262.

[8] Hewitt in *Journ. As. Soc.*, 1889. P. 308.

fishing.[1] In later times the Matsya occupied the lands now known as Alwar, Jaipur and Bharatpur.[2] In the Mahabharata, where the Kuru appear as confederates of the Madra, the king of the Matsya comes to their help " with his mountaineers ".[3]

All the above enumerated tribes arouse our interest amongst other reasons on account *of their migrations in later times*, where we find them in Central and in South India, and with the same names for their settlements as those which designated their ancient dwelling places in North West India. They were the more able to preserve their originality, since the central table land, on which these migrating tribes rallied, especially the highland districts of Ranghur and Chota Nagpur, are admirably adapted by nature for seclusion and defence.[4]

Habits of some Munda and Dravida Tribes.

Turning over even quite superficially the leaves of books of recent days, dealing with these peoples and certain Indian castes, we may notice at once facts which offer abundant inducement for *a future thorough study*; it is not impossible that interesting results may ensue concerning the connection of the Maori, and possibly also of the Magyar, with India. For instance the ancient habit of the Maori to eat by mere veneration their old and invalid parents, may be met also among the *Munda* Birhur of Chota Nagpur.[5] Another reminiscence of the Maori is the singular custom, prevalent amongst some tribes of the *Munda* Kharia (Kuru), of extreme exclusiveness with regard to cooking and eating; especially in association with the " hariah ", the eating pot.[6] Some men do not allow even their wives to cook for them; and if a stranger enters a house in which are kept their earthen drinking and cooking vessels and water pots, every vessel becomes " polluted " and all is thrown away or destroyed.—Amongst the Oraon [7] of Orissa, a Dravida-Turanian half caste people of immigrants, numbering about 600,000, with strong traces of their Northern origin,[8] there exists a habit of eternal bonds of friendship between girls, the ceremony attending which is called " gui ". Now " kui " is a ceremonial address for women and girls in New Zealand.[9]

[1] Their very name is said to be derived from Sanskrit " matsya " = fish.

[2] Keith. In Chapt. IV of Rapson's *Cambr. Hist. of India*. Vol. I. P. 84.

[3] A mere mnemonic list of the Sixteen Great Powers or Sixteen Great Nations, referring to the pre-Buddhist period, let us say to the seventh century B.C., make mention of a nation " *Maccha* ".—Rhys Davids. In Rapson's *Cambr. Hist. of India*. Vol. I. P. 172.

[4] Dalton: *Ethnology of Bengal*. P. 163.

[5] Ibid. P. 158.

[6] Ibid. P. 160.—In Maori " horo " means: to eat greedily; " horonga ": food eaten by the priest in the ceremony of removing the " tapu " of a house (Tr.).

[7] The name is derived from " orang " = the forest man.

[8] Hewitt: *The Ruling Races*. P. 45.

[9] Bhandarkar: *Lectures on the ancient History of India*. P. 27.—Also " koki " is an Indian address for girls, and Maori " ko " means: girl (Wi.).

The neighbours of the Oraon, the Munda (employing exceptionally this term not as the collective term, but as restricted to one tribe only),[1] used the name "Konk *Pat* Munda"[2] as a national denomination. Let us remember here too the "*Patu*-pai-arehe" people of the old fatherland of Maori tradition. For the Korwa, another neighbouring tribe, "*pat*" is the name for a mountain god, a spirit of the mountains. The most popular deities of the Bhuya tribe, once rulers of the present Bhagalpur, of the Ganges-delta and of Kathiawar, near to the mouth of the Indus, a tribe said to be closely allied to the Takka, are: "Dasum Pat," "Bamoni Pat," Koviar Pat," and "Boram." "Pat, Paz"[3] is also a term for deities among Ugro-Finn people.[4]—There is also an extremely interesting peculiarity in the music of the Bhuya, a tune wandering about through all keys and generally showing a cadenza of twenty or thirty notes every second or third syllable.[5] The popular music of the Magyar has the same.—Among the Kherwar, also neighbours of the Oraon, there is a strange rule of religious origin, forbidding the flesh of sheep and the use of wool for clothing. This may be compared with the peculiarity of the ancient Magyar, mentioned on page 93, according to which the wool of sheep was never used in clothing, in spite of the extreme cold.—With the Oraon we make acquaintance with an important deity: *Dharmesh.*—*Damasek* (Damases) was also the name of an ancient god of the Magyar (Et.).[6]—The headman of an Oraon-village is the "pahn"[7]; he deals with all its business, the "banata"; the administration itself is called "chalata". The ancient Magyar had also an official for public administration called *bán* (*rabonbán*), and *családosság* was their term for patriarchy (Et.).—The priest of the Oraon is the "byga", and *bü* (by) means in Magyar: magic, *bűvölö*: magician.—Marriage ceremonies also show some analogy. A bridegroom party called *barat* and carrying red and white flags fetches the bridegroom,[8] and thereupon dances the national dances of Játra and Khariah.[9]—Of *similar superstitions* let us mention one in which a sick person (especially a woman in labour) must be prevented from seeing a cat.[10]

[1] In the following we will describe the Munda *tribe*, as distinct from the Munda *race* as a whole (see page 113), as "Mundari".
[2] Dalton. P. 165.
[3] Hewitt: *Journ. As. Soc.*, 1889. Pp. 277, 273.
[4] Kandra. P. 91.
[5] Grierson: "Some Bhoj'puri Folk-Songs" in *Journ. As. Soc.*, 1886. P. 207.
[6] Of a god Dumu-si of the Indian Gond-tribes we learn by Hewitt in his *Ruling Races of Prehistoric Times*.
[7] Dalton. P. 247.
[8] "barát" denotes in Magyar: friend.
[9] Dalton. P. 245.
[10] Ibid. P. 248, resp. Kandra. P. 154.

Needless to say, all these small data have not been quoted for the purpose of drawing immediate conclusions, but solely with the intention to indicate the trend of closer investigation. So before dealing with the important *Munda* people of the Santal of Bengâl, mention should be made of the *Munda* Savar (also: Saura or Saur), close neighbours of the Bhuya and the Oraon. This tribe, called by Ptolaemeus the Sabarae, lived in bygone times near the Lower Indus, right up to the sea-shore.[1] On the other hand, Cunningham, in his Archeological Reports,[2] informs us that *the name Savara covered in early times all the different divisions of the Munda peoples.* They are told to have extended as far as the present districts of Azingarh and Ghazipore; their last traditional king is said to have belonged to the Treta-Yuga, the second age of Hindu Chronology. And even to-day some of the Munda tribes are called by others "Savara"; e.g. the *Munda* Mahla-Paharia people *term the Santal in this way.—Savarti, (Savarti-Asphali) is also a name amongst ancient Greek writers for the Magyar.*

The Santal. The *Santal* are at present one of the most numerous tribes of Bengal. They count about 2 millions of souls and inhabit an area of 5,470 square miles, the so-called Santal-Pargana, North of Calcutta, to which they migrated only about 100 years ago; their former home being the district of Hazaribagh in Chota Nagpur. The Santal are typical of those Indian races who remained *unaffected by foreign immigration.* According to their tradition, the ancient stock to which they trace their origin, as well as the Bhumij, the Mundari, the Turi, the Korwa, the Ho and other Munda tribes, was called *Kherwar or Kharwar.*[3] If the Santal are asked for their name and caste, they usually adopt the title "Manjhi" (headman).[4] Like some other Munda tribes, they also call themselves "*horoko*" (= men), from "horo"[5] (= man), and their language "horo kai".[6] Among their sagas is one of a wild goose coming from the great Ocean, alighting at "*Ahiri Pipiri*" and laying there two eggs, the male and the female, from which were hatched their first parents.[7] Now "Pipiri" is a very common place-name in

[1] Hewitt: *Journ. As. Soc.*, 1889. P. 256.—Thurston in *Tribes and Casts of Southern India*, Vol. VI, P. 304, derives the name of the Scythian "sagar": an axe, with reference to the axe which they use to carry in their hands.

[2] Vol. XVII. P. 139.—See also Roy: *The Mundas and their Country*. P. 52.

[3] Konow, in Grierson's *Linguistic Survey of India*. Vol. IV. P. 8.

[4] Concerning the name "mansi", which the *Vogul* use for themselves, reference may be found in Munkácsi's work under the word "magyar". See also page xii.

[5] For "horo" and its root "had" see also Skrefsrud: *A Grammar of the Santhali Language*. P. V.

[6] Maori: "koro" (Tr.): man; "korua": an old man. Magyar: "koros" = elderly; "kajdász" = to scream, to be noisy; "gajdol" = to shout with joy, to exult.

[7] Dalton. P. 209.

New Zealand (e.g. Pipiriki, Pipiroa, Piraki, Piriaka, Pirinoa, Piripiri, Pirongia).[1] Dalton draws from the above quoted saga the conclusion that the forefathers of the Santal came from the Sea in a white-sailed vessel; but other authors think they must have come across Assam to Central India, whilst others trace them back to the North West. According to Skrefsrud [2] they are supposed to have once lived *in the Punjab*.[3]

The Santal—as the Munda tribes in general—are said to be "amongst the most lovable of peoples". In their primitive and unsophisticated state, they are like big children; frank and sincere, honest and straightforward, gentle and peaceful by disposition, hardworking enough to meet their simple needs, loving flowers, loving mirth and music, loving dance and song, generally with strong family attachments, living a clean and healthy life in the midst of nature: they may be a primitive people, but not at all a savage one and possess a culture of their own. Their life, with its socio-religious institutions, its periodical festivals and gatherings, its music, its rude style of ornament, its sense of wonder for the life around, in the passing on of its tales and traditions from generation to generation, has kept up this culture as a living thing. Their songs (especially those of the Mundari, this tribe very akin to the Santal) are amongst the most beautiful specimens of poetry of the simple and primitive type: they are "among the fairest flowers in the garden of Indian poetry".[4] Their songs generally allude to birds and flowers, and unlike the lyrics of their neighbours, are remarkably free from obscenity.[5] [6]

South Indian Tribes.

The language of the Santal will occupy our special attention later on (Chapter XIII). Here we want only to shortly refer to two other tribes, both of South India. The first is the haughty, tall and well-built *Parawa, Paurawa*; at present fishermen and seafaring folk, who are said to descend from the Puru, the ancient foes of Alexander the Great. They originally lived in the province of Oudh, and at a time previous to the war recorded in the Mahabharata, therefore certainly not later than 900 B.C. their territory was bordered by the Jumna.[7] One of the most

[1] New Zealand Index. P. 339.

[2] Skrefsrud: *A Grammar of the Santhali Language*. P. VI.

[3] Roy, in *The Mundas and their Country*, P. 42, tries to show that the Mundari, with the Santal the most akin tribe, must have migrated from N.W. India more than three thousand years ago.

[4] See Chatterji: "The Study of Kol." *Calcutta Review*, 1923. P. 460.

[5] Man. *Sonthalia and the Sonthals*. P. 31.

[6] Specimens of Mundari songs will be found in Roy: *The Mundas and their Country*. P. 508. For Santali poems see further Bodding: "Studies in Santal Medicine and connected Folklore." *Mem. As. Soc. of Bengal*, 1925. P. 1.

[7] Thurston. Vol. VI. P. 141.

important Maori tribes in New Zealand also bears the name "Parawa".

Although counting but a few hundred souls, the South India *Toda* are noteworthy for their light coloured skin, regular features, very strongly developed pilous system and perfect teeth,[1] qualities shown also by the Maori of New Zealand.

Emigrations from India.

The East coast of India, from Tinevelly up to the Bay of Bengal, was the starting point of many *emigrations* by sea. According to tradition, the first expedition of colonists from this coast reached *Java* probably in the first century B.C. or even, according to other versions, as early as 300 B.C. This first expedition was followed "25 years later", but certainly not before the first century, by a second invasion led by a prince Watu Guning, of *Sangala*, who "subjugated" the first invaders.[2] As we have seen above, Sangala was the capital of the *Madra*. In any case, it is probable that the fine *bay of "Madura"* in Java has borrowed its name from that South Indian capital. In the people settled there and in Bali, some authors recognize an old Parawa colony. Since Smith fixes the time of Maori emigration from India to Sumatra and afterwards to Java at an earlier period, about 475 B.C., there may have been possibly three migrations instead of two to Java, the first of which was perhaps a "Maori" migration. In the Mohammedan Malay annals of the middle of the XVIIth century, record is made of another great influx from India across the sea. According to these, Arvistan Shah, a son of Alexander the Great (?), conducted in 290 B.C. 20,000 families from the *Kling coast or Tel-lin-gana* to Java. At the same time one of his rajahs (leaders) entered into a campaign "to subdue China", but finally the main body is supposed to have turned South, i.e. to Further India.

Further India.

Besides, *Further India* was the goal of many other emigrations from India. Thus already in the Vth century B.C. colonists were supposed to have settled there.[3] They were called Tchampas, Cyampas, also Tsam-bas, reminding us of the already mentioned "pat, paz". Later on, the same Indian colonists are found as the rulers of Cyam-bod-ia the territory of the present Cambodja.[4] As an ancient wrestling ground of various races, Futher India is at least as remarkable as Nearer India, or has become even more

[1] Ibid. Vol. VII. P. 121.
[2] Forlong. P. 96.
[3] Majumdar: *Ancient India*. P. 287.
[4] Keith, in Rapson's *Cambridge History of India*, P. 117, speaks of "Kamboja"-tribes, which lived N.W. from the Upper Indus, in a country adjacent to the present Kashmir. It seems noteworthy that the architectural remains of Cambodja, Further India, bear a considerable resemblance to those of Kashmir.

so since *Schmidt's* sensational fundamental researches [1] into its natives, *the Mon-Khmer people*, in whom he found a link between the populations of Polynesia, Melanesia, Indonesia and those of Nearer India. These natives are the more interesting since it seems to be certain that there is at the bottom of a considerable portion of the population of Further and of Nearer India a *common substratum*, over which there have settled layers of later immigrants, but which nevertheless has retained such strength, that its traces are still clearly seen over the whole area.[2]

Moreover, a comparison *between Mon-Khmer and ancient Magyar skulls* deserves attention. If an arithmetical average is taken from the measurements published by Schmidt,[3] we obtain from eleven skulls, measured by Maurel, the average values of 79·8 for the length and breadth index, of 52·4 for the nasal and of 86·1 for the orbital index.[4] The average of the two measurements carried out by Zaborowski, which Schmidt also publishes, gives 82·0, 46·9 and 87·4 respectively.[5]

Dixon however distinguishes [6] types of two strongly contrasted varieties in the Mon-Khmer speaking population of Further India: the first of these is fair-skinned, with straight or wavy hair, a narrow nose and a non-Mongoloid eye, the second, a long-headed variety, is dark-skinned, short, with curly or even frizzly hair, a broad nose and thick, negroid lips. Even Caucasian elements have been found, e.g. in Upper Tonkin, in the mountains between the Cao-Bang River and the Ba-Bé Lake.[7] They exist among the *Man-tribes*, numbering to-day only about 50,000 souls, of which the approximately 8,000 Man-Tien are the most remarkable. Their physical appearance does not recall at all the traits of the yellow race, and their traditions refer to their cradle-land as " far away to the West ", where their forefathers lived many thousands of years ago with a people of " white blood ".[8] In contrast to the races dwelling around them, these Man-Tien even now have no settled habits, but are addicted to nomadism.[9] The Man-Tiens believe in a spiritual existence and call the souls " hon " and the spirits " ve ".[10] A French scholar [11] supposes *the cradle-land of the Man-tribes* to be somewhere in the

[1] Schmidt: *Die Mon-Khmer Völker, ein Bindeglied*, etc. (The Mon-Khmer People, a Link, etc.)

[2] Kuhn, quoted by Konow in Grierson's *Linguistic Survey of India*. Vol. IV. Introduction.

[3] Schmidt. P. 30.

[4] Measurements of height are not given.

[5] Compare page 90.

[6] Dixon: *Racial History of Man*. P. 275.

[7] Billiet: *Deux Ans dans le Haut-Tonkin*. Vol. II. P. 78.

[8] Keane. P. 198.

[9] Billiet. Vol. II. P. 198.

[10] Abadie: *Les Races du Haut-Tonkin*. P. 137.

[11] Ibid. P. 106.—The Maori of New Zealand call " Honi-o-te-Warua " the cradle-land of the spirits.

great mountain range rising above the valleys of the rivers Si-Kiang and Yang-Tse-Kiang and covering the Chinese provinces of Hu-peh, Hu-nan, Kwang-si and Kwey-tsow.

Extension of Wanderings.

From all these rather disconnected considerations one fact nevertheless stands out: the enormous extent of the wanderings prior to our era and the immense distances covered. A people whom we find in dark primeval days in the cold and dreary highlands of the Himalaya, appears some centuries later thousands of miles more to the South, in the scorching heat of South Indian coasts. And even there the settlement is but a temporary stay, at least for a portion of them. The snow-capped highlands deter them just as little, as the obstacles of the endless sea. Six centuries before our era Indian warriors are found fighting far from their own country, in the armies of the Persian king Cyrus; whilst on the other hand his mortal wound is due also to Indian weapons. The sixth and also the fifth century B.C. especially, represent important historical movements and migrations. In this very epoch Lao-tse and Kung-fu-tse are stirring up China. The Phoenician Hamilcar is sailing from the Sidonian Carthago as far as England, and Hanno is leading 30,000 colonists to the Canary Islands. It is the age in which Belgians, Danes, Scandinavians begin to move. Jews go into Eastern captivity and Babylon falls to the new and first Aryan empire. Darius the I. and his successors raid then through North West India as far as Lahore. It is not surprising to find the Indian population also throwing off colonies southwardly and eastwardly. And even towards the North and West we find them; the excavations of *Sir Aurel Stein* in Khotan leave no doubt that there were about two thousand years ago regular Indian colonies in that region.[1]

[1] There is a tradition recorded by Hsüan Tsang to the effect that Khotan was first colonized by exiles *from Taxila*, banished by Asoka. (The latter died in 231 B.C.).—See Marshall: *A Guide to Taxila*, p. 11, who quotes Stein: *Ancient Khotan*. I. P. 156.

Chapter XII.

NOTES ON SOME LANGUAGES OF INDIA.

Dravida Languages suggested to be "Ugrian".—Munda Languages; their Fundamental Difference from Dravida.—Distribution of Munda Languages.—The "Austric" Family of Languages.—Some Terminal Sounds Characteristic of the Austric Family. Magyar shows the same.

Dravida Languages suggested to be "Ugrian".

Caldwell, the famous pioneer of research into the Dravida [1] languages, in a study published in 1858,[2] grouped them with "the Ugrian family of Turanian (Uralo-Altaian) languages", an opinion accepted since by other linguists also (C. Mueller, Lepsius, etc.).[3] As far as more especially the Magyar language is concerned, the idea of a Dravida-Magyar connection had been advanced, and this with great ardour, particularly by Bálint. In a study published in 1888 [4] he strongly advocated the deep relationship between Magyar and Tamil and tried to prove his theory by quoting a number of supposedly analogous words in both languages. It would be *very easy* to find for the same words corresponding Maori terms, just as it would be equally easy to show an affinity between certain Magyar terms and Sanskrit. We have here a first class example of *how insufficient mere comparisons of words are to prove the relationship of two languages.* The Hungarian Academy of Sciences was quite right in reply to Caldwell, that there is no relation whatsoever between Magyar and the Dravidian languages. In any case, in the course of our researches we have found nothing to suggest a revision of this verdict.

Munda Languages; their Fundamental Difference from Dravida.

Matters stand quite differently *with the Munda languages*, a family which also got its name from a single branch, namely "Mundari", a name which was extended by *Max Müller*—as simply a conventional one—to the whole. He was also the first scholar to discover not only the lack of identity, but the *obvious difference*

[1] This name of "Dravida (Dramila, Tamil)" (see also page 113) belongs as a matter of fact only to one branch of the family, "Tamil," the language of about 20 millions of people. But Caldwell extended it to the whole family of fourteen languages, and it has since been generally used in this sense. (See Grierson: *Linguistic Survey of India.* Vol. IV. Part II.)

[2] Caldwell: *Comparative Grammar of the Dravidian Languages.* Third Edition.

[3] "The Scythian family to which, on the whole, the Dravidian languages may be regarded as most nearly allied, is the Finnish or Ugrian." Caldwell. P. 67.

[4] Bálint: "A tamul Nyelv a Turáni Nyelvek Sanskritja, vagy van-e a Magyarnak Testvére?" (The Tamul Language as the Sanskrit of Turanian Idioms, or has the Magyar a Sister-Language?). In the Periodical *Erdélyi Muzeum-Egylet Kiadványai.* 1888.

between Dravida and Munda. So far as we know, no attempt has yet been made to establish a relationship between Magyar and Munda.

The presence of many expressions common to the Dravida and Munda languages may be explained by the intercourse of Dravida and Munda tribes as neighbours and by their manifold fusions, as shown in Chapter IX. In the same way may be accounted for the many *loan-words from Sanskrit* (*Hindi*) found in these languages.[1]

The *Munda family* is strikingly compared by Dalton to a river whose course is occasionally subterranean, to appear again in distant regions as a stream from the same source. In its idiomatic structure it is *absolutely different* from Dravida. This difference becomes most perceptible when we consider certain characteristics as adduced in the *Linguistic Survey of India*, edited by Grierson, Vol. IV, Part I. (Written by Konow.) Especially turning to the *verbs*, every trace of analogy between the Munda and Dravida families disappears, as the Dravida system of verbs is very simple, only comprising two or three tenses, whilst in Munda we find an almost bewildering mass of conjugational forms. The Dravida verb can be characterized as a noun of agency; the Munda verb is an indefinite form which may be used indifferently as a noun, an adjective or as a verb. The most characteristic features of the Munda verb, the categorical "a" and the incorporation of the direct and indirect object in the verb, are in absolute discord with Dravida principles. The Munda languages, on the other hand, do not possess anything corresponding to the Dravida negative conjugation.

This language has often different forms for the *masculine and feminine* singular of nouns denoting rational beings, whilst Munda makes no difference whatever. Further in Dravida differences exist also in the *formation of the plural*; Munda does not make any. The Munda languages make use, besides prefixes and suffixes, also of *infixes*; Dravida have nothing corresponding to the latter. The formation of cases is also quite different in the two; again Munda possesses nothing corresponding to the Dravida oblique base.

Concerning the first person of personal pronouns, "en" in Dravida and "in, ing" in Munda, the *Linguistic Survey* tells us that "the base of the Dravida word for the English "I" is probably "e", whilst the *essential part of the Munda pronoun*

[1] It seems that linguists have not sufficiently taken into account these facts, notably those who tried to find "Aryan elements" (loan-words) in Magyar. It is surely not enought to assert that a word is of Aryan origin simply because it is found in Sanskrit, or even in the dialects of the Vedas; they may be equally of Dravida or Munda source, borrowed by the Arya. Khittel e.g., is his *Kannada-English Dictionary*, gives a list *of 401 words, which Sanskrit* (*Hindi*) *had borrowed from Dravida languages.*

is " *n* ", etc. Finally Munda phonology has a striking feature: there exist so-called semi-consonants. There is nothing corresponding to these in Dravida languages.

Distribution of Munda Languages.

Although the Munda family of languages is not so widespread as the race itself, many tribes of Northern India who originally spoke Munda having been aryanized in the meantime,[1] and even if it is the least numerous of the four linguistic families, which divide among themselves the bulk of the population of India: Munda is still spoken by more than three million people. These are found mostly in the Santal Parganas and Chota Nagpūr; also in the Mahadeo Hills of the Central Provinces and in the Northern districts of the Madras Presidency. Munda is at the same time the basis of a number of mixed languages, forming a chain along the Himalayan slopes from the Punjab to Bengal.[2] Traces of an old Munda element are apparently also met with in several Tibeto-Burman dialects spoken in the Himalayan region.[3]

" Munda " is spoken [4] by

about	2,200,000	souls	speaking	Santal,
,,	600,000	,,	,,	Mundari,
,,	450,000	,,	,,	Ho,
,,	170,000	,,	,,	Savara,
,,	120,000	,,	,,	Kurku,
,,	460,000	,,	,,	Bhumij, Korwa, Karia, Gadaba, etc., etc.

However these dialects are not the exclusive languages of the territories where they are found. As a rule *they are spoken only in the hills and jungles*, whilst the plain and valleys are inhabited by people speaking some Aryan dialect.

As already shown on page 125, the tradition of the Santal traces back the origin of their own tribe, as well as that of the Mundari, Ho, Bhumij, etc., to the ancient stock of the Kharwar, Kherwar.[5] Some Danish scholars have therefore attributed to that subdivision of Munda languages, to which belong the above mentioned tribes and some others, the collective term of " *Kharwar* ", a denomination which has since been generally accepted. The dialects of this subdivision or group only little differ, and about 88% of the whole Munda-speaking people use it. The other branches (dialects) of the Munda family, more slightly

[1] As for instance the Chero of Behar and Chota Nagpur, etc. (*Encyclopedia Britannica*).
[2] Rapson. In Chapt. II of his *Cambridge History of India*. Vol. I. P. 48.
[3] Konow. In Grierson's *Linguistic Survey*. Vol. IV. P. 9.
[4] Census of 1901.
[5] Traced back to the Santali " horo " = man. See also page 125.

connected with this group are: Gadaba, Kharia, Kurku, Nahali, Savara and Juang or Patua. On the other hand, these latter branches show a more intimate relationship than those of the Kharwar group *to the Mon-Khmer family* of languages, a family of which more will be said later on.

The kinship of the dialects of the Kharwar group may be the best realized by the following schedule copied from the *Linguistic Survey of India.*

KHARWAR GROUP

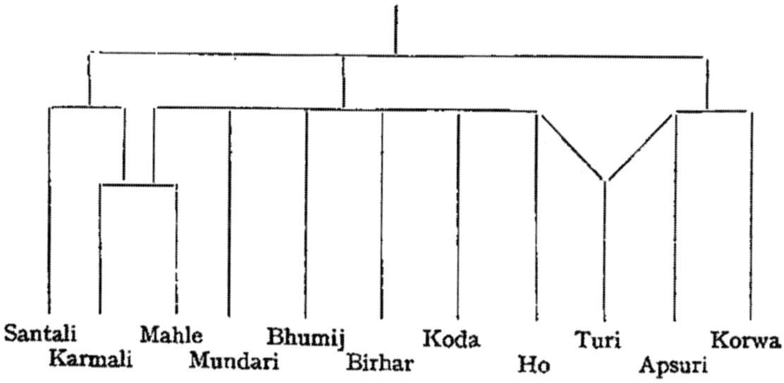

The "Austric" Languages.

That the Polynesian, Melanesian and Indonesian languages all appertain to one large class, has already been mentioned.[1] This class is termed the "*Austronesian*"; it is supposed to have originated *in Cambodia.*[2] Now, in a way which scientific authorities describe as "masterful", *Schmidt*[3] showed that a family of another class of languages stretches, although with many interruptions, from the Southern end of Further India, and right through to Nearer India, where it joins a *second family of races and languages.* This again is spread over the whole breadth of India, and traces of it may be found even in the Central and Western region of the Himalaya. The first family is composed by the *Mon-Khmer* and other, closely related aboriginal languages; surviving in the Khasi Hills of Assam, in certain hilly tracts of Upper Burma, in the coastal regions of the Gulf of Martaban in Lower Burma, in the Nicobar Islands, and in some parts of the Malaccan Peninsula.[4] The second family of this great class of languages is represented by the already examined *Munda,* with its several branches; the entire class has been termed by Schmidt the "*Austro-Asian*".

[1] See page 23.
[2] Skinner: "The Origin and Relationships of Maori Material Culture and Decorative Art." *Journ. Pol. Soc.*, 1924. P. 229.
[3] Schmidt: *Die Mon-Khmer Völker* etc.
[4] Rapson. In his *Cambridge History of India.* Vol. I. P. 48.

Whilst the Dravida family of languages form an isolated group, as there are no traces of connected forms of speech in the surrounding countries of Nearer India,[1] comparative philologists agree that the Munda and Mon-Khmer languages contain *a common substratum*; a stock of which no traces can be shown to exist in the Dravida form of speech. Both Munda and Mon-Khmer are derived from the same base. Each group has, however, had an independent history of its own, under the influence of various foreign elements. The Munda languages probably developed the tendencies of the common parent tongue with the greatest fidelity, as the tribes speaking them have led a more secluded existence than the Mon-Khmer.[2]

It is also the merit of *Schmidt* to have coined the term "*Austric*", as a collective name for both the *Austronesian* and the *Austro-Asian* classes. Thus *the "Austric" group embraces languages spread over the largest area in the world*, and its homes stretch from Easter Island near the South-American coast to Madagascar and from New Zealand up to the Punjab,—if not perhaps as far as Central Europe.[3]

Some Terminal Sounds Characteristic of the Austric Family. Magyar shows the same.

Schmidt indicates as the *most intimate characteristic* of the Austric languages *certain terminal sounds*, which appearing without exception in each branch of them, always give rise to the same signification. He says[4]:

"The most striking feature to our mind when investigating the Austric languages is the constant reappearance of *the terminal sounds p* in roots, etc., denoting to embrace, to contain, to squeeze, to pinch; further to bite, eat, chew, in general to indulge in anything; also to drink, to cover and "together" in general; to shrink, to shrivel, to become defective. In an analogous way the *terminal sound m* has the same meaning for words which express assemblage, a mass, whilst the terminal sounds *p* and *m* very often are interchanged."

"If thus attention is attracted, and researches extended to other terminal sounds, it will be also at once realized that *the c-sounds*[5] denote "away", "below", then to decrease, to decay, to deteriorate; similarly it is found that the *terminal*

[1] Excepting the Brahui tongue in Baluchistan, mentioned already on page 113.
[2] Grierson: *Linguistic Survey of India*. Vol. IV. P. 14.
[3] The fact that Cambodia is considered by many as the cradle-land of the Austric languages, calls for our special interest, if we bear in mind that in the opinion of geologists the earliest relics of civilized man are to be found in countries immediately adjoining to the Southern Hemisphere (Hewitt: The ruling Races . . . etc. P. VI).
[4] Schmidt. P. 54.
[5] Corresponding to the Magyar letters "cs", "gy", "s" and "zs".

sound s[1] serves as an expression for removing, a scratching off, rubbing away and others, and that both these sounds also are interchanged."

"Perhaps even more striking is the regularity with which words with *the terminal sound n* express the meaning of: from one another, pell-mell, into one another, there and back; and especially practically all verbs denoting weaving or plaiting end with this sound. In the figurative sense the terminal *n*-sound is found in expressions indicating unrest, inward agitation, anger, yearning."

"Finally, *the terminal sound t* appears in words which represent the idea of: into anything, insertion; intersection; then cutting in general, and also cutting off."

These criterions, which apply neither to the Uralian, nor to the Altaian languages, are very explicitly shown in Magyar, as may be proved by examples, such as the following.[2]

TERMINAL SOUND P:

to grip, squeeze, pinch	csip	to beat, strike	csap
to seize, grasp	kap	to fling, throw	dob
to comprise, fit, join	szab	to bite	harap
prisoner	rab	molar tooth	záp
ferry	kerep	eating, food	táp
to tear	tép	crumb	dereb
mash	pép	together, entire, complete	ép
bean	bab	picture	kép
oats	zab	settlement	telep
honeycomb	lép	people	nép
beautiful, pleasant	szép	more	több
to dance	rop	rotten, stinky	záp
little bell, rattle	kolomp	to whet	kop
to suck	szop	to shrink, fade	töp
to sip	hörp	hump	púp
to spit	köp	neglected pasture	gyep
drop	csöpp	mud	iszap
tap (for liquids)	csap		
headgear	kalap		

TERMINAL SOUND M:

to grow	terem	soot, smoke-black	korom
the main body	zöm	weeds	gyom
feast, repast	tom	track	nyom
drinking bout	iszom	mill	malom
to cram, stuff	töm	harness	hám
number	szám	embroidery	hím
species, kind	nem	turnpike, crank	gém
litter	alom	drag-net	gyalom

[1] It corresponds approximately to the Magyar letters "c", "sz" and "z".

[2] The English meaning of these Magyar words does not correspond always to the sense in which they are used nowadays, but to notions they represented in ancient times, as shown by historical dictionaries (Sz.S. and Et.).

TERMINAL SOUND C AND S (MAGY.: CS, GY, S, AND C, SZ, Z):

to draw off	húz	erroneous	más
to carry away	visz	filth, rot	gaz
to take away	(el-) tesz	bad sweep	csuhez
to expel	űz	bad mixture	abajdóc
guide	kalauz	dirt	dancs
ransom	sarc	gout	csúz
to take off	vesz	cramp	görcs
wick	mécs	diarrhoea	fos
match	kanóc	tumour	dagás
to fall	es	complaint	panasz
to crawl (up and down)	kúsz	little	kevés
autumn	ősz	small	kis
hoary	ősz	almost nothing	csipisz
done for	kész	useless thing	encenbenc
mourning	gyász	exchange	drincs
bare	csupasz	to scratch off, torn piece	konc
bald	kopasz	to scrape away	karc
leafless	gulacs	bumpy	rapacs
to dry, wither	asz	bark of lime-trees	hárs
bad	rossz	fold	ránc
miserable	csörc	gristle	porc
malignant	gonosz	chisel	ponc
to wash	mos	knife	kés
to rob	koboz	to cut down, to mutilate	nyes
to jolt, to shake off	ráz	carpenter	ács
to rummage	motoz	to dig	ás
to dishevel	tibáz	slot	rés
shaggy	gubanc		
rough cloth	daróc		

TERMINAL SOUND N:

to turn upside down	hán	ache, pain	kín
hither and thither	hun	weak	halaván
to go, start asunder	mén	arid, meagre	sován
to come	jön	useless	hiún
to disappear	tűn	private, detached	magán
wilderness	vadon	to whet, sharpen	fen
in vicinity of	rokon	to smear	ken
outside	künn	spoon	kalán
separated	külön	bore	ún
to pull	von	sin	bűn
sleigh	szán	to confess	gyón
to regret	szán	instinct	ösztön
to worry	bán	to plait, to twist	fon
to desire, wish	kiván	flax	len
relative	rokon	nettle	csalán

TERMINAL SOUND T:

to begin	kezd	frame	keret
to kindle	gyújt	garden	kert
insertion	betét	to collect, to gather	gyüjt
to pour (in)	önt	to disseminate	hint

to sow	vet	to spread wide	tát
dew	harmat	to split	hasít
stick	bot	chisel	ispót
pole	rúd	to cut	arat
buckle	csat	furrow	gerezd
to sink	süpped	sword	kard
to dip	márt	to slay	sujt
to penetrate	hat	to wound, to hurt	sért
to germinate	fakad	to whip, to chastise	suhod
to tear along	ránt	to demolish	bont
to stagger, to break	ront	to carve	met
asunder	szét		

Many other such examples might be given.

Chapter XIII.

IS MAGYAR A MUNDA LANGUAGE?

Phonetics.—Grammar: General Remarks. Gender of Words. Formation of the Plural.—Suffixes and Infixes.—Articles. Pronouns.—Verbs. Their Conjugation.—Comparison of Munda (Santal) and Magyar Words.

If a connection exists between *Maori and Magyar*, and if at the same time *Maori and Munda* are allied—both belonging to the "Austric" languages—it is reasonable to expect a connection between Munda and Magyar also.

Phonetics.

We have already seen in the preceding chapter, that the terminal sounds in Magyar seem to correspond to the general law governing Austric terminals. With regard to *Magyar initial sounds*, some interesting peculiarities may also be pointed out. In the Ugrian languages, or, as Müller terms them, the "languages of the nations of the Ural" (Uralvölker), there is no word beginning with "h", whereas an initial "h" is as common in Magyar as in Munda.[1] Further no word in the "Altaian" languages, i.e. Mandzu, Mongol and Turkish, begins with "r", and very seldom with "n" or "p", whilst in Magyar and in Munda this occurs constantly.[2] Groups of two consonants as initial sounds, occurring frequently in Ugrian languages, such as Lapp, Mordwinian, Tcheremissian, etc.,[3] are quite exceptional features in ancient Magyar and Munda. When incorporating into their own language foreign words beginning originally with a consonant, Munda and Magyar habitually prefix a vowel to this consonant; so the English "sponge" becomes in Munda (Santal) "ispanj", and "school" becomes "iskul",[4] just as in Magyar the Latin "scola" or the German "Schule" changes into "iskola" and "spongia" into "espongya". Each language abounds in vowels, short and long, and in both when it is desired to emphasize the meaning, short vowels are frequently lengthened. On the other hand, long-vowelled monosyllables, when an accented syllable is added, have their long vowel shortened.[5]

[1] Müller: *Grundriss der Sprachwissenschaften*. Vol. II. P. 199.
[2] Ibid. P. 266.
[3] Müller. P. 199.
[4] Campbell: *A Santali-English Dictionary*. This work will be hereafter referred to as: (Ca.).
[5] Grierson. P. 36.

Comparing a Munda (Santal) text from the Chakai Thana, District Monghyr,[1] with the most ancient Magyar text,[2] we find for a total number of 365 vowels the following results:

	MAGYAR.	MUNDA (SANTAL).
Consonants approximately . .	456	437
Semi-consonants (l, r) approximately .	75	70
Labials (b, f, p, v in Magyar, b, p in Munda) approximately . .	45	46
Aspirant (h) approximately . .	17	21

The accent is similar in both languages, i.e. on the first syllable in disyllabic words.[3] Further the *law of harmonic sequence*, so characteristic of Magyar—a law which affects the vowels in consecutive syllables so as to make their sounds agree—is also traceable in the Munda family, especially in Santal and Mundari.[4] For a more thorough investigation of this interesting point, for instance for exceptions from this law existing in both, Magyar and Munda, readers may be referred to Grierson's *Linguistic Survey of India*, and to Hoffmann's weighty *Mundari Grammar*. But one assertion of the latter may be quoted at once: that the vowels of tense-suffixes never undergo any changes for the purpose of harmonizing with the root vowel, as he shows by the examples of "do-akad", "de-akad", "ti-akad", "nu-akad"; "akad" as well as "ked" being described as a "*continuative-present*" *suffix*.[5]—Similarly, we shall find in Magyar: "*gyan*-akod-(ik)," "*biz*-akod-(ik)," "*von*-akod-(ik)," "*huz*-akod-(ik)," the denominative (and reflexive) verbal-suffixes "akod" as well as "ked" being there also a kind of continuative-present formatives.

Grammar: General Remarks. Gender of Words. Formation of the Plural.

Just as when treating phonetics we restricted ourselves to points of striking interest, so with regard to the Munda grammar we will confine our attention to a short enumeration of some of the more prominent features, and this only for Santal and its so strongly related Mundari, as, even the ancient vocabularies of both have been partially replaced by an Aryan one, their old grammatical principles are said to assert themselves strongly till the present date.[6]

Already in Chapter XII, when comparing the *general characteristics* of the Dravida and Munda languages, it was obvious

[1] Ibid. P. 67.
[2] The "Halotti Beszéd", (Oratio Funebris).—See also page 27.
[3] Grierson. P. 39.
[4] For more details see especially Bodding's *Material for a Santali Grammar*. (A work of first class importance.)
[5] Hoffmann. Pp. 4, 163, 164.
[6] Konow. In Bodding's *Santal Folk Tales*. Vol. I. P. XIV.

that, whilst there was no accord whatever between Dravida and Magyar grammatical principles, for Munda and Magyar the case is quite different. Let us now examine it rather more in detail. In Munda as in Magyar, the same root can be a noun, an adjective or a verb.[1] In both languages nouns do not take any particles (suffixes) indicative of gender. Equally with pronouns, the same form denotes both masculine and feminine. Thus in Mundari "i, e, ae" means "he" as well as "she"; and "ni": "this one," denotes both "celui-ci" and "celle-ci".[2] Adjectives also (as well as some tense-forms used as participial adjectives) never take any suffixes indicating gender. Further, adjectives or participial adjectives, when placed immediately before the noun, take—just as in Magyar—no suffixes indicative of either number or case.—Whilst, according to Müller, in all Uralian languages "other than Magyar" the plural is formed by adding the suffix "t", *in Magyar, as in Munda*, this suffix is "k", or more exactly: in Mundari "ko". Hoffmann derives this "ko"[3] from the indefinite demonstrative "oko" = more than one, a certain number, some; he adds that the initial "o" of the latter is always *very short.* Now, in Magyar, we have for instance *vágás* (= a cut), the plural of which is *vágások* with a very short "o" in spite of the two preceding long "a"-s; or *tapasztalat* (= experience), the plural of which, in spite of the law of harmonic sequence, is not *tapasztalat-ak* but *tapasztalat-ok*; etc., etc.

Suffixes and Infixes.

Let us consider some other Munda formatives. These are mostly found nowadays as suffixes; but *in the opinion of scholars*[4] *prefixes seem to have played a considerable rôle in the history of the Munda languages.* The various Magyar suffixes we dealt with in Part I, Chapter V (B), can, apparently, be found in Santal also. It was there said, that *féle* meant "eiusmodi". Campbell gives for "phalna, phạlni"[5]: a certain, used when the speaker wishes to avoid particularizing.—The Magyar suffix *-hoz, -hez*, the ancient Magyar *-hon*, means in English "to", whereas Santal "honte, hontere" means: there, over there, yonder.—For the suffix *-h, -ha, -he*, used to indicate a wish in Magyar (*óhaj* being the noun for wish) "haya" appears in Santal, Campbell's dictionary giving for it the meaning: to feel a desire for, to long for. *-int, -ent* denotes in Magyar manner, mode, procedure; in Santal "ente" is: in that way.—Both the Magyar suffix *-kor*

[1] See pages 33 and 147.
[2] Hoffmann. P. 5.—Magyar "ő" means: he or she, and "(ez)ni" indifferently "celui-ci" or "celle-ci".
[3] Page 21.
[4] E.g. "ạ-ñu": to give to drink. Grierson. P. 23.—Compare with Maori "inu" and Magyar "in".—Santal ñ corresponds to the Magyar letter *ny*.
[5] Santal ạ corresponds very closely to the Magyar ő.

and Santal "kar" are words for: time. *-nyi* bears a comparative meaning in Magyar; in Santal "ne" is described as a particle signifying: like the speaker, like myself, like ourselves.[1]—The Magyar suffix *-lag*, *-leg*, corresponding in its comparative and restrictive sense to the English "like", is said to have originated from the noun "alak", i.e. shape, figure. Santal "ol" is: to draw patterns, figures, and Hoffmann gives[2] for Mundari "leka" the English: like. He also says that this suffix "leka" turns the Mundari adjective into an adverb of manner[3]; the same is the case in Magyar, where for instance *lehető* means: possible, and *lehetöleg*: possibly.

Further Santal suffixes—called by Grierson "most common ones"—also suggest Magyar. Thus the suffix "tat" is used in Santal "in order to form abstract nouns." In Magyar *-tat* *-at* play a similar róle; there "akar" is: to want, and "akarat": the will, "tapasztal": to experience, and "tapasztalat": the experience.—Another common Santal suffix is "ak", used in forming inanimate nouns. In Magyar *ék* holds the same place, "marad" being: to remain, and "maradék": the rest; "kever": to mix, and "keverék": the mixture, etc.,[4]—The Santal suffix "ich" is used for inanimate nouns, nouns of agency and the like. In Magyar we have, arising from "kap": to catch, "kapocs": a hook; from "sző": to weave, "szőcs": the furrier, etc.; and we shall find the terminal sound "cs" in many other nouns of agency, like "kovács" = (blacksmith), "szakács" (= cook), "ács" (= carpenter), etc.—Patronymics and proper nouns are formed in Mundari with "i"[5]; the same is the case in Magyar.

In Santal, by adding "an, n", possessive adjectives are formed, "especially in the sense," says Grierson, "that a thing is provided for, has got it," and he describes these as a kind of verbal adjectives. In Magyar we may find this kind of "verbal adjectives" in such forms as "tártan": open, in an open manner, provided with an opening, from "tárt" = the past tense (praesens perfectum) of "tár": to expand, to open, etc.; and perhaps the Magyar suffix—*tlen*, *tlan*, showing that a thing is *not* provided for, has *not* got it, may have also to deal with this case, "erő" being, e.g. "strength" and "erő-tl-en": "strengthless," etc. Grierson further asserts that this "n" can be added almost to every word ending in a single vowel. The

[1] "no" means also: "a little"; used only in composition. Magyar does with "nyi" (once "nyé") the same.

[2] Hoffmann. P. 20.

[3] Ibid. P. XXIX.

[4] Even the form *ák* exists in obsolete words, as "fúl", to bore and "fulák', a sting, etc.

[5] Hoffmann. P. 9.

same is true of Magyar, where "kicsi" or "kicsin", "piczi" or "piczin" (both meaning: small, little), etc., etc. can be used indifferently.

This "n" appears also in the *Munda numerals* as Santal numerals in the successive groups of tens are often formed by adding "khan" = more [1]; "gäl-khan-ponea" (Grierson) is: ten more four, i.e. fourteen; in Magyar it is: "tiz-en-négy," where "tiz denotes: ten, and "négy": four.—"gäl" being in Santali: ten, it is interesting to record that "kil-enc" is in Magyar: nine. "n" occurs further, though not as a suffix but as an infix, (supposed to be derived from a prefix "en"), in the formation of *Santal collective numerals*,[2] and in a similar way we shall find in Magyar from "négy"–"négyen": all the four; from "hét" –"heten": all the seven, etc.—In the shape of fractional numerals there exists in Santal and Mundari only the word "tala" or "tara",[3] meaning: to halve, to divide into equal parts; in Magyar "tör" is: to break, to divide, and "tört": a fraction.—An important numeral in the Munda languages *as the Munda counted in twenties*, is twenty; "hisi" in Mundari, "isi" in Santal; and "húsz" is the Magyar term for twenty.[4] Hundred is termed in Santal and Mundari "sae"; in the Korwa-dialect "sais". Magyar "száz" is hundred.

Some Magyar *frequentative verbal-suffixes* are also suggestive of Munda, e.g. *-ereg* (*-orog*), *-gál* (*-gal*), *-dál* (*-dal*), *-dos* (*-dös*), *-kod* (*-köd*), *-oz* (*-öz*); all suffixes which give to the Magyar verb a sense of the repetition of an action. Thus Santal "erok" is: to sow, to scatter ("arak": to loose, to set free, to let go), and in Magyar "hent*ereg*" means to roll free, "bizs*ereg*": to prickle; "hab" is a billow, a wave, and "háb*orog*": to wave.

Santal "kalkal" means numerous, very many ("ghalok": including, enumerating). Magyar "húz", to draw becomes "húz*gál*", i.e. to draw and draw again, to draw many times; "hajít", to throw, "hajít*gál*," "haji*gál*": to throw one after the other, to throw repeatedly; etc., etc.

Santal "dal" has, between others, the sense of "to split in pieces". Magyar forms from "vág", to split–"vag*dal*", to split in pieces; from "szab", to cut–"szab*dal*", to cut in pieces; from "tép", to slit–"tép*del*", to slit in pieces; from "tör", to break–"tör*del*", to break in pieces.—"szúr" is to stab, and "szur*dal*": to stab again and again; "lép": to make a step, and "lép*del*" to divide in some way his walk, to walk step by step; (in contrast to "lép*ked*", which we will see later and

[1] We saw Magyar "-hoz", "-hon" for Latin "ad", i.e. to, to augment, more.
[2] Grierson. P. 44.
[3] Hoffmann. P. 68.
[4] In Santal we have: "his, hisa": share, portion, to divide.

which means also to walk, but making the steps in a more continuous manner).

Santal "dhacal", "dhucul" is: to bob backward and forward, up and down. Magyar has "röp*dös*": to fly up and down, backward and forward, from "röp", to fly; "lop*dos*": to steal here and there, from "lop": to steal; "lök" means to push, and "lök*dös*" is the manner in which one pushes e.g. oneself through a crowd.

"kadae" in Santal is an expression for "*always* on the move, going about *continually*". In Magyar "röp*köd*", in opposition to the former "röp*dös*" bears a more continuous sense; just as well "lop*kod*" is to steal again and again, continually or "csap*kod*" to beat in a continuous manner, e.g. as a bird of prey with its wings (from "csap", to beat), whilst "csap*dos*" will be used, if this bird will distribute hits with these wings.

"oste" ("osto") is a Santal term for "gradually, continually". Magyar says "bot*oz*", to strike, from "bot" a stick; "fol*toz*" to patch, to repair, from "folt" a patch, etc.

-an is a Magyar suffix indicating a sudden and momentary action; "vill*an*" is the sudden lightning (from "vill", to splash); "durr*an*": to crack as a gun (from the sound of cracking "durr"). On the other hand Santal "ancot" is "suddenly, unannounced".

-hat is the Magyar verbal-suffix for "possibility"; thus the verb "ír" means to write, and "ír*hat*": to be able, to have power to write. This suffix is said to originate from a verb *hat*: to effect, to bring about, to operate, to act upon (and also to affect). Santal "hotere" ("hotete") corresponds to "by means of, through, and the dictionary gives for "hat chut": active, energetic, quick in movements, especially on the hands.

A most frequent Magyar particle, extensively used also as a verbal *prefix*, is *meg* (*mög*); it is thought to originate from "mögé": behind, after, postponed. Santal "makup" means to be postponed, deferred.

Besides prefixes and suffixes, Munda languages make use of *infixes*. So the infix "p" is employed in Santal for collective nouns. Magyar "bb" has a meaning of "more"; it is the suffix for the first comparative degree.—An important Santal infix is "k"; inserted after the first vowel of verbs it has intensitive effect. Grierson adds that it is also often inserted for the same purpose in demonstrative pronouns *beginning with* an "n", e.g. "nui": this man here, and "nukui": just this man here. Some Magyar verbs are intensified also through the infix "k"; so "rí" is : to cry, whilst "rikít" is: to yell and "rikolt": to scream; "ád, od" means: to give, and "okád" to give in masses, to vomit; "lő" is: to shoot (sagitto), and "lök": to push, to thrust (peto, jacio). In the same way we have Magyar "ni" as a general adverb of direction,[1] and "neki", i.e. against him, in a more decidedly personal and limited meaning.

Many other Munda suffixes, especially such indicating *local and causal relations*, recall also the Magyar grammar. Hoffmann, under the title "Postpositions", deals at great length with a group of them for Mundari.[2] It would be outside our scope to follow him here; we shall confine ourselves therefore to a few examples only; for instance to "*re*", both in Mundari and in Magyar a postposition for space-relations, such as "in, on, at", as well as for time relations, such as "before, ago"; to "*ta*", denoting: permanence, continuation, and suggesting a comparison with Magyar *tart*: to continue; or to "*lo*", which in Mundari is used both for space and time, meaning in the first case: together with, with, along, and in the second: simultaneity (a word which suggests a comparison with Magyar *va-l, ve-l*: with, along).[3] For more details the reader may be referred to Hoffmann, pp. 33–63, etc., or to Edmonston Scott's interesting "The Basque Declension: its Kolarian Origin and Structure"[4]; in view of our present purpose we prefer to confine our attention chiefly to the articles and pronouns.

Articles. Pronouns. Where in English the indefinite article "a, an" or the phrase "a certain" would stand, Mundari uses often, especially in narration, the numeral "mi-ad" (Santal: "mit"): one. It has already been mentioned[5] that the Magyar *egy*: one, is supposed to be derived from *ed*.

The Mundari (Santal) pronouns deserve special mention in view of Müller's statement[6] that in the "Uralic" languages, i.e. in Finn, Lapp, Tcheremiss, Mordwin, Syrjan, Ostjak, Esthonian, Votjak, Vogul *and Magyar*, the roots of the pronouns are "indubitably":

first person singular: *ma*
second person singular: *ta*
third person singular: *ta* (sa).

But the Magyar pronouns are:

first person singular: *én* (ín); accusative: *en-ge-m* (ín-ge-m);
second person singular: *te* (tí); accusative: *té-ge-d* (tí-ge-d);
third person singular: *ö*.

[1] See page 43.
[2] Hoffmann. P. 33.
[3] "le", considered by Hoffmann as a weak form of "lo", is at the same time a Mundari future tense suffix. In Magyar "lesz" is the future tense of the verb: to be.
[4] *Bull. School of Oriental Studies.* 1920. Vol. I. Part III. P. 149.
[5] Page 44.
[6] *Grundriss der Sprachwissenschaft.* Part II. P. 215.

The above are in Mundari represented by:

first person singular: ing (in Santal: iń);
second person singular: me (in Santal: me);
third person singular: i (in Santal: e); the same for impersonal or neutral beings: a.

With regard to the first person singular, *Hoffmann*, in a very original dissertation,[1] gives interesting and valuable reasons for the idea that it may be a *compound word*, containing the personal pronoun of the third person singular as one of its constituents. According to him, the constituents of the first person would be: "i(e)" = he or she, plus "ne" = this, or here, and "ge" = another original demonstrative, having an emphatical suggestion of something near.[2] In Magyar *ő*, *ni* and *ge* have similar meanings as have the Mundari i(e), ne and ge.[3]—(*Bodding* thinks that this personal pronoun may have *two parallel forms*, one with "i" and one with "e".[4])

In Mundari possessive pronouns (adjectives) are formed from the personal pronouns by adding the suffix of the genitive, "a".[5] In Magyar "é" plays an analogous rôle; "én," (I), becomes "eny-é-m"; "te" (thou): "ti-é-d" (thine); "ő," (you): "ő-v-é" (yours.) When in Mundari the pronoun "ing" is followed by this "a", the "n" of the word *ing* becomes transformed into a so-called "n-mouillé", the *g* disappearing. Similarly in Magyar we have in the same case from é-*n*: I, e-*ny*-é-m: mine.[6]

The *plural* (dual) in Mundari has manifold forms. "bu" means: you and I; "le": they and I; "pe": you; "ko": they, and also an inclusive dual form, "I and thou," exists: "*lang*". Now, Mundari inserts pronominal direct and indirect objects in the very body of the predicate word[7]; a process entirely unknown in the Finno-Ugrian languages, except *Magyar*. There we find, even if only in a single case, but nevertheless most significantly, e.g. from *vár*: to wait, forms like *vár-lak*: I am awaiting thee; *vár-ta-lak* (praesens perfectum): I have awaited thee; *vár-á-lak* (praeteritum): I had awaited thee; *vár-ná-lak* (praesens optative conditional): I would await thee, etc., etc. We may notice en passant that "t" is the suffix of the Magyar past tense; and Hoffmann thinks that all the tense suffixes of Mundari are only variations of the roots "ta" and "ne".

[1] Hoffmann. P. 21.

[2] Campbell quotes for "ge" in Santal: indeed, certainly, of course.

[3] Magyar "ge" see under "de" in the *Magyar Etymological Dictionary*.

[4] *Materials for a Santali Grammar*. P. 23.

[5] The same is the case for Ho and Kurku, whilst Santal adds "ren".

[6] In Mundari and Santal pronominal suffixes are usually added to nouns denoting relationship. Thus in Santal e.g. they say "enga-ń": my mother, but very seldom "enga" in the meaning of mother alone. We have the similar case in Magyar.

[7] Hoffmann. P. XIXX.

Verbs. Their Conjugation.

Thus we have arrived at the verbs. The Munda recalls in many respects the Magyar and the Turk verb.[1] In both Magyar and Munda we find an "almost bewildering" mass of conjugational forms,[2] and in neither does there exist any negative form of conjugation, which is a common feature of many "Ugrian" languages, such as Finn, Mordwin, etc. In both languages, Magyar and Santal (Mundari), the primary root of the verbs remains perfectly unaltered through all the voices, moods and tenses of the conjugation. In both those of the formating elements which denote these voices, moods and tenses, remain unchanged through all numbers and persons, the pronominal subjects and objects alone undergoing the changes.[3] ("The wonderful intricacy of the Santal verbal system is a marvel to the student"—says Cole[4]—"and considering the mental calibre of the Santals of the present day, one is all the more surprised to find such a complex, and yet perfectly regular verbal system. Can it be they are the pillars of some noble edifice that has become more or less a ruin! the remains of a decayed language!") The most pregnant feature of the Magyar verb, its conjugation "without an object" and "with an object", seems to have a parallel in Santal in the latter's so called "active voice" and "middle voice". Thus, in the phrase: "Have you finished planting," the Santal uses[5] the active voice (e.g. cabakeda), just as Magyar would use here a conjugational form without object (e.g. *végezél*, instead the form with object: *végezéd*). In his answer the Santal states: "I myself have finished planting" (cabaiena), while the Magyar answering the same question would use the conjugation "with object" (i.e. *végezém*, instead of *végezék*, which is the form "without object"). Santal possess further a verbal form, which is described as a kind of passive; in this case a causative particle, "oco," is constantly added to notify causation. (E.g. "ńel": to see, and "ńelo-cońme": allow me, cause me to see it.) In Magyar the infixed particle *ass* (ess) has the same effect; there we shall find e.g. *néz*, to see: *nézessem*, i.e. cause me, allow me to see him (she, it).

As a general rule, in the Santal (Mundari) conjugation, the voice sign will stand first after the root (R), the mood sign second (M), the tense sign third (T), the "copula" (C)—a feature which will be explained later—comes in the fourth place, the pronominal

[1] "The only tongue with which I can compare the Munda languages"—says Grierson—"is Turki." *Linguistic Survey of India.* Vol. I. Page 36.

[2] The reader may find in Müller: *Grundriss der Sprachwissenschaft,* no less than 70 different conjugational forms of a Magyar verb.

[3] Hoffmann. P. 116.

[4] Cole: *Santali Primer.* P. 33.

[5] Ibid. P. 37.

subjects and objects coming last (Pr). In other terms, the general verb scheme will be (according to Hoffmann):

$$R + V + M + T + C + Pr$$

The Magyar verbal scheme is exactly the same; from *fut* (to run), for instance, we can get a figure like:

futtathattalak

(I might have let you run) i.e.:

fut (R) + *tat* (V) + *hat* (M) + *t* (T) + *a* (C) + *lak* (Pr.).

The above mentioned copula—always the sound "a"—is considered most characteristic for the Munda verb in general. The Munda root of course, as we have already mentioned, can be used not only as a verb, but also indifferently as a noun or as an adjective. Therefore it is not enough to suffix elements showing the voice, mood, tense, etc., to such roots: something more is needed to denote that the action really took place. This is obtained by the copula "a"; it gives them something finite to the verb. Hoffmann thinks, that this "a" is nothing else as the third person singular indefinite (neutral) pronoun "a".[1] It may be translated in most cases by the word "it".[2] Whilst in Ugrian languages, as Finn, Mordwin, Ostjak and others we do not find this copula, in Magyar it seems to exist. Thus we see *tár*, which means: to expand, to open (verb); further: expanded, open (adjective); finally: depot, magazine (noun); and *tárja*, is: he (she, it) expands, opens *it*, or *something*, i.e. we have an *effective* action.

Remarking finally that in the Mundari (Santal) *Syntax* the ordinary sequence in sentences is: Nominative + Dative + Accusative + Predicate, a series which is also seen in Magyar, we have come to the end of the few examples we wished to give as similarities in the two grammars: Munda (Santal, Mundari) and Magyar. They suggest the question ***whether Magyar is not much more closely allied to the Austric Munda languages than to any other family, and that it should therefore be classed with it instead of with the Finno-Ugrian (Uralian) family, even though it may possess some common features with the latter.***

Comparison of Munda (Santal) and Magyar Words.

The impression of the reader will be strengthened when comparing Magyar and Munda words also. For this purpose we will select from the Munda family its "Santal" dialect. As the Munda languages have not been extensively studied up to the present,

[1] Hoffmann. P. 125.
[2] Cole. P. 33.

it is not at all impossible that other Munda dialects, having little or no existing dictionaries, may show even more striking analogies than Santal.[1] It is imaginable that Mundari, Korwa, *Manjhi*,[2] or Savara for example may prove more akin.

When comparisons are made by scholars in order to prove that Magyar is an Ugro-Finn language, it is a habit of theirs to take words alternately from one or other of the many Ugro-Finn dialects; to quote now a Finn, now a Vogul, or again a Mordwin, Suryan or other word, just as it suits their desire to find analogies. We shall abandon such a wide method and shall confine ourselves *exclusively to Santal.* Our Santal words will be chosen at first from the somewhat limited material of word-comparisons contained in *Schmidt's* repeatedly quoted work.[3] Yet within these narrow limits many instructive features are obtainable, although the study is rather handicapped by the fact, that an accurate reproduction and valuation of Santal spelling has to be abandoned here. However, the numbers added in brackets to each Santal word indicate the place in which they may be found in Schmidt's book, thus allowing anyone wishing to undertake a more minute examination of the quoted examples, to do so.

SANTALI. (According to Schmidt)	MAGYAR. (According to Et., Sz.S., and Ba.)[4]
ASIT: exhausted (as plants in the winter, 316)	ASZOTT: withered
BAG: to intertwine, to curl up (195)	BOG: knot; BOG-OZ: to intertwine
DAKAL-DAKAL: motion of the body of Santali girls at dancing (33)	DAGÁL: pride (superbia), stately attitude. – (FARDAGÁLY: "tournure")
DAR: slit, fissure (158)	TÁR: to open, to expand
DARU: great (232)	DARU: tall and slim
DER: to stretch the body (159)	TÉR: space
DOMBOL-DOMBOL: to toss about as a boat on the high sea (207)	TOMBOL: to jump, to leap

[1] Attention may be called also to the "Shina" language, spread over the highland valleys of Gilgit, on the Upper Indus, next to the Hazara district mentioned on page 122; especially on its "Gilgit dialect", to-day the language of not more than 20,000 isolated people. Although this idiom is grammatically quite different from the Munda languages, as it may be classed with the Indo-Aryan, it is yet noteworthy for the many words, which for their sound and sense remind us of Maori. See Grierson: *Linguistic Survey of India.* Vol. VIII. Part II; and Lorimer: "Notes on the Gilgit Dialect of Shina." *Journ. As. Soc.* 1924.

[2] See Grierson: *Linguistic Survey.* Vol. IV. P. 145

[3] Schmidt: *Die Mon-Khmer Völker.*

[4] See page 47.

DIGIC: to hurt, to knock (42)	DIKICS: chopping knife, edge-tool
DOK: to preserve (138)	TOK: case, covering, box, sheath
GAD: deep.–GADA: depression of the ground, channel, river, stream (45)	KADA: an undermined hollow place in a river
GAHIR: to publish, to make known (in Khmer HIER: to overflow, to widen) (341)	HÍR: news, message (KIHIRDET: to publish)
GAND-GAND: diagonal, rectangular (46)	KANDAL: squint-eyed
GERWEL: ring round the neck (as for pigeons, etc.) (304)	ÖRV: ring round the neck (as for pigeons, etc.)
HABAK-DABAK: to raise and descend as waves on the sea (191)	HÁBOK: the waves of the sea
HADUI-HADUI: shaggy, bushy (156)	HADAZ: to shake the head, to nod
HAP: to eat, to get a bite (28)	HARAP: to bite
HAROP: to fit in, to grip tightly, conquer, surmount (in Bahnar ROP: to enslave; in Stieng ROBOT: "fouet" = whip) (251)	RAB: slave.–ROBOT: socage
HAT: to put a hand on, to arrest (Bahnar, KAET, KOT: to bind, gag; Stieng, KOT: to tie up) (25)	KÖT: to bind, gag
HATAR: to scrape the tongue, to cut off (121)	HADAR: to babble, to chatter, also: to hit, beat
HETET: to irritate.–GOTET: to touch (lightly) (106)	HAT: to excite.–KOTTY-FITTY: light touch, rap on the nose
HER: to rub off, polish (32)	HERÉCSEL: to rub, streak
HUL: to revolt (344)	HULL: to fall, to desert.–HULLONGÓ: tramp
INDIT: to suspect, reprimand (147)	INT: to reprimand
LADAK: to shut, close by drawing (a door) (139)	LAKAT: lock
LADUR-BADUR: careless, thoughtless (157)	BADAR: uncomprehensible, absurd (talk)
LENGET: slippery (71)	LENG: to slip.–LENGETEG: unsteady, light
LOCOK-LOCOK: to tremble, vibrate (53)	LOTYOG, also: LITYEG-LOTYOG: to totter
LOPOR: of the consistence of soft mud, soup, cast metal (Stieng, POR: soup) (184)	PÁR: lye
PASI: an *iron* joint on a wooden plough (in Mon iron is PASAI, in Malay BASI, in Battak BOSI; in Old and New Javan WESI, WSI, in Semang UWASE, etc.) (155)	VAS: iron
PAYAR: to go forwards and backwards (230)	JÁR: to walk.–BEJÁR: to pace off
PESET-PESET: tasteless, disgusting (316)	PESZMET: anything tasteless (preserved food)

PISKIC : to part with the tips of the fingers of one or both hands, as the hair ; to remove with the thumbnails (22)	PISZKÁL : to root, burrow, stir up
PIDIC-PIDIC : tiny (children) (95)	PICI, PITI : tiny, children
PUKPUKU : to swell, swollen (172)	PUKKADT : swollen
SURUN : to bore a hole into the rock (240)	SZÚR : to sting, to pierce
SUSU : to snip, to snort (201)	SZUSZOG : to breathe heavily
TE, TEH : to winnow, sift (84)	TESZ : to do, to set.–EL-TESZ : to put aside, to sift
TEP-TEP, DEP-DEP : hard, stiff (112)	TÖPPAD : to grow stiff (Sz.S.)
TI : hand (83)	TŐ : trunk (truncus) lowest part, foot (pes)
UAI : another, a stranger (9)	UJ : new, another.

Turning to *Campbell's " Santali-English Dictionary "*, a publication which registers the greatest number of Santal expressions, we are enabled to make further comparisons with Magyar expressions. The latter, together with their meaning *in Latin*, are quoted, with the exception of the unavoidable abbreviations, *exactly as they appear* in Gombocz and Melich's excellent *Etymological Dictionary* (words : A-Dunnyog), in Szarvas-Simonyi's *Historical Dictionary of the Magyar Language*, or occasionally in Ballagi's *Magyar-German Dictionary*. For the Santal words no phonetic signs are represented here except Ạ, which very closely corresponds to Magyar Ó, and Ṅ, corresponding to Magyar NY ; for the others consult Campbell directly. As far as pronunciation is concerned, we shall restrict ourselves to mentioning, that the letters " C " and " J " in Campbell's dictionary *correspond to the Magyar letters* " CS, GY, ZS, S " ; further Campbell's " S " to Magyar " SZ ", eventually to " C " and " Z ", (or even " S ").—Santal " B " and " P " have the counterpart in Magyar " B ", " P ", as well as in " F " and " V " ; Santal " Y " in Magyar " J ".—The " h " following certain capital letters in Campbell (e.g. : " Bh ", " Gh ", " Kh ", etc.) denotes only an aspiration in their pronunciation.

SANTAL. (Quoted from Campbell)	MAGYAR. (Quoted from Et., Sz.S., or Ba.)
AC : heat, flame (for instance in the Santal-phrase " ACAK-ME " : increase the heat !)	AZSAG ; ASAK, AZSAK : poker
ẠDAI : to give back, to collect money etc. due, to exact	AD : dare = to give.–ADÓ : vectigal, tributum = tax, tribute
AKA : to hang, to suspend	AKASZT, OKOSZT : suspendo, appendo, applico = to hang, suspend.–AGGAT : To hang repeatedly

ẠNTHUL: unconscious, stupified	ANTAL: stultus fit, animo in diversa rapitur, in meditatione defixus ambulat = to become stupid, to dream, to be given to day-dreaming
BAD: to accuse, to suspect, to accuse from ill-will, or a desire to injure	VÁD: crimen = accusation, impeachment.–VÁDAS: accusator = plaintiff
BHAND, BHOND: to defile, to corrupt, to defile ceremonially, to corrupt a holy day	BÁNT: impedire, offendere, turbare = to touch, offend, disturb.–BONT: turbare, corrumpere = to derange, destroy
BAO: calamity, distress, fair	BAJ, BAOS: molestia, fatigium, malum = trouble, fatigue, distress
BARE: may, oh that, please, do (e.g. in "Oh! that he would come!)	BÁR: esto, sane facito = well then, indeed
BẠTU, BẠTUẠ: a small bag used to carry small articles in, such as money, tobacco	BATYU, BATU: knapsack, bag, small parcel
BEMBHA: a simpleton, a muff.	BAMBA: stolidus, stupidus, stupore correptus = a simpleton, a muff
BICKẠU: to sprain.–BICLAU: to sprain, as an ankle	BICSAKL-IK: to sprain (the ankle)
BIKOL: uneasy, troubled (e.g. in "The mind will be troubled")	PIKÓ: ebrius = intoxicated
BODLA, BODOL: to exchange, to substitute	PÓTOL: suppleo, compenso = to complete, restore, compensate
BODO: stupid and unable to speak distinctly. - BODOC HANDI, BODOC MELA, BODOC SODOC: liquor obtained by squeezing the malted grain	BÓDÍT: stupefacere = to stupify.–BÓDÚL: errare, insanire, confundari, mente corripi = to err, to be benumbed, to be troubled in mind
BONDO: Foolish, stupid	BANDÓ: stolidus = foolish, stupid
BUJ: wisdom, understanding, sense	BÖLCS, BÖCS: doctus, consiliosus, sapiens = wise, understanding, clever
CABCAB: slushy, moist	CSÁP: watery, moist, damp
CAPADOK, CAPAT: to throw, to be thrown.–CAPOT: to seize prey by springing on it, as a tiger	CSAP: infligo, ico = to beat, hit.–LE-CSAP: precipitor = to rush down, precipitate on
CẠRI: a "lean to" roof, a verandah, a small house made by resting the roof on the wall of another house, a temporary shelter when engaged watching the crops	CSŰR: shed, barn
CETER: a thunderbolt	CSÜTÖRTÖK: Thursday
CHIN: appearance, shape, form, bodily representation, disguise, semblance, likeness	CSIN: decor, cultus, elegantia, situs, natura, structura = appearance, culture, smartness, figure, nature, structure
CIRI BIRI: into small pieces, thin, split into thin strips, to mince	CSIRIBIRI: exilis, minutus = insignificant, minute

COK : to kiss	CSÓK : a kiss
COTHRA, COTHRA POTRA, COTHRO : puny, ill-conditioned, half-starved	GYATRA : weak, wretched
CUBẠK : to have a mote in the eye	CSIPA, CSOPA, CSAPA : gramiae, lippitudo = sty, pus in the eye
CHUC : a needle.–CUICUI : pointed, tapering to a point in form of a cone	CSÚCS : cacumen = point.–CSUCSA : lancea, hasta = lance.–CSÚCSOS : accuminatus, cupidatus, turbinatus = pointed
DE : an interjection of entreaty, a very common particle giving emphasis or clearness.–DO : an emphatic or persuasive particle, used with the imperative	DE : sed, verum, atqui = but, yet, however. In exclamations it serves to prove or to emphasize. A particle of corroboration
DHUMA : stout, fat	DUMA : thick, fat
DUNDUN : to rise and fall like waves, to be piled up	DUN : to dam up, the rise of waters
EBHEN : to awake from sleep	ÉBREN : vigilanter = awake
ELAO : to have enough	ELÉG : sat est = it is enough
EN : that particular	ÖN, EN : in propria, suus, ejus, eorum = proper, own.–ÜNNEP : holiday. (NÁP, NEP : day)
GAD : the receptacle into which the rice to be husked is placed	KÁD : receptacle, tub, cask, barrel
GANDON : to think, to ponder, to consider	GONDOL : cogito, to think, to ponder, to consider
GHAS : grass, all the small species of Cyperacea, as well as nearly all Graminae are called " ghas "	GÁZ : grass, weeds
GOL : round, spherical	GOLYÓ : ball
GOROB, GOROBIA : heavy, indigestible, proud, conceited	GOROMBA : crassus, asper, rudus, ineptus = heavy, rough, rude, thick, nasty
HALA HẠLI : in exchange for, to recompense, a recompense, retribution	HÁLA : gratia = thank.–HÁLÁL : to be grateful
HALO : to scoop with the hand or some implement fish out of water	HÁLÓ : rete = fishing net
HASA : earth, soil, land, to bury, to become soil	HAZA, HÁZA : domum, patria = home, fatherland
HEJER : to roll the skin back from the prepuce ; to cut off (e.g. " Behead him ")	HEGYEZ : spiculo, acumino, fastigio, cacumino = to point, to taper
HEPER HENDE : to hang about	HEVER : cubito, desideo, otior = to idle away one's time, to lay idly
HO : also, even, too	HA : etsi = although, if, when
ILET : to apply an ointment to a sore	ILLET : applico = to apply (as an ointment to a sore)
IR, IROK : to reap	ÉR-IK, ÍR-IK : maturesco = to reap
ITI : this, this present	IDE : huc, hic = hither, here.–ITT : hic, tum = here, there
JAORE JAORE : imploring, earnestly, urgently	GYERE GYERE : come along !

JẠUSA JẠUSI : quickly	GYORS, GYARS : quick, swift
JEL : flesh, flesh meat	SÜLT : flesh meat
JENTHE : sticky, adhesive	GYANTA, GYENTÉR, GYENTÁR : resin, varnish
JHAR : liquor which oozes out of the malted grain during fermentation	SER, SÖR : beer
JORMA : small of stature (e.g. in " Two little people ")	GYERMEK : puer = child
JOS : to succeed.–JOE : victory	GYŐZ : vinco = to be victorious
KANKO : cloth	KANKÓ : garment
KAR, GHORI : time	KOR : time, age
KAR : side.–KẠRKẠRI : a lever with which a rope is tightened.–KẠRU : handles on a box or trunk by which to lift it	KAR : arm, lever
KẠR : an eruption appearing on the legs, mainly of children.–KARON : disease, malady.–KORRA : a renal disease	KÓR ; morbus = illness, disease
KARJA, KARJI : tall, high	KARCSU : gracilis = tall and slim
KẠSAI : a butcher	KASZAP : lamio = butcher
KHẠS, KHOS : itch, scabies, a kind of skin disease	KOSZ : scabies = scab, scurf
KHEN : impending calamity	KÍN, KÉN : mortificatio, cruciatus, tortura = torture.–KINLŐDÁS : vexatio, afflictio = pain, agony
KI : an interrogative	KÍ : quis, quae, qui, quae, quod = who, which (interrogatively)
KINCIT : a little	KICSIT : a little
KORPA, ARPA : to gather together by littles, perquisites received by yearly servants when harvesting crops, also by daughters previous to marriage	KORPA : furfur = bran ÁRPA : hordeum = barley
KOYA, KUYẠ : a wild dog.–KUTU : a dog, a puppy	KUASZ, KUVASZ : molossus = big dog.–KUTYA : caniculus = lap dog.–KUTAK : pumilio = dwarf
LABDA, LABDAO, LEBDA : to throw at, as a stick, to hit or knock down anything.–LAP, LAPLAP : to catch with both hands, as a ball thrown	LABDA, LAPTA : pila = ball
LAGAN, LOGON : preparations for a marriage	LAKZI, LAGZI : wedding
LẠJUN LẠJUN, LUJUN LUJUN : slow-paced	LASSU : slow.–LASSAN : slow-paced
LANGA : to be tired, to be fatigued	LANKAD : lassesco, torpeo = to be tired, fatigued
LAKER, LAKIR : to habit	LAK-IK : habito = to dwell
LEDER BEDER : to scamp	LEDÉR : lascivus, circulator = lascivous, fickle.–LEDÉRSÉG : nequitia, inprobitas = debauchery, disorderliness
LO : to burn	LOBB : flamma = flame

MACHA : resembling, like	MÁSA : resembling, like
MEN : An exclamation of warning, caution, admonition or alarm ; beware, take care, mind what you are about, look out.-(e.g. " Clear out of the way."-" Flee, there is a tiger." " Beware father ! Look out father ! etc., etc., respectful form used to elderly people.)-MENA : to exist	MENJ ! : " Go on ! ".-MÉN : eo, meo, pergo = to go.—MÉN : locum habeo = to have place. (ÁLTAL)-MÉN : permutor, vertor = change into, to become
MENTE : affixed to certain roots to form adverbs, implying sudden or single actions (e.g. in " He came at once ")	MENTEN : statim, protinus, continuo, ilicet = instantly, at once. " MENTEN MEGYEK " : pergo = I go without delay
MOT : method, way, mode	MÓD : modus, modalitas = kind, mode, way
NANA : aunt	NÉNE : aunt
NI : this particular (one of animate objects)	NI : eu, ecce = here, see ! EZ-NI : (just) this
OD, AD : to shelter, to protect	ÓD : cavere, tueri, defendere, protegere = to guard, defend, protect.-ODU : a shelter
OJ : reasonable amount	OLCSÓ, ÓCSÓ : facilis pretii = reasonable, cheap
ONTEN : yonder, that place	OTTAN, OTTON : inibi, ibidem = there, yonder, on that place
ORE : old, worn out	ÖREG : senex = old, aged, worn out.
PAL : a herd, a flock	FALKA : pars boum vel ovium = flock, herd
PARAK : to split, to crack	FARAG : sculpo, fabrico = to carve, cut, chisel
PETER : to twist, to screw, to writhe	PEDER : to twist, to screw, to writhe
POKHA : the part of the body under the ribs	BOKA : talus, tibia = ankle
RASAO : to solder	RÉZ : aes, cuprum = ore, copper
RẠSIA : partner, sharer, partnership	RÉSZES : partner, sharer, partnership
REGHA, REGHAO : to sing	REGE : vetus cantilena = old chant.-REGÉL : to sing an old chant
SAGAR : a cart having solid wheels	SZEKÉR : currus, vehes, plaustrum = cart
SAL : house, as in school house, shop, as in workshop, place, as in dancing place	SZÁLL : se conferre, se recipere, rivertor = to set out, to join, alight. - SZÁLLÁS : mansio, statio = house, station
SE : or.-SEM : or not	SE, SEM : neu, nec, neque = nor.-SEM : also not
SOBHA : beautiful	SZÉP : beautiful
THAG : to deceive, to oppose, to swindle	TAGAD : nego, infitior = to deny, disavow
THAM : a prop, a pier, as of a bridge	TÁM, TÁMASZ : pillar, prop, support

THASAO: to do for, used in threats (e.g. in "We will take you in court and do for you")	TESZ, TESZEN: facio = to do, execute.–TESZEK RÓLA: to manage (in a threatening sense)
TOA: milk	TEJ: milk
UJU UJU: true, accurate (e.g. in "Speak truthfully")	ÚGY: ita, sic = so, thus.–ÚGY-MOND: inquit, ait = "he said"

Other (some thousand) Santal expressions, taken from the same dictionary, suggesting comparisons with Magyar words, will appear as APPENDIX I at the end. Here only some *omonatopoeic* words of both languages may be still registered.

SANTALI.	MAGYAR USES.
BAKAT: to chatter, to jabber	BAKOG
BEHAJ, BEHAL: expression of wonder or astonishment	BEH
BEJEK BEJEK: suppurating liquid	PEZSEG
BHULKAU: to rise up, to spring as water	BULYOG
BHURKAK: to raise up earth, as beetles do	BURROG
BUGUR BUGUR: the sound produced by the blowing of the blacksmith's bellows	BÚG
CAI CAI: used when driving an elephant	CSÁ (vox ad stimulandos boves)
CATOK CATOK: sound of dog lapping	CSATTOG
CAUCHAL: a babbler	CSACSOG
CIRIC CIRIC: chirp of sparrow	CSIRIPEL
CIROC COROC: dripping, water issuing in small jets or drops.–JHOROK: oozing out of water	CSIREG-CSOROG
CORAN: to overflow	CSORRAN
DARRAO: To roll, to husk, as by grinding with a curry stone	DARÁL
DERE DERE: angrily	DÉR-DÚR
DHAPDHUP: to stamp the foot	DOBOG
DHOP DHOP: sound emitted by a drum	DOBOL
DOHLAO: to break out afresh as a fire that was apparently extinguished	DOHOG
GAGU: speaking through the nose and very indistinctly	GAGYOG
GURGURAU: to roll on the ground	GURUL
HABAK: to speak disconnectedly, indistinctly	HABOG, HEBEG
HAKAR HAKAR: applied to the wheezing of a person suffering from bronchitis	HÁKOG
HEK: to cut the wind or breath from one, as by a blow between the shoulders.–HAKA CAKA: to be surprised, taken aback, troubled	HÖK, (MEG)HÖKKEN
HARAS: sound of rumbling, as of thunder; bang, crash	HARSOG
JHABAR JHUBAR: dripping, as the clothes of one who has just waded through a river	CSEPEG-CSUPOG
JHAO JHAO: applied to the continued barking of dogs	CSAHOL
JHURU JHURU: to polish, to smooth	SÚROL
KATKATAO: to set and grind the teeth, as in convulsions	KATTOG

KHAROK KHAROK : sound of scratching	KARCOL
KHOK : to cough	KÖHÖG
KHORO KHORO : applied to the noise made by a bubble-bubble.-KARKUR : sound of rumbling in the stomach	KOROG
KOP : phlegm	KÖP
KHOTKHOTAO : to cackle as a hen	KOTKODÁCSOL
LABAN LUBUN : leisurely, slowly, applied mainly to the leisurely movements of wild animals	LABBAN, LAPPAG
LACAK PACAK : large drops of rain falling from the leaves of trees, etc.	LOCSOG (POTYOG)
LAWAK : to dangle, to spring up and down, to jerk up and down, to hand loosely	LOBOG
LOKOT LOKOT : the throat move with each respiration, as a hen panting.-LIKIC LIKIC : to shake, to vibrate	LÖK, LÜKÖG, LÜKTET
NE : a particle which signifies that something inanimate is being offered for ; " take "	NE
PACAK : to spread out, as anything soft falling on the ground	POTYOG
PAHUR : to be beaten	PÁHOL (to beat)
PARI : to turn about, to roll	PEREG
PATAN BATAN : to snap at, to reply testily	PATTAN, (FEL)PATTAN
PATAS : sounding of a slap	PATÉL
PHEC : to drop, to drip, to fall in spray.-PHICKARI : a syringe	FECSKENDŐ (a syringe)
PHECAN : to backbite	FECSEG
PHERE PHERE : to gush, to issue with violence and rapidity, as anything semi-liquid from confinement	FERCSEN
PHORPHOR : imitative of the sound produced by a strong flame	FORR
PHUPHUAU, PHUPUA : to blow	FÚ
POSON : to leak as bellows	POSZOG
RABAC RUBUC : heavily, without elasticity, without spring, as a heavy creature walking	ROBOG
RAGAT : rough, as speech	REKEDT
RAK : cry or note of a beast, bird or insect	RÁKOG
REC : imitative of a slightly rustling sound, creaking as of boots, cracking as of dry leaves, etc.	RECSEG
RIPRIPI : to flap the wings, as a bird of prey hovering over its prey	REPDEZ
ROPOT : to creak, as shoes	ROPOG
RUP : to collapse, to fall down	ROPPAN
SERE SERE : fizzing sound, as that produced by fresh firewood when burning.-CERE PETE : explosive sound produced by wood when burning	SERCEG
SETE : imitative of a suppressed bubbling sound	SETTEG
SODOR SODOR : sound produced by pouring water.-CODO CODO : sound of water falling in a stream	SODOR
SOKOC : to shog, to shake up, to toss	ZÖKÖG

SOKOR: sound produced by an obstruction in the wind pipe or nostrils, to gurgle, rattle in throat	ZOKOG
SOSU: to breathe heavily	SZUSZOG
SUGUI SUGUI: gently, as wind	ZÚG
SURKAU: to sniff, to suck up	SZÜRCSÖL
SUSUẠ, SUSWẠU, SUSNẠU: to shiver	ZÚZ
TABA TUBU: imitative of the sound produced by striking the water with the feet	TAPOS
TERE TERE: to vaunt or boast, applied to insignificant persons	TERE-FERE
THER: to peal, as thunder	DÖRÖG
TIPIK TIPIK: tripplingly, said of small females	TIPPEG

For further onomatopoeic words see the APPENDIX I.

Strange is, at least, also the resemblance of some religious, mythological, etc., expressions of the Santal and of such of Magyar tradition. Thus we find:

SANTAL.	MAGYAR.
BAHAL: the holder of an office.	BÁN, BÁHÁN: the holder of some office of the ancient Magyar.
BONGA: a demon (the name given by the Santal to the spirit they worship).	BENGA: a spectre, a devil.
DẠN: a witch, witchcraft.	TŰNDÉR: magus, prestigiator = a witch, witchcraft, sorcerer, fairy. (TŰN: evanescere: to disappear, to change one's body.)
GURU: teacher (in medicinal questions=a quack).	KURUZSOL: to quack.
JILA: a district, a division of a country for administrative purposes.	GYILÁSZ: the holder of some important office in Magyar tradition. (Coming in grade after the "kende".)
KARANATH SIM: a black fowl, with black flesh and black bones. (SIM: a fowl.)	KERECSET: a mythological bird of the Magyar.
KHARKHARI: clever, expert, energetic, keen, adept, skilled.	KÁRKÁSZ: a holder of some office (a kind of tribal chief ?) of the ancient Magyar.
KOENDA: the name of a race of traditional kings of the Santal.	KENDE: the traditional chief-king of the Magyar.
MON: spirit.	MANÓ: an evil spirit (a good spirit ?).
MUN: a mythical semi-divine being.	MÉN MARÓT: a traditional Magyar chieftain. – MÉN: a stallion. (The sacrifice of a stallion was as well a Santal as a Magyar habit.)
TATOK: a sorcerer, a juggler.	TÁTOS: the priest of the olden Magyar.

CHAPTER XIV.

INDIA AND THE MAGYAR.

POSSIBLE REASONS WHY MAGYAR PHILOLOGY HAS NEGLECTED INDIA.—MAGYAR PLACE NAMES IN INDIA.—SOME RELATIONS OF ANCIENT MAGYAR CULTURE WITH INDIA.—RELIGIOUS CONNECTIONS.—INDIA IN OLD MAGYAR CHRONICLES.—THE ORITES.—THE "SCYTHIAN".—POINTS OF VIEW WHEN JUDGING THE RELATIONSHIP OF THE MAGYAR TO INDIA.

Possible Reasons why Magyar Philology has Neglected India.

We must not be astonished if Hungarian scholars, who in other ways are devoting themselves with such profound knowledge and praiseworthy zeal to the study of the primitive history of their kinsmen and their language, have hitherto taken no notice of the many features common to Magyar and Munda (Santal) and of the apparent close relationship of the former to the great *Austric* family. Since the scientific authorities of Hungary had established, and rightly so, that there exists no relation between Magyar and the Dravida languages, and as they were obviously undeterred by the profound difference in the grammars of Dravida and Munda : it was natural that they should have no inducement to search again for possible Indian connections. It must be borne in mind, that it is only within the last few years that the grammar of the Munda family of languages has been rendered widely accessible, by the publication, in 1906, of Vol. IV of the *Linguistic Survey of India*; and *Schmidt's* standard work on the Mon-Khmer languages is not of much earlier date. (Nevertheless the first assertion which represented the Munda family of languages as quite different from other Indian linguistic groups, from Arya and Dravida, was made as far back as 1854 by the eminent linguist *Max Müller*.)

The similarities between many *Magyar* words and words of alleged *Sanskrit* origin, a relationship also pointed out by the great scholar *Alexander Csoma de Körös*,[1] may be due to the borrowing of Munda words by the invading Arya.[2] In the same way the instances of apparent relationship which attracted the attention of Caldwell in the Dravida languages,[3] may be

[1] Duka: *Life and Works of Alexander Csoma de Körös*. P. 217.—See also Schmidt. In *Kőrösi Csoma Archivum*. P. 8.
[2] See Chapter X.
[3] Caldwell: *Comparative Grammar of the Dravidian Languages*.

easily explained by the close intercourse, not to say the fusion of Dravida and Munda tribes, in consequence of which an exceptionally large number of Munda words have been incorporated in Dravida.[1] Connections of Finno-Ugrian nature in Dravida might be considered as remnants of the supposed ancient Dravida emigration from Akkad and Sumer.[2] However it would lead us too far were we to enter here into the problem of all such connections. It may suffice to mention that presence of many *Akkadian words* in Magyar has already been noticed.[3] (It should be added, that according to Lenormant,[4] Assyrian documents refer to a people "*Maga*", a mother-worshipping race, living on the coast, and speaking "the language of the fishermen, which differed from the Turanian tongue of the Akkadian and the Semitic speech of the Aryan".) Of course it is obvious that in many parts of the world the mere use of any particular language *does not at all involve a lineal descent* of its present speakers at an earlier period.[5] It is impossible, without historical evidence, to be certain that the language spoken by any particular people was the language of their ancestors.[6] For many students language is more an integral part of the history of culture than that of race.[7] Tribes in a low state of civilization, especially, change their language very readily. How quickly such a process may occur even within 50 years, can be proved by some striking examples.[8]

Magyar Place Names in India.

There are still other than linguistic instances suggesting relationship between India and the Magyar. It has already been emphasized (page 84), that comparisons of geographical names are, as a rule, not very reliable. Nevertheless they must not remain unnoticed, when they occur, recalling Magyar names in great numbers, as they do, within the districts inhabited by Munda tribes in the Indian provinces of Bihar, Orissa, and especially of Chota Nagpur: namely the region of Hazaribagh, the homeland of the Santal. We will quote only a few instances[9]: *Bagodha, Banki, Bano, Biru, Choka Hatu, Ichak, Kalna, Katangi, Kenda, Korba, Kot, Mand*

[1] See Chapter X.

[2] Comp. Cserép: *A Magyarok Eredete* (The Origin of the Magyar). P. 34.

[3] Kápolnai: *Az Ősmagyarok Mivellsége, etc.* (The Culture of the Primeval Magyar).

[4] Lenormant: *Chaldean Magic.* P. 437.—See also Hewitt. In *Journ. As. Soc.* 1890. P. 720.

[5] Szinnyei: *Die Herkunft der Ungarn.* P. 22.

[6] Rapson. In Chapt. II of his *Cambridge History of India.* Vol. I. P. 66.

[7] Kennedy. P. 502.

[8] Gait: *Census of India.* P. 328.—Even the surroundings and the conditions under which a people lives, whether in forests or in villages, may alter the racial character. Examples are quoted in Thurston: *Tribes and Castes.* Vol. I. P. XVII.

[9] According to Andree's *Handatlas*, 3rd Edition.

(river), *Mor* (river), *Nara, Orda, Porba, Tarnol, Toposi, Torba,*[1] etc. Or *Bankota, Chapia, Dobra, Hatwa, Ghat, Gonda, Kot, Sikra,* etc.; all on the right bank of the Rapti, where Munda tribes are also said to have once dwelled. All these and many other names of localities in the above mentioned areas often occur in Hungary of to-day as well as in its pre-war territories, and this always in *purely Magyar districts*, such as the countries Baranya, Heves, Szolnok, Somogy, Tolna, Zala, etc., and in the Székely land of Transsylvania.[2]

When noting all these Indian place-names, and when recalling that the original home of the Munda is supposed to have been in North Western China, one is less astonished to find a noted Hungarian scholar asserting most decidedly that one of the two great rivers of the "cradle-land" mentioned in ancient Magyar chronicles, is identical with the *Hoang-Ho.*[3]

Place names sounding like Magyar are found apart of the Eastern part of India also in another region of Asia: on the South Coast of Persia. We shall return to this point later on; in the meantime let us look at the right bank of the Lower Indus.

Magyar Tribal Names in the Indus Region.

It has been already mentioned (page 14), that at the time of the conquest of their present homes on the Danube, the Magyar were divided *into 108 tribes*; the names of these tribes have been preserved.[4] However unreliable such legendary records—we repeat—may be [5] and how little scientific proofs such comparisons may afford, nevertheless the fact exists, that on the right bank of the Lower Indus and to the West of it, in a relatively small area limited by the river (on the right of which a "*Mantschar*"-Sea can be found [6]), the sea-coast, lat. 62°, and longt. 29°, that is to say about as far as the Bolan Pass, over an expanse of about 90,000 square miles: many geographical names appear which recall old Magyar tribal

[1] Hahn, in his "Dravidian and Kolarian place names in Mirzapur, Shahabad and Gaya" (*Journ. As. Soc. of Bengal.* Vol. LXXII. Part III. P. 9), points out as Kolarian (Munda) place-names such as end in "da'a": water; printed in the maps as "da" or "dag", and thus because a Hindu cannot pronounce the hiatus in the word da'a. (Hence the pronunciation "da" or "dag".) Hahn also considers as either Munda or Dravida place-names ending in "gara".

[2] Comp. Jekelfalussy: *A Magyar Szent Korona Országainak Helységnévtára,* and others.

[3] Fejér: *Beiträge zur Erklärung der auf Skythien bezüglichen geographischen Angaben der ungarischen Chroniken* (Contributions to the Comments on geographical Data about Scythia in Magyar Chronicles). In *Kőrösi Csoma Arch.* P. 40.

[4] These tribal names can be found in Jászay: *A Magyar Nemzet Napjai.* P. 179.—See also Cseh: *Tudományos Gyűjtemény.* Vol. V. Pp. 79–89. Etc.

[5] According to *Kerékgyártó,* P. 14, the following tribal names may be taken as reliable: Ákos, Bastek, Berend, Bor, Csák, Csaba, Csanád, Érd, Kadocsa, Kalán, Keled, Kevi, Levente, Maglód, Mike, Ompod, Othmár, Rosd, Simánd, Szemény, Szemere, Szoárd, Tátony, Torda, Turul, Zombor.

[6] According to Andree's *Handatlas.* 8th Edition.

names.[1] The similitudes of place and river names also acquire importance from the fact, that the Magyar, like other wandering and colonizing people, brought these names from their ancient homes and again and again attributed them to their new settlements. This particularity should be borne in mind when recalling the historical tradition, according to which during the wanderings of the Magyar, *a division took place*,[2] a part of the nation remaining in Asia. The same part is said to have settled "somewhere in Persia, near to great swamps". This Asian empire of theirs was called by the chroniclers, besides "Hungaria Magna, Hungaria Vetus", often also *Bascardia, Pascatir*, and by Arab chroniclers *Badjgerd*.[3] Now the name of "Bascardia", etc., could be possibly derived from the country of *Baschakerd, Baschkird*[4] in the present South Persia, an area extending from the Gulf of Oman to the great swamps of Djhas Noriam Hamum, as this area shows, as already said, once more numerous place-names of Magyar sound.[5]

Some Relations of Ancient Magyar Culture with India.

But all we have just discussed, is somewhat in the *nature of guesswork*; let us consider less speculative things. The ancient Magyar culture also bears manifold allusions to South Asian bonds. "Whilst Magyar historical research is sticking fast in the swamps of the Meotis"—says Huszka[6]—"the cultural traces lead us to India." Thus the classical Székely

[1] Following the sea-coast we see (the Magyar tribal names are added in brackets): Pitiani (Pudány), Karatschi (Koros), Tscharna (Csornag), Ormara (Othmár), Chor Kalmat (Csór), Gadagan (Katapán), Tular (Turul), Gwadar (Kádár), etc. In the interior: Bani (Bana), Nag (Negol), Bolida (Bodli), Taradun (Torda, Tordos), Kei (Kevi), Las (Laca), Botschapir (Bucsoha) Djerind (Győr), Kalat (Kalata), Samiran (Szemere), Ges (Géc), Wad (Bád), Kirta (Kürt), Gordja (Gordon), Djhalawan (Gyula), Betan (Botond), Tscheba (Séva), Chakar (Csák), Nattal (Nádasd), Ratha (Rátha), etc. It will be agreed that fragile as may be such a basis, the great number of instances seem nevertheless to justify further investigation.

[2] The Santal tradition also refers to a division of their people, and Madhosin is said to have been the name of the person who broke up their unity.

[3] See especially Gombocz: "A Magyar Őshaza és a Nemzeti Hagyomány" (The Magyar Cradle Land and the national Tradition). In *Nyelvtudományi Közlöny*. Vol. XLV and XLVI.

[4] Andree's *Handatlas*. 8th Edition.

[5] Alleged descendants of the Magyar remaining in Asia were met by a traveller, in 1235, on the banks of a river called "Etyl", near the town of "Bunda", in the land of "Vela, Velat". Up to now neither the town, nor the land have been identified. Concerning the river, some scholars think "Etyl" may be the Dniester. (See Fehér: Atelküzü Területe és Neve—Territory and Name of Atelküzü. In *Századok*. 1913. P. 682). It would be worth while to investigate, whether this "Etyl" was not the *Hilmend*, the "*Etymandros*" of the ancient. The historian Moses Choremi describes the river Etyl as of 70 branches, a characteristic more applicable to the Hilmend, with its many channels of irrigation, than to the Dniester. Along the former some towns recalling "Bunda" may be found.

[6] Huszka: *Magyar Ornamentika*. P. 13.

porch [1] in Transsylvania with its characteristic ornaments had its origin in India.[2] It is quite sufficient to compare its richly intertwined motifs with those published by Skinner in his "Origin and Relationship of Maori Material Culture and decorative Art" [3] *as samples of Indian art*: to become convinced of the truth of the above assertion. It is further corroborated by the fact, that certain constructive details of Székely doors cannot be discovered anywhere else but on the doors of some Indian rock-temples.[4]

The important ornamental element of *spirals* in ancient Magyar tomb relics, etc., has already been mentioned.[5] Hadden, in his *Evolution of Art*,[6] holds the opinion that the motif of the spiral derived from the lower leaves of the holy *lotos-flower* of India.[7] In *Huszka's* opinion this flower is the most important element also of Magyar decorative art. He tries further to prove that the ancestors of the Magyar must have lived for centuries, together with nations of the "second Persian empire". Now the North West and West of India, up to the present Deccan, was for centuries *under Persian rule.* The well-known rock inscriptions of Darius I at Behistun mention amongst 37 provinces of the Empire, 5 situated in the region of the *Indus*; the "India Satrapy" paid to this sovereign a yearly tribute in gold of the value of one million pounds; etc., etc.[8] Other motives of Indian origin, such as the peacock, and peacock feathers,[9] are so predominant in the Magyar decorative art, that a sort of symbolical meaning must be attributed to them. And in this respect Huszka calls attention to the peculiar fact that "this is not the case with any other Scytho-Ugrian people related to Magyar".[10] He expresses also his astonishment, that, reminding how fond the Magyar were of *horses*, this motif is very rarely found in their ornaments. But we find it just as rare in Indian art also. Considering the importance of horse-sacrifice amongst both people,—the sacrifice of white horses is a Munda habit [11]—one would expect this motif to appear. Old Magyar names, like

[1] See page 86.
[2] Huszka: *Tárgyi Ethnographiánk östörténeti Vonatkozásai* (Primeval Connections of our material Ethnography.)
[3] *Journal Pol. Soc.* 1924. P. 243.
[4] Huszka: *Tárgyi Ethnographiánk*, etc. P. 27.
[5] See page 87.
[6] Quoted by Newman. P. 278.
[7] See also the most characteristic figures in Annandale: "Plant and Animal Designs in the Mural Decorations of an Uriya Village." *Mem. As. Soc. of Bengal.* 1924. P. 239.
[8] Williams Jackson, in Rapson's *Cambridge History of India.* Vol. I. Pp. 328, 335, 337.
[9] In Magyar the peacock is called "páva"; in Maori "pawa" (Tr.) means: arched, bow-shaped, anything bended in a bow.
[10] Huszka: *Magyar Ornamentika.* P. 6.
[11] See Hewitt in *Journ. As. Soc.* 1888. P. 311.

Kupa, Tana, etc., are even to-day often met amongst the Munda.[1]

Religious Connections.

Much might be said about the religious links connecting ancient Magyar with India. Here we will restrict ourselves to instancing the *cuckoo*, enjoying, with the peacock, very great veneration there, and also said to be one of the main figures of old Magyar mythology.[2]

We may be justified also in asking whether in certain Magyar names for localities, or in other Magyar expressions traces are not to be recognized of the Indian *Bud* (*Bod*) *cult*. The name of the town *Buda* is quoted sometimes by old Magyar chronicles as "Bodvariam",[3] and its situation on a steep hill, near the edge of a forest-region, at the bifurcation of river-branches recalls in a most striking manner the description given by Forlong of the abodes of the Indian Bod cult.[4] At any rate, it is probable that Bod, Bud, Buda was not an original place name found by the immigrating Magyar, but a name given by them to the place, as the chronicler Anonymus writes: " . . . que per linguam Hungaricam dicitur *nunc* Buduuar," [5] i.e. that the town is called *now* in Magyar, etc.—Among Magyar expressions containing the root *bod*, let us mention: *bodró* = the young shoot of a tree on which the fruit grows: *bodoró* (Et.): to be delivered of a child (both expressions referring to generation); and perhaps even the popular saying: *kis ember nagy bottal jár* = the little man is walking with a "big stick". In connection with the Bud or Phallus-cult, also vestiges of *serpent-worshipping* may be found in the ancient Magyar mythology. Here snakes are esteemed as mighty and most useful beings, and there is even a story of a serpent-king. In Körmöcz the popular faith still believes in the existence of a white snake in each house, as its sentry and guardian.[6]

Knowledge of Metals.

The assertion that the ancient Magyar had no knowledge of *iron* up till our era, cannot lead to important conclusions, even if it should be proved correct.[7] Although iron and probably steel were known from earliest times [8] in India, it has to be borne in mind that their use was by no means general. Thus the historians accompanying Alexander the Great relate about the

[1] Kuba, Dana.—See Roy: *The Mundas and their Country*. P. 48.
[2] Ipolyi: *Magyar Mythologia*. P. 319.
[3] Podhradszky: *Béla Király névtelen Jegyzőjének Idejekora és Hitelessége* (The Age and Authenticity of King Béla's Chronicler Anonymus). P. 84.
[4] See page 116.
[5] Gombocz: *A magyar Őshaza és a nemzeti Hagyomány*. P. 133.
[6] Kandra. P. 14.
[7] Karácsonyi: *A magyar Nemzet Őstörténete* 896-ig. P. 17.
[8] Heath: "On Indian Iron and Steel." *Journ. As. Soc.* 1889. P. 395.

Orites,[1] a people living West of the mouth of the Indus, that they did not know of iron. Besides, how rare this metal must have been may be judged by a description of Quintus Curtius [2] of the presents offered by Indian rulers to Alexander, where amongst other precious gifts, such as 300 horses, etc., mention is made of "ferri candidi talenta centum", i.e. about 25 lb. of "white metal" (steel ?).

India in Old Magyar Chronicles.

How far descriptions of the old homeland given by ancient Magyar chronicles may be accepted as historical truth and whether certain instances are not simply borrowed from chronicles of other nations and attributed to the Magyar, cannot be examined here. However if the records of these chronicles are regarded as correct, there are two features which deserve our special attention, because they seem *to allude to India*. These are first: the description of the old homeland, secondly: the names of the enemies who were there "put to flight" by the ancestors.

In one of these chronicles the ancient fatherland is described [3] as a country where "sunt serpentes diversi generis, ranae velut porci, basillisci, et plura animalia toxicata; tigris et unicornis ibi generantur", i.e. there are to be found snakes of all kinds, frogs as large as small pigs, basilisks, many venomous animals; also *tigers and rhinoceroses*. The chronicles, further, speak of great quantities of gold, silver *and pearls* to be found in the old homeland and say that this country was one "of a fertile soil, where groves, woods and meadows flourish, extremely rich in all kinds of game, a country where the natives are fond of a quiet life, where they are vain and haughty, show tendencies to licentiousness and robbery, and whose complexion is more dark than fair.[4] The big frogs—obviously tortoises—and pearls mentioned by the chroniclers suggest a sea-coast; and gold was produced in those days in very great quantities in *Cashmere*.[5]

[1] It should be noted that ancient authors very often describe territories even beyond the Indus as parts of India, as for instance Plinius (Lib. VI, Cap. XIII) who considers as belonging to India: Gedrosia, Arachosia, Aria and Paropamisus, i.e. the greatest part of Baluchistan and Afghanistan. Later on Oriental geographers speak also of Gedrosia, the present "Mekrân" district of Baluchistan, as belonging to "Sindistan", i.e. to India.

[2] Lib. IX, Cap. VIII. 3.

[3] More can be found by Gombocz, in *Nyelvtudományi Közlemények*. 1917–1921. P. 135.

[4] See Jászay. P. 17.—"Dark skin," as one of the characteristics of the inhabitants of the ancient fatherland, is referred to also by Adhemar of Angoulème, when describing the journey of a brother monk to a province called "White Hungary" (the present home of the Magyar) in opposition to "Black Hungary", whose population have a dark skin like Ethiopians.—See also Horváth: *A Magyarok Története* (History of the Magyar). Vol. I.

[5] Bevan. In Chapt. XVI of Rapson's *Cambridge History of India*. Vol. I. P. 414.

It is tempting to compare these descriptions with that given by *Quintus Curtius* about [1] the country traversed by *Alexander the Great's army* to the North of the present town of Jhelam, and eastwards, near Rawalpindi, as well as in the present Hazara district of Cashmere, *i.e. the ancient home of the Madra and the Takka.*[2] According to this writer there were "serpents of unusual size, also rhinoceroses, an animal rarely found elsewhere (rarum alibi animal) ; . . . the air is very healthy, and the heat of the sun is tempered by the coolness of the shade and by abundant springs. The forests also were full of snakes the scales of which had the glitter of gold ; none are so poisonous, etc."

The fact that the old Magyar chronicles refer to the *tiger*,[3] seems remarkable, as this animal is not even mentioned in the *Rigveda*,[4] his haunts being in the region of the Ganges,[5] in Bengal, and not in North West India, on the road followed by the Aryan invasion. On the other hand the *lion* is left unmentioned by the Magyar chronicles ; as a fact he lived *eastwards* of the lower course of the Sutlej and the Indus.[6] These considerations would lead to the conclusion that the general line of Magyar migration passed from Bengal up the Ganges valley, along the slopes of the Himalaya to North West India, and thence to regions beyond the Indus.

It should be remembered that, apart from purely linguistic considerations, the alleged Finn-Ugrian relationship of the Magyar is based, amongst other things, upon the idea that the *Ural range* must have been their cradle-land, because there may be found the "*great quantity of gold*" referred to by the chroniclers, and because *the pine*, well known by the ancient Magyar, is the prevailing tree in that region and westwards along the track of their migrations. But in those bygone times, India was certainly better known as a gold-producing country than the less civilized and less explored Ural-region ; further the pine-tree holds exactly the same important position in the slopes of the Himalaya as it does in Northern Europe or in the Siberian mountains.

Let us now consider the statements of the chronicler that the

[1] Lib. IX. Cap. I.

[2] Smith : *The early History of India.* P. 82.

[3] The wearing of tiger and panther skins has kept to this day in Hungary a national character.

[4] See Das : *Rgvedic India.* P. 87.

[5] In his comments to the chronicle of Kézai, Podhradszky speaks (P. 8) about the Ganges, saying that " . . . maiores nostros ex Africa in Asiam, et quidem in orientalem quoque Indiam concessisse, *vetus ergo Persia ad Gangem usque* exporrigebatur . . ." (Our ancestors proceeded from Africa to Asia eastwards as far as India, thus spreading formerly from Persia as far as the Ganges.) And ibid. (P. 155) is also stated, that "nomen Pesio a fluvio Phison seu Gangen *unde Hungari commigrarunt* . . ."

[6] Berriedale Keith. In Chapt. IV of Rapson's *Cambr. Hist. of India.* Vol. I. P. 81.

Scythian ancestors of the Magyar "put to flight" such mighty enemies as *Cyrus, Darius and Alexander.* Anonymus relates[1] that the ancestors ignominiously draw back Darius, who fled panic-stricken as far as Persia. They (the Scythian) also killed Cyrus and "item Alexander Magnum turpiter fugaverunt". Now, attention should be paid to the *sequence*, as Darius is mentioned before Cyrus, although he ruled after him. Obviously, the success won over the former was considered the more important one. As a matter of fact, only Darius and Alexander reached the interior of India in the course of their campaigns, whilst there is no record that Cyrus ever crossed the Indus. He is said to have been killed in 528 B.C., probably not far from the North West frontier of India, and by a warrior of the *Indian* auxiliary troops of his enemies.[2] The Indian origin of these auxiliary forces is proved, besides, by the fact that they had war-elephants within their ranks. (Cyrus lost an army between 545 and 539 B.C. in the country of the above mentioned Orites, a nation who gave much trouble also to Alexander the Great.[3] But as the chronicler definitely alludes to the *killing* of Cyrus, there appears to be no connection between the two events.) *Darius and Alexander,* in the course of their campaigns, both reached the region of the present *Lahore*[4] and had there to turn back. Alexander was obliged to abandon the conquest of the "Eastern Nations" because his troops refused to follow him; these "Eastern Nations" were people who were under the suzerainty of the Empire of Maghada and its ruler Dhana (Tana ?).[5]

The Orites.

The above named Orites are found in the area inhabited to-day by the Brahui,[6] i.e. in the region beyond the Bolan Pass up to Cap Madara, near Bashkerd, on the Persian Gulf. The Orites were not only inhabitants of the sea-shore, since Arian refers also to them as "inland" Orites.[7] Further, the name is said to denote "mountaineers" in general.[8] Their funeral obsequies

[1] Gombocz: In *Nyelvtudom. Közl.* 1917–1921. P. 133.

[2] Ctésias: *Histoire de Perse.* Chapt. VII (Extraits donnés par Photius, traduits par Bouchon).—See also Jackson. In Chapt. XIV of Rapson's *Cambridge History of India,* Vol. I, P. 330, and Katz: *Cyrus, des Perserkönigs Abstammung, Kriege und Tod* (Origin, Campaigns and Death of Cyrus, the Persian King).

[3] Diodor. XVII. 105.

[4] Rapson. In Chapt. XIII of his *Cambridge History of India.* Vol. I. P. 313.

[5] Of the Nanda dynasty, descendants of the *Munda* Ciçu-Nagas.—See Rapson in Chapt. XIII and Bevan in Chapt. XV of the above mentioned *History of India.*

[6] Tomaschek: "Topographische Erläuterungen zur Küstenfahrt Nearchs." (Topographical comments on the Coasting of Nearchos) in the *Records of Sittings of the Viennese Academy of Sciences,* 1890. P. 18.—The *Encyclopaedia Britannica* describes the origin of this people as an ethnological mystery.

[7] Arrian, VI: 22 (3) and 24 (1); VII: 5 (4).

[8] Panckouke's *Comments on Plinius' Natural History.* Vol. V. P. 289.—Comp. the Magyar "orom" and the Maori "oro" (Smith. P. 55), both = top of a mountain; further Maori "oruga" = high up (Ch.).

consisted in the exposure of corpses on wooded hills.[1] Although their clothes and weapons were the same as those of the Indians, their social institutions were quite different and *their speech completely dissimilar.*[2]

The "Scythian". The designation of the Magyar by ancient chroniclers as "scythica gens" and the name "Scythian" certainly do not exclude the possibility of an Indian origin. We know now, that the term "Scythian" was for the Greeks and Romans nothing more than *a collective name* for alien and uncivilized races, just as later on the word "barbarian" was applied in general to people from the East. So under the vague name "Scythian" a large number of very different races were embodied; including all important branches of the Mongolian type as well as some Westasian and Easteuropean nations.[3] This variety of races becomes more obvious when considering the different descriptions given of the Scythians by ancient authors. Herodotus, Strabon and others make mention of Scythian tribes where the death penalty was exacted for the most trivial delinquencies. On the other hand Anonymus relates that "Scythae gentes fuissent sapientissimi et mansveti, qui terram non laborabant et fere nullum peccatum erat inter eos . . .",[4] a description much more applicable to the peaceable Munda races than to the wild and bloodthirsty foes of Rome. What has been said about the nation, applies to the *Scythian language.* "The denomination Scythian"—says Hopkins [5]—"is a very unhappy one. The Scythian words which have been handed down by Greek writers are distinctly Iranian, i.e. they belong to the Indo-European family. But nevertheless the word has been used as a common designation of all those languages of Asia and Europe, which do not belong to the Indo-European or Semitic families. Moreover those languages cannot by any means be brought together into one linguistic family."

For a long time it was also believed, and this is due to Herodotus, that the Scythian were mainly a people of the plains of Eastern Europe, of Central and of Northern Asia. So nobody took the trouble to search for them in the South of Asia also. Especially concerning India their first appearance there was supposed to be their well known invasion in the second century

[1] According to Plinius (Panckouke). P. 77.—Likewise the Maori according to Best. Vol. II. P. 63.

[2] Nagy, in "Századok", 1897, p. 426, asserts that *instead of "Magyar" formerly the term "Magyari" was usual.* (He derives the word from "mad" and "eri" and the latter from the Scythian term "oior" (= man) in Herodotus, (IV. 110).—Concerning "mad" see what is said about Madra on page 122 and page 183.)

[3] Keane. P. 168.

[4] Podhradszky. P. 67.

[5] Hopkins. In Chapt. XII of Rapson's *Cambridge History of India.* Vol. I. P. 282.

B.C. And yet there were "Scythian" in India *much earlier.* Hekateos of Miletos, who lived in the time of Darius I, i.e. between the Vth and VIth century B.C., describes that region of India where the town of Kaspapyros was situated, as a sea-coast belonging to Scythian.[1] Strabon also has something to say about Scythian tribes living on "islands".[2] (Parts of the Massagaetes.) From the records of Herodotus we may learn that Scythian women used *incense* in their "toilette", and this was undoubtedly more easily procurable from the Upper Indus-region or from Cashmere, than from Arabia.[3] As a proof of the large dispersion, if not of the great mobility of the Scythian, it may be mentioned that Bactrian coins of the period of 200 B.C. were found on the coast of Madras.[4] A scholar has been led even to ask: "Are we not induced to assert what has been said already about Phoenicians: that they were chiefly commercial travellers?"[5]

After all, it would be erroneous to draw far-reaching geographical conclusions from the terms "scythica gens". The wild hordes of the Lower Danube were just as well "Scythian" as the Parthian[6] of the Lower Indus, whose royal flag proudly carried the image of the "naga", the Snake.[7] Scythians were just as likely in the South of Asia, as in the North. And the Magyar tradition is not opposed to this, on the contrary it supports it: chronicles speak of a "torrida zona" in the old Magyar fatherland, and in ancient Magyar sagas, in striking contrast with the other Finn-Ugrian nations, *snow plays little part.*

Points of View when Judging the Relationship of the Magyar to India.

Whatever opinion we may have of these different questions, three points of view at least should be borne in mind when trying to arrive at sound conclusions concerning the relations of ancient Magyar to India. First of all we must not forget that reliable records of the history of the Magyar, at least such as bear *an undoubted reference to them,*

[1] Jackson. In Chapt. XIV of the *Cambr. Hist. of India.* Vol. I. P. 336.—Sir Aurel Stein holds the view that Kaspapyros, the present Jahangira, was situated on the confluence of the Indus and Attock.

[2] Lib. XI. Cap. 8 (7).

[3] *Encyclopaedia Britannica.*—Parts of the "Scythians" very likely dwelt in districts of the far Northern springs of the Indus. See Jackson in Rapson's *Cambr. Hist. of India.* Vol. I. P. 338.

[4] Foulkes: "The Pallavas." *Journ. As. Soc.* 1885. P. 209.

[5] Vignier: *L'aventureux Art Scythe.* P. 11.

[6] According to Cuno: *Forschungen im Gebiete der alten Völkerkunde.* P. 192, the name "Parthian" denotes: exiled. Comp. the Magyar "pártos" = revolting.—It is also noted that in the troop of 50,000 horsemen sent against Antonius by the Parthian there were but 400 free men.

[7] Hewitt. In *Journ. As. Soc.* 1889. P. 708.

are not available before the IXth century A.D.[1] Yet many events and connections mentioned here date back some fifteen hundred years earlier. If more distinct traces of the Magyar are not found in Indian documents and literature, we must not allow ourselves to be discouraged, as old literature always deals more with systems of faith, than with nationalities; thus in Indian works no mention is made of even such important events as the invasions of Darius I and Alexander the Great.[2] The exodus of Israel from Egypt may be taken as a further analogy. What a mighty event it was in the history of this people and yet Egyptian chronicles did not find it worth mentioning.

Next, we must not forget either that migrations in those bygone times were not extraordinary events, but almost of daily occurrence. Curtius records that the population of entire districts of Northern India fled before Alexander the Great[3]; and Strabon describes the journey of Aristobulos,[4] who suddenly found a district of more than 1,000 towns and villages entirely deserted by their inhabitants because the Indus had changed its course and irrigation became impossible. Intercourse throughout Asia was as free and complete in a 1,000 B.C. as it is to-day; throughout the East caravanserais, and tracks called roads, existed then as now.[5] One did not go "into the wilderness" when departing on a journey, but on the well-known tracks of individual wanderers. And how intensely this Inner Asiatic traffic was developed, may be judged by the disciples of Buddhism, those missionaries of the VIth century B.C., who chose by preference the subterranean vaults next to the road-passes for their propaganda, because they were certain of always finding resting travellers in great numbers there.

Finally, it should be considered that relapses in the civilization of a nation are not impossible.[6] The absence of needs and of incitement from the outside leave man at liberty to forget and to drop any earlier acquirements, as they have become useless and no longer necessary for the satisfaction of his daily needs. Tribes reduced by surrounding circumstances to the strict satisfaction of the wants of nature, are certain to lose any previous knowledge and arts, as these are henceforth of no use to them.[7] On the other hand no one can pretend that the Magyar, when

[1] Zichy: *A Magyarság Őstörténete és Műveltsége a Honfoglalásig* (Primeval History and Culture of the Magyar up to their Home-Conquest). Budapest. 1923. P. 1.

[2] Rapson: In Chapt. II of the *Cambr. Hist. of India*. Vol. I. P. 57.

[3] Lib. VIII. Cap. X.

[4] Lib. XV. Cap. I.

[5] See also map 2„in Rapson's *Cambridge History of India*. Vol. I. P. 26.

[6] Herman: "Az Ősfoglalkozások Kérdése" (The Question of the primeval Occupations). In *Budapesti Szemle*. 1897. P. 417.

[7] Terrien de Lacouperie: "Beginning of Writing in and around Tibet." *Journ. As. Soc.* 1885. P. 473.

they ultimately reached the banks of the Lower Danube, were entirely devoid of traces of a previous culture. On the contrary, their rich, poetical language, full of colour, their tasteful and manifold decorative arts, and several other details, as for instance the dignified behaviour of their envoys to the Byzantine Court, *give proof of an important history and of a quite considerable degree of civilization attained in the past.* One feels inclined to agree with Huszka's opinion, that the immigrating Magyar were in many ways *more cultivated* than the settled populations they encountered and subjected in the Carpathian region.[1] How anybody, with an exaggerated modesty, could see in this nation, even at the beginning of our era, simply a " hunting and fishing nomad folk ", is just as unintelligible, as the suggested closest relationship with the Suryan, Mordwin, Lapp, Ostyak and other anthropologically entirely different people. As it was already mentioned at the beginning of this chapter, this may be due to the fact that with regard to the classification of Magyar, scholars came to a definite conclusion, *before* great Asiatic families of Languages, like that of Munda, had been investigated ; further scientific research being based simply upon the unshakeable dogma of a *predominant* Finno-Ugrian linguistic relationship.

[1] Huszka : *Tárgyi Ethnographiánk*, etc. P. 1.

Chapter XV.

INDIA AND THE MAORI.

Migrations of the Maori.—The Original Home of the Maori on Asian Mainland.—The Maori as Seafarers.—Seagoing Vessels of the Maori.—Possible Double Composition of Crews.—The Manahune.—Akkad and Sumer.—Connections with Further India. The Site of the Old Homeland.—Stone Culture.—A few Religious Connections with India.—Astronomy.—Ornaments. Inscriptions.

Migrations of the Maori.

The Maori tradition emphasizes, that when their great navigator *Kupe* discovered New Zealand, in about A.D. 950, he did not find a living soul there.[1] Hence it was supposed, that the island had been uninhabited for all time, and that it was the successive arrivals of Kupe's sailor-brethren which were responsible for the first human population on this soil; the last immigration of them occurring in about A.D. 1350.[2] Recent archeological discoveries (Avanui Swamps, etc.) have given a strong denial to this theory [3] and have shown that already in prehistorical times a large culture must have existed in New Zealand. Nevertheless, the fact encounters no scientific contradiction, that those *Polynesian*, those "*Maori*" who form to-day the bulk of the indigenous population of so many islands of the Pacific, migrated thither "per mare", and that one at least, if not the most important migration must have come *from Indonesia*. Besides, it is generally recognized that the spreading of the wandering Maori over the South Seas began from *Samoa*, this group situated so centrally with respect to the islands on the outside. Samoa was known to them at least as early as A.D. 400; some scholars even think,[4] that it must have been, during a probably large interval, *the scene of two settlements of people both speaking the same language*. The dissentiments between the old inhabitants and the newcomers would give a reason for the other migrations. Further, it is most probable, that the route of the migration from Indonesia to Samoa led through *Micronesia*, and not through

[1] Smith: "History and Tradition of the Taranaki Coast." In *Journ. Pol. Soc.* 1907. P. 169.

[2] Te Rangi Hiora (Buck), in his "The Coming of the Maori", *Journ. Pol. Soc.* 1925, P. 379, suggests three migrations of them to New Zealand, the first of which got there "much before" A.D. 1150, the last very likely A.D. 1350.

[3] Brown: *Peoples and Problems of the Pacific.* Vol. I. P. 159; Vol. II. P. 142.

[4] Churchill: *Polynesian Wanderings.* P. 20.

Melanesia. Otherwise an advanced and warlike people like the Maori would scarcely have left such rich islands, sparsely peopled, in favour of the poorer and more distant ones of the Central Pacific.

The Original Home of the Maori on Asian Mainland.

Indonesia is considered by very many explorers as only a temporary abode, whilst the real cradle-land of the Maori is supposed to have been on the mainland of Asia. According to some, it was in India, to others in Central Asia, to others still in countries further to the West: but in every case *their way led through India.* The scholars who think that Asia was the Maori original home are very numerous. We shall mention (partly relying on Tregear): Balbi, Beechey, Best, Bory St. Vincent, Bougainville, Bovis, Brown, Bülow, Calderon, Chamisso, Churchill, Cook, Cowan, Crawfurd, Diffenbach, Dixon, Dumont d'Urville, Fenton, Fleurieu, Fornander, Gaussin, Gobineau, Gudgeon, Guignes, Hale, La Pérouse, Luschan, Lütke, Macdonald, Mager, Marsden, Molina, Newman, Raffles, Rienzi, Skinner, Schaffer, Smith, Te Rangi Hiroa, etc., etc. In spite of this respectable number of scholars, really precise and scientifically irrefutable assertions are so far not available. A reason for this appears to be *a want of sufficient collaboration* between the experts on Pacific questions and those interested in India. This circumstance may also explain how it is, that many, including so distinguished ones as Fornander or Tregear, always search for "*Aryan*" *connections only*, although there existed in India quite other, and much older civilizations.

The most interesting and in some respect pioneer work concerning the original homeland, was Smith's "*Hawaiki, the Original Homeland of the Maori*". His assertions are based mainly upon oral tradition. In this case traditions, however, have a special value,[1] as the Maori attached a particular importance to their *precise* maintenance: in olden days any incorrect reproduction was even visited by capital punishment. Another book published since, by Newman, *Who are the Maoris?* tries to prove that almost every object of daily use on New Zealand can be traced back to India. Unfortunately this work is of less scientific value, because it shows a regrettable lack of system, and is deficient in the quotation of its sources. Moreover Newman's one principal endeavour is to find out "Aryan" connections.—Not without interest is Luschan's point of view on the old homeland,[2] that there is no necessity to any recourse to linguistics and ethnography, because even without

[1] See also Te Rangi Hiora (Buck): "The Value of Tradition in Polynesian Research." *Journ. Pol. Soc.* 1926. P. 181.

[2] *Journ. Pol. Soc.* 1924. P. 78.

their aid, *merely examining their physique, it becomes evident that the Polynesian came from Asia.*

And really, these Maori can never be studied enough, because they offer so many worthy and interesting traits of character. " Imagine a portion of our race "—says Emerson [1]—" cut off from the thought-currents of the great world and stranded on the island specks of the great Ocean, as the Polynesians have been for a period of centuries that would count back to the times of Charlemagne, with only such outfit of the world's goods as might survive a 3,000 miles voyage in frail canoes, reinforced by such flotsam of the world's metallic stores as the tides of Ocean might bring them,—and with such limited capital to start with in life, what should we judge, would have been the outcome of the experiment in religion, in morals, in art, in mechanics, in civilization or in the production of materials for literature, as compared with what the white man found in New Zealand, Hawaii, etc., at their discoveries in the last quarter of the eighteenth century ? "

The Maori as Seafarers.

The respect we must have for this people is increased if we regard their material achievements, especially as seafarers. This point is the more important since it may enable us to find the key of the problem, as to how it was *technically possible* to accomplish oversea migrations of such importance. It may be said to-day without any hesitation that *the Maori were the greatest sailors, " the most hardy race of daring navigators,"* [2] *that the world has ever known.* At a time when our European ancestors were still timidly hugging the shores, the Maori, in their matchless self-confidence, boldly took the risks of the high seas. They used for their guidance the stars, or such shore-sighting birds, as when released would indicate by their flight the direction of land.[3] When sailing in complete canoe flotillas, they resorted to a fan-formation, each vessel within sight of the next neighbour, thus increasing considerably the range of vision. In the Sunda Archipelago, where it was almost possible to sail without losing sight of land,[4] navigations were easier; but when they had to venture upon the open sea, and especially in the case of individual voyages of great distances, their achievements compel real admiration.

[1] Emerson. P. 261.

[2] Churchill: *Polynesian Wanderings.* P. 18.

[3] Such birds were known already since the Vth century B.C.—See also Hornell: "The Origin and Ethnological Significance of Indian Boat Design." *Memoirs of the Asiatic Soc. of Bengal.* 1918. P. 207.

[4] In this Archipelago, where most of the islands are forest-clad down to the water's edge to this day, the water was the principal highway, and this necessitated the constant use of canoes. So Indonesia became the school in which the Polynesian learned to become great navigators. (Churchill: *Polynesian Wanderings.* P. 54.)

This is true first of all of *Tama-reti*, who according to Maori tradition, explored 109 generations ago, thus before 1300 B.C. "with his ship *Uruao*, the first vessel even built by the Maori ancestors,[1] a large part of the world," that is the world known to the Maori of those times. A worthy successor was *Ui-te-rangiora*, who in the VIth century A.D. must have already penetrated into the *Antarctic regions*, because he reported having met polar bears, walruses, etc.—An equally great navigator was *Kupe*; he discovered, as has already been said, New Zealand about A.D. 950. Truly a bold seafarer must have been *Tangaia*, in the middle of the XIIth century; tradition speaks of his cruisings on the South Seas, covering a total distance of at least 12,000 miles.[2]

Sea-Going Vessels of the Maori.

So we see there was no lack of enterprising leaders for the migrations of this nation across the Ocean. We can show now, that there also existed vessels, allowing of extensive transports, even of families with all their household equipments. Already at the beginning of our era, boats were known near the mouth of the Ganges with 100 oars.[3] In New Zealand at the time of its discovery by Cook, the standard type of the Maori war-canoe had a crew of 140 oarsmen.[4] They built sailing vessels of 150 feet in length,[5] and a tradition of the Arawa tribe in New Zealand speaks of three-masters.[6] At any rate, sea-going vessels *of great tonnage* must have existed in South Asia some time before, because on the occasion of a raid, in 550 B.C., "mounted troops," i.e. elephants were carried from the head of the Bay of Bengal to Ceylon.[7] So, it does not seem at all impossible, what Maori tradition says: that on double canoes of 100 or more feet, *complete houses* were transported. Such vessels were called in Samoa: "alia."[8] (A vessel like this, from Tonga, may be seen in a drawing of the time of Cook.[9]) Caillot records[10] about the natives of Mangarewa, that they undertook high-sea voyages on floats capable of carrying even

[1] Smith. P. 115.
[2] Ibid. P. 169.
[3] Newman. P. 112.
[4] Quatrefages. P. 126.
[5] Best. Vol. I. P. 34.
[6] Cowan. P. 4.
[7] Hornell: *Memoires As. Soc. of Bengal.* 1918. P. 210.
[8] Comp. the Magyar word "alja" = the lower part, the bottom of something. —Bülow, in *Die Bemühungen um die Feststellung der Urheimat der Polynesier* (The Endeavours to locate the oldest Home of the Polynesian) is of opinion, that the word "alia" must mean "Häuptlingsschiff" (chieftain's ship), and he traces "alia" to the "Old-Polynesian": "aria," in Rarotonga "karika", thus the true translation of the word being, *according to him*, "Arierschiff" (ship of the Arya).—In: Globus. Vol. XC. 1906. P. 64.
[9] Cowan. P. 44.
[10] Caillot: *Mythes, Légendes et Traditions des Polynésiens.* P. 161.

1,000 persons. In cruises on the high seas, often a daily average of 150 miles and more was covered by the Maori.[1, 2]

Now, it is very curious to note, that there are certain indications, which give ground for the idea, that *the Maori originally were not seafarers.* Traditions tell us [3] that they were instructed in the art of navigation by another race, having more experience of maritime life than their ancestors. On the other hand, we may learn from the ancient writings of India, such as the *Rigveda*, that their writers were acquainted *with river-navigation only*, and had no knowledge at all of the sea and its traffic.[4] This is in some way corroborated by the tradition of the Maori of the Marquesas, who call themselves "Take", and according to which they spread first from "Take-hee" to "Ahee-tai" (and further to "Ao-nui", etc., etc.). Comparing the Magyar term "hegy" [5] with Maori "heie": summit of a mountain, and "heio": the ridge of a hill (Tr.), it seems possible that "Take-hee" is identical with "Take-hegy" i.e. "Mountain of the Take's or Taka's" (Taxila ?), while the word "tai" denotes in Maori: the sea. ("Ao-nui" might be translated as "the wide world".)

Very important, as bearing on the relation between the Maori and India, are the results of a study made by *Hornell*, Inspector of sea-fishing in Madras.[6] He originally started on the task to investigate the connections by sea between India and the Phoenician. But his work led him to surprising results:

[1] Smith: *Hawaiki*. P. 174.
[2] See also Best: "The Maori Canoe." *Bull. Dominion Museum.* No. 7. 1925.
[3] Smith. P. 26.
[4] *Das*, in *Rgvedic India*, P. 32, strongly opposes this view and publishes many quotations from the *Rigveda* in support of his opinion. Further, he thinks, that Munda and Dravida tribes never dwelled at all in N.W. India; that the Arya there had not immigrated, but were autochtones; finally, that their *Rigveda* is as old as at least 5,000 B.C. (P. 66).–The question seems to be here: *is the Rigveda fully and exclusively an Aryan work?* Is it not partially a recollection of the sacred hymns of the Non-Aryan peoples which the Aryan newcomers met in N.W. India; the "poetical soul" of the Munda, e.g. being notorious? Is *Das* right, so many traditions of Munda and Dravida tribes, pointing out to this part of the country are inexplicable. On the other hand, if it is true, that the Arya invasion was a numerically relatively small one, and that it began with the infiltration of the Brahmans (see p. 111), and these men, as good diplomats, accepted, if not tolerated the religions they found, thus securing also the training of the children: it is conceivable, that they have not rejected the songs and hymns they found there, but that they, in some way "built them out". (And then it is not astonishing if they did not recall in the hymns their foreign origin: equally an evidence in Das's eyes for the autochthonism of the Arya.) It may be noted also that even women and people of the lowest classes of society are mentioned as composers of some of these hymns. (See Majumdar: *Ancient Indian History.* P. 92.)—See also Viswanatha's most interesting developments in *Racial Synthesis.* P. 19. (For him it is not much evidence that the Aria used ships in the Vedic times.—For the cradle-land of the Arya see ibid. P. 19.)
[5] See also page 59.
[6] In the *Memoires of the As. Soc. of Bengal.* 1918.

he discovered no evidence whatever of any Phoenician trade influence, and he was even less prepared—as he points out—to find the extreme weakness of Malayan connections. On the contrary, he was brought in face of very vigorous Polynesian affinities; affinities far too strong to have been traceable simply to the extremely limited scale of ancient commerce. The type of vessels employed are also decisive: on the one side those with simple outrigger, used by the Polynesian, and those with double outrigger by the Malay.[1] Hornell concludes that it must have been the same sailors who used single-outrigged boats in the South Seas, who introduced this type of boat on the East Coast of India (they are not known on the West Coast), and that these sailors came to India from the West of Sumatra. (Where, in Mantawei, there still exists a Maori colony.[2])

Possible Double Composition of Crews.

Interesting as are Hornell's conclusions, we must not lose sight of the eventuality, that the people who built and navigated the ships, were not necessarily of the same origin as those who sailed in them; examples abound in ancient history of professional navigators. Attention has been already drawn to the possibility, that the Maori were originally no seafaring nation at all, and a New Zealand legend serves to corroborate this. According to it, the ancestors were compelled to leave " Hawaiki ", their original home, owing to a great war there, one in which they were probably not involved. Before they started on their flight, they took counsel and determined *to build canoes* in which they could go and discover new lands in which to dwell.[3] Obviously, at the time they had no canoes and had never thought before of voyages of discovery. Thus probably they were obliged to apply to other people, forming a sort of guild of navigators, whose profession it was to undertake such transports. These navigators may have come from Indonesia, and were perhaps no other than Hornell's above mentioned sailors from the West of Sumatra. Tradition relates also, that on their migration the Maori sailed in a space of 11 days from " Irihia "[4] to " Tawhiti-roa ", which latter has been identified as Sumatra.[5] It is also possible that the navigators, who according to Hornell came from Sumatra to India, were already Maori who simply returned to the old homeland

[1] See also Best: " Did Polynesian Voyagers know the double Outrigger? " *Journ. Pol. Soc.* 1923. P. 200. Further the same author's " The Maori as Deep-sea Voyagers ". *Journ. Pol. Soc.* 1924. P. 329.—Concerning the boats with single-outrigger, the " waka-ama's " and the double canoes, the " pahi's " as typical vessels of the Polynesian see more in *Journ. Pol. Soc.* 1920. P. 202.

[2] More will be found about this Maori colony in a study of Rosenberg, in *Internationales Archiv für Ethnographie.* 1888.

[3] White: *The ancient History of the Maori.* Vol. IV. P. 29.

[4] " Vrihia " was an old name for India.

[5] Best. In *Journ. Pol. Soc.* 1923. P. 17.

for a visit; there has always been a strong connection between the country known in ancient days as "Kalinga", the land extending from the Godaveri to Gaunjam, and the opposite coast of the Malay Peninsula. From the port of Kalingapatam, for long the greatest shipbuilding centre of the East Coast of India, emigrations started since time immemorial; thence came the "Kling's" to the Malay Peninsula and from there also the people who emigrated from Telingana (Telungana), the land of the Telugu, to Burmah and Pegu, etc., etc.

To what an importance *a guild of sailors* may grow in a nation, and how indispensable they may become: is proved by an example offered by the Maori of Mangarewa. Whilst they are extremely skilled in building houses, these islanders are, curiously enough, incapable of building canoes. The reason may be, that the shipbuilders of this little and sparsely populated island either were once shipwrecked, or for some other reason never returned home, and thus the art of canoe-construction was lost.[1]

The Manahune.

That the Maori vessels carried also people of at least one other nation, is shown once again by their very traditions. These refer to a people of Manahune or Menehune: one of the most interesting ethnographic elements in the Pacific. They, or their traces, may be found everywhere in the South Seas: in Hawaii, Tonga, Rarotonga, Paumotu, etc. In New Zealand the tradition mentions a strange people called "Manauna". They are present in Tahiti also, where one of their kinsmen, "Ta'aroa", attained, 38 generations ago, the rank of a chieftain and became thus the founder of an entire lineage.[2] Besides this individual case, they represented obviously a less eminent class of people, as may be inferred also from a description of them in a Hawaiian tradition. According to this tradition,[3] the Manahune were "small indeed, short in stature and rotund: they were known to be powerfully built, stout and muscular; their skin was red, their body hairy, their nose short and thick set, and their low, protruding forehead was covered with hair. They had big eyes hidden by long eyebrows, and their set countenance was frightening, so that they were unpleasant to look upon. Unsightly was the appearance of their eyes, yet they were not angry or quarrelsome men; on the contrary they were a good natured people who molested no one without cause. They were great builders, even in stone. Their conversation

[1] Churchill: *Easter Island*. P. 80.—In the same way in New Zealand the art of building that special type of high-sea canoes in which the ancestors reached the island has completely disappeared.

[2] Dixon: "A new Theory of Polynesian Origins." *Journ. Pol. Soc.* 1921. P. 82.—See also Smith: *Hawaiki*. P. 150.

[3] Thrum: "Story of the Race of People called the Menehunes of Kanai (A Hawaian Tradition)." *Journ. Pol. Soc.* 1920. P. 70.

was a kind of murmur like the low growl of a dog; yet their laughter was loud voiced. They were in perfect accord in all their undertakings and manner of living. Although they mainly lived in forests, they were clever builders of watercourse with stone".

One cannot refrain, when reading this quotation, from turning one's thoughts to *the Munda Santal*, as portrayed e.g. in Dalton's *Ethnology of Bengal*, to their agglutinative speech, to their good-natured mental disposition, and above all, to their skill as stone-builders.[1]

The "red skin" as well the speech "like the growl of a dog" recall even the description of the Veda given of some Non-Aryan tribes "who are reddish in appearance and utter fearful yells."[2]

With the Munda we get, speaking generally, a very strong impression, that their characteristic good nature inclined them to easily accept to follow, even in large numbers, groups of men of other nations with more initiative and enterprising spirit. Their traditions contain references to such things too; they state that they accompanied "King Ram" on his expedition to Ceylon, etc., etc.[3] As we have seen in Chapter X, it was sometimes *Dravida people* who "encadred" the *Munda.* This latter circumstance gives one reason more to throw a short glance with respect to the Maori Asiatic homeland, also on the old Akkad and Sumer: since Dravida are supposed by some to have reached India from these spots.

Akkad and Sumer.

Some scholars place the ancient home of the Maori on the shores of the Persian Gulf,[4] especially in the region of the Euphrates and the Tigris.[5] The Maori tradition mentioned on page 176, according to which the exodus of this people from the ancient fatherland was due to *a war waging there,* tells us also, that this war was carried out between He-ta and Ue-nuku, and that the battle was called the battle of Ro-to-rua, the battle of the double sun-set, i.e. coinciding with an eclipse of the sun.[6] Now the Sumero-Akkadians called themselves "the black-headed sons of Hea, the fish-god"[7]; and the mother city of the land of the Euphratean delta is said to have been called "Unuk"[8]. Another Maori tradition relates that their ancestors lived in

[1] See also page 181.
[2] *Rigveda* I. 133, 5.
[3] Campbell: *English-Santali Dictionary.* P. 110.
[4] Fornander: *Polynesian Races.*
[5] Others, as Macdonald and Fenton, suppose them to have dwelt even farther to the West. The latter, in his *Suggestion for a History of the Maori People,* even as far as the old Saban, on the South Eastern Coast of Arabia.
[6] White: *The ancient History of the Maori.* Vol. IV. P. 29.
[7] According to Sayce.—See also Hewitt: *Journ. As. Soc.* 1889. P. 385.
[8] Hewitt, in *The Ruling Races.* Vol. I. P. 141.

"Uru",[1] and Ur was the well-known town of the Akkado-Sumerian Empire.[2] From "Uru" they say they migrated, owing to a state of war, to "Irihia", i.e. India, and there to a country ruled by "Kopura". The followers of this latter were so numerous, that a local saying was: "Yonder they move like unto sands of the Ocean."; upwards 750 chiefs were under Kopura's sway.[3] A legend even embodies that the Maori wandered under the chief "Ngana-te-ariki" from Uru to Irihia.[4]

Other allusions also to the *South-Persian Coast* may be found in Maori legends. The white people of the "Turehu", with whom the Maori assert that they lived for ages,[5] had no knowledge of the cooking of food; on the same coast some fishing folk, the "Ichtyophags" of Greek authors, were known as "raw-eaters". The eating of old relations as a sort of veneration, this ancient Maori habit, is mentioned by Herodotus in connection with the population of the same Persian shores.[6] Finally, it is most curious, that many of the objects of Akkadian worship have Polynesian significations, or similar names are found in the sacred lore of the Polynesian.[7]

Connections with Further India. The Site of the Old Homeland.

We have seen Maori traditions recording migrations from Akkad and Sumer. But we must not fail to bear in mind, that many scholars think *differently*. Though they admit migrations from the West to *India*, they consider the *original home* of the "Austric culture", including Austric language, to have been East of it, namely in Cambodia, in *Further India*. From there, in their opinion,[8] this culture passed into *Indonesia* and was also dispersed into Assam, Chota Nagpur and Ceylon westwards, and to Melanesia, Micronesia and Polynesia eastwards. Unfortunately no conclusions whatever can be drawn about Further India from the *geographical terms* [9] contained in the

[1] Best: "The Origin of the Maori." *Journ. Pol. Soc.* 1923. P. 13.

[2] The word "uru" means in New Zealand: the West.

[3] Inscriptions near the mouth of the Kistna, thus on the East Coast of India, mention a king "Kubera", who likely ruled in about 200 B.C.—See Rapson. *Cambridge History of India.* P. 529.

[4] Smith. P. 108.

[5] Best. Vol. I. Pp. 167, 206.

[6] Bevan. In Rapson's *Cambridge History of India.* Vol. I. P. 395.

[7] See Tregear: "Asiatic Gods in the Pacific." *Journ. Pol. Soc.* 1893. P. 130. (He enumerates there 16 names.)—It would be also worth while to investigate the names of the ancient Akkadian Signs of the Zodiac, as quoted by Hewitt in *Journ. As. Soc.* 1889, P. 58, because they seem to be very similar to Maori.

[8] Skinner: "The Austric Languages and Austric Culture." *Journ. Pol. Soc.* 1924. P. 79.

[9] Besides "Hawaiki" and "Irihia", these terms are: Pulotu, Tawhiti, Mataora, Wawa, Pali, Kalana, I Hau, Ola, Hihiri Pipiri, etc.—Some of these words suggest *Indian* connections: e.g. Hihiri Pipiri recalls the Santal tradition of a homeland "Ahiri Pipiri" (see page 125). Further, ancient Chinese travellers

Maori traditions, whilst for the West such terms as Uru and Ue-nuku have been seen.[1] The proofs for an old Maori culture in Further India are to be found in other directions: one of them is supposed to be revealed through the recent *excavations* there, with discoveries dating back several centuries B.C.[2] The chisels, gauges, axes, adzes and other implements of this kind which were dug up, show a remarkable resemblance to Maori implements. Also fish-hooks found there bear a close resemblance to Maori workmanship. The arrow-heads excavated are of bone and never of stone, bearing in this respect a likeness to the arrows of the Pacific.[3] Noteworthy is further the fourfold division on a great number of excavated jewelry (ear-rings); we have seen [4] that this is a characteristic of Maori ornaments. An explanation may be found in these excavations also for the well-known lack of metals amongst the Maori, as they revealed no trace of iron and as the bronze implements discovered were as simple as they were primitive. Thus it is not surprising, that after the few metal tools brought originally by the Maori on their migrations had become worn out or lost, this people never thought of reproducing them.

Another proof of the connection with Further India, or at least with Indonesia is seen in the *cocoa-nut*. Hornell hints that the cocoa-nut is not a native of India; it reached the country by way of Ceylon and Indonesia. Hence we may infer that the people living by its cultivation must have introduced it from the same region. The Maori tradition says that the cocoa-nut was brought from the *old fatherland*.

In any case, it seems beyond all doubt, that the Maori lived at some time in Indonesia.[5] It is supposed, that they arrived there about 450 B.C. and started in A.D. 65 on their new migration. It would be also an interesting question whether there were not two emigrations from Further India to the South Seas,[6] one in very early days by a race which carried with it the *original speech*, and a second which first started from Cambodia to the West and on to India. In this place a mingling may have taken place with Dravida races coming from the West, and later a new

mention a country "Po-liu" or "Pou-lou" westward from Udyana, with its capital on the banks of the river "So-i". (See Levi and Chavannes: "L'itinéraire d'Ou-K'ong." *Journal Asiatique.* 1895. P. 377.)—It is also not bare of interest, that the very numerous "Hawaiki" legends known throughout Polynesia, are entirely missing in Melanesia.

[1] See pages 68 and 178.

[2] Excavations executed at Somron-Seng and Longprao by the Service de Géologie d'Indo-Chine. See Mansuy: "Contributions à l'Étude de la Préhistoire de l'Indo-Chine". In *Bulletin du Service Géologique de l'Indo-Chine.* 1923. No. III and 1925, Nos. VII, VIII.

[3] Barron: "Excavations in Cambodja." *Journ. Pol. Soc.* 1924. P. 335.

[4] See page 88.

[5] Smith: "The Polynesians in Indonesia." *Journ. Pol. Soc.* 1921. P. 120.

[6] See also page 171.

migration may have started with an already somewhat altered language across the sea to Indonesia and from there onwards.

Light upon this darkness may best be thrown by Philology. Churchill has already undertaken [1] to fix the situation of the "ancient homeland" on philological bases. The vision he gives on the greater "Hawa", based upon merely linguistic deductions, is shown by him as follows: "It is a land so high that the air is chill and folk gather round the fire comfort. It is a surface sloping towards the West and the setting sun. It is scored with gullies, sometimes dry channels of rock, and on booming banks with the spate of torrential streams. The Eastern prospect is bounded by a distant sierra, so remote that its outlines are but faintly shown by the rising sun. Between the inhabited Hawa and this limiting sierra is some commonplace natural barrier, which prevents further advance of the people in that direction. The sea it may hardly have been, perhaps it is the impassable drought of desert land, where is no food or water." So far the general sketch of the ancient homeland, to which many other features might be added, collected from the roots and seeds preserved in the language; thus to mention simply one instance: "arisi," the ancient term of Tamil language for rice,[2] must have been familiar to the Maori of New Zealand, as "ari" is the name there for a small seed and a prized food product of the old homeland Irihia.[3]

Stone Culture. When examining the cultural connections between India and the Maori lands, the first, if not the most important features attracting our attention are the *stone-monuments*, such as megalithic stones, monoliths, dolmens, platforms, paved roads, places of refuge, tombs and temples,[4] found repeatedly, and always showing the same character both in India and in the Pacific. The stone implements, which starting from Central India, Chota Nagpur are distinctly traceable through Eastern Bengal, Assam, Further India, the Malayan Peninsula, Indonesia to the Maori lands of the South Seas, and which reach their culmination in the curious stone statues of *Easter Island*,[5] show such a similarity, that, in the opinion of the archeologists they appear to be the work of one and the same race. These implements perhaps are the milestones of a wandering nation, as Parry connects [6] the works of the stone

[1] Churchill: "Root Reductibility in Polynesian." *Journ. Pol. Soc.* 1906. P. 123.

[2] Hewitt: In *Journ. As. Soc.* 1889. P. 205.

[3] "Words and Expressions not included in published Dictionaries of the Maori Tongue." *Journ. Pol. Soc.* 1896. P. 67.

[4] Brown: *Peoples and Problems.* Vol. II. P. 148.

[5] For details see Routledge: *The Mystery of Easter Island*, or Churchill's Appendix to his *Easter Island*, etc.

[6] Perry: *Megalithic Culture in Indonesia.* (An extract by Smith in *Journ. Pol. Soc.* 1921. P. 27.)

using people of the Pacific directly with those of the Khasi of Assam and Eastern Bengal. And Forlong, alluding[1] to the wonderful hill and cave shrines constructed two or three centuries B.C. by *Munda* Nagaists at El-Ura, Ajanta, etc., in India, asks, "who else but these clever builders could have reared the beautiful and massive cut stone-structures of Easter Island?" In the South Seas we find massive stone-works[2] in the Tonga Islands (Tonga Tabu); truncated pyramids of great size in Tahiti; stone statues in Hawaii, Tubuai, Raivavae and in the Pitcairn Islands as also in the Marquesas (Hivoa); stone groves in Tonga, Rarotonga and Niue. Brown says[3] that *nothing could surpass* the symmetry of the design of a stone temple situated 2,000 feet high and recently discovered in the Marquesas. He further draws —and rightly so—attention to the fact, that in the islets of the Pacific it is still more difficult to understand, than even in *Egypt*, how the small communities could afford such tremendous labour as would be necessary for the shaping and transport of stone blocks, many of which are scores of tons in weight.

At this point it is interesting to note, that Maori legends record the existence of big stone works in the ancient "Hawa".[4] They speak about a gorgeous temple "Koro-tua-tini", which was erected by "Tu-te-rangi-marama" and which had a height of 12 fathoms, and was enclosed by a stone-wall.[5] Such legends prove incidentally, that the Maori have a traditional recollection of a higher civilization which once prevailed amongst them.

A Few Religious Connections with India.

To draw up religious parallels between India and the islands inhabited by Maori would supply plenty of material for a voluminous manuscript. Here only a few random comparisons can be dealt with. About the goddess *Miru*, the guardian of the Gates of Death, the Maori legend relates, that "before the deluge" she dwelt on earth in a "pa" (a Maori fort). The "Mount Meru" was on the other hand the Olympus of the Indians, and its site is supposed to have been near the upper course of the Indus.[6] "Miru" is also the name of a prominent clan of Easter Island.[7] Further,

[1] Forlong. P. 119.

[2] See between others Tautain: *Notes sur les Constructions et Monuments des Marquises*, and Mager: *Le Monde Polynésian*. P. 77.

[3] *Peoples and Problems*. Vol. I. P. 240.

[4] Smith. P. 137.

[5] In Maori "tini" means: very many, a host, a multitude, a myriad, and may be connected with the name "Tinevelly" of the Southern Coast of India. On the other hand Bevan writes (in Rapson's *Cambridge History of India*. Vol. I. P. 424), that the name of the extreme South of the Indian Peninsula was the country of "Kori". Here lived the sailor-folk of the Parava; and "Parawa" is the name of an important tribe in New Zealand.

[6] Hopkins: In Rapson's *Cambridge History of India*. Vol. I. P. 253.

[7] Routledge. P. 232.

an Indian term for deluge is "kalpa"[1] and the Maori of Mangarewa denote by "kare, kale": the surf, breaking water, a billow. Traces of the Indian *Bud-cult* may be found amongst the Maori too, e.g. in New Zealand in names of mountain peaks, as Putahi, Puta matakohe, Putanaki, etc.[2] On the coast of the island there is a cliff considered as the "bud" of the national hero Kupe. Besides in the Maori language "puta, putake" means: to be born, the origin; "Pute" is a mythical creator.[3]

A connection between the Maori and the ancient *Naga of India* (or even the present Naga-tribes of Assam, hinted at by Smith for the first time) may be presumed by the prefix "nga, ngati" (= descendants of) of several tribes in New Zealand.[4] Curiously, in the Sanskrit texts the Naga are referred to as a semi-mythological people of *islanders*, having their seat in the waters in the nether regions.[5]

In the same way traces of the *Indian "Mad"-cult* may be found.[6] In India the religious intoxicating drink prepared from the "Mahwa"-tree[7] was called "madhu". (Hence the name of the great drinkers, the Munda "Madra".) In Maori they have tree names such as Mahoe, Mahi, Mahuri, Mahowea, etc. (Tr.). In New Zealand "matewai" means: thirsty and on Tonga "mete": benumbed. They have there also "maihi": uneasy in mind (Tr.); in Samoa "mate" (Vo.) is: "être engourdi, stupéfié", to be benumbed.

Astronomy. The *Maori cult of the Pleiads* had its correlative in South India. Further, astronomical traditions permit of other interesting conclusions. According to Maori tradition, the shooting stars were created first, afterwards the Moon, followed by the Sun and then in succession the constellations of Perseus, Auriga and Gemini. Now, the three latter are stars of the *Northern firmament*: thus the conclusion seems to be justified that this people came from the Northern hemisphere. Their cosmogonic tradition tells us also, that the sky was originally "much lower" and was lifted later on by the gods, and propped upon 10 pillars, all of which were stars. These ten stars have since been identified as known fixed stars; and seven of them belong again to the Northern firmament.[8]

In India as well as in the Assyro-Akkadian calendar, there was for each day a god, to whom the 33, or sometimes only 30 days

[1] Hornell. P. 232.—According to Campbell, in Santal "kalapani" is: the sea.

[2] See: *New Zealand Index.*

[3] Best. Vol. II. P. 392.

[4] The Maori "nga, ngati" has the same meaning as "pu" = to take breath. Besides "pu" denotes also: tribe (Tr.).

[5] Viswanatha: *Racial Synthesis.* P. 79.

[6] See also page 122.

[7] Hewitt: In *Journ. As. Soc.* 1889. Pp. 255, 278.

[8] Henry: "Tahitian Astronomy." *Journ. Pol. Soc.* 1907. P. 101.

of a month were consecrated.[1] Similarly the Maori had special names for each moon-night of their Lunar chronology, and we find that these numbered 28 or 30; in one case even 33.[2]

Ornaments. Inscriptions.

Certain features of the Maori ornaments might be traced back to Indian influences, especially the very popular motif of spirals,[3] as well as the triangular scallops, recalling the pattern of Indian snake-skins. In this connection, very instructive results could perhaps be attained by a thorough investigation, whether motifs of Maori tattooing could still be found in India. E.g. an old, though long ago abandoned method of Maori tattooing consisted of short straight lines, always arranged in *groups of three*. Women, always more conservative where decorations are concerned, are said to have formerly had in New Zealand their eyelids tattooed[4]; a custom of the Oraon of Chota Nagpur and of the Kherwar women of the same region.[5] *Knotted cords* as means of communication were used by Maori[6] as well as by the Munda Santal[7] and their neighbours, the Bhuya.[8]

Concerning the old characters found in *Easter Island*, Terrien de Lacouperie holds the view that they were decayed forms of the South Indian alphabet, the "Vaihu" characters of the Vengi-Khalukya inscription.[9] For the elucidation of the latter problem, another point ought to be taken into consideration, as it may prove an inducement to a renewed research into the origin of these inscriptions. Towards the end of the last century Major Dean, Deputy-Commissioner of Peshawar, had brought to light on the Northern border of his district and in the independent territory beyond it, inscriptions on rocks, an account of which was published by *Sir Aurel Stein*.[10] Some of them,—especially those numbered 55 and 60, found in the Upper Swat region, just above Ramora Fort, on the right bank of this river and on the boundary of the Adenzai Valley (thus not far from that Hazara country which we have repeatedly referred to); further, inscription No. 34, lying close to the village of Chargam in Purau, a country above Boner (thus probably connected with "Mount Meru" mentioned on page 182, and in this way with the clan "Miru" of Easter Island)—show characters of a most decided

[1] Hewitt: In *Journ. As. Soc.* 1889. P. 556.
[2] Best. Vol. II. P. 180.
[3] See page 162.
[4] Best. Vol. II. P. 549.
[5] Dalton. Pp. 160, 248.
[6] Best. Vol. II. P. 201.
[7] Terrien de Lacouperie: "Beginning of Writing in and around Tibet." *Journ. As. Soc.* 1885. P. 428.
[8] Dalton. P. 144.
[9] Terrien de Lacouperie. *Journ. As. Soc.* 1885. P. 444.
[10] In *Memoirs of the As. Soc. of Bengal.* 1889. P. 1.

affinity with some of those composing the mysterious inscriptions of the Easter Island tablets.[1]

In a general fashion, this island is the most interesting of all places inhabited by Maori, because here, on an area of a few square miles only, great riches of almost mysterious relics of bygone times have been preserved. Hewn stone-heads, 23 feet in height, are scattered about in quarries, next to abandoned tools,[2] just as if a secret power of nature had suddenly cast a spell on this activity, stopping it with all its wonderful masterpieces! Brown, dealing in a noteworthy way with this subject,[3] gives us interesting explanations. In his view, the motive power for the Easter Island achievements is especially to be found in an exceptionally strong autocratic power of the leaders, and in a similar strong religious fanatism of the mass influenced. Where could we find more striking examples for autocratic power and religious fanatism even to-day, than in India?

[1] Published amongst others by Routledge. P. 302; by Smith. P. 31; by Newman. P. 256.

[2] Compare also with the *Munda* Ho memorial-stones, huge pillars of rock varying in height from four to fourteen feet, as seen in Bradley-Birt: *Chota Nagpore*. P. 101.

[3] Brown: *Peoples and Problems*. Vol. I. Pp. 288–307.

CONCLUDING REMARKS.

Thus our wanderings between the Antipodes are ended. The subjects included in the study might be divided into three categories.

The first, and by far the largest, comprises material which is naturally not sufficient as yet to justify any definite conclusion: it has been published simply with the idea of giving eventual starting points for future research.

The second, and much smaller category, contains such material as, if carefully used and adequately supplemented, may already allow to expert scholars certain definite deductions.

A third category will supply even to the uninitiated a number of immediate conclusions. If the author restricts himself to one conclusion only: *to the close relationship between Magyar and Munda, and thus to a relationship between Magyar and Maori*,[1] the reason of his reserve may be frankly stated. The present work, especially in its linguistic part, deals with matters about which there already exist very definite and settled theories. Moreover, on these foundations important and complete scientific edifices have been erected. So it is possible, that architects of such edifices may select and expose mistakes and errors of the author not so much with the idea of exhibiting these special cases, but to use them to discredit the whole new theory. It is therefore in the interest of science itself—as the aim of the work is to stimulate further study—that we have avoided bringing forward presently any other conclusion beside the one already mentioned.

In so doing the writer has been guided by no feeling of self-sufficiency whatever. The caution he shows is considered by him as a mere duty towards the men, whose unflinching ardour and self-denying assiduity alone have furnished him with the material for his "Munda-Magyar-Maori". Above all to those propagators of the gospel, who in distant and inhospitable lands laboriously compiled the first Polynesian, as also the first Munda dictionaries. Their work and their life full of self-sacrifice can never sufficiently be appreciated; and if the author has succeeded in suggesting some possible new points of view, the merit is all due to them and to the other first pioneers.

What shall we say of an Alexander Csoma de Kőrös, who started on foot from Hungary to India, to discover there the "lost brethren" of his nation!

[1] Let us say: a Magyari-Mundari-Maori interdependence.—See also page 167, foot-note 2.

And what about the difficulties which scholars have to meet even to-day, as Colenso, the publication of whose imposing Maori Dictionary had to be suspended for the lack of £300; or if we learn from Ray, that though the material of the Oceanic languages is completely collected, it runs the risk of being lost, as nowhere, not even in Australia or in England the importance of its preservation by publication is sufficiently realized.

If his study can contribute in any small way to encourage the furthering of such scientific efforts, the author would consider it as the amplest reward for the pains bestowed on them.

BIBLIOGRAPHY.

"The Times" (London) of the 25th May, 1920.

BOOKS.

Abadie: Les Races du Haut-Tonkin de Thong-Tho à Lang-Son. Paris. 1924.
Arrian: Expéditions d'Alexandre. (Bouchon) Paris. 1837.

Ballagi: Magyar-Német Szótár (Magyar-German Dictionary). Budapest. 1905.
Bartucz: Honfoglaláskori magyar Koponyák (Magyar Skulls from the Age of the Home-Conquest). Budapest. 1926.
Best: The Maori. Wellington. 1924.
Bhandarkar: Lectures on the ancient History of India. Calcutta. 1919.
Billet: Deux Ans dans le Haut-Tonkin. Lille. 1898.
Bodding: Materials for a Santali Grammar. Dumka. 1922.
Bodding: Santal Folk Tales. Oslo. 1927. (Preface from Sten Konow.)
Bopp: Über die Verwandtschaft der malayisch-polynesischen Sprachen mit den indisch-europäischen. Berlin. 1841.
Bradley-Birt: Chota Nagpore, a little-known Province of the Empire. London. 1903.
Brown: Maori and Polynesian. London. 1907.
Brown: Peoples and Problems of the Pacific. London. 1927.
Budenz: Magyar-ugor összehasonlító Szótár (Magyar-Ugrian Comparative Dictionary). Budapest. 1873, etc.

Caillot: Les Polynésians orientaux. Paris. 1909.
—— Mythes, Légendes et Traditions des Polynésiens. Paris. 1914.
Calderon: Tahiti. London. 1921.
Caldwell: A comparative Grammar of the Dravidian or South-Indian Family of Languages. 3rd Edition. London. 1913.
Campbell: A Santali-English Dictionary. Pokhuria. 1899.
Chadurne et Guierre: Marehu Rehu. Croyances, Légendes, Coutumes et Textes Poétiques des Maoris d'O-Tahiti. Paris. 1925.
Churchill: The Polynesian Wanderings. Washington. 1911.
—— Easter Island. The Rapanui Speech and the Peopling of South East Polynesia. Washington. 1912.
Colcott and Havea: Proverbial Sayings of the Tongans. Honolulu. 1922.
Cole: Santali Primer. Pokhuria. 1896.
Colenso: A Maori-English Lexicon. Wellington. 1898. (Letter "A" only.)
Cowan: The Maoris of New Zealand. Christchurch. 1910.
—— Fairy Folk Tales of the Maori. Auckland. 1925.
Cserép: A Magyarok Eredete.—A turáni Népek Őshazája és ókori Története (The Origin of the Magyar.—The Cradle-Land of Turanian Nations and their primeval History). Budapest. 1925.
Ctésias: Histoire de Perse. Extraits donnés par Photius. Traduit par Bouchon. Paris. 1837.
Cuno: Forschungen im Gebiet der alten Völkerkunde (Researches in ancient Ethnologies). Berlin. 1871.

Dalton: Descriptive Ethnology of Bengal. Calcutta. 1872. (Also in German by Flex. Berlin. 1875.)
Das: Rgvedic India. Calcutta. 1927.
Déidier: Précis grammatical de la Langue Maori. Barcelone. 1885.
Deniker: Les Races et Peuples de la Terre. Paris. 1900.
Diodori Siculi Bibliothecae Historicae que supersunt (Dindorf). Paris 1855.
Dixon: Racial History of Man. London. 1923.
Dordillon: Grammaire et Dictionnaire de la Langue des Iles Marquises. Paris. 1904.
Duka: The Life and Works of Alexander Csoma de Kőrös. London. 1921.

Emerson: Unwritten Literature of Hawaii. The sacred Songs of the Hula. Washington. 1909.
Encyclopaedia Britannica. London. 1911.

Forlong: Short Studies in the Science of Comparative Religions. London. 1920.
Fornander: An Account of the Polynesian Race, its Origin and Migrations, etc. London. 1878.

Gait: Census of India. Calcutta. 1911.
Gombocz and Melich: Magyar Etymologiai Szótár (Magyar Etymological Dictionary). Budapest. 1914, etc. (Published as far as the word "dunnyog").
Grierson: Linguistic Survey of India. Vol. IV. Calcutta. 1906. (The part on Munda written by Konow.) Further: Volumes I, II, VIII.

Haddon: Les Races humaines, etc. (Translated from English.) Paris. 1926.
Hall: The ancient History of the Near East. 6th Ed., London. 1924.
Hampel: Altertümer des frühen Mittelalters in Ungarn. Braunschweig. 1905.
Herman: A magyar Halászat Könyve (The Book of Magyar Fishing). Budapest. 1885.
Herodot: Histoire. (Debure.) Paris. 1902.
Hewitt: The ruling Races of Prehistoric Times. Westminster. 1895.
Hochstetter: Neu-Seeland. Stuttgart. 1863.
Hoffman: Mundari Grammar. Calcutta. 1903.
Horváth: Magyarország Történelme (History of Hungary). Pest. 1871.
Huart: La Perse Antique. Paris. 1925.
Hunfalvy: Magyarország Ethnographiája (Ethnography of Hungary). Budapest. 1876.
Huszka: Tárgyi Ethnographiánk őstörténeti Vonatkozásai (Primeval Relations of our material Ethnography). Budapest. 1898.
—— A székely Ház (The Székely-House). Budapest. 1895.
—— Magyar Ornamentika (The Magyar ornamental Art). Budapest. 1900. (Published also in German, translated by Seemayer, Berlin. 1902.)

Ipolyi: Magyar Mythologia (Magyar Mythology). Pest. 1854.

Jacobson: Arier und Ugrofinnen. Göttingen. 1922.
Jászay: A magyar Nemzet Napjai (Days of the Magyar Nation). Pest. 1855.
Jaussen: Grammaire et Dictionnaire de la Langue Maorie. Dialect Tahitien. Paris. 1880.

Jekelfalussy: A magyar szent Korona Országainak Helységnévtára (Index of Place-Names in the Domain of St. Stephen's Holy Crown). Budapest. 1892.

Kálmány: A Hold Nyelvhagyományainkban (The Moon in our linguistic Traditions). Szeged. 1887.
—— Mythologiai Nyomok a magyar Nép Nyelvében és Szokásaiban (Mythological Traces in Speech and Habits of the Magyar People). Budapest. 1887.
—— A Csillagok Nyelvhagyományainkban (The Stars in our linguistic Traditions). Szeged. 1893.
—— Világunk Alakulásai Nyelvhagyományainkban (The Cosmogony in our linguistic Traditions). Szeged. 1893.
Kandra: Magyar Mythologia (Magyar Mythology). Eger. 1897.
Kápolnai: Az Ösmagyarok Miveltsége a Sinaiakkal való Érintkezésük elött. (Culture of the ancient Magyar prior to their intercourse with the Chinese). Budapest. 1897.
Karácsonyi: A magyar Nemzet Östörténete 896—ig (Primeval History of the Magyar Nation up to A.D. 896).
Katona: Historia Critica primarum Hungariae Ducum. Pestini. 1778.
Katz: Cyrus, des Perserkönigs Abstammung, Kriege und Tod. Klagenfurt. 1898.
Keane: Man, Past and Present. Cambridge. 1920.
Kerékgyártó: Magyarország Müvelödésének Története (History of Hungary's Culture). Pest. 1859.
Kézai: De Originis et Gestis Hungarorum. (Published and commented by Podhradszky.) Budae. 1833.
Khittel: Kannada-English Dictionary. Basel. 1898.

Macdonald: Oceanic Languages. London. 1909.
Majumdar: Outline of ancient Indian History and Civilization. Calcutta. 1927.
Man: Sonthalia and the Sonthals. London. 1867.
Marshall: A Guide to Taxila. Calcutta. 1921.
Martin: Catalogue d'Ouvrages relatives aux Iles Hawaii. Paris. 1867.
Missionaires Maristes: Dictionnaire Toga-Français, etc. Paris. 1890.
Morgan: L'Humanité préhistorique. Paris. 1924.
Munkácsi: A magyar népies Halászat Műnyelve (Terminology of Magyar popular Fishing). Budapest. 1887.
—— Árja és kaukázusi Elemek a finn-magyar Nyelvekben (Aryan and Caucasian Elements in the Finn-Ugrian Languages). Budapest. 1901.
Müller: Grundriss der Sprachwissenschaft. Wien. 1882.

Nagy: A magyar Viseletek Története (History of Magyar Costumes). Budapest. 1900.
Newman: Who are the Maoris? Christchurch. 1920.
New-Zealand Index. Every Place Name in New-Zealand. Dunedin. 1925.
Ngata: Complete Manual of Maori Grammar. 3rd Ed. Auckland. (Year of publication not mentioned.)

P.A.C. (Prêtre Mariste): Vocabulaire Arorai. (Iles Gilbert.) Paris. 1888.
Perry: Megalithic Culture in Indonesia. London. 1918.
Pittard: Les Races et l'Histoire. Paris. 1924.
Plinius: Histoire naturelle. (Commented by Panckouke.) Paris. 1830.

Podhradszky: Béla Király névtelen Jegyzőjének Idejekora és Hitelessége (Age and Authenticity of the Chronicler Anonymus of King Béla.) Buda. 1861.
Pulle (F.): La Cartografia antica Dell' India. Firenze. 1901.
Pulle (G.): Historia Mongolarum. Firenze. 1913.

Quatrefages: La Polynésie. Paris. 1866.
Quintus Curtius: Rebus gestis Alexandri Magni. Paris. Hachette. 1912.

Rapson: The Cambridge History of India. Vol. I. Ancient India. Cambridge. 1922. (With contributions from Bevan, Barnett, Charpentier, Giles, Hopkins, Jackson, Keith, Macdonald, Mackinder, Marshall, and Rhys Davids.)
Ray: A comparative Study of the Melanesian Island Languages. Cambridge. 1927.
Reclus: Nouvelle Géographie Universelle. Paris. 1885.
Reischek: Sterbende Welt. Leipzig. 1924.
Rémy: Histoire de l'Archipel Hawaiien. Paris. 1862.
Risley: The Tribes and Castes of Bengal. 1891.
Rivers: The History of the Melanesian Society. Cambridge. 1914.
Rohonyi: A Honfoglalás Története (The History of the Home-Conquest). Budapest. 1896.
Routledge: The Mystery of Easter Island. London. 1920.
Roy: The Mundas and their Country. Calcutta. 1912.
—— The Birhors: a little-known Jungle Tribe of Chota Nagpur. Ranchi. 1925.
Ruggiera: Homo Sapiens. Wien. 1913.

Schmid: Die Mon-Khmer Völker ein Bindeglied zwischen Völkern Zentralasiens und Austronesiens. Braunschweig. 1906.
Simonyi: A magyar Nyelv (The Magyar Language). Budapest. 1889.
—— Magyar Nyelvészet (Magyar Linguistics). Budapest. 1905.
—— Die ungariche Sprache. Geschichte und Charakteristik. Strassburg. 1907.
Skrefsrud: A Grammar of the Santhali Language. Benares. 1873.
Smith (P.): Hawaiki: The original Home of the Maori. 4th Ed. Auckland, etc. 1921.
Smith (V.): The early History of India. Oxford. 1904.
Strabonis Geographica. (Müller and Dübner.) Paris. 1853.
Szabó: A magyar Vezérek Kora (The Age of the Magyar Vezirs). Pest. 1869.
Szarvas and Simonyi: Magyar Nyelvtörténeti Szótár (Historical Dictionary of the Magyar Tongue). Budapest. 1890.
Szinnyey: Die Herkunft der Ungarn, ihre Sprache und Urkultur. Berlin, etc. 1923.
Szirmay: Hungaria in Parabolis. Budae. 1828.

Tautain: Notes sur les Constructions et Monuments des Marquises. Paris. 1898.
Thierry: Attila und seine Nachfolger. (Translated from French.) Leipzig. 1867.
Thurston: Castes and Tribes of Southern India. Madras. 1909.
Tregear: The Maori-Polynesian Comparative Dictionary. Wellington. 1891.
Trumpp: Grammatische Untersuchungen der Sprache der Brahui. München. 1881.

Vaggioli: Storia della Nuova Zelanda e dei suoi Abitatori. Parma. 1892.
Vignier: L'avantureux Art scythe. Paris. 1925.
Violette: Dictionnaire Samoa-Français-Anglais, etc. Paris. 1879.
Viswanatha: Racial Synthesis in Hindu Culture. London. 1928.

Waddell: The Indo-Sumerian Seals deciphered. London. 1925.
White: The ancient History of the Maori. Christchurch. 1874.
Williams: A Dictionary of the New Zealand Language. Wellington. 1915.
Wilson: The Persian Gulf. An historical Sketch from the earliest Times to the Beginning of the Twentieth Century. London. 1828.

Zichy: A Magyarság Őstörténete és Műveltsége a Honfoglalásig (Primeval History and Culture of the Magyar up to the Home-Conquest). Budapest. 1923.

Periodicals.

Akadémiai Értesitő (Informations of the Academy). Budapest.
Az erdélyi Muzeum-Egylet Kiadványai (Publications of the Trans-sylvanian Museum-Society). Kolozsvár.

Budapesti Szemle (Review of Budapest). Budapest.
Bulletin of the Dominion Museum of New Zealand. Wellington.
Bulletin of the School of Oriental Studies, London Institution. London.
Bulletin du Service Géologique de l'Indo-Chine. Hanoi.

Calcutta Review. Calcutta.

Ethnographia. Budapest.

"Globus." Illustr. Zeitschrift für Länder-und Völkerkunde. Braunschweig.

Internationales Archiv für Ethnographie. Leiden.

Journal Asiatique. Paris.
Journal of the Polynesian Society. Wellington.
Journal of the Royal Anthropological Institute of Great Britain and Ireland. London.
Journal of the Royal Asiatic Society. London.
Journal of the Asiatic Society of Bengal. Calcutta.

Keleti Szemle (Eastern Review). Budapest.
Kőrösi Csoma Archivum. Budapest.

Memoirs of the Asiatic Society of Bengal. Calcutta.
Memoirs of the Archaeological Survey of India. Calcutta.
Memoirs of the Bernice Pauahi Bishop Museum. Honolulu.
Mitteilungen der Gesellschaft für Erdkunde zu Leipzig. Leipzig.

Nyelvtudományi Közlemények (Linguistic Publications). Budapest.

Proceedings Pacific Congress 1924.

Sitzungsberichte der Akademie der Wissenschaften. Berlin.
Sitzungsberichte der Akademie der Wissenschaften. Wien.
Századok (Centuries). Budapest.

APPENDIX I.

MUNDA-MAGYAR COMPARISONS.

(Expressions taken from Campbell's *English-Santali Dictionary* and Magyar expressions which may be usefully compared with them.)

APPENDIX I.

The *Munda* languages of India are older than the *Aria* and the *Dravida*.

Grammatically they differ essentially from both the younger; but, on the other hand, the latter borrowed extensively words from Munda, which thus passed into Sanskrit, Hindi, Tamil, etc.

The Munda languages have been little studied up to the present. No exhaustive dictionaries have been compiled, merely lists of words; except in the case of *Santal,* of which the Rev. A. *Campbell* published in 1899 an English-Santal dictionary of a few hundred pages.

This dictionary contains a rich collection of Santal roots and expressions; moreover, numerous examples illustrate their meanings by the quotation of sayings, proverbs, maxims, etc., thus increasing the value of the work.

Side by side with the *Santal words* of Campbell, *Magyar words* have been placed. The latter, as well as their corresponding Latin (German) meanings, are taken from the great *Magyar Etymological Dictionary* of Gombocz and Melich, of Szarvas-Simonyi's *Magyar Linguistic Historical Dictionary*; and occasionally also from Ballagi's *Magyar-German Dictionary.*

Both, the Munda (Santal) and the Magyar expressions have been quoted word for word as they there appear, except for unavoidable curtailments, and, for Munda the complicated phonetical signs, save Ạ, which very closely corresponds to Magyar Ö, and Ń, corresponding to Magyar NY. Thus for a more thorough study readers must consult Campbell himself; and for the exact pronunciation of Munda such special works as those of Skrefsrud, Cole, Konow (in Grierson's *Linguistic Survey of India*), and especially that of Bodding.

Here it may suffice to mention that Campbell's

B	corresponds to the Magyar letter	B (sometimes to V, or even to P, F).
C	corresponds to Magyar	CS (GY, S, TY, ZS),
J	" "	GY (CS, S, ZS),
P	" "	P (B, F, V),
S	" "	SZ (C, Z, and occasionally also S),
Y	" "	J.

The letter h after an initial consonant denotes simply aspirated pronunciation. (E.g.: Bh, Ch, Gh, Kh, Ph, Th, etc.)

The value of the Santal-Magyar comparisons now to be given is lessened through the following circumstances :

The *Magyar Etymological Dictionary*, which otherwise offers a full, extensive, and most meritorious basis, has been brought up only as far as the letter D (the word " dunnyog ").

Concerning the Santal side, it is a defect that words other than of Munda origin may appear also ; Campbell admits himself not to have distinguished between them. (Even a few Santalized English words are quoted by him.) [1]

Further, there is no proof that of all dialects of the Munda family *Santal is the most akin to Magyar* ; a greater degree of affinity with other tongues of this family of languages is also quite possible.

Finally, the cases quoted are far from exhausting the whole vocabulary ; this would require a considerable time, and they must be regarded *only as examples*.

Naturally, an exhaustive study may result in the discovery, that many words which seemed to the author worth comparing, have, in fact, no relation at all. Nevertheless, he thinks, that what he has shown is already sufficient to be of use to those who wish to explore possible connections between the Austric and the Uralo-Altaic groups of languages.

From the special Magyar point of view—a nation which since all time has sought " the brethren lost in Asia "—it may, one day, lead also to historical results.

[1] It would have been evidently possible to make a selection and e.g. to exempt the words known as Aryan ones from the beginning. But it seemed more instructive not to do so. Firstly, because it is obvious if many words considered now as Aryan (Sanskrit, Hindi), were at the advent of the Arya in N.W. India not borrowed by them from the numerically many times stronger Munda tribes ; secondly, as some chronological conclusions might be eventually drawn from the circumstance, if the same Arian words appear in Santal as well as in Magyar.

A

A	Yes
A	Yes.
ABOD	Young, ignorant.
APRÓD [1]	Parvulus, puer = child.-Tyrunculus, famulus, opificium = tyro, novice.
ABOSTA	To waste.
ABÁZOL, ABÉZOL, OBÉZOL	To waste, to lavish, to squander.
ABOT	Not broken to work, untamed.-ABE TABE: Just at the time of.-APRE: I, the speaker, myself, ourselves, commonplace. (E.g. in: "He is like myself." Or in: "Do you see the bride? Yes, she is just like ourselves.")
ÉP	Integer, intaminatus = intact, entire, untamed.-ÉPEN: Just at the time of; just like (myself, ourselves).
AC	Heat, flame.-ACAKME: Increase the heat! (By stirring the fire.)
AZSAG, ÁSAK, AZSAK	Poker.
ḌADAI	To give back, to collect money etc. due, to exact.-ADHON MADHON: To sell at sacrifice, below value, for anything. (E.g. in: "At last I sold it for what I could get.")
ADÓ	Vectigal, tributum = tax, tribute.-AD: To give, to sell.
ADHAPADHA, ATRA PATRA	Imperfectly; imperfect work; to half do a thing, to leave some out, to scamp work.
ÁTABOTA	Disorderly.-ÁTABOTÁBAN: Obiter, negligenter, huc-illuc = superficial, careless, indolent.
AGRA	Blighted, as an ear of dhan. (DANA: Gram.)
AGGFŰ, AGGSZÉNA	Blighted grass, blighted hay.

[1] See the analogy between Santal EBHEN and Magyar ÉBREN.

AGU, NAGU	To bring, exact, charge, deprive. Very common in conjunction with other verbs, giving idea of motion, up to a certain time or place.
NÓGAT	Impello = to exact.–GAT: A very common verbal affix, giving idea of motion to a certain time or place.

AGYO	A skin disease.
AGOS	A child with skin disease.–AG: Skin-maggots.

AHAL AHAL	Distressed, as through hunger.–AHA: To bewitch by looking at one while eating.–AHRA: An edible root.–ATWẠSI PATWẠSI: Famishing, hungry.–(See also ATA SATA and ITẠT.)
ÉHÜL	Famesco = to become hungry.–ÉH: Fames = hunger.–Famelicus = hungry.

AHAP	Quickly, hurriedly.
AHAJT	Instantly, at once.

ẠHLA	Emanation, presence, radiation, motion.
IHLET	Spiritus = spirit.–IHL, EHL: Inspiro, afflo = to inspire, to breathe upon.

ẠIGU	An interjection of annoyance, used by women only.–ẠIYO, ẠIYO GE: An exclamation of annoyance.
AJ, EJ	Annoyance, trouble, inconvenience.–EJNYE: An exclamation of annoyance.

ẠIKẠ	But only, but certainly, with this provision. (E.g. in: "Only it will bite when it grows up; i.e. though it does not bite now.")
AKKOR, AKKO, AKKÓ, AKOR	Tunc = then, only then.

ẠIMẠI	A woman.
EME	Famella: animal femineum = little wife, little woman; a feminine animal.

ẠITẠU	To sift rice, etc. in a peculiar way with hatak. (HATAK: A winnowing sieve.)
EJT	Sino labi = to let fall.

AJARE	To go about gossipping.–AJAR : Heavy ; trouble, bother.
ÁCSOROG	To go about.–AGYAR : A tusk (of an elephant, of a boar).–AGYARKOD-IK : Machinatur = to be underhand, tricky.

AJGUT	Used to express surprise at anything.
ÁSINGOL, ÁSIT, ÁSOYT	Stupescere = to be surprised, amazed.

AJHNAR	Wife's elder sister.
ÁNGY	Sister-in-law ; wife of an uncle or great-uncle or any elder relative.

AJIJ	To implore, to entreat, to beseech.–AJAK : To importune, to beseech, to beg hard, to clamour for. (E.g. in : " He importunes for the book.")
ES-IK, ESENG	Obtestor, oro = to implore, to beseech.

AK	A bow.–AK : Sugar cane.–(See also OK.)
ÁG, AGG	Ramus arborum, frons, propago = branch, bough.

AK	A figure, a numeral.–AKHOR : A letter of the alphabet.–AKUT BAKUT, ANKUT BANKUT : Zig-zag.
ÁKOMBÁKOM	Scribble.

AKA	To hang, to suspend.–OKOT : Hinder, to impede.–OTKAO : To delay.
AKASZT	Suspendo, appendo, applico = to hang, to suspend. -AGGAT : To suspend repeatedly, to suspend by and by.–AKADÉK : Impedimentum, remore obex = obstacle, hindrance.–(MEG)-AKASZT : To delay.

AKAR	Free, exempt, scot free.–AKHIR : End, finally, in clauses to express courage and independence. (E.g. in : " Happen what may.")
AKÁR, AKAR	Libet = as you like.–AKÁR-(MI) : (Happen) what may.

AKASOK	To go to heaven. (ASOK : To wander.)
ÉG	Heaven.

AKHAT	To dispute, to bear ill will, to be at daggers drawn.
ÁKÁCIÓS	Quarrelsome, querulous, litigious.
AKHOR	A short song, one of a course, a dancing stance; the place where an ojha (a charm doctor, diviner) sits with his pupils.
ÁKOROG	To sing in a false voice.
AKO	They, they themselves.-AKOAK: Theirs, their.
ŐK	They, they themselves.-ÖVÉK: Theirs, their.
ALA ẠLI	Tired, run down mentally and physically.
AL, ALAJ, ALJ, ALJAS	Deterior, vilis = decayed, vile (also mentally).
ALAC OLOC	Stupid. - ALAP BAKAP, ALAP OLOP, ALBAKAHA: Unintelligent. - ALABASUA: Deficient in intellect. - OLO: Ignorant, foolish.-(See also AYAK OYOK.)
ÁJUL, ALIUL	Stupeo, stupesco = to be amazed, stupified.-ALAMUSZI: Slow, narrow minded, awkward.-ALANGYÁR: Stupid.
ALAK JHALAK	Conceited, dandified, putting on airs to attract the notice of the other sex, lascivious.
ALAK	Amatia, pusis = darling, pet.-Pretty.-Form, figure.-ALAKOS: Putting on airs.
ALAN	The tongue.-(See also ELAN.)
LÁNG	Flame.-LÁNGOL: To fork (as flames).
ALDHOM, ALDOM	To suppress the truth, tell only the half.
ÁLT	Fallo, seduco = to deceive, to cheat.
ALE	To be satisfied.-ALAO, ALA ẠLI: To give in, to be beaten, to have enough, to be wearied, to be tired.-ALEKHA: Without number, that cannot be numbered.-(See also ELAO.)
ELÉG	Satis, sat = enough.-ELÉGTELEN: Insufficient.-ALAFÁL, ALAPÁL: To beat.-ALANGYÁR: A wearied coat.-ELÉG A: Without number. (It is sufficient.)

ALEC, ALET	To scold.
ALÁZ	Improbo = to scold.

ALGA, ALGAO	To assist, to make lighter for another, to think lightly of. (E.g. in : " Do not trifle with God.")
ERKÖLCS, ELKECH	Mos = moral.

ẠLMẠL	Confused, at a loss to know what to do.–ALMẠLAO : To be perplexed.–ULMẠL : To be perplexed, to be troubled.
ÁLMÊL	Stupere = to be perplexed.–ELMÊLKED-IK Contemplor, meditor, considero = at a loss to know what to do, to contemplate, to speculate.–ELME : Mens, ingenium = sense, opinion.

ALO, ALOALO, ALOGE, ALOTET, ALO BARE	Not, in prohibitions, final clauses and unfulfilled conditions. (E.g. in : " If only it is not lost.")
EL	A, ab (prefixum verbis) = on, away off, forth.–ELLEN : In contrarium = on the contrary.–ELLENEZ : To prohibit, to hinder.

ALOP, ALOP ALOP	A little, a very little. (E.g. in : " He took very little.")–ALAP ALAP : To be fatigued, to be worn out.–ALAK CHOTAK : Imperfectly, to leave out a part.
ALIG, ALEG, ALIG-ALIG, ALIGON ALIG	Vix = scarcely.–ALIGOS : To be fatigued.

AMẠLI, AMLA, AMOLI	Authority, office, title.
EMEL	Exalto, cligo = to heighten, to rise, to choose, to elect.

AMAR OMOR, AMBAR OMBOR	To take up anything lying about, as a child does to busy about.–(See also ELEM CELEM, EPEL, UMẠR and UPEL.)
EMEL	Levo = to take up.

AMAR, TUẠR	An orphan, to become orphan.
ÁRVA	Orphanus = an orphan.

AMDAJ	To make a rough estimate, measure, approximately.–AMADANI : Very much, much.–ẠNU ẠNU, UNU ẠNU, UNU UNU : Of many kind, diverse, different.
ANNYI, ANNA, ANE, AMANNYI, AMANNYA	Tantus, tot = as much, manyfold.

ẠMELẠ	Abundant, unlimited, great in quantity or number.
ÖMÖL	To pour forth, to stream in great quantity, to overflow.

AMKA, ẠMKI	The veiled name by which a child is referred to in the Chatiar (cleaning after child-birth) ceremony.–(See also UMẠS.)
EM-IK	Lacteo = to suckle.–CSECSEMŐ : A suckling infant.

AMOL	Time.
ÁMOLYOG	Otiari, cunctari, moras trahere = to pass idle the time.

AMOL	Acidity of stomach, dyspepsia, to eructate through acidity of stomach.
ÉMELY	Nausea = nausea.

AMPA OMPO	Hurriedly, fussily.
AMPULA	Tortuoso agito = to talk confusedly, to whirl about.

AN	An affix indicating possession.–APATAN : Having a father.–AN : A privative prefix equivalent to the English in, and un.
APÁTLAN	Having no father. (APA : Father.)

ANDA MANDA	To go about aimlessly, to wander about, to be confused. (MANDAMANDE : To stand in the way of others.)
ANDALOD-IK	To indulge in reveries.–ANDALOG : To go about absorbed in thoughts. (MENDEGÉL : To go slowly.)

ANDAK	A method of cooking by roasting.
ANDACS	The broiled and kneaded potatoes of an alcohol-distillery.

ANDHA DHUND	Furiously, severely, with all one's force. This word possesses intensifying force.
ANDOROD-IK	To become suddenly zealous at work, to grow warm, to fly into passionate work.

ẠNDIẠ	Male of animals.–ANDGA, ANDGE : Testicles.–ANDRA : Not effectually castrated.–ANDWẠR : Utter.
ONDÓ	Sperm.

ANGEN	To disappear, to be spirited away by water spirits.–ẠNGIR, ẠNGRA ẠNGRI : To elope.–ANKHER : To absent oneself, to be out of sight.–(See also AŃSET).
ENYVES	Opacus, umbrosus = dark shady, shadowy.–ENY : Praesidium = shelter, protection.

ANGOC, ANGHACAO	To admit, confess, acknowledge.–ẠNGIKAR : To agree, to accept, to take responsibility.
ENGED	Cedo, concedo, consentio, permitto, indulgo = to give assent to, to admit, to allow, to consent, to indulge.

ANGOT BANGOT, ANGOT PANGOT	Aimlessly, carelessly. (E.g. in : " He speaks at random.")–ANKOTHA ANBETHA : Unintelligible, inaccurate, thoughtlessly.–ANKHA ẠNKHI : Disturbed in mind.
ÁNGÓ-BÁNGÓ, ANGÓ-PÁNKÓ	Blockhead.–ÁNKÓ : A good for nothing fellow, dull, stupid, careless.–ÁNKÁL : To work in a lazy manner, aimlessly.

ẠNGRA	Flirtation, gallantry, coquetry.
ENYELEG	Nucor, jocor = to flirt.

ANJAN	An ointment.
ENYV, ENYŐ, ENYŰ, ENE	Gluten, colla = an adhesive substance, glue, lime.

AÑJET	To dry up, to run dry, to die.–(See also ANGEN.)
ENYSZ, ENÍSZ	To vanish, to disappear, to waste away, to perish, to die.

ẠNHUT	Independent, self-willed, opinionative, to persist in opposing.
ÖNHITT	Opinionative, conceited.

ANMAN	Guess, inference, appraisement, measure, estimation, taking careful notice. (E.g. in : " To all appearances, i.e. taking a good look at him, he resembles a Hindu.")
AMANNYA, AMANNYI	Tantus, tot = as much as.–AMÁJA : Certe = certainly.–" AMMÁN Hindu " = " That's a Hindu."

ẠNTHUL	Unconscious, stupified.
ANTAL	Stultus fit, animo in diversa rapitur = to become stupid, to become unconscious.

AORA BẠS	Girlhood. (BẠS : Age, the female breast.)
ARLA	Virgo = virgin.

AP, ABOK, ABUK, ABUN	To wash hands and feet, also hands and mouth after eating.
ÖBLÍT, ÖBÍT	To wash, to rinse (as the mouth).

APA	Father.–ENGA APA, ENGAT APAT : Parents.
APA	Father.

APASUL	To support, to maintain, to nourish, to supply the necessaries of life. (E.g. in : " I brought him up.")
ÁPOL, APOL, APUL	Curare = to tend, to nurse, to foster, to take care of.

APAT, AT	To lose.–AP ; To alight as a bird on tree, house, etc.–APNAO : To cool down after a fit of anger.
APAD	Diminui = to lose.–Decrescere = to decrease.–ALAP : Bottom, base. (AL : Inferus = the lower part.)

APHOTI	Calamity, distress ; to raise objections.
EPESÉG	Acerbitas, anxietatila, negotia = what embitters a persons life, trouble, apprehensiveness.

APTAR	To be littered, to be dirty, litter, leaves etc. lying about.-ABJOR : Litter or rubbish lying about.-APẠI : Fault, rough, irregular.
ABAJDÓC, ABANAJC, ABAJ, OBA	Litter, rubbish.

AR, ARTET	More, in addition to, and, also, other.
ARRA, ARA	Ad hoc = in addition to.-Ad id = and.

ARAK	To loose, to set free, to let go, to allow, to give way, to make way for.-OREC : To tear, to rend, to cut cloth to sew in a garment.-(See also ER.)
ERESZT	Mitto, emitto, dimitto, concedo, crescere sino = to send, to let, to let go, to allow, to allow to grow.-(MEG)ERESZT : Laxo, relaxo, retendo = to make loose or spongy.-ERESZTET : A stitch, a needle-hole.

ARAK	Red, scarlet. (E.g. in : " The fruit has begun to ripen.")-ARAK JHAR : Hematuria. (JHAR : Liquor.)-ARAK PORDHOL : Blood from womb passages. (PORDHOL : Menstrual disorder.)-ARDHẠNGI : Hemiplegia.-HARA : To grow, to increase.-HARATẠL : To become of full age, adult.-(See also IR.)
ÉR-IK	Maturesco = to ripen (as fruit). (SÁR : Mud, filth.)-ÉR : Vena = vein.

ARẠMIN	Outsiders, non-relatives, public.
ARRAMENŐ, ARAMENŐ	Belonging to the public, outsiders (the ambulants). -ARRA, ARA : Ad hoc. (MÉN : To come, to go.)

ARẠNI DAN	A measuring rod.-ẠRI : A measure.-ARPA : The distance between the tips of fingers when both arms are stretched to full length.
ARÁNY	Proportio, dimensio = proportion, measure.-ARASZ : Palmus, spithama = a span.

ARAO	To clothe.
ARASZ	Panni genus = light woollen cloth.

ARAP, AROP	Slightly, to glance off, to miss by a hair's breadth, to graze. (E.g. in: " I shot at him, but only grazed him.")-(See also ARGAT.)
ÉR	Tango, contingo = to touch.-ÉRINT: To touch slightly.

ARDA	In a state of nature, fallow, unbroken. (E.g. in: " Primeval forest.")
ERDŐ, ERDE	Silva, saltus = forest.

ARDU	Of enormous size, applied only to tigers.
ÖRDÖG	Daemon.

ARE	To dam up, to erect a dam, ridges round rice fields, etc.
ÁROK	Fovea, fossa = ditch, trench.

AREC	To bale out water, to throw out water.-ARA: A flock, an army, a crowd.-ẠRIC: Much, many.
ÁR, ÁRASZ	Fluctus, aestus, inundatio = flood.-ÁRASZT: Exundere facio = to let overflow.

ARGAT	Proper time, favourable moment, in good time, morning, early.-ARJAO: To gain, acquire, earn.-(See also ARAP.)
ÉRKEZ-IK	Vaco, vacat mihi = to arrive at, to have time.-ERKEZES: Proper time.-ÉR: Parvenio, pertingo = to reach, to gain, to attain.

ẠRIT, URIT	To see, to look.-ẠRIT KURIT; To stare round about, to look carefully.
ŐRIZ	Specto = to see, to look.-Custodio = to look carefully round about. (KÖRÜL: Round about.)

ARO	In composition has the same meaning as re in English, repetition, again. (E.g. in: " To re-make." Or in: " To beat again.")-ARHO: More, again.-(See also ẠRUK DHẠRUK.)
ARRA, ARA, ORA	Ad hoc = more.-UJRA: Again, re.

ARPA DAHNA	A small quantity of grain given daily to a labourer. (DANA : Grain, food, gram.)-(See also KORPA ARPA.)
ÁRPA	Hordeum = barley.

ARRA ẠRRI	To bellow, to howl, to growl.
ERREGET	(Canis) ringitur = the dog mutters, grumbles.

ARSE	Presents or perquisites given at time of marriage to certain relatives of the bride by the bridegroom.-AKRA : Dear, high prized.
ÁR, ÁRA	Pretium valoris = value, price of something.

ARSEŃ TORSEŃ, ERSEŃ TORSEŃ	Uncomfortable feeling of a person after having eaten too much, or of a person suffering of dropsy ; to be unable to rest at night owing to heat.-PẠRIS, ẠRISI : To trouble, worry, annoy, bore, bother, disquiet, disturb, plague, badger. (E.g. in : " They don't find work a burden.")-ẠRISIẠ : Easily annoyed or troubled.
ÉRZÉS	Sensus = feeling.-ÉRZŐ, ÉREZŐ, ÉRZÉKEN : Facile movendus = sensible.

ẠRTHI PẠRTHI	Odd corners that are not cultivated every year for want of water. - (See also ẠUNTHI PẠUNTHI.)
ÁRPART	Brink of floods. (PART : Bank, shore.)-ÁR : Tide flood.

ẠRUK DHẠRUK	Here and there, everywhere. (DẠRUK : Quickly.)-(See also ARO.)
ARRA, ARA	Eo, istac, illac = there.-ARUNNAN : De eo = from there.

AS	Aim, to take aim.-AS US : To reply sullenly, as a person awaking from sleep.-ASAM USUM ASAN USUN : Half-awake, drowsy, sleepily.-ẠSUK : Uncomfortable in mind.-ASBAS, ESTO BESTO : Confused, perplexed.
ÉSZ	Mens, animus, prudentia, sapientia=mind, understanding, sense, intelligence.-ESZMÉL : Evigilio = to awake.-Reputo, considero = to think, to consider.

ẠSIN	September, October.
ŐSZ	Autumnus = autumn.

ASOK TAYOK, TAYOK	To wander.–ASA JAWA : Coming and going.
	ỵ. AKASOK.
ÖSVÉNY, ÖSZVÉNY	Semita, limes = path, footpath, track.–Diverticulum, frames = crossing of roads, crossway. (TÁJÉK : Tractus, regio = tract of country.)

AT	Zealous, vehement, forcible, strong, intense, vigorous, loud ; to insist, to incite, to persist.
ÁTALL, ÁTU, ÁTOLKOD-IK	Se obfirmare, pertinacem esse = to persist, to insist.

ATA SATA	Food, victuals.–ATA TALSA · Food, such as taben (a kind of parched rice), khajari (parched rice), satu (meal, flour) etc.–ATA : Flour, meal.–(See also AHALAHAL and ITẠT.)
ÉTEL	Cibus = food, victuals.

ATA ẠTI	To dispute.
ÁTÁNKOD-IK	To attack one with words.

ATAL GONDAL	A large assortment of clothes of various ages, qualities, and colours.–ATAR : In composition gives the idea of indifference, outright.–AT TOT : Without certainty, at random.–ATHE ATHON, ATHE ATHWAN : Very close, together, thick. (E.g. in : " He is covered with sores.")–ATRẸ : To plough a field in section, a double rig.–ẠTUR : To hang over, to lag behind.–AT ẠPAT : The very image of each other.
ÁTLÓS	Large.–ÁTALÁNOS : Universalis, generalis = general.–ÁTALÁBAN : In genere, directe, omino = in general, quite.–ÁT : Per, trans, ultra = trough, away trough, throughout, tither, by, by means of, across, during, owing to.–ÁT VAN : To be full and full with . . . , to be covered.–ÁTALOS : In sections (?).–ÁTURU : From behind.

ATAN	To receive, to take, to hold.–ATAN DAK : Water caught in a vessel. (DAK : Water.)–UDẠI : A small bamboo basket.–UDIA : A kind of bamboo basket.
EDÉNY, EDÉN	Vessel.

ATET	A bed.–ATGATE: Strait, narrow, cramped.–AJGAR: Strait, pinch; great, vast.
ÁGY	Torus = a bed.–Area, pulvinus = a vast place, a border.–A channel, a river-bed.

ATO	A village.
ÁTA, ATA, ATÓ	A frequent name for Magyar settlements, or a part of their name.

AṬU	To flow, to shed, to float.
ÁZIK, ÁTÓ, ATTOU	Humectare, macerare = to water.–ASZÓ, OSZU: Fluvius, rivulus = stream, rivulet.

ẠU	Of inferior quality, worthless. (E.g. in: "There is only timber of inferior quality on this hill.")
Ó, AV	Parvus, vetus = inferior, old.

ẠULẠ ẠULI, ẠULẠ KẠULI, ẠULẠ SẠULẠ, ẠULẠ SẠULI	Disordered.
ÜLLE-FÜLLE	Vulgivagus = vagabond.

ẠUNTHI PẠUNTHI	Odd corners and edges which are not cultivated every year for want of water. (PẠUNCHI: To raise a ridge of earth to prevent water to come in.)–(See also ẠRTHI PẠRTHI.)
ÖNT	Fundo = to water.

ẠURẠ, ẠURẠ ẠURI	Vainly, thoughtlessly.–ẠURI, ẠURIAK, ẠURINAK: False, in vain, carelessly, indefinitely, ordinary, unqualified, unfixed, unspecified, ineffective. (E.g. in: "A day not fixed.")–ẠURI SẠURI: Thoughtlessly, in vain, serving no purpose. (E.g. in: "Thou shalt not take the name of the Lord thy God in vain.")–ẠRIC: To pour off liquid so as to retain the solid particles.–URIẠ: To clean out a house.–URMẠL: Small, hollow spheres. (MALA: Beads.)–ẠURI, ẠR: Straw from which the grain has been thrashed by beating it against a piece of wood.–(See also OAR.)
ÜREG, ÜRES	Vacuus, cavus = empty, void, cleared out.–Inanis = vain.–ÜRESKED-IK: Otior, nugas fatior = to idle, to do things serving no purpose.–ÜR: Vacuum = emptiness.

AWALA	Conditioned.
AVVAL	" With it." (" Under the condition.")

AWAR, AOWAR	After-birth, placenta of animals.
ÉV, EV	Pus, sanies = matter, pus.

AWẠSI	An heir.
AVAT, AVÉT, AVÍT	Inaugurare, introducere = to induct, to introduce.

ẠWIL, ẠVIL	To raise the arm, to stretch out the arm.
EVEZ	Remigo = to row.

AYA	Really, truly, without mistake of a truth. (E.g. in : " Of a truth I saw him steal, still he will not admit it.")
ÁJANG, AJONG	Ambigo, fluctuo = to doubt, to admit a mistake of a truth.–AJOG : " Vociferatur, seu ore et labiis operatur, aperiens os suum clamat."

AYAK OYOK, AYAK UYUK, AYOK TAYOK, AYUK TAYUK	Bewildered, at a loss, engrossed, overcome, without resource.–(See also ALAC OLOC.)
ÁJUL	Territus, confusus, stupefactus = bewildered, engrossed, stupefied.

AYAT	A verse, a sentence.
EJT	Profero, pronuncio = to express, to pass sentence on.

ẠYUP	Evening, nightfall.
ÉJ	Nox = night.

ẠYUR	To lead, to conduct.
ELJÁR, EJÁR	Perambulo, pervagor = to wander. (JÁR : Ambulat, eo, gradior = to walk, to go.)

B

BA	Or, either.-BHẠI : Or, whether.-BAKHAC : Or else, otherwise.-BAJE : Some . . . others, sometimes.-BANSE, BASE : Is it not so ? (E.g. in : " Is it not so that you have left us for a long time ? ")-BANKHAN, BANKHAC : Or else, if not, otherwise, of course.-(See also BAN.)
VAGY, WAGH	Seu, vel, out, sive = or, either, otherwise.-VAGY SE, VAN-SE ? : Is it not so ?-VAJJON, VALLYON : Whether.-Nunc (?) = " I wonder if." (?)

BABER	Twine, string.
BÁB	Fasciculus filorum = a skein of twine.

BAC	To deliver.-BOC : To drawn from sheath as a sword, to pull off, to slip off.
BOCSÁT, BACHAT	Dimittere, permittere = to let go, to release, to dismiss.

BACA	To decide upon ; to receive an answer of a witch doctor ; to find out.-BACAO : To choose, to select.-BEJHA : To blame.-BECOL : Of bad behaviour, of bad character, unreasonable. (See also JA.)
BECS	Aestimatio, valor, pretium = value, price.-BECSÜL : Aestimo, censeo = to value, to estimate.-Honesto = to appraise, to honour.-BECSMEL : Viliprendo = to blame.-BECSTELEN : Of bad character, of bad behaviour.

BACHA	A bull calf ; a term of endearment ȧpplied to a child, or younger person.-BAKRA, BAKRU : A male lamb.
BAKSA	A bull kid, less than one year old ; a bull lambkin, one year old.-The male of animals.

BAD	To accuse, to suspect, to accuse from ill-will or a desire to injure.
VÁD.	Crimen = accusation, impeachment.-VÁDAS : Accusator = plaintiff.

BẠDẠI	To be proud, to be vain glorious, to be bumptious, to play the fine gentleman.
BADÁR, BADI	Proud in the manner of a common, rustic person; snappish, foppish, arrogant; elegant, smart.

BADAR	Very dense low jungle.-BADHA BẠDHI: To get hotter, as a quarrel.-BADRAK: With great force or momentum. (E.g. in: "I dashed him down with great force.")-BADRAK BADRAK: Thoughtlessly, nonsensically.-(See also PHADA.)
VADON	The wilderness.-VAD: Indomabilis, effrenatus, intractatus, efferus, ferus, ferox = wild, savage, ferocious, fierce.-Fera, belua, bestia = a wild animal, a beast.-VADON, VADAN: Ferociter, efferate=fiercely, with great force.-VADAS, VADOS: Stultus = foolish, nonsensical.-BADAR: Obscurus = thoughtless, foolish.

BAE	To store, to lay by, to keep shut up, to put in a safe place.-BAHA BAHI: Heaped, piled up, a pile.
PAJTA	A granary, a store.-PÁHÓ: A depot, a magazine.

BẠGHIN	A common thorny climbing shrub. (Mezoneurum cucultatum.)
BAGIFONA	Carduus = thistle.-BAGRÉNA: Acacia, locust tree.

BAHAL	To appoint to an office.-BAHẠLI: An office, a position, an appointment.
BÁN, BÁHÁN	The holder of a certain office.

BẠI	A fit, convulsions, the falling sickness, delirium, insanity, madness, unconsciousness.-BAYOK: To be seized with convulsions.-BAO: Calamity, distress, fear, cholera.-(See also: BANDOR BẠI and BUYUT BUYUT.)
BAJ, BAOS	Molestia, fatigium, malum = trouble, fatigue, distress.-BAJKÓ: Vesatus, stultus = crazy, lunatic.

BAJ	To entangle.–BAJHAO : To entangle, to entrap.
BOGYÓ	Flayer.
BAJA	The fibre of the pericarp of the fruit of the cocoa-nut and palmyra palms ; stringy, as a fruit.
BECSÜ (Ü), BÉCSŐ	Tegumen, triticum, siliqua, folliculus = pod, legume, wheat, the hull, shell, husk.
BAJAR	A market.–BAZAR : A market.–BAJAR KURI DIN : All day long, the whole day.
VÁSÁR	Mercatus = a market.–VÁSÁROL : Emo, mercor = to buy.–VASÁRNAP : Sunday.
BAK	To hook on, to catch on a thorn, etc. (E.g. in : " Look out, you'll be caught by a thorn.")–BAKHOR : An instrument for cutting.–BAKHRA : To share, to divide.–BHAGAO : To divide. (E.g. in : " We will divide this goat in pieces, for convenience of sale.")–BHAGAO : To overcome, to conquer, to gain.
VÁG	Caedo, concedo, seco = to cut, to intersect.–BÖK : Pungo, figo = to pierce, to cut, to stab.
BAKA	Crooked, twisted, bent.
BÖKE	Curvus, flexosus = crooked, twisted, bent.–BIGE, BÜGE : Oxen with small, twisted horns.
BAKARNA	Fit to be weaved.
BAKÓ	Twine winded up on a ring.–BAKOL : To use a hemp-brake.
BAKAT BOKOT	To chatter, to jabber.–BAKBAKAOK : To chatter, to prate, to gabble, to talk idly, talk at random.–BAKHNAO : To talk idly, to prate, to babble, to jaw.–BAKBAKUR : To coo as a pigeon.
BAKOG	Balbutire, haesitare = to jabber, to stammer.–(AZON) BAKSÁG : Gabbling.–BAKARÁSZ : To talk in a confused manner.–TURBÉKOL : To coo as a pigeon.
BAKHER	To invoke, to pray, to beg, to petition. (E.g. in : " They severely scolded their gods in their prayers.")
BEKÉR	Exigo = to call in, to demand. (KÉR : To beg, to petition.)

BAKHERA	Wrangling, vain disputation, a war of words, a row, bragging, quarrelling.-BAKHARIA: Wrangling, disputatious.
BAKAFÁNTOS	Quarrelsome, disputatious.-BAKAFITYERE: A quarrelsome child.
BAKI, BUKI	An insect pest, which injures the young rice plants.-BAKDULU: A species of dragon fly.-BAKJUNU: The fire fly.-BUKU: A white ant.
BOGÁR, BUGÁR	Insectum, vermis = insect, worm.
BAKLAK	The bark of a tree; rind of certain fruits (unripe fruits).
BAKLÓ	Unripe berry of an apple.
BAKOLI	A poetical name for the white paddy bird.-BAK: The white paddy bird.
BAGOLY, BOGOL, BAGUL	Owl.-Falcon.-Hawk.
BALAI	Abundant, so very much as to cause surprise; wonderful. (E.g. in: "He is very wealthy." Or in: "He spoke a great deal.")-BHAL BHAL, BHALE BHALE: Good, rich, wealthy, great, respectable.
BÁLVÁNY, BALUUN, BOLUAL, VÁLVÁNY	Ingens, permagnus = very great. - VÁLASZTIGEN: Magnopere, multum, satis = abundantly, enough.-VALÁL: Possessio = possession, wealth.-VALL: Habeo = to have.
BALBAL, BALBAL DAK	Perspiration, sweat. (DAK: Water.)-BALBAL JIRIJIRI JOROK KANA: "The sweat trickles down."-BAL GADA: Sand washed on to a field by a flow of water.-BALI: Iron stone sand. (The Kol, i.e. Munda iron smelters wash the ore from the sand in the river beds.)
VÁL	Separor = to separate.-VÁLADÉK: Secretum. (ZSIR: Grease.-CSOROG: To trickle down.)-VÁLYOG: Lutum = diluted sand, mud, ooze.
BALE DABI	The ridges of the scapula, or shoulder blade.-(DABI: The shoulder blade.)-BALGAR: Strong, vigorous, mighty.-BOLMAN: Strong,

	well developed, strong and vigorous.-BẠLIS: A pillow.
VÁLL, VÁL	Humerus = shoulder.-VÁLLAS: Latos habens humeros = broad-shouldered.-VÁNKOS: Pulvinar = pillow. (KAS: A basket, a hamper.)-BÁLVÁNY, BOLUAL, BALUUN: Ingens, permagnus = enormous, huge.

BALOK	Young, immature.
BALEK	Simpleton, fool. (In the language of schoolboys: the novice.)

BAN	Not, no (asserting); to deny, refuse. (E.g. in: "Why are you angry.")-BANOT, BONOT: To agree, to be of one mind.-KANA: Present tense of verb "to be", predicative form. (E.g. in: "He is a Santal.")
VAN, VAGYON	Verbum supplendi = a substitution, a complementary word, always in an asserting sense.-Habeo = to have.-Sum, existo = to exist.-VISSZA-VAGYON: Discordo = to be not of one mind.-(See also BA.)

BANA CERE	A bird so named.-(CERE: Bird.)
BENE	A moor-snipe, Scolopax gallinago.

BANAO	To make, to fashion, to prepare, to agree, to live in harmony.-BANGAM: To finish, to do for, to make an end of.-BẠNIJ: To trade, to obtain with some trouble, to search for.
BÁN, BÁN-IK	Tractat, se gerit = to handle, to manage, to treat, to manipulate somebody or something, to be occupied with.-NEM BÁNOM: "I agree"; "well then."-Reliquias colligit, racemat = to glean.

BANBAN, BONBON	Wide, gaping; a rent, a wide hole.
BÁNYA, BANA, BONYAK (?)	Fodina = mine, pit.

BAND	An embankment.
BENT, BÖND	Agger contra eluviones fluviorum = an embankment.

BẠNDHA	Foolish, dull-witted.
BANDÓ	Stolidus = foolish, dull-witted.

BANDOR BẠI	Restlessness, St. Vitus dance, convulsions during which the patient grinds his teeth.–(See also: BẠI.)
VÁNDOROL	Vagor = to wander round, to hover round. (BAJ : Malum = sickness.)

BẠNUA	Unsocial, solitary, hermit-like.–BAN : Sorcery.
BANYA, BÁNYA	Anus, vetula = old hag.

BARAC BURUC	To go about, to run here and there, to go in and out from place to place.
BARANGOL	To go about, to run here and there, to go in and out from place to place.–BARANG : The nomad.

BARAC BURUC	To rise in bubbles.
BURROG	To rise in bubbles.

BARAO	To decompose as hot lime ; to fall down as earth in water.
BARATYOL	To mix something with water, mud.–BARA : Puddle, slough.

BARDURUC	A bat. (DHURUC : Stunted, undersized, puny.)
BŐREGÉR	A bat. (EGÉR : A mouse.)

BARE	May, oh that, please, do ! (E.g. in : " Oh, that he would come ! ")– BAH : Bravo ! Well done !
BÁR, BÁ	Esto, sane facito = well then, indeed.–Utinam = if, only.–May, oh that !

BARLANGA MAT	A species of bamboo. The nodes are far apart, and the hollow within the bamboo large. It is used to make flutes. (MAT : A bamboo.)
BARLANG, BÁRLANG (?)	Cavea = a hollow.–BARLA : Fulcrum = a stick, a baton. (NÁD : A bamboo.)

BAS	Smell, odour, scent; to smell, to scent.–BẠSI: Stale, fusty.–BIS: Poison.–ẠIS: A bad smell.
BŰZ, BÍZ	Odoramen = odour.–Foetor, putor = bad smell, stench.–BUZGALÓ: All kinds of poisonous plants.

BASAN	To heat water.–(See also PELPEL.)
FŐZ	Coquo, lixo, elixo = to cook, to boil.

BASLA	A species of fish.
BASZÁR	A species of fish.

BATA	A quail.–DAK BATA: A snipe. (DAK: Water.)
BATLA	Black snipe.–Tern.

BẠTU, BẠTUẠ	A small bag used to carry small articles in, such as money, tobacco, etc.
BATYU, BATU	Knapsack, bag, small parcel.

BAYAR	A small buffalo kept for breeding purposes.–BAYAR SẠNDI. A cock kept for breeding purposes. (SẠNDI: A cock.)–BUYA: The female organ.
BAJOL	To copulate.–BUJA, BŰJA, BUJÁN, BUJNÁN: Lascivious, voluptuous, unchaste.

BAYAT BUYUT	To let out a secret, to let the cat out of the bag, to peach.–BURYUN: To slip out of a hole, as a snake or fish.
(KI) BÚJ-IK	Prorepo, se evolvere = to creep out, to slip out.–BÚJ, BÚ: Se recipere, se abscondere = to hide, to conceal, to absconder.–(KI) BOJT: Emanare = to emanate.

BEC	To vomit, to be sick, used mainly of children.–TOA BECKEDAE: He vomited milk.–(See also PHEC.)
FECSKEND	To spurt up. (TEJ: Milk.)

BEHAJ, BEHAL, BEJAE	Expressive of wonder or astonishment.
BEH, BEG	Interjectio: eheu quam! quam! = Expression of wonder or astonishment.

BEJE BEJE	Loquacious, garrulous.
BEZSE	Gingrire = to chatter.

BELE	To gather as an abscess, to suppurate, to mortify, to fester, pus.–BALAUNDI : Goats dropping.–BELE : An egg, to lay eggs.–BOL : Strength, might.–BOLE : To ripen.–BOLO : To enter, to go in.–BELA : Time, the sun.–BELA BELA : Time after time, continually, often.
BÉL	Intestina, viscus = intestine, bowels.–Medulla = kern, pip, stone, of fruit, pith, pulp, essence.–Pars interior, animus, sensus, significatio = the interior, mind, disposition, meaning, sense.–BELÉ, BELE : Intro, in = into, in, to enter.–KÖRÜL-BELÜL : Approximately (also for time.)–BELE-BELE : Time after time.

BEMBHA	A simpleton, a muff.
BAMBA	Stolidus, stupidus, stupore, correptus = a simpleton, a muff.

BER	The sun, the distance between the sun and the horizon. (E.g. in : "The East.")–BER ÑOK-KATE : When the morning advances a little.–BARAN : Refulgent as the sun's light before he appears above the horizon.–PIRIT, PIRIT PIRIT : Glistening, resplendent, dazzling, shining.–(See also BEREL and PIẠN PAYAN.)
VERŐ	Sol, radii = the sun, the rays of the sun.–(HAJNAL) PIR : Dawn.–PIROS, PIRÓK, VEṚES : Rubber, rubens, rubicundus = red.–PIRIT : Torreo = to roast.–PERGYÓ : The open air, the free horizon.

BEREL	Raw, unripe, uncooked, fresh, cold. (E.g. in : "The wound is becoming raw.")–BEROT DUK : Any disease or illness, the name of which is not known. (DUK : Trouble.)–(See also BER.)
VÉR	Sangvis, cruor = blood.–VÉRES : Bloody, raw.

BERGA	Small of stature, under-sized, as an ox, etc.–BHIRKẠI BHIRKẠI : A game played by children.–BHIRKẠ ENEC : A children's game.
BIRKA, BIRGE BERKE	Ovis = sheep. (ÉNEK : A song.)

BERHON	Daily wages paid in kind to agricultural labourers. (HON: Daily.)–BARPHẠI: Profit, gain, benefit.
BÉR	Merces, salarium, premium = wages, salary, benefit.

BES	Good, well.–BE-SOK, BE-SAK: Assuredly, without doubt, certainly.
BEZE	Certe, juste = good, well.–BEZZEG, BEZEG: Sane, certe = assuredly, without, doubt, certainly. (Used also to show displeasedness.)

BESAHA	To traffic, to sell, to dispose of.–(See also PẠSIND.)
VESZ, VESZEN	Commercor, emo, capio = to traffic, to buy, to take.

BET	A cane, to flog with a cane, stroke of a cane.
BOT, BATH	Baculus, fustis = stick, cane; stroke of a cane.

BETA	An affectionate form of address.
BADÁR	An affectionate form of address.

BETHA	Pain, to pain one in body or mind.–Inflammation of lungs, or membranes thereof.–BATAR: Unwholesome, inducing illness.–BEDON, BEDNA: Pain, grief, distress.–BED: Adverse influence or hindrance of supernatural kind.–BONGA BETA: Intercostal neuralgia.
BETEG, BETEK	Aeger, aegrotus = ill, sick.–BEDA: Vae = woe.–BENGÁS: Out of health, affected with chest disease.

BEJAE	An adjective or an adverb possessing intensifying force. (E.g. in: "He strives vigorously.")
BEGYES	Headstrong, obstinate.

BEJAR	To suffer from an attack of fever; to be ill.
BEGYÓ	Morbidus = sickly, unhealthy.

BEJHA	To blame.
BECSMEL	Vilipendo = to blame.

BHADES	To be haughty, or supercilious, to spurn, to depreciate, to look down on, to revile.
BÜDÖS	Superbus, arrogans = haughty, arrogant.

BHADET BHADET	Knock-kneed, to walk as one weak in the knees.-BHADIẠL : Knock-kneed.
BEDŐLT, BEDŰTT	Falling in.

BHAG	Fortune.-BHAGAN : Fortunate.
VAGY, VAGYON	Bona, facultates = fortune, capacity.

BHẠIẠDI	Near relatives.
FAJ, FAJTA	Genimen, stirps, genus = species, family.

BHALA	Well, good, well then, you don't say so, let me see then, it does not signify, it matters little.
VÁLLAL, VÁLAL	In se recipere = to undertake, to assume (the responsibility).

BHAND, BHOND	To defile, to corrupt, to defile ceremonially, to corrupt a holy day.-BHANDAO, BHANTAO : To destroy, to lead astray, to pervert.-To defile, to deflower.
BÁNT	Impedire, offendere, turbare = to touch, to deflower, to offend, to disturb, to shock, to wrong, to trouble.-BONT : Turbare, corrumpere = to derange, to destroy.

BHẠNKUR	The sound emitted by anything struck when drawn tight.-(See also PẠIONGẠN.)
BENG	Tunnire = to sound, to clink.

BHAO	To prophesy, to explain, to speak as a person possessed with a spirit of divination, spell, enchantment.
BÁJ	Magia, incantatio, veneficium = magic, spell, sorcery.

BHARO	To be astonished, amazed, to wonder.
VARÁZS	Fascination, enchantment.

BHARSA, BHAROSA	Hope, expectation.–BHARTI HORMO: Pregnant. (HORMO: Pregnant.)
VÁR	Expecto = to expect.–VÁRANDÓS: Pregnant.

BHASA BHARRA	Thoughtlessly, to rave as an insane person. (See also BHOS BHOS.)
VESZETTÜL	Stolide = foolish, silly.–VESZETT (KUTYA): A raving (dog).

BHE BHE	To bleat as a sheep.–BHEBHAO: To bleat as a goat or as a sheep.
BEKEG	Balare = to bleat, as a goat or as a sheep.

BHẠI, BAYA, BOEHA	Brother.
BÁ, BÁTYA	Frater germanus natu major = an elder brother.

BHEK BHOK, BHAK BHOK	Said of a drunken man who has lost control of his mental and bodily faculties.
BÖKKEN, BEKKEN, BÜKKEN	Titubo, vacillo, talipedo = to reel, to stagger, to vacillate.

BHITẠR	The inner apartment of a Santal house.–BHITAR: Inside, within, indoors, to be inside, to put inside, to include.
PITAR, PITVAR	Atrium, vestibulum, triclinium, propylæum = porch, vestibule, entrance hall. (UDVAR: Courtyard.)

BHITUẠK	The petiole of a leaf.
BÜTYÖK	A petiole.–BÜT: Finis = the end.

BHOCO	Stupid, foolish.
BOSÓ	Crazy, foolish.

BHOC BHOCAO	Plentifully, liberally.
BŐ, BÖÖS	Adcopiosus = plentiful.

BHODA	Dull witted.–(See also BHOTO and BODO.)
BEDA	Dull witted.

BHODOR BHODOR — Continuously, without intermission. (E.g. in: "He annoys by continually speaking.")–BOHI: Flowing.–BOHI DAK: Running water.–(See also POLOC.)

FOLYTON, FÓTON (?) — Continually, without intermission.–FOLY-IK: Fluo = to flow, to trickle.–FOLYADEK: A liquid.

BHOE — Fear. (E.g. in: "To be afraid.")

FÉL, FÉ — Timeo, metuo, paveo = to fear, to be afraid.

BHOK — To bark as a dog.

BÖKÖG, BAKÁKOL — To bark as a dog.

BHON — To explain, to decipher, to interpret, to give the gist of.

BONT — Dissolvo, disseco = to dissolve, to decipher, to dismember.

BHOS BHOS — Thriftlessly, thoughtlessly.

BASZUTA — Stupid, awkward.–BASZKA: Foolish.

BHOSA — To pierce through, to stab.

BASZ-IK — Futuere = to have sexual intercourse.

BHOSDON, BHOSNDON, BHASUDAN — Slovenly.

BUSZMOG — To do something slovenly, tediously.

BHOTO — Stupidly, ignorant, dunderhead.–(See also BHODA and BODO.)

BOTOR — Hebes, stolidus, stupidus, bardus = stupid, block-headed, simpleton.

BHUBHUK, BHUK — Distress, sorrow, affliction.

BÚ — Moror, tristitia, dolor = distress, sorrow, affliction.

BHUC BHUCI — Pride, obduracy, contumacy, dogged resolution, headstrong desire.

BÚSAN, BÚSÁSAN — Self-willed, headstrong, obstinate.

BHUCER	To excess, over much.
BÚSAN, BÚSÁSAN	To excess, over much.
BHUK, BHUGẠK	A hole, an opening, a cave.
BÚG	(?) Cavea = bird-cage.
BHULẠ BHẠTUẠ	Wandering about as a half-witted person, thoughtless, negligent, heedless.–BẠUL: Mad, insane, crazy.
BALGATAG, BOLGATAK (BOLOG-ATAK)	Erraticus, absurdus, delirius, bardus = erratic, lunatic, foolish, stupid.–BAL, BALU: Laevus, sinister, scavea = left, awkward.
BHULKẠU	To gush out, to flow out, to rise up, to spring, as water. (E.g. in: "Water rises up from the earth.")
BULYOG	To gush out, to flow out, to rise up, to spring as water.
BHUMBUK	To issue as water in a fountain, to bubble up, as water.
BÖMBÖL	To blubber.
BHUŃCAMPA, BUŃ CAMPA	A spinning top. (CAMAOTA, CAMPTA: A strap or strip of raw hide.)–(See also UŃ.)
FON, FONY	Filo, necto, texo = to spin. (CSOMBÓ: A strip of raw hide.)
BHUNDẠ	Far, large, corpulent.
BUNDA	Far, large, rich (harvest).
BHURKẠK	To raise up earth, as beetles do.–BURBUDUC, BHURBURAU: To bubble, air bubbles to rise to the surface of water when some creature is breathing below.–BURUC BURUC: To rise, as small bubbles in water.
BURROG	The hum of cock-chaffers.–BUBORÉK: Air bubbles rising to the surface of water.
BIBI	Anything living that frightens or hurts, said to and by children only.
BIBE, BIBI	"A word of the children, ulcusculum, vulnus parvulum = a very little wound."

BI, BIK	To be satisfied, to be satiated. (E.g. in: "I gave him sufficient to eat.")
BŐ, BE, BIJJ	Ubertus, copiosus = plenty of, sufficient.–Amplus, largus = ample, wide.

BICẠR	To judge, to consider, to contemplate, to ponder, to devote the mind, thoughts, or attention to. (E.g. in: "A judge.")
VIGYÁZ	Vigilio, excubo, lucubro, speculor = to watch, to contemplate, to devote the mind to.–VIGYÁZÓ: Circumspectus, attentus = prudent, mindful.–VIGYÁZÓ: Episcopus = bishop.

BICKẠU	To sprain.–BICLAU: To sprain as an ankle.
BICSAKL-IK	To sprain (the ankle).

BIJHẠUK	To travail in birth.
VISEL	Partum fero = to be pregnant.

BIJIR BIJIR	To be separated into very small particles, to fly as sparks from an anvil, to scatter as rain drops falling on a hard surface; to separate into small globules, as mercury; very fine, as spray.–BEJEK BEJEK: Foul, as a suppurating sore; liquid filth.
BIZSEG, PEZSEG	To swarm, to abound.–BIZSEREG: To prickle.–PES, PÖS: Urina, lotium = urine.

BIKOL	Uneasy, troubled. (E.g. in: "The mind will be troubled.")
PIKÓS	Ebrius = intoxicated.

BILIK BALAN, BILIT BALAN	To glitter, to flash, to sparkle, to twinkle; resplendent.
VILLOG, VILLAG, VILLAN	Mico, corusco = to sparkle, to glitter, to glance.–VILLÁM: Fulgor = lightning. – (BALÁN: White.)

BINHAK	Falsely, illegally.–BHINGORA: A deceiver.–BHINGRẠU: To pervert, to lead astray.–BIN: The snake. – PUN: Virtue, merit, religious merit.
BŰN, BIN	Peccatum, culpa = sin, vice.[1]

[1] In the Bible the snake is the symbol of *vice*; for the Indian snake-worshippers it is the symbol of *virtue*.

BIR	Jungle, forest.–Further very common in tree names.–BURU : Common in tree, as well in plant names.–BERENJO : A hedge plant.–BEREN PHUL : A pretty flowering plant.
PÖRÖS	A jungle of reed.–BURJÁN : Jungle.–Herba inutilis = weeds. – BIRKE : Grove, bushes, thicket.–BIRITTY : A thorny bush.–BÜRGE : Thick stalked (grass, weeds). – BURJA, BURNYA : Weeds. – BÓR-FENYŐ, BŰR-FENYŐ : A kind of spruce.–VIRÁG : Flower.

BIRẠJ, BIRIJ	To worry ; to harass.
BIRIZGÁL	To worry ; to harass.

BIRI	A fetter.–BIRI HOR : A prisoner. (HOR : A man.)
BÖRTÖN, BERTEN	Custodia = prison, jail.–BILINCS : A fetter.

BIRIT	Trade, calling, profession. – BIRBANTA : A mighty man of valour.–BIROT : At variance, at enmity with each other.
BÍR	Possum = to be able, capable.–Validus sum, valeo = to be mighty.–Possideo, habeo, teneo = to possess, to hold.–BIRKÓZ-IK, BIRIKOZZI-IK : Contendo, certo = to quarrel.

BIRLẠN	To keep a sharp look out on all sides, to be on the alert against enemies from any quarter.
VIRRASZT, VIRROGAT	Vigilo, excubo, pervigilo = to watch.

BISOE	Regarding, concerning.
VISZONY	Relation.

BISPOHOR, BISPHOTKA	Eczema, boils.
VISZKET	Prurio = to itch. – VISZKETEG : Pruritus, scabies = itch, scab.

BISBISWẠS	Certainly, without doubt, without fail.–BISWẠS : Faith, belief.
BÍZ	Fido, confido = to trust, to believe.–BIZALOM, BIZÁS ; Confidence, trust. – BIZVÁST : Fidenter, confidenter = undoubtedly, certainly, without fail.

BITA̤	A span, the distance between the tips of the thumb and little finger when stretched out.
BÜTYÖK, BITIAK	The thumb.

BITON BITON	Separate, distinct, belonging to different castes, or localities.
BITANG	Cattle separated from the rest; belonging not to the herd.

BOAR	A species of fish.
PÉR	A kind of fish.

BODLA, BODOL	To exchange, to substitute.–(See also POD.)
PÓTOL	Suppleo, compenseo = to complete, to restore, to compensate, to substitute.

BODO	Stupid and unable to speak distinctly.–BODOC HANDI, BODOC MELA, BODOC SOTOC: Liquor obtained by squeezing the malted grain.–(See also BHODA and BHOTO.)
BÓDIT	Stupefacere, confusum facere = to stupify.–BÓDUL: Errare, insanire, confundari, mente corripo = to err, to be benumbed, to be troubled in mind.

BOHOK	Head. (In Mundari: BOK.)
BÓKOL	Nicere, nutare = to nod the head (in sleeping).–BÓLINT, BÓLANT, BÓLOG: Nutare = to nod the head.

BOKA	Foolish, stupid.
BÓKA	Foolish, stupid.

BOKOM BAHA	An ornamental tree, the Persian lilac. (BAHA: Flower.)–BHOGA KASKOM: A cotton plant extensively cultivated. (KASKOM: The cotton plant.)
BOKOR	Dumus, dumetum = shrub, small wood, bush, thuft, thicket.

BONDO	Foolish, stupid.
BANDÓ	Stolidus = foolish, stupid.

BONGA	The name given by Santals to the spirits they worship, a demon.
BENGA	Spectre, devil.

BOLAO	To stir up, to interfere with. (E.g. in : " Do not stir up the snake.")
BOLYGAT, BOLYÁSZ	Vexo, turbo = to trouble, to stir up.

BOLIDAN	A sacrifice, an offering.–BULAU : A method of exorcism.
BÁLVÁNY, BOLUAL, BOLUUN	Superstitiosus, idolis inservio = superstitious, to idolize.

BOMBO	Stupid, ignorant, unsophisticated.–BEMBHA : A simpleton, a muff.
BAMBA, BAMBU	Stolidus, stupidus = stolid, stupid.

BOŃBOŃ	Extended to full length ; long.–BONTOBOTOC : A long line or strip, long extending in one direction.–PANTA : A line, a row. (E.g. in : " He can sit in one line as the raja.")
VON	Traho = to draw, to trail.–VONTAT : Produco = extend to length.–VONÁS : Linea = line.–FÖL-VON : Extendo = to extend.

BONGA BARCHI	A common annual plant.–BONGA CAREC : A common grass.–BONGA SARJOM : A common scandent shrub.–BONGA TAENI : A common jungle plant.
BONGOR	Tuft of trees, grass.–Kitchen garden.

BOSERTAK	Incapable, incapacitated ; bungling.
BUSZTOR, BOSZTOR	Bungling.

BOTE	Certainly, correct, true, as you say.
VOLT, VÓT	" It was." (As you say.)–VOLTAKÉPEN, VÓTAKÉPEN : Serio, re ipsa = certainly.

BOTOC	End of a turban, or any part of cloth hanging down behind, resembling a tail.
BOJTOS	Hairy, shaggy, downy.–BOJT : Fimbria pendula in vestibus = tassel.
———	
BOTOR	Fearful, to be frightened, fearsome, terrible, frightful.
BOTOR	Tramp.
———	
BUDA̩	Stock, root, clump, stalk.
BUDA	" Some stalk, used in a game."–BODA : Capsulus, manubrium = handle, stalk.–BODORÓ, BODORU : Proles monogena = the one who has but one child.–BODRÓ : The shoot on the hazel-bush, on which nuts are growing.
———	
BUDA̩K	To break up ground with the plough, to be broken up, as a mud or floor into holes.
BUDÁK	A sort of quadrangular chopping axe.
———	
BUDUC BUDUC, BADAC BUDUC	To bubble up, as water boiling.–(See also BUJUK.)
BUZOG	Bullo, bullio = to bubble up, as water boiling.
———	
BUGUR BUGUR	The sound produced by the blowing of the blacksmith's bellow.
BŰG	Strepere, fremere = to howl, to bluster, to buzz.
———	
BUJ, BUJ SUJ	Wisdom, understanding, sense. (E.g. in : " He speaks with reflexion.")–BUJHANTAR : Wise, clever, sharp.–BUJ BUJHA̩U : To understand what is right and what is wrong.
BÖLCS, BŐCS, BŰCS	Doctus, consiliosus, sapiens = wise, understanding, clever.
———	
BUJRI	Slovenly in dress, cloth round waist too low down, unshapely in waist.
BUGYOGÓ	Wide trousers, baggy breeches.
———	
BUJUK	To spill, as grain out of a hole in a bag, a basket, etc.–(See also BUDUC BUDUC.)
BUGYOG, BUGYAG	Strepo = to rustle, to bubble.–To spill, as grain out of a hole.

BUKẠ CURRUC	A child's game.
BUKKOS	A child's game.–BUGATTYU: Lusus puerorum = a child's game.

BUKU	A white ant.–BOK: The pedicle of the cocoon of the tassar silk worm.
PÓK	A spider, a cantharide, a tarantula.

BUKUR BUKUR	The motion of erd-worms raising up earth from underneath by jerks.–BUKẠ: A bag in a fish or hair net, into which the fish or game drop.–BUGUR: Soft as earth or quicksand into which the foot sinks.–BHUKUR BHUKUR: To bubble up, as water in a spring.
BUK	To jerk.–BUK-IK, BUKÁZ: Lapso = to drop in.–Mergere = to sink.–(FEL)BÚK-IK: To bubble up, as water in a spring.

BUL	To be drunk.
BŰRBUJ	Halfdrunk.

BULKẠU, BHULKẠU	To spring as water, to bubble up, to well up.
BULYOG	To spring as water, to bubble up.

BURHU	To wind twine into a hank, so as to be easily pulled off.
BERHE	" The hank in the twine."

BURI	A small ball, a pill. (KONDHA, KOHNDA: A species of pumpkin.)
BURGONYA	Potato.

BURUI BURUI	To drizzle.
BURDUGA	Drizzling.

BUSAR, BUSER	To be born, to be brought into the world.
BUZULDUG (?)	Abortivus = abortion, monstrous.

BUSKĄ	A species of termite which is very destructive to the rice plant, where there is an insufficiency of water.
BÜSZKE	A large red ant.

BUSKU	To rouse, to exasperate.
BUZDUL	To rouse.–PUZDURI : Irritable, rousing.–BÖSZ : Vesanus, „furiosus, insanus = roused, exasperated. = BÖSZIT : To incite.–BUSZÁMOD-IK : Furiously getting at something.

BUTĄ	The trunk of a tree.
BUTUK	Trunk of wood.

BUTRA, BUTRI	Short in stature, dumpy, dwarfish.–BUTUR : A child.
BUTURA	Misshapen.

BUTUC	Short, applied to the ears of rice, oats, etc.
BUTA, BUTU	Short (?).

BUYUT BUYUT	To prick, to pain, to throb.
BAJLÓD-IK, BAJÓD-IK	To pain.–(See also BĄI.)

C

CABA	All, the whole.
CSUPA	Merus, totus = all, the whole.

CABCAB, CABHCABH, COBCOB	Slushy, moist (E.g. in: "The soil is wet to slushiness.")-COBCOB, CHOBCHOB: Drenched, well moistened, slushy.-CHAP CHAP: Shallow, just covering the surface, as water.-JAB JAB, JABJABAO: Damp, wet, moist.-JABAR JUBAR: Dripping, drenched.-JABDẠHI: Moist, as a field; wet, as a puddle.-JẠPUT: Applied to the raining season's rain; the raining season.-CAPOS CAPOS: Unpalatable, badly cooked.-(See also CẠBUK, CHEPKO, and JHABAR JHUBAR.)
CSÁP	Watery, insipid.-Moist, damp.-CSÁPTOS: Wet, covered with dew (a cloth).-CSAPADÉK: The (raining season's) rain.-CÁPOLOD-IK: Vadare = to walk in mud.

CẠBUK	To dip the tips of the fingers into and transfer what adheres to them on to something else. (E.g. in: "Dip your fingers into the oil and transfer what adheres to them to the palm of the other hand." Preparatory to anointing a person.)-JEBE JOBE: Drenched, dripping.-JHIPIR JHIPIR: Continuous drizzle.-CHEPKO, CHEPRA, CEPRE, CEPROT: Low, small of stature, deficient in height.-JOPOR: Of equal size. (E.g. in: "They are growing at the same pace.")-See also CABCAB, CHEPKO, and JHABAR JHUBAR.)
CSEPP, CSEB	Gutta, stilla = a drop.-CSÖPÖG: Stillo, destillo (both: transitive and intransitive) = to drip.-CSEPEREG: Continuous drizzle.-CSEPÉR: Increscere, adolescere = to grow.

CACO	To toddle, the first walking of a child.
CSOSZA, CSESZA	Toddling.-A little child.-CSÁCSOG: To babble as a child.

CAEKOP, CẠIKUP	Scantily supplied with raiments, as a beggar in hard times.
CSAJINKÁZ	To live in penury.

CAHAL CAHAL, CAHAR CAHAR, LAHAR CAHAR	Quickly, hurriedly.–CAHAP CẠTUR : Excited.
CSAHIN	Alacer, vivax = lively, vivacious.

CẠI CẠI	Used when driving an elephant.
CSÁ	" Vox ad stimulandos boves " = an exclamation used to drive oxen.–CSIGET : To drive.

CẠKI	The patella or knee cap.
CSUKLÓ, CSIKLÓ	Junctura = a junction.

CẠKU	A kind of clasp knife with a handle resembling that of a razor.
CSÁKLYA, CSÁKJA	Mattock.–BICSAK : A clasp knife.

CALA, CALAK	To go, to move, to walk, to pass away.–COLOE BOLOE : Wander about, a vagrant.
GYALOG, GYALAG	Per pedes=to walk.—CSALNIKOZ : To move, to wander about.–CSALÁMBOZ : To wander about, to move here and there. (BALLAG, BALAG, BULLOG : Deambulare = to walk.)

CALAK	Clever, expert, deceitful, fraudulent.–CALAKI : Fraud, trick, deception, knavery.–CHOL, CHOLE : Fraud, deception, knavery, artifice.–DHAL : To obtain goods on credit in the name of another and keep them oneself.–JHALI : A snare, trap, net ; to snare, to trap, to net.
CSAL, CSOLÓ, CSALU	Fraudo, fallo, allicia = to fraud, to deceive, to cheat.–CSÁL : Dolus = trick, ruse.–CSALI : Cunning, sly, tricky.–CSELFES : Versutus, astutus, callidus, fraudulentus = sly, ruse, fraudulent.–CSÁL : Decipula = a trap, a snare.

CALAO	To set in motion, set agoing.–To impel, drive, direct, urge.–To conduct, manage, administer, guide.–To forward, advance, hasten, expedite. To prosecute, carry on.–To meet a demand, pay.–CAL : Conduct, behaviour, life and conversation, character. (E.g. in : " His conduct is not good.")–(See also CELE.)
CSELEKSZIK, CSELEKÖD	Ago, facio, efficio, exerceo, struo = to do, agitate: make, cause, prosecute, construct.–CSELEKVŐ, Agens = active. - CSELEKMÉNY : Actio = action.–Virtue.

CAMEK BAI, COMOK BAI	Spasms with unconsciousness, convulsive witching. (Said to young people when scolding.)-COM : to suffer.-CENBAI : Colic.-CENGA PATHA : Colicy pain in the stomach.-CHAN CHAN : Burning, stinging, smarting, as pain.
CSÖMÖR, CSEMER, CSEMEL	Nausea = nausea, disgust. (Said to young people when scolding.)-The name of some sickness.-CSOMA : The pest.-A kind of devil.-Burning pain. - Diphtheria. - " Tophus podagricus." (BAJ : Sickness.)

CAMPTA	A strap, or strip of raw hide.-CUMKAK : To assemble, to be gathered together. (E.g. in : "A compact village." Or in : " A clump of tree.")-JOMKA JUMKI : All together, in a body.-JOMOK : Together, in a body.-(See also JAM.)
CSOMBÓ	A strip of raw hide.-CSOMÓ : Caterva = a group, a body, all together.-Fasciculus = a bundle.

CAMRIA	A skin disease, in which the cuticle peels off.-Papula, herpes = a pustule, a pimple, a pock.
SÖMÖRGŐS	Pustulis affectus = papulous, pustular.

CAOLE	To husk grain.
CSÉPEL	To trash (as grain).

CAOLE GHURA	A species of fish.-CALHA, CALKA : A species of fish inhabiting rivers.
CSELLE	Phoxinus levis = white-fish.

CAOWAR	The long hair of the tail of the cow or horse.
CSÓVÁL	Caudam movere = to wag the tail.-CSÓVA : Tail.

CAPAR	To be possessed, as by a spirit. -(See also COPAO.)
CSÁBA, CSÁPA	Delirious = possessed.

CAPAT, CAPADOK	To throw ; to be thrown.-CAPOT : To seize prey, by springing on it, as a tiger : to seize and devour.-CABHAO : To swallow.-CAPOS CAPOS : Sound of bellows when being blown.-CAPAE CUPUI : Pressing the feet down alternately, as when working a treddle.-CABUK : A horse whip, a driving whip.-CABUK,

CẠBHUR: Splashing, plumping into water.-CHAP: To print, to seal.-CAPAO: To place one thing on another, to pile up, to increase.-CAPEL, CEPEL: To rise and fall, as water without breaking into waves; moving as a large expanse of water.-CAPCAPA: Wide spreading, extended.-CHẠPILMAN: To overflow.-CABA: To complete; all, the whole.-CEPEL: To fill full, brimful, quite full.-COPA KUTẠ: Rascally, scoundrelly. (KUTẠ: Measured, estimated.)-JABA, JABU: To cut the throat.-JAPAK: To shut to, as a door.-JẠPUT: To pounce suddenly, as a bird.-JHAPTAO: To overrun, to make a descent upon, to attack suddenly.-(See also JAPAN JUPUN.)

CSAP — Infligo, ico, peto, ferio = to throw, to beat, to hit, to cut, to dash, to whip (horse.)-CSAPOD-IK, CSAPAT-IK: To be thrown (intransitive and transitive).-CSAPÁS: Ictus, flictus = a blow, a cut, a strike.-CSAPOL: Promo = to tap (fluid).-CSAPA, CSAPÁS: A spur.-The print of a cart-wheel.-CSAPÁS: A lot of merchandise.-CSAPIG: Brimful.-(BE)CSAP: Invado, irruo = to overrun, to make a descent upon.-Claudo = to shut the door.-To behave rascally, to deceive.-(FEL)CSAP: Deglutio, devoro = to devour.-To put one thing on to another, to pile up.-To rise and fall (as a flame, or waves.)-(LE)CSAP: Prosterno, dejicio = To spring on a prey.-(KI)CSAP: To overflow.

CAPOT SIRIS — A large forest timber tree, Dalbergia lanceolaria. (SIRIS: A large forest tree.)

CSÁP — A very tall, young spruce.

CAPRAS — A badge.

CAFRANG, CHAPRANG, CHAPRAG — Exornat = to decorate.

CẠPRI — A small beetle.

CSEPRŐ — Pertenuis = small.

CẠR SIRA — A large forest tree.-CORCO: A common forest tree.

CSER — Quercus, robur, ilex = name of various species of oak.

CARA	A young plant, a seedling.
CSERE, CSERJE	Frutex = a shrub, a bush.–CSERÉNY : Silva novella = young wood.

CARA DANRA	Cattle taken to a distance to graze and not brought home at night.–CARAPIA, CARAPIA DHON : Live stock, as animal that grazes.–CARA : Forage, fodder, food. (DANRA : An ox, a bullock.)
CSORDA, CSARDA, CSARADA	Grex, armentum = a herd (cattle).

CARAT, CARAT CARAT	Sound of snapping or slapping.–CARCAR, CAR CARAO : Noise of scratching, rending of a branch.–CARCẠRI : A scourge.–CERE PETE : Noise produced by grain bursting when being roasted ; explosive sound produced by wood when burning.
CSARTAT	Strepitum facere, fragorem edere = to make a noise, to clatter, to rattle, to rustle, to crack, to crackle.–CSÁROG : To make a noise.–CSERGET : Scutica personare = to crack or to click with a scourge.–SERCEG, CSERSZEG Explosive sound produced by wood when burning.

CẠRHI	A mane.
SÖRÉNY	A mane.

CARMANDO	To half thresh, as grain.–JHORA : To drive game, to beat for game.
CSÓR	Percutio, verbero = to beat, to thresh.–CSÓRÁL : Frumentum ventilo = to shake grain.–Moveo, agito = to move, to drive, to brandish.

CARORIŃ	A red and black beetle which eats flowers.
CSERE BOGÁR	Bruchus = cock-chafer. (BOGÁR : A beetle.)–CSIRI : A sort of red bug.

CẠLCUL	Separating.
CSALA	Having separating ears (as oxen).

CẠRI	A " lean-to " roof, a verandah, a small house made by resting the roof on the wall of another house, a temporary shelter when engaged watching the crops.
CSŰR, CSÜRÖ (?)	Horreum = shed, barn. – CSÁRDA : Shed, verandah, shelter.–An inn against the heath.

CARNAO	To flog, to whip, to lash.
CSARNA-KÖTÉL	The shroud. (KÖTÉL: Rope.)

CAS	Cultivation, growing crops.–CARWAḤI: Pay of a shepherd.
CSÖRC, CSŐSZ	Guard of crops.–Shepherd.

CẠTẠI	A meeting.
CSŐDÜL	Confluo, concurro = to meet, to crowd together.

CATAI	A measure, both liquid and dry.
CSÁTKÁL	To measure liquids.

CATOK CATOK	Sound as of a dog lapping.–CAT CATAO: Cracking or wrenching sound, as when a branch is being broken.
CSATTOG CSATTOG	Said of the lapping of a dog.–CSATTAN, CSATAN, CSATAG: Percepare, crepitare = to crack repeatedly.

CẠUCHẠL	A babbler.
CSACSOG, CSÁCSAG	Blattare, garrire = to babble, to chatter.

CAWAOK	To ferment, to be distressed, to froth.–CHALE: Scum rising to the surface of any liquid.–TOA CHALE: Cream.–(See also SABAK.)
CSÁVA, CSÁVÓ	Lixivium, nautea = tanning bark, corrosion.–CSÁVA: Pinch.–CSÁVÁBA KERÜLNI: "To be in a fix . . ."–SAV: Acid.–SAVÓ: Serum, lac emulctum = whey, cream. (LÉ: Juice, liquor.–TEJ: Milk.)

CAYA	A stinking, flying bug, said to leave a smell on grain on which it may alight.
CSÁJA	Name for various kinds of bug.–Cock-chafer.

CEK	Squeal of some animals.
CSEKEG	Gannere = to bark, to yelp.

CELE — Who, what (animate). (E.g. in: " Who is he ? " Or in: " What is it ? A tiger."–" It is not known what it may turn out, whether a cock or a hen.")–CEDAK: To do, used generally when fault finding. (E.g. in: " What were you doing ? ").–CEDAK: Why, wherefore. (E.g. in: " Why have you come ? ").–CETAT: What thing, something.–CEKA: What to do, what to happen. (E.g. in: " What will happen to me ? " Or in: " They will do nothing.")–CEKAN: What sort.–CEKA LEKA: Like what, like how, in what way. (E.g. in: " I do not know what they may do to me.")–JAHA: Any, whatever.–JATE: In whatever way.–(See also CALAO.)

(MI)CSODA, (MI)CSEDA, (MI)CSE — Quodnam ? Quidnam ? = What ? Qui ? Quae ? Quod ? Qualis ? = Which kind of, what kind of ?–(KI)CSODA, (KI)CSE: Who ? (LAG, LEG: Like, like how, in what way.)–(CSELEKEDET: What to do, the action.)

CELKO MELKO — Wanton, flirting, smart, applied only to females.–CEMKEC: Tidy, clean, trim, prepossessing of young women only.

CSALINGÓS — Wanton, flirting.–CSEMPESKED-IK: To flirt.–CSECSE: Pulcher, venustus = pretty, nice, neat, dainty.

CEMAT — To be proficient, to master anything, such as carpentry, dancing, etc. (E.g. in: " He has mastered a well.")

CSINÁL, CHENÁL — Facere, agere = to make, to master.–Conficere, condere = to make, to fabricate, to construct.

CEPA — A piece of turf.–(See also COPO TORO.)

GYEP, GYEPÜ — Herbetum = turf.

CEPEL — Low, as ridge of rice field, etc.

CSEPEL — A frequent name of localities.

CEPRE — A kind of earring.

CSERCSE — Inaüris = earring.

CEPTHE — To stick or adhere together.

CSEPZ-IK — To stick or adhere together.

CERE	A bird.-JHOROJHOC: The Pied Crested Cuckoo. (Coccystis jacobinus.)
CSÉR	A bird.-CSINCSERE: A bird. (Parus.)-CSIRA, CSÓR, CSŐRÉSZ: A bird.-(Larus.)-CSIRE: A bird.-(Hydrochelidon.)-CSÉRJA: A bird. (Sterna.)-CSERKA: A duck-like, aquatic bird.-CSERKÓ: A bird. (Sterna hirundo.)
CEREA	Undersized, stunted, small.-COROETHO: Puny, stunted.
CSŐRE	Undersized, stunted.
CERKA BERKA	Spotted.
TARKA BARKA, BARKA	Variegatus = spotted.
CEROBERO	To twitter, as birds; applied also to the chatter of children.
CSERE-CSURÁL	To chatter, to babble.
CET	Miserly, niggardly.
CSETTEN, MEGCSETTEN	Desperare = to despair.
CETAK	To slap.-CEWAK: To chop, to cut through by chopping.
CSETTEG	To slap.-CSETTEN: Sound of cracking or rending. (VÁG: To cut.)
CETE CETE	Talkative, always putting in one's words.
CSETRES	Garrulus, loquax = talkative, tattling.-CSETE (CSETE-PÁTÉ): Dispute.
CETER	A thunderbolt.
CSÜTÖRTÖK CSETERTEK	Thursday.
CEWAK	To do, used when finding fault. (E.g. in "Where and in what mischief were you.")
CSÉVELYEG, CSÉVELEG	To rove about.

CHABHA	A small earthen-ware pot.
CSOBA	An earthen-ware drinking pot; the pot.

CHALA BADLA	Pack bullock.
CSÁLÉ	An oxen-name.

CHALE	Cataract; also applied to blindness from corneal opacity.
CSOLLÁK	Ụnoculos = having only one eye.-Strabo, luscus = squint-eyed.

CHẠLIẠ, CHẠILẠ	A game played by children.
CSÁBLÉZÁS	Lusus puerorum = children's play.

CHATAR	A framework attached to the rafters on which the thatch is laid.-CHOTOR: A cloth umbrella.-CHẠLDẠRI, CHOLDORI: A small one-ply tent.
SÁTOR	Tentorium, velaria = tent.

CHEŃCHEŃ	Tinkling sound, as that of cracked cymbals, or steel struck by steel.
CSENG	To tinkle

CHENCHAO	To flog, to chastise.
CSENDERIT	To flog (with a whip).

CHEO	To wound, to bruise. (E.g. in: "They cut and wound me.")
SEB	Vulnus = a wound.

CHEPKO	Low, small in stature, deficient in height.-COPA: Puny.-COPOT: Low.-JHAP: A bribe.-(See also CABCAB, CẠBUK, and JHABAR JHUBUR.)
CSEPKE	Parvulus = small in stature, deficient in height.-CSEPP, CSEB: Paululus = very little, small.-A bribe.-CSOPAK: Of small stature.-CSOPÁK: Cattle of little size.

CHIẠK	Low, despicable, contemptible.
CSIÁPOL	Aegroto, tabesco = to vegetate, to pine away, to live in misery, despicably.–(On plants, sick animals or even as a cannibal.)

CHIK CHOK	Bright, plump, looking glossy as the skin of a well fed and well groomed horse. (E.g. in: "The horse is fat and glossy skinned." Or in: "The bright heavens.")–CI HO HO: Neighing of horses.
CSIKÓ	Hinnulus, pullus equineus, equleus = mare, filly.–CSILLOG, CSILOG: Mico, corusco = to shine, to beam (as the heavens).–CSIHI, CSIHÓ (?): To urge a horse to start.

CHILBILẠU	To rush hither and thither.
CSILLAT	To let leap about (a horse).

CHIN	Appearance, shape, form, bodily representation, disguise, semblance, likeness.–CUNU MUNU: Dainty, neat and tiny.
CSÍN	Decor, cultus, elegantia, situs, natura, structura = appearance, culture, smartness, figure, nature, structure, bodily representation.–CSINOS: Concinnus, ordinatus = well arranged, dainty, neat, elegant.

CHIP	Highest point, top pinnacle, as of a tree or steeple.
CSÍK, CSÍP (?)	Cacumen, vertex montis = highest point, top pinnacle of a mountain.

CHOT	Band to bind sheaves when harvesting.–CHONT: Band to bind a sheaf.
CSÓT, CSAT	Hamus, fibula = buckle, clasp.–CSATOL: Confibulare, connectere = to strap, to bind.

CHUC	A needle.–CUICUI: Pointed, tapering to a point in form of a cone.
CSÚCS	Cacumen = point.–CSUCSA: Lancea, hasta = lance.–CSÚCSOS: Accuminatus, cupidatus, turbinatus = pointed.

CHUCHKAR	To speak kindly, to allay fear or suspicion, to coax.
CSUCSOGATÁS	To coax.–To act in order to allay fear or suspicion of a horse.

CIẠP CIẠP	Cheaping of chicken.
CSIÁPOL	Pipio=cheaping of chicken.

CIGURI	An apparatus for raising heavy beams when beyond the height to which men can reach, consisting of two poles crossed at the top and securely tied.–JHIK: To tighten a rope by twisting it with a piece of wood as lever.
CSIGA	Lifting jack, pulley ("quaedam instrumenta ad bombardos nostras pertinentia, vulgariter chyga vel czweg appellata.")–CSIKAR, CSIKOR: Torqueo = to wind.

CIHIK BẠI, CIHKI BẠI	Nervous spasms, twitching, starting suddenly, shuddering.
CSIHARI	Epilepsy.

CIKAN, CIKON, CIKAR	Smooth, glossy, slimy, polished, glazed, perfect.–SIKIL: To polish, to burnish.–SOKA SUKI, SOKHA SUKHI: On the same level, equal, even.–JIKI, JIKIC JIKIC: To move while in a sitting posture, dragging the posteriors along the ground.–(See also SIKIL.)
SÍK	Lubricus, levis = smooth, even.–SIKAM: Locus lubricus = a slimy ground.–SIKÁROL: Poligo, levigo = to smooth.–SIKIT: Deplano, explano, complano = to smooth, to plane, to level.–SIKLIK: To slant.

CIKHNẠ	A sign, a memento.
CSÍK	Stria = a stripe.

CINDẠR CANDAR	Artifice to attract the notice of the male sex. (E.g. in: "She goes about giving herself airs.")
CSINDSA, CSANDSA	Strabosus = leering. – CSÍNTALAN: Lascivus, petulans, protervus = lascivious, frivolous, wanton.

CIPẠ BATA	The lath by which each row of thatch is fastened to the framework of the roof.–CIMTA: Pincers, to seize with pincers. (BATA: A bamboo lath.)
CSÍP	Vellicare = to pinch.–CSÍPTETŐ: Tendicula, volsella = pincer, tong, loop.

CIPẠ CAPE, CIṔO COPO	To walk gingerly, with short steps.
CSIPE, CSOPA, CSIP	Minutim, per exiguas quantitates = piecemeal, trifling.

CIPOC COPOC	Getting old, advanced in years.
CSIPEREDIK, CSEPEREDIK, CSÖPÖRÖDIK	Increscere, adolescere = to grow up, to become adult.

CIRẠ, CIRO	To split, to tear, to rend.
CSIRA	Germinasco, pillesco, pullulo = to germinate, to shoot forth.

CIRI BIRI	Into small pieces, thin, split into thin strips, to mince.
CSIRIBIRI	Exilis, minutus = insignificant, minute.

CIRI CUNTHI, CIRI HURI	To tear or rend, as a tiger its prey.
CSIRINKÜL	To cling on someone's neck.

CIRIC CIRIC	Chirp of sparrow.
CSIRIPEL	Cbirp of sparrow.

CIRIT	Narrow, strait.–(E.g. in : " Enter it at the strait gate.")
SŰRÍT	Spisso, denso = to compress, to condense.

CIROC COROC, CIROC CIROC, COROC COROC	Dripping, water issuing in small jets or drops.–CORO CORO : Sound of running or pouring water, as of a pipe.–SORO : To soak through, to fallow interstices, as water.
CSIREG-CSOROG	To flow, to purl, dripping.–CSOROJ : Fons = a fountain.

CITẠR KABAR	Spotted, variegated. (KABAR : Spotted variegated.)
CSIT	Telae genus = a sort of gay-coloured linen.

CO, CON — Perhaps, expresses doubt or uncertainty, used to emphasize an affirmative statement.–JA : Dubitative suffix ; perhaps, perchance, may be.–JAKHON : When.

CSAK, CSA, CSOK — Tantum, solum, saltem, sane, perinde, tamen = but just, even, only, yet, merely, indeed.–(UGYAN)CSAK : Also, as well.–CSAK(HA) : When.–(HA)CSAK : Nisi = perchance.

COCKO — The female organ, human and bestial.–CUCU, CUCUK : The female organ.–CUCẠ : A term of disparagement.

CSECS — Mamma, uter = breast, bosom, udder.–CSICSÓK : Lascivio = lascivious.–SUSKÁS : In rut, lascivious.–SUSPUS : Shame, disgrace.

CODO CODO — Sound of water falling in a stream.–CODOR : To pour out a libation.–(See also SODOR SODOR.)

SODOR, (VÍZ SODRA) Stream, current of water.–CSATORNA : Channel, drain.

COE — Part of female private member.

CSÁVEL — Coitus cum femina = coit with a woman.

COENDA — Ill-natured, bad tempered.–CONDHO : Scoundrel.

CSANDER — False.–Ill-natured, bad tempered.

COK — A kiss.

CSÓK — A kiss.

COPAO — Addicted, accustomed to. (E.g. in : "They are greatly addicted to beer and spirits.")–(See also CAPAR.)

CSÁBA, CSÁPA — Inducere, pellicere, corrumpare = to reduce, to tempt, to attract.

CORAN — To overflow. (See also JOROK.)

CSORRAN — Usque ad affluvium = up to overflow.

CORHOT, CARHAT — To shuffle, to drag the feet ; sound of shuffling.

CSORSZOG, CSORSZOL — To shuffle, to drag the feet.

CORPOT — Corrupt, rascally, scoundrelly.–CORCOTA: Passionate, cruel, short tempered.

CSORVASZ — Lout, ruffian.–Ill-tempered, wicked (?).

COT — Above, high.

CSÓTÁN — The highest side panel of a planked car.

COTHAO — To do, used only when quarrelling.

CSATA, CSATAJ — Proelium, pugna = battle, struggle, fight.–CSATÁS: Avidus certamini = eager for fighting.

COTHRA, COTHRA POTRA, COTHRO — Ill-conditioned, half-starved; exhausted, unfertile soil.

GYATRA — Weak, wretched.

COTOK — To dress up, to embellish.

CSÓTÁR — Fimbria ephippi = ornaments of the harness.

CUBẠK — To have a mote in the eye.

CSIPA, CSOPA, CSAPA — Gramiae, lippitudo = sty, pus in the eye.

CUCHUNDAR GHAO — Chancre, specific sore.–(GHAO: A sore.)

CSUCSORDUD-IK — Sarcoma = chancre.

CUDI — To go backwards, to keep to the side, squeezing into as little space as possible.

CSÓTOL — To thwart.

CUKẠU — To have finished or completed.

CSUK — Claudo, occludo = to lock, to shut up, to close.

CUKRUC — A folded leaf used as a spoon, drinking cup, etc.–CUIKUP, CUIKUT: Shrivelled, shrunk, rolled up, said of leaves.

CSOKROS — Crisped, plaited, crinkled.–CSUKORGAT: To shrivel.

CULUN	A small piece or quantity.
CSULA	A cow with little horns, a sheep with small ears.–CSOLESZ : A small vessel.

CUNGUR MUNGUR	To be restless, moving here and there, never still. -COŃCOL : Fickle, restless.
CSÁNKÁL, CSÁNGÁL	To move, to spring ; to wander.–To be fickle, to be restless.

CUNI	Small, stunted, smaller than other, said of fruit, grain, etc.
CSONI, CSUNI	Porculus = a small pig.–CSONKA, CSUNKA : Small, stunted, said of a forest, etc.–CSUNYA, CSUNI (?) : Deformis = stunted.

CUPI	Tail of a bird or fish.
CSÚPOS	Fastigiatus = pointed.–CSÚP, CHUPYA : Apex vel cacumen montis = peak or top of a mountain.

CUPUT	To close the fist, to receive as much as can be held in the hand when closed, to close the hand upon.
CSUPORGAT	To join, to fasten together (with the fist).

CURCURIẠ	To fry in oil.
CSÚRDÍT	To fry lard.

CURIẠK	A small earthen vessel.
CSERÉP, CSERIÉP	A small earthen vessel.

CURU BURU	Brimful, full to overflowing.
CSURO (VÍZ), CSÚR(VÍZ)	Permadeus = to be thoroughly drenched.

CUTHẠR, CHUTHẠR	A carpenter.
CSUTORÁS	Tornator, cornuarius = turner, turner in horn.

CUTKI	A little piece, a fragment.
CSUTA	Short, small.–CSUTKA, CSUTIKA : A fragment.

D

DABAK DUBUK	To shake the head or body, as an old man through weakness.-DABAC DUBUC: To sink and rise again and again.-DAP DUP: To tilt up, to alternately rise and descend, as the arm of a balance.-DAPADOPO: Slow, sluggish in movements (as a man).
DÁBBOGÓ	Having a gauche, clumsy walk.-DIBBEG-DÁBOG: To walk with slow, sluggish movements.-(MEG)DOBBAN: Permoveor = to be shaken, mowed.

DABAO	To press down, to snub, to chide, to keep under, to check, to curb, to restrain.
DÍBOL, DÉBOL	To knead, to press down, to keep under, to destroy, to grub up.

DAC DUC	To fine, to impose a penalty, to leave one without anything.
DÉZSMA, DESMA	Tributi seu vectigalis species = a kind of tribute or tax.-DÉZSMÁL: To pinch off, to curtail, to steal from.

DACAN DACAN	Quickly, flying from place to place, ubiquitous. (E.g. in: "That man moves very rapidly.")-DHARA DHẠRI: Quickly.-(See also JẠUSẠ JẠUSI.)
GYORSAN, GYARSAN	Propere, mobiliter, volubiliter, celeriter, velociter = quickly, easily moving, rapid. - DORCS, DORCSÓ, DORCSE: Quickly.

DẠDURHAM	Bushy, hairy.
DADVAS	Bushy, hairy.

DAEKA DEREN	Long, spreading horns with an upward turn.
TEKEREDETT	Long, with an upward turn (horn).

DAEYOK DAEYOK	Taking long steps and lifting the feet high, as a camel does when walking.
DAJBAS	Of sluggish, lazy walk.

DAG	To cremate, to burn the dead, used generally of the completed operation.–DAGI : Spotted, stained, blemished in character or reputation.
DÖG, DÖK	Cadaver, lues, pestis = carcass, dirt, pestilence, plague. Applied also to persons as a sign of contempt.

DAG DAGAO	To grow well, to grow luxuriantly, to flourish.–DOG DOGO : Heavy, indisposed to move, as one who has gorged himself with food.
DAGAD	Extumeo, superbio, se inflare = to swell, to flourish, to puff out.

DAH	Enmity, ill-will, envy.–DAHOK : Envy, spite, malice. (E.g. in : "Suppressing your anger for the time being, pay us a visit.")
DÜH	Rabies, furor, mania = rage, fury, mania, anger.

DẠHGI	Race, tribe, family, stock. (E.g. in : "He is of their stock.").–DAK DAK : A very distant relative.
TAG	Socius = member.–Corpus = body, bulk.–(VÉR) TAG : Germanus = brothers and sisters. TÁG : Large, distant.

DAHLE	Curd milk.
TALLÓ, TARHÓ	Oxygala = curd milk.

DAK	Water.
-DÉK, TÉK, TAK-	In words like FOLYADÉK : A liquid.–TAJTÉK Foam (as of the sea).–VÁLADÉK : Secretum.–TAKONY : Mucus of the nose.–Etc.

DAK	To tighten, or make taut.
DAGASZT	Tumefacio = to make taut.

DAKA DAK	A wooden trough used for feeding pigs, watering cattle, and at times for bathing. (DAK : Water.)–(See also TAGAR.)
TEKENŐ, TEKNŐ	Capisterium, trulla, labrum, alveus = a trough.

DẠLIL	Extra work, as punishment.–DALMAL : To excite, to agitate.–DAL : To strike, to thresh

	grain with a flail, to split into two or more pieces.–TALGATẠUAK: To crush, to bruise, to disintegrate.
DOLOG, DALAG	Opus, labor = work.–DOLGOLÓD-IK: Agito = to excite or agitate.–VAGDAL: To thresh repeatedly, to split into two or more pieces. (VÁG: To thresh, to split.)–SZABDAL: To cut continuously, to cut into pieces. (SZAB: To cut.)–CSIPDEL: To twitch again and again.–HARAPDÁL: To crunch, to crack repeatedly.–(MEG)DOLGOZ: To strike.

DALPAN	Clothed with a garment shorter than the usual worn.–DẠLPUN: A short quilted cloth.
DOLMÁN, DOLMA	A short Magyar garment.

DANAN	To conceal, to hide, to disappear, to depart the life.–DẠN: A witch, witchcraft.
(EL)TŰN-IK	Evanesco, se transformare, figuror = to conceal, to hide, to disappear, to change one's body.–TÜNDÉR: Magus, prestigiator = witch, witchcraft, sorcerer, fairy.–DANA(?): Devil.

DẠNAI	To judge, to consider. (E.g. in: "Judge for me.")
DŐNT	To decide, to arbitrate, to pass sentence.

DANGA	To fight or strike each other; a free fight, to assault.
DÖNGET	To strike, to beat repeatedly; a free fight.

DẠNGẠURA	A rubbish heap, a heap of rubbish.
DŐNG	A heap, a pile.

DANGOK, DANGOT	Humorous, jocular.–DON ENEC, DOM ENEC: A kind of dance.–DONGER: A dance by men only on the evening of the first day of an annual hunt.
DÁNOMOZ	To be in gay spirit.–DINOM-DÁNOM: Compotatio = a feast.–TENGER TÁNC: Some dance. (In a popular saying: "EGYETEM-BEGYETEM-TENGERTÁNC.")

DAR	A fissure, a rent, a trench.–DER: To stretch oneself, as one who has sat in one position

	for a long time.–DAṚIAU, DOREAO: The sea, ocean, large river, like an inland sea.–(See also THAR.)–TIAR: To stretch.
TÁR	Aperio = to open.–(KI)TÁR: Expando = to stretch oneself.–DERMEDEZŐ: To stretch one's limbs.–TERPESZKEDŐ: Stretching.–TÉR, TER: Regio, plana = a plain.–Spaciosus, planus = spacious, large, ample.–TÉRES: Amplus = ample, large. (?)–Tumidus = tumid. (JAU, JÓ: Water, river.)

DARA	To come.–BOLO DARA: To enter on the way coming.
TÉR, TÉRÜL	Eo = to come.–BELE TÉR: To enter on the way coming.

DARAE DARAE	Sound of thumping, clammering, clanking. (E.g. in: "The door is being slammed.")
DÖREJ	The uttering of a low, dull sound; to thud, to resound, to thunder; the noise made when slamming a door.

DARAE DHAMPAE, DARAE DHAPAE	Busy, diligently, hastily, without delay. (E.g. in: "He is hurrying to see him.")
DÖRÜ(L)	"To set oneself in operation with full strength."

DARE	Strength, power, might, ability. (E.g. in: "An able bodied man.")–DARSAR, DHARSAR: Slope of a hill.–DARAHARA: Fine, large, substantial, applied to houses.–DHARA: The side, from the armpit to the tight.–DHAREN: A beam which supports the ridge pole of a house.
DERÉK, DAROK, DARIK	Excellens, electus, aptus, martialis = excellent, select, fit, powerful.–Via principalis = main road.–A compartment of a house constructed of wood.–Pars corporis superior, truncus pectus = the body, the trunk, the upper part of the body.–The trunk of a tree.–TOR: The chest.

DARAN	White hot.–(See also DHARRA.)
DARU	Greyish white.

DARJA	Property, house and stock.–TAR, TAL: Subject, topic, theme.
TÁRGY	An object.–A subject, topic, theme.–TÁR: Suppellex, utensilium congeries = property, house and stock.

DARRAO	To roll, to husk, as by grinding with a curry stone.
DARÁL, DERÁL, DARÁLL	Crassius molo, comminuo = to rough grind.–DARASZOL: To husk, to rub off (?), to scrape off.–DARASZLÓ: (?) A plane.–DÖRGÖL: Contero, detero = to rub, to grind.

DAṢI	A fringe.–THOSOK: Splendour, grandeur. (E.g. in: "He has built a very great house.")
DÍSZ	Decus, ornamentum = an ornament, a fringe.–Splendour, grandeur.

DASI	A servant.–DESPODA: A wanderer, one who does not work, but spends his time visiting friends and living on them.
DECOK	Companion, attendant. (POTYA: What costs nothing.)

DAWAHI	Clamorous, importunate.
DÁVORIKOL, DAVARIKOL	To clamour.–DÉVAJ: Petulans = wanton, petulant.

DE	An interjection of entreaty, a very common particle giving emphasis or clearness. (E.g. in: "Now my girl, do be quick." Or in: "Do, listen to my prayer.")–DÓ: An emphatic or persuasive particle used with the imperative.–DÓ: Corrective suffix, but, however; used between others with a limitative function (as far as that is concerned, so far as that goes.)–GE: In comp. emphatic. (E.g. in: "Not they, but these." Or in: "It was even he.") HE GE: It is even so, certainly.–HE: Yes, to assent.–HE GE CON: Yes, surely.
DE, GYE, GE	Sed, verum, atqui = but, yet, however.–In exclamations it serves to prove or to emphasize.–A particle of corroboration.–Used between others with a limitative function (so far as that goes).–IGEN: Yes, to assent.–HIGYE: Believe it, it is even so.

DEH	The body.
TEST	The body.

DEHET — To put off time, to loiter.–TEHE MEHE: To linger, to put off time, to dawdle.–DẠHUR BULẠU: Give invitations to join a hunting party, fishing meet, etc. (BULAU: To divert, to amuse.)

DÖHÖD-IK — To divert, to amuse oneself.–To put off time. (MULAT: To divert, to amuse oneself.)

DEKHENSE — Let me see.–(See also TAKAO.)

TEKINTSEM — Let me see.

DEPER — To copulate, to have sexual intercourse.–DHẠKUC: To have sexual intercourse with, to copulate.

TEKER — To copulate, to have sexual intercourse.

DERE DERE — Angrily.

DIRRE-DỤRRE, DÉR-DÚR — Fragose, rigide, rixore = surly, angrily, sulky.

DESE — Conveys the idea of entreaty.–DESE ANJOM TIṄME: Do listen to me, or grant my request.

TESSÉK, TESSEN — Conveys the idea of entreaty. (Do please.)

DET — Small, little.

DED — (?) Small, little. (In composition.)

DHAB — A hollow, a large moist rice field. (E.g. in: " He followed up the hollow." Or in: " Water has collected in the hollow.")

DOBRA — A hollow, washed out by water.

DHABE DHOBE — Beautifully, excellently.–DHABA LUMẠM: Good, 1st class cocoons. (LUMAM: Cocoons.)

DÉVÁLYOS — Good, 1st class, excellent.

DHẠBIC — Till, until, as far as, as long as.–DHABLU: Broad.–DẠPTHU: Large.–DABDABA: Broad, wide.–DAP DAPA: Very wide, broad.–THABU: Large, big, very large, very big.–TAPHAT, TOPHAD, TOPHAT: Distance, distant, separate, far away, removed.–DAGOR:

	Large.-TAOGAR : Elastic. - (See also TEGE TEGE.)
TÁVIG	Till, till the distance of . . .-TÁVOL, TÁVUL : Eminus, longe procul = far away, distant, remote.-TÁVLAT, TÁV : Distance.-TÁG : Amplio, amplifico = to enlarge, to amplify, to augment.-TÁG : Large.-TÁGUL : To enlarge, elastic.

DHAKAO	To cover, to obscure.
TAKAR	To cover, to obscure.

DHAL	A shield, a buckler.
TÁL	Patina, catinus, paropsis, scutula = a plate.

DHẠLU	Slope, to slope.-(See also DILDAL.)
DŰLŐ	Slope (of a hill).-Sloping.

DHAMAS, DHAMASTE	Influence, power exerted on men or things, force, forcefulness, impression produced, influence exerted. (E.g. in : " Owing to the impression produced, the people are afraid.")-THAM : A prop, a pier, as of a bridge.
TÁMASZT	Creo = to create, to produce.-Sustineo = to help.-Moveo = to cause.-Resuscito = to exert.-TÁMASZTÉK, TÁMASZ, TÁM : A support.-Influence, help.-A prop, a pier, as of a bridge.

DHANDHASEŔ	To destroy, or ruin, to be overthrown. (E.g. in : " I will overthrow the temple.")
DŐNT	Dejicio = to overthrow.

DHANGA, DHẠNGI	Tall, long-shanted. (E.g. in : " She is a big, tall woman.")
DÁNGÓ	Big, tall.

DHARAO	To owe, to be in debt.
TARTOZ-IK	To owe, to be in debt.

DHẠRMUS, DHURMUS	An instrument used to beat down earth.
DORONG, DURONG, DŐRÖNG	An instrument used to beat down earth.-Phalanga, fustis, pertica, palus = a bar, a stake, a pile, a post.

DHARRA, DHAṚRI	Under side of the body more or less white, the rest black; applied to goats and sheep.–(See also DARAN.)
DERES	Coloris murini = mouse-coloured, greyish-white.–Applied mostly to horses.–DÉR: Pruina = hoarfrost.

DHAT	An exclamation of vexation.
TOTT	(?) Inquam = I say.

DHAWA	A guirland, etc., for adorning cattle.
DÉVÁLYOS	Adorned.

DHENKA	A species of crane.
DANKA	A bird.–Larus ridibundus L.

DHEO	A wave. (E.g. in: " If the river becomes flooded waves will be formed.")
TAJTÉK	Spuma = foam, froth.–Bubble.

DHER	To increase.
TEREM	Cresco = to increase.

DHOB DHOBO, DOBE DOBO	Big bellied, like a snake that has just swallowed a meal.–DHOBEA, DOBEA: Applied to a person who has a protuberant stomach.–DHOPSA, DHOPSAHA: Suffering slightly from dropsy, body swollen.–DOBDOBO: The feeling after a rather full meal.
DOBÁR, DOBASZ	Swallowed, swollen, full (stomach).–DOBOZI, DOBRI: " One who eats very much."–DOBZÓD-IK: Commessori = to feast, to gormandize.–DOBSA: Immodicus = immoderate.

DHOCOR	Proud, froward, self-willed.–DHACRAR: Self-willed, restive, as an imperfectly broken-in bullock.–DHAṬHI: Persistent, inexorable. DHADNAS: Bravado, pretence.
DACOS, DACHOS	Contumax, obstinatus (equus, homo) = obstinate, froward, self-willed, restive.–Superbus = proud, haughty.

DHOLO	Fat and lazy, applied to women.
DALMOS	Fat, stout, corpulent.

DHONGA A boat made from a hollowed out tree, a wooden trough.

DONGA Asserculus = a small stop-plank, a small beam.

DHOP DHOP, THOP THOP Sound of rapping or tapping, to rap, to tap.–Sound emitted by a drum with a hole in it, or one that requires lacing.–DAP DUP: Sound produced by light objects falling in succession.–TOPOK: To drop.–DHAPDHUP: To stamp the foot, sound of tramp, or the thud on the ground of a blind man's stick.–DABA DUBU: Noise made with feet and hands when swimming.–TOPO: To immerse.–(See also HABAK DABAK.)

DOB A drum.–Jacio = to drop.–DOBOG: Palpitare = to tap.–DOBLÁS, DOBLOM: Pulsare, tundere = to drum.–DOBÁSZKOL: To tread something with the flat side.–DOB: A part on a fishing implement (net-implement).

DHOROT DHOROT Worn and cracked, as feet with much walking; cracked as a plank, earthenware vessel, drum, etc.; footsore.–TOROT TOROT: Noise produced by old and battered shoes.–DHARÁR: Sound of creaking, or of cracking.–DHARA DHẠRI: To pull, to offer violence. (E.g. in: "The moneylender knocked me about.")–(See also TARA.)

TÖRÖTT Worn and cracked, as feet with much walking; cracked as a plank, earthenware vessel, drum.–TÖR: Frango, tero, tundo = to pull, to ruin, to bruise, to crush, to break, to fracture.–DÖRÖCKÖL: Subigo, pilo = to mill, to thrash.

DHORSOT MORSOT Ugly, unprepossessing and dirty.

TORZA-BORZA Miserandus = wretched, contemptible.–TORZÁS: Hispidus = to be dishevelled (hair).

DHUKẠ DHUKI To altercate, to dispute violently.

DULAKOD-IK Luctari, concertari = to dispute violently, to wrestle, to have a scuffle.

DHUMA Stout, fat, corpulent.–DUMERAE, DUMKE: Stout.–DUDHMA: Fat, rolling in fat.

DUMA Stout, fat.–DÖME: A big, corpulent man.–DUMANO: A corpulent girl.–DUDDÓU: Having a heavy, clumsy body.–DUDLA: A woman rolling in fat.

DHUNẠU	To strike by jerking up the head.
DUMÉ	To strike with the fist on someone's back.

DHURIẠU	A method of curing sores, also of rendering the poison of snakes harmless.
TÚR	Ulcus saniosum = ulcer, sore. (JÓ, IAU : Good.)

DHURUP, DHURPẠU	Mid-harvest, busiest season, in full swing, at the greatest height, as work in harvest.
DERÉK	Pars precipua, principalis, media = the principal part, the middle.–Media aestas = the middle of the highest summer.–DEREKA (A MUNKÁNAK) : Mid-harvest, busiest season.

DIL	Courage, pluck, bravery.–DILGẠR, DILGẠRIẠ, DILMAN : Brave, plucky.
DÜLEKED-IK, TÜLEKED–IK, DULAKOD-IK	Luctari, concertari = to ring, to fight.–DÚL : Vastere, depredari = to devastate, to destroy.–DALIA, DELIA : Heros = hero.

DILDAL	Rock about, sway, waddle, body to tremble with fatness when moving, as a fat ox.—DOLE : To bob up and down on the surface of the water, to sway from side to side, as a lightly laden boat.–DOLOE DOLOE : Shaking gently, swaying, nodding, dangling.—DOLOP DOLOP : Swaying, shaking.–DULUN DULUN : To toddle, to walk as a little child.–DHẠLUI DHẠLUI : To dangle.–DHILO DHOLON : Loosely, slack, opposite from firmly.–DHIL DOKOC : Loose, slack.–DHULUC DHUPUC DHULUK DHUPUK : The head and body to shake as of very old people when walking.–THẠLI : To sink as in a bog, quicksand, mud.–TULẠ : Scales, a balance.–DIKẠ DAKE, DIKO DOKO : Unstable, shaky, loose ; tossing, staggering.–DUK DUK : To go pit a pat, to throb.–(See also DHẠLU.)
DOL, DÉL, DÜL, DÖN	Ruere, corruere, procidere, labi = to fall, to tumble down, to descend, to sink.–DÜLÉDÖZ, DÜLÖNG : Sensim ruere, vacillare = to rock about, to shake, to sway, to waddle, to be loose.

DIMẠK DIMẠKI	Unwilling, idle.
DIMOS	Unwilling, idle.

DINI	Give, give to me or to us, used with animate objects only. (E.g. in: "Then give to me.")–DINMAS: The end of the agricultural year, when engagements terminate and accounts are made.
DÍJ, DÍ	Reward, payment, salary, wages.

DIPNI	A stopper.
DÓP, DUP	A stopper.

DOBO	Large, big.
DUBI, DÓBER (?), DÓBÁR (?)	Large, fat.

DOGA, DUGI	A cutting of sugar cane for planting.
DUG, DAG	To stick in.

DOHLAO	To break out afresh as a fire that was apparently extinguished.–DAHGAO: To blaze, to flare up.
DOHOG	To mutter (as fire).

DOHO	A tumor, excrescence, a camel's hump.
DUHAD	To protrude.

DOK	To shelter, protect, preserve.
TOK	A sheath, a covering.

DOLAO	Damp, limp, lean.
DOH, DOHLIK, DOLLIK	Putor, putredo = fustiness.

DOLDOL	A lullaby sung to babies by Santal mothers.
DALOL	To sing.–DAL: Cantus, modulamen = singing, song, melody.

DOMAO	To strike, to beat.
DUMÁL	To beat with the fist in the back.

DOMBOK	Little balls of bread.–DOMBE: A knot, an excrescence on a tree.–DHOMPO: Lump, knot,

mound.–DHOPO : A hillock.–DHUMBAK : A ball, a clump.

DOMÓ — A ball of bread.–DOMB, DUMB : Tumulus, tumor terrae, tuber = an excrescence, a hill, a knoll.

DOMBAL DOMBOL, DOMBOL DOMBOL — Rising and falling as a boat on the waves, heaving up and down as a boat on a rough sea.–DOM ENEC : A kind of dance.–(ENEC : To dance, to dandle.)

DOMBOL, TOMBOL — Exculto, tripudio, persulto = to leap, to spring, to jump, to dance.–TOMP : Salio = to jump.

DOMDOM — Heaped up, rising above the surface.

DOMOS — Raised, elevated, heightened.

DONDHA — A mass. (E.g. in : "The ants are massed together.")–DAN : A heap, a pile ; to pile up, to heap. (E.g. in : "You have crowded here.")–DUNGEL, DUNGER : In vast numbers, in crowds, a party, a group.

DANDÁR, DONDÁR — Cohors, caterva, phalanx = a party, a group, a brigade.–DONDA : Clumsy.

DOPKA — A basket with which water is raised for irrigating purposes.–TUPLAK : A small bamboo-basket.

DOBOZ — "A kind of pot-shaped straw-basket."

DOPYO — Old and weak.

DOPONYA — Grandmother. (ANYA : Mother.)

DORASA — Slightly.

DERÉCE — "What slightly can be ploughed."

DORMOD, DORMOC, DORMAD, DORMADI — Ill, ailing, out-of-sorts, anything wrong with any part of the body.

DERMED — Emori, interire, obrigescere = to die by and by, to become torpid, benumbed, to stiffen, to freeze.

DOROB, DOROP, DARAP — Metal, excluding iron.–DOROBOS, DURUBUS : All the necessaries of life. (E.g. in : "She has everything she needs.")

DARAB — Fragmentum = a piece.–Pars = a part.–(?) Cattle.

DOROK, DOROGOK — In comp. be done with it, have it over, let it take its way, it can't be helped. (E.g. in: "Bear it, it can't be helped.")–THIR: To become quiet or still, to cease, to stop, to stand still.

TŰR, TÖR — Patior, perpetior, tolero = to bear, to endure, to tolerate.–(MEG) TŰRKŐZ-IK: Se abstinere = to abstain, to forbear.

DORPAT — A flaw.

TORPADÁS — A flaw.

DOWA BOWA, DHOWA BHOWA — Doubtful, uncertain, hesitating.

TÉTOVA — Doubtful, uncertain, hesitating.

DOYO — Slightly.

DEJ, DEJI — Approximately, nearly, about.

DUC — Small, dwarfish.–DUC HOR: Little folk. (HOR: A man, a human being, a Santal.)

DOCSER — Little farmer. (EMBER: A man, a human being.)

DUDHWẠ, DHUDHWẠ — A small earthenware pot.

DUDU, DUDULLÓ — An earthenware pot.

DUDURGUC — To draw oneself together through being cold.–DEREC DEREC: To shiver, as on the approach of an attack of fever.

DIDERGŐS — Shivering through cold.–DIDEREG, DEDEREG, DUDÖROG: Frigutio = to shiver with cold.

DUHẠU — To milk.

TEHÉN — A cow.

DUL — To pour, to cast metal in a mould. (E.g. in: "This river flows into the sea.")

DÚDOL, DUDUL — To pour (?).–To flow in (?).

DUNDI — Foolish, ignorant.

DUNDI — Awkward, gauche, stupid.

DUNDUN	To rise and fall like waves, to pile up.
DUN	The rise of waters.–To dam up.

DUГẠI	To tremble, to shake, to be in tremor.–(E.g. in: "I am trembling with fear.")–DHUPUC, DHUPUCOK, DHUBUJOK: To be frightened. –DUBHẠU: To spring, to issue, as water from a spring.
DOBAJ	Palpito = to tremble, to shake.–Subito adesse = to spring.–DÜBBEN, DEBBEN: Terreri = to become frightened.–TOPLA: Terror = fear.

DUR	To put from one, to reject.–DURE: The scrotum of a boar.
TÚR	Egero, regero, proruo = to eject, to vomit, to reject, to push forward.

DURAO	To begin, to set to, to engage in.
DURÁL, NEKI DURÁL	To begin, to set to, to engage in.

DURATHAN	To destroy, to spoil. (E.g. in: "They tramped over it and spoiled it.")–DHUR: Drought cattle, plough cattle.–TOR: To sting.
TÚR	Rostro humum fodio = to root, to grub up, to turn up the ground, to stir up, to sting.

DURHẠK, DHURHẠK	An exclamation of annoyance or vexation.–DUR KARAHAK: How foolish!
DŐRE	Insipiens, stultus = foolish.–DŐRÉK: The fools! (An exclamation of annoyance or vexation.)

DURI	A species of fish resembling an eel, and very slippery.
DURBANCS, DÖRGÉCSE	Acerina cernua.–Gobio fluviatilis.–Perca fluviatilis.

DUSMAN	An enemy, an ill wisher.–DUSTAMA: Hatred.–DUSKO: Affliction. (E.g. in: "He is sorely afflicted.")
DUZZAD, DUZMAD	Contumesco, efferveo, excandesco = to puff up, to get furious, to get angry.

E

E	The abbreviated form of the third Personal pronoun, he, she, him, her.
Ő	He, she.
EA	Used in addressing inferiors, or when rebuking.–EI : Employed to call attention.
HÉ, HEH	Used in addressing inferiors, or when rebuking.–HEJ : Employed to call attention. Holla !
EAE	Seven.–ETWAR : Sunday, the first day of the week.
HÉT	Seven.–The week.–HÉCZER : Seven times. (SZER : -times.)
EBHEN	To awake from sleep.
ÉBREN	Vigilanter = awake.–ÉBRED : To awake from sleep.
EC	To take glowing embers from the fire and put them in a vessel, to carry away glowing embers.–IC : Dross, slag from a smelting furnace, rust, excrement. (E.g. in : "The star voided excrement."[1]–IPIL : A star.–CANDBOL IPIL : A comet. (CANDBOL : A tail.)
ÜST, IST	Kettle.–Boiler.–ÜSTÖK : Tuft of hair on the head.–ÜSTÖKÖS : A comet. (TÖK : Head ?)–IPRIK : Excrement.
ECKOC	Beyond one's means.
EZKÖZ, EZKÜZ	Medium, instrumentum = means.
EDEBEDE	Intricate, involved, complicate. thick, indistinctly.–ECOC : Indistinctly, inarticulately, as a child learning to speak.
EGYEBUGYA	Pell-mell, intricate.–Misshapen.–Heavy, clumsy.–HEBEG, EBEG : To speak indistinctly.

[1] A shooting star is regarded by the Santal as the excrement of another star.

EDE EDE	To watch, applied oftenest to children who hang about where cooking, etc. is going on. (E.g. in: "You are watching here, you won't even go to herd.")–(See also IDU.)
IDŐZ, EDŐZ	To stay, to sojourn.
EGAR	To begin, to put one's hand to a thing, to undertake. (E.g. in: "Trying to make it better, I made it worse.")
AKAR	Velle = to be about, to have in view, to intend.
EGOR OGOR, AGAR OGOR	To move as one out of breath and fatigued, used mainly of animals run down at a hunt.
AGÁR, AGAR	Canis venaticus = greyhound.
EH	An interjection of surprise, Oh! what; indeed! really!
EH	Papae = really !–EHE: "A word of surprise or pleasure."
EHE	Hist! Hey! look here! halloo!; used to call attention.
EHOL, IHEN	Eu, ecce = hey! look here!
EHE EHE, EHE TALAN	So much, so large a quantity, the idea being completed by signs.
EZ, E, EH	Hic = this. – Hujusmodi = such. – ENNYI, (?) EHENNYI: Tantus = so much, so large a quantity. (TALÁN: Approximately, perhaps.)
EHE RE	Used when calling attention to boys; Hey! hey you!
ERRE	Hac, isthac = (hey !), in this direction!
EHO	Used to call attention.
EHOL, EHÓ	Here it is!
EKA	One (indefinite).
-IK	A frequent verbal suffix (especially with reflexive verbs.)–EGYIK, EGYIKE: One (indefinite).[1]

[1] Magyar EGY, ED may be in connection with Santal MIT, MI–AD.

EKA HARIA	One yoke oxen. (HARIA : A harrow or clod crusher, drawn by one pair of oxen or buffaloes.)
IGA	One yoke oxen. (HARIT : To cleanse, to scour, to furbish.)

ELAN	Heat, flame.–(See also ALAN.)
LÁNG	Flammus = flame, blaze.

ELAO	To have enough.–EBE TEBE, EBE TUBE: More than sufficient, used always with " JOM " : to eat.–ODGEL : Not to the full, short of, insufficient, used in comp. with verbs.–OKULAṆ: Insufficient, inadequate, too little, not enough.–(See also ALE.)
ELÉG	Sat est = to have enough.–ELÉD, EBÉD : Prandium = meal. (GYOMOR : Stomach.)–ELÉGTELEN, ÉGTELEN : Insufficient, not enough.

ELEM CELEM	Used generally of children watching for an opportunity to take something, and at times of wild animals, such as jackals waiting for a favourable opportunity to seize something.–EM : To give.–EM SEHOT : To help by giving.–EM HALA : To repay.–(See also EPEL, AMAR OMOR, UMAṚ and UPEL.)
ELEMEL	Amoveo, dimoveo, tollo = to take something and to carry it away.–EMEL : Levo, erigo, aufero = to lift, to erect.–(EL : Away.)–IM, EM, IME, EME : Ecce, eu = see, here ! (Accompanying a gift.)–(SEGIT : To help.)

EMAN, EMON	Such, such like, such as, so.
EMON, EMOLYAN	Such like, such as.

EN	That particular.
ŐN, EN	In propria, suus, ejus, eorum = proper, own.–AZON, EZEN : That particular, this particular.–ÜNNEP : Holiday. (NAP, NÉP : Day.)

ENEC	To dance, to play a game, to dandle, to pacify.–(E.g. in : " A snake charmer.")
ÉNEK	Cantatio, musica = song, singing, music.

ENGA	Female, mother.–ENGAM: Thy mother, a term of abuse, an expletive.–(Bodding, in *Santal Folk Tales*, Vol. I, P. 290, quotes for this expletive the form ENGATE, pronounced sometimes with stress on the initial vowel, sometimes with stress on the much lengthened A. He notes further, that most of the expletives used by Santal men seem to have reference to the sexual functions or natural functions.)
ANYA	Female, mother.–ANYÁD: Thy mother, a term of abuse, an expletive.

ENGEL PENGEL	The feeling of one tired with many things still to do.
INGEREL	Irrito, exaspero = to irritate, to exasperate.

ENKA, ENKAN	Thus, in such a way, like that, as that. (E.g. in: "Let it remain as it is.")–ENKA ENKATE: By degrees, by that way, in that direction, in that way, thus.–ENKATHAE: Used to introduce a statement, that is to say, namely, as they say, that is.
EKKÉNT	Sic = in such a way, by degrees, by that way, thus. Often used to introduce a statement.

ENTE	For because.–ENAN: A little while ago, a previous part of the same day.–ENDE, ENDETE: Then.–ENDE, ETE: There, in that place. (E.g. in: "Remain there for the present.")–ENE: Now.–ENEC: Not until.
INNÉT, ENNÉTEN	Hinc = for, because.–Inde = thence.–INNÉNT, INNÉNTEN: Paulo ante, proxime, dudum = a little while ago.–ITT, ITTEN, ITTIGEN: Hic = in that place, there.–IME, EMI: Now.–AMIG (?), EMIG: Till (not until).

EPEL	To rise or lift up, to strike as a stick. (E.g. in: "He raised a stick to me.")–(See also ELEM CELEM, AMAR OMOR, UMAR and UPEL.)
EMEL	Levo = to raise.

ER, EROK, EROGOK	To sow, to scatter; to be sown or scattered.–(See also ARAK.)
ERESZT	To swarm. (Bees.)–To lose.–ERREGET: To set free, to sow, to scatter.–EREG, -OROG: A verbal suffix connected with the idea of propagation or circulating, e.g. BIZSEREG: To prickle.–HÁBOROG: To wave.

ERA	Wife, female, applied to women only, and generally as a mark of respect.
ARA	A female relative. (Applied generally as a mark of respect ?)

ERE	To deceive, to lie, to pretend.
ÖRV, ÖRÜ, ÖRI	Pretextus = a pretext.

EREM EREM	Hankeringly, looking wistfully on.
ÖRÖM, EREM	Gaudium, laetitio = delight, pleasure.

ERGO	A species of field rat.–(See also URIC HON.)
ÜRGE	Cuniculus, curculio = a species of field rat.

ERO, IRU	To tantalize, as a child holding out a piece of sweetmeat to another, and when he puts out his hand to take it, puts it in his own mouth.
ŐRÜL	Deliro = to become mad.–ŐRJÍT: To tantalize.

ERON	On account of.–ERPHER: To exchange, to alternate.
ÉRT, ÉRETT	On account of.–Pro = in exchange.

ESEL	Fair, light coloured.
ŐSZ	Canus = grey (of hair).

EWER	To fan.
ELVER, EVER	Profligo, percello, dispergo = to beat, to cudgel, to break into pieces, to disperse.

G

GAB GAB	Deeply, to sink deeply. (E.g. in: "The feet of the bullocks sink deeply in the mud.")
GÜBE	A deepening in a reservoir, basin.–GÜBÜ: Mud, swamp.

GABDHAO	To bring forth dead offspring, applied to animals only. (E.g. in: "They struck her with the result that her calf was born dead.")
GEBED	To die, applied to animals only.

GABHA	The middle, the centre.
KÁPA	Umbo sellae = pommel of a saddle.

GABHAND, GAMHAND	The ear formed within the sheath, and beginning to protrude, applied to all graminæ.
GABNA, GABONA	Frux, frumentum, fruges, seges = corn, grain (applied to all graminæ).

GABRI	A fool.
KÁBA	Stultur, fatuus, hebes = foolish.

GAD	The receptacle into which the rice to be husked is placed.
KÁD	Receptacle, tub, cask, barrel.

GADA	A depression or hollow, a pit, a trench, a hole, a river, a stream.
KADA	A hollowed, washed away place in streams.–GADAJ: Caverna = a cavern, a pit.–GÖDÖR: Caverna, fovea = a cavern, a hole.

GADA CAṄCIR	The wagtail. (CAṄCIR: The tit-lark.)–GEDE: A duck.
GÖDÉNY	A kind of water-fowl.

GADAE GUDUI	Long, flowing garments, superfluity of cloth. (GUDUI : Long, shaggy, loose, baggy, as clothes.)-GADLE : A garment worn round the waist reaching below the knees.
GATYA, GATTIA, GAGYA	Femorale, feminale, subligor, perizoma, subligaculum, calliga = pants. (The Magyar "GATYA" are flowing trousers, with superfluity of cloth, reaching below the knees.)

GẠHNDI	A herd, a flock, family, company.
KONDA	A herd of swine.

GAJAR	Noise, turmoil, tumult, din.-GAJA GUJU : Numerous, crowds.-(See also KẠJIẠ.)
KÉSA	Tumult, mutiny.-GÖGY : Noise, din.

GAL GALAO	To be moist, to run as a sore.-GALAO : To melt, to decompose.-GHALGHALAO : To mortify, to spread as a malignant sore, to waste as time.-GẠLID : Mash, mush, mashy, mushy.-GILẠ : Moist, mushy. - GHALOK, GHALOKTE : Including, reckoning, enumerating.-(See also KHẠLIS.)
KEL	Fermento = to ferment.-Tumesco, inflor = to swell, to increase by swelling.-Consumor = to be wasted (as time).-In usu esse, valere = to be current, marketable.-KÖLT : Fermentatum = fermentation, bubbling up.-KELÉS : Apostema, ulcer, tuber = an ulcer, a sore, a tumor.

GALAK SALAK, GALAT SOLAT	Stupid, dull-witted, unintelligible.-GALASAN : Unconscious. (E.g. in : "This man is in a heavy sleep." Or in : "He is very ill with fever, he is laying in an unconscious state.") GALTA GOLAT : Dull, vacancy of mind, stolidity, want of intelligence.-(See also GOJRA and KALOBALO.)
GALABÓGYI	A blockhead.-GYALABELI : Dull-witted, clumsy, awkward. - KALAKÓCA : Crack-brained. - KELEKUTI, KELAHAJTI : Foolish, crazy, mad.-KALANTOS : Benumbed, drunk.-KOLCSAGOS, KÓCSAGOS : Ebrius, potus, delirious, ameus = drunk, stupid, unconscious.-GAJOS, GAGYOS : Drunk.

GALAN	To plait, to braid.–UP GALAN : To braid the hair.
GALAND, GALANT, GALLAN	Taema, taemiola = a braid of hair.–A band, a linen band, a lace.–KALLANG : A band.–KELEKOLA : Plaited.–KELEM : The binder.

GALAN GULUN	Slowly. (E.g. in : " He moves along slowly.")
KULLOG, KULLAG, GULLOK	Ambulo resistans, procedo pedentim = to move along slowly.

GALAT GALAT	Dirty, ill-looking, applied to large sores.
GALÁD	Nequam, sordidus = dirty, sordid.

GALGAL, GALGALAK, GALGUL	Din, tumult, loud murmuring as a crowd.–GAL : To boast, to brag, to speak.–GALA : Voice.–GAL GOLPA, GAL GOLPO : Tittle-tattle.–GALKẠTUẠ : Boasting, bragging ; a boaster, a braggart.–GẠGU : Speaking through the nose and very indistinctly.
GALAGYOL, GAGYOG	To stammer, to speak thick, to babble.–KOLO-KOLOG : Glotoro, crepito = to chatter, to click.

GẠLI	A loop, a method of tying. (A method employed to tie the feet of a pig when it is desired to carry it on a pole between two men when alive.)
KALAFA, KALODA	A block of punishment.–KALAFÁZNI : A method of tying on a pole. (FA : A pole.)

GALOC CERE	The hawk cuckoo. (CERE : A bird.)–KARA-NATH SIM : A black fowl having black bones and black flesh. (SIM : A fowl.)
KELECSEN, KERECSEN, KERECSET	The gerfalcon (?).–A mythical bird of the Magyar.

GALOC SALOS	Higgledly piggledly, in confusion. (E.g. in : " The dhan is all lying different ways.")
KALANGYA, GELIM	Heap of corn made (disturbed ?) by the wind.

GAMAO	To recognize, to diagnose, to remember.
KAMALIT	Animadverto = to recognize.–KÉM : A spy.

GAMCHA HASA	A kind of earth with which cloth is dyed, a light reddish brown colour. This is the Hindu and Buddhist sacred colour. (HASA : Earth.)
KÁMZSA	Amictorium = waistcoat, jacket, short dressing gown. (Generally of reddish brown colour.)

(BINDI) GANAK	A spider's wed. (BINDI : A spider.)–GAK : To stretch twine, thread, etc. from one point to another.–GEND : A ball.
GÖNGY	Ball of twine, thread.–GÖNGÖLITGET : Voluto = to coil (as twine).–GÖNGÖRIT : Evolvo = to twist.

GAŃJON, GAŃJAN	To annoy, to render life miserable.–GAŃJA GẠŃJI : To mix up, to break up and mix. (E.g. in : "They have mixed up the matter, i.e. confused it." Or in : " They badgered me terribly.")–GANGUN : Having an impediment in speech, dumb.–GAN : A contused wound, a blind boil.–Impedio (?) = to annoy, to hinder.–(See also KHONOS.)
GÁNCSOL	Mendum, defectus = fault, defect.–Trica = impediment.–GÁNCSOS: To find fault continually.

GANTHAR	The inner skin of fruits, the film underneath the shell of an egg ; the placenta of animals ; an inner wrap of filmy nature.
GÁNYOL	Togo = to cover, to protect.

GẠR	Difficulty, strait.
GERÉB	Hindrance, impediment.

GARA JALA	Black and heavy, as clouds.–KARI : Black.–KARYO : Black, dark colour.
KOROM	Thick, foggy air.–Soot.

GẠRI	To push from or towards, as a fish net with a handle, to draw towards, as with a rake.
GEREB, GEREBLYE	Rastrum, sarculum = a rake.

GATAE	An itching or irritating sensation of the throat.
GÖTHÖS, GOTHOS	Sick (on the chest, on the throat).

GARAJ, GOROJ	Interest, concern, necessity, occasion, want, need. (E.g. in : " If a thing is urgently required by the purchaser the price asked by the seller is high." Or in : " What interest have you here ? ")
KERES	Acquiro, paro = to earn, to gain, to get, to win, to procure, to provide, to supply with.–Quero, inquiro, contor = to require, to scrutinize. KERESKED-IK : Negotior = to negotiate.

GARDAN, GORDON	The neck, the back of the neck.
GERINCZ, GERENCZ, GERÉCZ	Spina dorsi = backbone.–The neck.

GAREC	To trifle with, to despise, to make light of. (E.g. in : " Do not trifle with God.")
GAR	Arrogantia = arrogance, pride, haughtiness.–GARA : The critic.

GARHA	Bed of a watercourse, a hole, a pit, a hollow.–GARHA GORHO : Full of holes or pits.
GARAT, GARAD	Alveus = bed of a watercourse.–GARANGYIKOS : Rough, bumpy.

GARMAT, GARMAK	Difference in dialect, in pronunciation, accent.[1]
GYARMAT	Colony.

GURU	A teacher. (A quack.)
KURUZSOL	To practise quackery.

GASMANDAO, GHASMANDAO	To disorder by rolling.
KÁSZMÁL	To entangle, to disorder by rolling.–KASZIBÁL : To disorder.

GEHET GEHET	Slow of speech, slow and mild of speech, and reserved.–Hoarsely speaking from the throat.–(See also KHOK.)
KEHETES, KEHES	Dampy, muffled (as drums).–Short-breathed, asthmatic.

GEJER	To smash into atoms.
KÖSEDÉK	Very little (atoms).

[1] The Santal term so the other Munda-tribes, as the Mahle, Koda, Birhor, Kamar, etc., etc.

GEL	Ten.
KILENCZ	Nine.

GELE	An ear of grain, as of rice, wheat, etc.-To flower, applied only to Indian corn and the Matkom-tree. (E.g. in : " The rice is about to shoot into ear.")
KEL	Adnascor, accresco = to grow, to shoot up.-KALÁSZ : Spica = ear of corn.

GENEC GENEC	Natty, neat, trim, pretty and little.-DHAṆI : Rich, precious ; a term of endearment ; an interjection of surprise. (E.g. in : " Where are you going to, dearie ? " Or in : " What, can he go ? ")-(See also GHANE GHANE.)
GYÖNGY, GENG, GÖNY	Margarita, gemma, unio = pearl.-GYÖNGYÖS : Charming, sweet, dear, beloved.-JÖN, GYÖN, GYÜN : It comes (an interjection of surprise).

GERWEL	A ring round the underside of the neck, said of birds, such as the ring dove, the quail, etc.
ÖRV	A ring round the underside of the neck, said of birds, such as the ring dove, etc.

GESER GESER	Quickly, as when in a hurry. (E.g. in : " The buffalo goes stamping about.")
GESZTEL	To trot.

GHAGOR	Shrewd, smart, scheming.
GŐGÖS	Superbus, arrogans = superb, splendid, arrogant.

GHAṆL	To wound.-JAKHAM, JOKHOM : A wound, to wound.-JHUK : Vigorous, impetuous. (E.g. in : " He works vigorously.")-GOC, GUJUK : To kill ; to die.
GYILKOS, GYIKOS, GALKOS, GELKOS, GYOLKOS	Sicarius = murderer. – Mortifer = deadly. – Very vigorous.

GHANE GHANE	Repeatedly, time after time, every now and again. (E.g. in : " You come to me time after time.")-DELOI : Come.-(See also GENEC GENEC.)
JÖN-JÖN, GYÖN-GYÖN	To come time after time.-GYERE, DELE (?) : Come.

GHAR GHAṚIẠ	A very steep incline, steep.
GARAT, GURDÓ	Slope of a mountain.

GHARWA	The sparrow (passer indicus).–GAṚUR : The adjutant bird (ardea argala). KARE : A bird, the maena of starling.–KARKOR : A species of bird.–KURIT : The Bengal kite (falco cheela).
KARVALY, KARULY	Nisus, nisus falco = the sparrow-hawk.—KERRA : The gos-hawk.–KORÁCS : The Egyptian vulture.–KORGÁLY, KORGÓ : The agami bird (psophia).

GHAS	Grass, all the small species of Cyperaceae, as well as nearly all Graminae are called "ghas".–GHASIARA : A grass cutter.
GAZ	Grass, weeds.–GIZGAZ : Weeds, rubbish.–(ARAT : To cut.)

GHASA GHASI	Rubbing one against the other, as people in a crowd.
GÁZOL	Vado = to wade.–To trample.

GHAT	A way down to a river, a difficult pass through hills, a narrow way of access.–GHUTU : A mound, rising ground, bank of a river.–GHATAC GHUTUC : Many ascents and descents, as at unbridged rivers, etc.–GHATAL SANJ : Emergency.
GÁT	Agger perpluvium, moles, impedimentum = a dam in the water, an obstacle, hedge, fence.–GÁTOL : To impede, to make difficult.

GHERAO	To encircle, to surround, to hem in.–GHAR GHAṚI : A pulley wheel.–GHAR GHURHẠ : To fence round securely.–GHURANT : Circuitous.–GHURCI : To coil up, to curl up.–GORNA : A fence.–(See also KEROT.)
KERÍT	To encircle, to surround, to hem in.–KÖR : A circle.–KERÉK : A wheel.–KERT : Septum, septimentum = a fence, a secure fence.–GORÁNY : To turn a somersault.–GORNYA : Curled up.–GÁRGYA : Septura = enclosure, hedge.

GHESA	Friendly, familiar.
GÉZA	Peaceful, friendly (?).

GHET	To tie up anything in a cloth, a knot on a string.–GAT: A knot, a nob, a node.–TOL GATKADAE: He has knotted it.–GATAO: To plait, to set bricks or stones in mortar, to accept, to take.–Arrange with someone to do his work.
KÖT	Lingo, vincio = to tie, to make a knot.–KÖTÖTTE: He has knotted it.–KÖTÉS: Ligament.–(MEG)KÖT: To arrange.

GHIGRIN	A species of lizard.
GYÍK	Lacerta = a lizard.

GHORAO	The change produced in an egg by incubation.–GHORAO BELE: An egg which has undergone the change produced by incubation.–GẠRIẠ: Doer or agent; in comp. possessed of.
GERJED, GHEERYED	Succendor, flammesco = to inflame.–ERJED: To ferment.–GERJ: Motion, impulse, agitation.

GHUL GHUL	To suffer for want of air; close, oppressively close, air or breeze excluded.
FÚL	To suffer for want of air; to suffocate.

GHUSẠU, GUSẠU	To hide with a wish to shun or shirk work, etc.; to pass as time.–GHUSIẠU: To enter humbly. (E.g. in: "She crept into the house and keeps still.")–GHASKAO: To move along the ground. –GHASGHASAO: To rub or slide along in a sitting posture, as down a steep rock.
KÚSZ	To climb, to clamber, to scramble up.–KUSZKÓ: A hiding place.–KÖZ: Tempus, spatium temporis = time, meantime.

GIDAR, GIDRA	Children, little children.–GEDRA, GIDRI: Small of stature.–GEDA, GIDI: Short, undersized.
GIDA, GIDRA (?), GIDÓ	Capella = kid, fawn.

GIJRI	Curdled, sour, as milk.–KẠC KẠC: Bitter, acid.–KASA: Bitter, adstringent.–(See also KACAR.)
KESERÜ	Amarus, acerbus = sour, bitter.

GITIL	An insect that burrows in the sand in river beds.–An invisible insect said to burrow under the toes during the rain.–GICHO: Earthworm.
GILISZTA	Earthworm.

GOCA, GOJA	A mixture, such as a Santal marrying a Kol, or Indian corn and rice cooked together.–(See also KACUR MACUR.)
KOTYMA, KOTYVASZ, KOTYLÉ	A bad mixture, a squash.

GOCO	A beard, the pistils of the flower of Indian corn.
KACS	Tendril, runner, shoot.–KÓCOS : Pilosus = hairy.–KÓC : Tow ; oakum.

GOHA	A witness, to bear witness.–GOHAK : To depose.–GACAO : To confess, promise, vow, to agree.–GACHAO : To acknowledge, to admit.
GYÓN, GYOHON	Confiteor = to admit, to confess.

GOJRA	Sleepy-headed.–(See also GALAK SALAK and KALOBALO.)
KÓCSAGOS	Ameus = sleepy-headed.–GAGYOS : Benumbed.–KASUKA : Weak-minded, simple.

GOKHNA	To give a by-name, to give a name to, make fun of.
GUGG	Mockery.

GOL	Round, spherical.–GULAND : Round, spherical.–GULI : A ball.–GULU MULU : Round, spherical.
GOLYÓ, GULÓ	Sphaera = a ball, a sphere.–Testiculus = testicle.

GOM	A cultivated fruit tree.–JAMA : Applied to fruit that do not become detached from the tree when ripe ; complicated.–JAMBAL : Offspring.
GYÜMÖLCS, DIMILCS, DIMELCS	Fruit. (CSOMÓS : Knotted.)

GORHON	To carve, to engrave wood.–GARHAO : To make, to fashion, to carve.
KORHÁL	To cut wood.

GOROBIA, GOROB	Heavy, indigestible, proud, conceited.
GOROMBA	Crassus, asper, rudus, ineptus = heavy, rough, rude, thick, nasty.

GORTOROC	To introduce extraneous subjects into a discussion.
KERTEKURÁL, KERTEL (?)	To introduce extraneous subjects into a discussion.

GOROM	Grand, as in grandfather, grandmother.
KOROS	Magnus = great, aged.–GÓR : Grand.

GOSO ISIN	To cook over a slow fire. (ISIN : To cook ; to be inflamed, completion of fermentation.)–GẠSIC : To make or pass wind.–GHẠSIC, GHOSIC : To break wind.
GŐZ	Vapor = vapour ; musty exhalation ; fume ; steam. (IZZÓ : Fervens, fervidus, exaestatus = very hot, hot to boiling.)

GOSON	To follow after.
KÖZEL	Proximus = the next.

GOSRE, GHOSRE	Dull, sluggish, careless.
KOSZLOBÁR	" A man who is frivolous, inconsiderate, null."

GOTHAO	To collect cattle together.–GUTIẠU : To keep to oneself, to arrange it in order.–GUTEK, GUTKE : Very much, many. (E.g. in : " The river is in flood.")–GUTEK UTẠR : An immense number, very much, very many. (UTẠR : Added to other words is intensive, implying highest in degree, perfection, completion or absoluteness ; very. GUTU : To sting, as bees.–JUTẠU : To assemble.–JUKTẠU : To amass, to accumulate.–JẠORA : To assemble, to collect.–JẠUHAR : To assemble in large numbers.
GYŰJT, GYÖIT, GYEIT, GÖIT	Acervo, cumulo, colligo, congrego = to assemble, to accumulate, to collect.–GYŰL : Convenio, congrego = to assemble. - GYÜLEKEZET : Multitudo = a multitude.

GUCHI	Straw from which the grain has been trodden out by cattle and afterwards so drawn out, as to lay it lengthwise. It is then tied up into small bundles ; a small bundle.–GUJ GUJ : Crowded. –GUJẠ : A wedge.

GUZSOL	Exprimo = to press, to cram.-GÚZSOLÁS: Jugamentum = knotting, bond.-GÚZS: Fetter. -KOCSOL: To wedge.

GUJRẠU	To pass, as time. (E.g. in: "They spend the day anywhere and come home at meal times.")
KÉS-IK	Commoror, demoror = pass, as time.

GULI	Brown, reddish brown.
KULI	A cow with black horns.

GUM BẠI	Flatulence. (BẠI: Sickness.)
GUMÓ	A protuberance, a hump. (BAJ: Sickness.)

GUND	To ponder, to think over.-GUNDI: To cast about in one's mind, to consider, to think deeply over, to reason in one's mind.-GANDON: To think, to ponder, to consider.-GANDUK SANDUK: Careless of appearance through sorrow.-GANDUC SANDUC, GANDAC GUNDUC: Forgetful, as old people sometimes are, as one very busy or in deep sorrow.
GOND	Cogitatio = thought, opinion, care, meditation.-Cura = sorrow.-GONDOL: Cogito = to think. -Perpendo, reputo = to ponder.-Meditor = to think deeply over.-Curo = to care, to sorrow.

GUNGA	Dumb.
KUKA	Dumb.

GUNGU	A covering for the head and back of leaves pinned together, worn principally by women when planting rice.-GUNGUT: To cover with cloth, with the wings, with the body.-GUNPALAN: Panniers and panniers' saddle cloth.
GUNYA	Vestis, pannus = dress.-Sarcina (?) = cloth.

GUNTHI	The knee. (E.g. in: "They are sitting with their knees touching.")
KÖNYÖK	Elbow.-Knee.

GUPI	To tend cattle, sheep, goats, etc.
GÖBÖLYÖS	Custos armenti = a tender of cattle.

GURGURAU	To roll on the ground.-GHUR GHURAU: To cause to whirr or revolve.-GARGARAO: To roll as a ball.-GARGARAO: To revolve as a wheel in motion.-GARDA GURDẠ: Rolling on the ground one above the other.-GUDUR GUDUR, GUDRUC GUDRUC: Applied to the motion of anything small, as a wheel.
GURUL, GURDUL, GORDUL, GÖRDÜL	Volvor, volutor = to roll, to rumble (as a wheel in motion).

GURHAK	To be costive.
KORHADT	To be dryed up (as wood).

GURU	A teacher, a leader.
KURUZSOL	Incanto, ope magiae medeor = to quack.

GUSUC, GHUSUC	In amongst; to push oneself in between, to force a way in.-GHASEN: Amongst, in the middle of.-GHUS GHUS: Internally.-GUSTI: Family, tribe. (E.g. in: "The whole family are witches.")
KÖZ	Medius = in the midst of.-Communis = familiar, common. - Spatium, intervallum = space. - KÖZÉ: Inter = in amongst.-KÖZTI: Belonging to them.-KÖZTÜK: All of them.

GUTHLA, GUTRA	Short in stature, a dwarf.
KUTAK, KUTAG	Short in stature, a dwarf.

GUTI	Small pox.
(VÖRÖS) GUTA	Erysipelas.

GUYUN MENTE	Without warning, unexpectedly.
KIJÖN MENTEN	It comes out without warning.

H

HABADIẠ	A glutton, to eat greedily.
HAPSOL	Devoro cum festinatione et cum quondam sonitu = to eat greedily.

HABAK CUBẠK	Disconnectedly, indistinctly, carelessly. (E.g. in: "You speak disconnectedly." Or in: "You are leaving one piece of work before you have finished it and taking up another.")
HABAHURGYA, HEBEHURGYA	Praeceps = thoughtless, inconsiderate, heedless, giddy. (CSEVEG: Argutor, garrio = to tattle, to chatter, to gossip.)–HABOG, HEBEG: Balbutio = to stammer, to speak disconnectedly.

HABAK DABAK	To rise and fall, like the waves of the sea; to heave, as the water of a river in flood; to swell, as the sea; applied also to a crowd moving gleefully along with drums beating.–(See also DHOP.)
HABOZ, HÁBOROG	Undis agitor = to rise and fall, like the waves.–HAB: Fluctus, unda = flood, waves of the sea. (DOBOL: To beat drums.)

HABHAB	Heartily, gleefully, with zest. (E.g. in: "When rain falls they plough with zest.")
HÉV	Fervour.–HÉVEN, HEVEN: Fervide = gleefully, with zest.

HACAR HACAR	Hurriedly, quickly.–HACPACAO: To hurry, to harass, to ill-use.
HESSENGET	To chase, to drive away, to scare away.–To waste, to lavish, to squander.

HACHUC	Quietly, without saying anything.–HATAR Meanwhile, for the present, used only in combination with other verbs. (E.g. in: "Do not hinder me, let me go.")–HATKAO: To lessen, to hinder. (E.g. in: "Do not hinder me, let me go.")
HAGY, HAD	Sino = to let, to permit (without saying anything.)–HADD! HAD! Sine = let it! HAGYÁS: Omissio = omission.

HADAC HUDUC To walk as if lame or weak.

HEDEREG To wag, to rock, to totter, to waddle.

HADAM HUDUM Early in the morning, before daylight, before sunrise.

HODȦI Matutinus = matinal.–HOL, HOLDA, HOTA: Aurora, matuta, tempus matutinum = early in the morning.

HADAR HADAR Rustling or grating sound, as that produced by dragging a dry hide, or Palmyra palm leaf along the ground.–HODOR HODOR: Sound produced by dragging a piece of wood, etc. along the ground, to drag.

HEDER To sweep, to brush, to scour.

HAD HẠMUS Anæmia, pain in the bones. (HẠMUS: Anæmia.)

HAGYMÁZ Typhus. (HÁT: The neck.)

HẠDUI HẠDUI, HȮDO HȮDO, HODGO Shaggy, bushy, as hair.

HADAZ To shake the head.

HAE, HAE HAE An exclamation of sorrow or pain, alas!

HEJ Alas! Ah!

HAGAE HUGUI Rustling of cloths, as when the wearer walks.–HAKA HẠKI: To bid against each other, as at an auction.

HÁG Scando, ascendo = to walk, to climb, to rise.

HAHA Stop, stop; hold, don't; an exclamation of prohibition.

HÓ HÓ Stop, stop; hold.

HẠI Won't you, yes, used also to call attention.

HEJ, HÉ Won't you, yes, used also to call attention.

HAK HAK To laugh, to guffaw.–HIHI KOKO: Flirting, laughing and speaking with men. (E.g. in: "You spend your days in frivolity.")

HEKKES Foppish, alert, impudent.–HEKLE HUKLA: Continual babbling, foolish, foppish talking.

HAKA CAKA — To be surprised, taken aback, troubled.–HEK: To cut the wind or breath from one, as by a blow between the shoulders. (E.g. in: "He spoke so loud as to quite take away my breath.")

HÖK — Repellentis vox = stop !–(MEG) HÖKKEN: Percutio, stupefactio = to stop short, to be taken aback, to be confused.

HAKAO — To boast. (E.g. in: "He challenged them and said, Who is the man that can kill me?")

HÉJAZ, HAJAZ — Superbio = to boast. – HEKKES: Forward, impudent

---

HAKAR — To call to each other when watching crops, etc. at night.

HÉKA — Do you hear?–HÉKÁS: My dear!

HAKAR HAKAR — Applied to the wheezing of a person suffering from bronchitis.

HÁKOG — Screo, excreo = to clear one's throat, to spew out.

HAKO — A fish.

HAL — A fish.

HAL — Moisture, sap. (E.g. in: "The moisture in this place does not soon dry up.")

HALVÁNY (?) — Moisture, sap. (?)

HALA HAḶI — In exchange for, to recompense, a recompense, retribution.

HÁLÁL — To recompense.–HÁLA: Gratia = gratitude, reward, prize.

HALA ÑULAK — To wander about, as one forlorn.–HALHALAO: To press, to be urgent, to hurry.–HAL SAL: Within the year, the present year.–HAḶI SALI: A short time ago, a few days ago.–HOLA, HOLANOK: Yesterday.–HAḶI: Modern, recent, new, present, now. (E.g. in: "Current expenses.") (ÑULAK: Indistinctly.)

HALAD — Prodeo, progredior = to succeed, to go on well, to advance.–Praetereo, differeror = to postpone, to delay, to retard.–HALABURDA: Praeceps = hasty, rash.–(IDŐ) HALADÁS: Temporis preteritio = course, laps of time.–HOLNAP: Cras = to-morrow.

HALER	To ruin or destroy, applied mainly to the destruction of crops, etc., by animals grazing on them.
HÊLA	Spica inanis, granorum expers; avena fatua, avena sterilis, aegylops = sterile crops.

HAḶI	Modern, recent, new, present, now. (E.g. in: "At the present time, just now.")–HAL: Circumstance, state.–(See also HELAO.)
HELYI	Actual, present.–HELY, HEEL: Locus, spatium, situs = spot, space, situation.

HALO	To scoop with the hand or some implement fish out of water.–KHALOE: A fish basket.
HÁLÓ	Rete = a fishing net.

HALOBALO	To keep moving the arms about.
LÓBÁL	To move slowly (the arms) there and back.

HAMET	To take all, to keep oneself what belongs to others.
HAMIS, HAMAS	Iniquus, injustus = unfair, unjust.–False.

HAMOR, HAMER	A granary, a grain storehouse.
HOMBÁR, HAMBÁR	Granarium = a granary, grain-storehouse.

HANA NHA	This and that. (E.g. in: "How are you speaking? This thing and that thing? Say one thing.")–HANE, HAN: There, yonder, away, over there.–HOLE, HALE: Thus, in this state, under the circumstances.–HUNẠR: Of all kinds, of many kinds. (E.g. in: "All sorts of merchandise.")–(See also HULUK.)
HUN, HON, HOL	Tum-tum = this and that.–Ubi = there.–Ubi (conjunction) = thus.–HUN VALÓ: Res, reculae, utensilia, suppellex = little things, household furniture of all kinds.

HANAK	Epilepsy.
HÁNYÁS	Vomitus = vomiting.

HAPARAO	To contest, to strive for victory.–HABA DUBA: To rebuke, to reprove, to threaten, to frighten. –(See also HẠR.)
HÁBORÚ	Bellum = war.–HÁBORSÁG (?): Jurgium, rixa = contest, quarrel.

HAPEN	By and by, in the future.–HẠBIC : As far as, till, until, up.
HÉBEN-HÓBAN	By and by, in the future.–HÊBEKORBA : Now and then. (KOR : Time.)

HẠPSI	To joke, to ridicule. (E.g. in : " They are ridiculing me.")
HEPCIÁS	Braggart (?) ; blustering, swaggering (?).

HAR	To rub or chafe.–HORIOR, HORYOR : To glide over the surface.–HURIT : To scrape off.–HURTIR : To rub the teeth with the finger.
HORZSOL	To rub, to stroke.–To glide over the surface.–HERÉCSEL : To rub, to chafe.

HẠR	To overcome.–HARAO : To conquer, to defeat, to beat.–HẠRIT : To be vanquished, beaten.–HARKA HẠRKI : Quarrelling, altercating.–HAROP : To vanquish, to overcome.–(See also HAPARAO.)
HARZSOL, HARSOL	Certo = to fight, to quarrel.

HẠR	To draw towards oneself by the hand or any implement, to collect together, to lift and take away.
HÁROGAT	Congero = to collect together.

HẠR	Bhil, marsh.–HURUT : A fungus which grows mainly on tree stumps.
HARASZT, HOROSZT	Silva, quercetum, dụmus, dumetum = forest, oak-forest, briers, brushwood.

HARA LATAR	To overtop, to outgrow. (E.g. in : " You have outgrown me, you are taller than I am.")–HIR HIR : Tall, as a man. (LATAR : To put under or underneath.)
HÓRI-HORGAS	Longurio = very tall grown. (LETÁR : To put under.)

HẠRIBOL	A shout given during the marriage-ceremony.
HÖRE, HÖRÉSZ, HÉRÉSZ	The after-wedding.–HERE : Wedding.

HAṚIA, EK HAṚIA	Once round, as in tying a rope; a harrow or cold crusher drawn by one pair of oxen or buffaloes. (E.g. in: "Tie it by putting the rope once round.")
HUROK	Nodus mobilis, laqueus, pedica, tendicula = a (running) knot; noose, loop, mesh, tendril. (EKE: A plough.)-HARISNYA: Stocking.

HARKET, HARAKAT, HARKHA HAṚKHI	To irritate, to tantalize.-HARAN HURUN: Hastily, as a person enraged.
HARAG, HARAGUTT	Iratus = irritated.-HERGEL: To irritate.

HARMAD, HARMADIA, HARMAND	Scoundrelly, rascally, base.
HARAMIA	Praedo, latro = robber, highwayman.

HAṚMAṚ, HURMUR	Hastily, quickly, rapidly, industriously.
HAMAR, HAMMAR	Properus, cito, subito, celeriter = hastily, in a hurry, quickly, rapidly.

HAROP	To join closely, to place in or on anything forked; to vanquish, to overcome.-HADAP: To nibble; to take grain out of the husk with the teeth.-HAP: To eat, to take a bite.-HURUR: To strip off, as flesh from bone.
HARAP	Mordeo = to bite.

HAṚSUR	To become low, as a fire.
HARAP	Fire spreading in low herbs.

HARTA	Skin, leather, a hide.
HÁRTYA	Membrana = skin, parchment.

HARTA, HARTAO	To serve out food, to place food before one.
HÉRIC	The feast (after the fasting).

HAṚU	The small flies found in some fruits.
HERNYÓ, HERNYÚ	Worm, grub, vermin.-HERE: A drone.

HARUN	To weep and groan.
HÖRÖG	To have a rattling in the throat.

HARWAHA	A ploughman, a person who ploughs.–HURUT : Stump of a tree in ground. (E.g. in : "Stumps and roots.")
HORVASZT	To hew out, to lop, to root out.–HOROL : To root out, to grub up.

HASA	Earth, soil, land, to bury, to become soil.–SEBEL HASA : Good, fertile, soil.
HAZA, HÁZA	Domum, patria. (SZÉP : Good, fertile.)–HÁZ : Domus, taberna, familia = house, lodging, residence, family.

HAS GADLAK	A pit from which earth has been dug. (GADLAK : Having holes or hollows here and there.)–(See also HUCAK.)
HÉZAG	Cavus, inanis = hollow, empty.

HAT CUT, HATH CHUTI	Active, energetic.–HATIAU : To take, to lay hands on, to help oneself to.–HUT, HUTHA : Strong-headed, self-willed, independent.–HUT HUTU : High, lofty. (E.g. in : "Elephants are high when they stand.")–(See also HOTERE.)
HATALOM, HATAM	Pollentia, valentia, energia = might, energy.–(KI)HATÓ : Activus = active.–HAT, HOT : Possum = to have power, to be able to.–Possideo = to possess.–HATALMAS : Vastus, grandis = great, considerable, high.

HATA	A piece of ground, surrounded by a ditch.–A compound.
HATÁR	Territorium, ora = district, domain.–HATÁROL : Termino, limito = to bound by, to limit.–(ÖSSZVE) HADAR : Commisceo = to mix, to mingle, to compound.

HATA BADI, HATA BAJI	To vie, to contend, to contest ; rivalry. (BADI : Enmity, hostility.)
HAD	Bellum, pugna, proelium = war, contention. (BAJVIVÁS : Duel.)

HATAK	A winnowing sieve, used also for sifting grain. The " hatak " is oblong in shape and has a raised rim round three sides.
HATAKOS	Having a distended, sticking out shape.
HATAO	To push back or away, to overcome.–HATAORI : A hammer.
HADAR	Ferio, peto, percutio = to push, to hit, to drive into.
HAT DAHAR	The Milky Way. (DAHAR : A cart track, a road made by use.) – HATAHUT : One beyond another, clustered.
HAD ÚT, HADAK UTJA	The Milky Way. (ÚT : Road, way.)
HATE	Hear, listen. (E.g. in : " Hear, a fruit is fallen.")
HALLD, HAD (?)	Hear, listen.–HALL, HADLAVA : Audio = to hear.
HATKHAṚI	A method of divination, resorted to during illness.
HAT	Credo, commendo = to confide, to entrust to. (KÓR : Illness.)
HATOK, HOTOK	The neck.–HADI : Aching pains in the neck or shoulders.–HATAHUT : One beyond another.–HATLAK : Armpit.
HÁT	Dorsum, tergum = the back, the neck. (LUK : Fovea = a hole, pit.)
HATOKAETE, HOTOKAETE	Carelessly, without circumspection.
HATLAT	To work carelessly, without circumspection.
HAYA	To feel a desire for, to long for.–HIROHI : To long for, to sigh for.
ÓHAJ	To feel a desire for, to long for, to sigh for.
HE	True ; yes, to admit, to agree, to assent.–HIẠ : Love, solicitude, liking.
HŰ	Fidus, fidelis, creditor, credo = true, faithful, to believe, to admit.–Good, true-love.

HEBEN	Unpalatable, as some kind of wild herbs.
HIBÁS	Defectu laborat, vitiosus = defective, vitiated.
———	
HEJ	Disrespectfully, tauntily, detractingly, disparagingly.
HEGYKE, HETYKE	Taunting, disparaging, impudent, presumptuous.
———	
HEJ HEJE	To straddle.
HEZSETEL	To move convulsively, to sprawl, to flounder.
———	
HEJER	To roll the skin back from the prepuce.–To cut. (E.g. in : " Behead him.")–HAIAR : A pointed piece of wood or bamboo, used to dig up roots, tubers, etc.
HEGYES	Pointed.–HEGYEZ : Spiculo, acumino, fastigio, cacumino = to point.
———	
HELAO	To move on. (E.g. in : " He has put them to work.")–HELA : A large area covered thickly with cut brushwood.–(See also HALI.)
HELYEZ, HELYHET	Loco, pono = to move on.–HELY, HEEL : Area, spatium locus, situs = place, spot, area.
———	
HEMKHEM	To delay, to loiter, to waste time. (E.g. in " What are you wasting time for ? Do the work at once.")–HIMAN, HUMAN : To confess, to admit.
HÍM, HÉM	Fucatio, circuitio = round about way, disgression.–HIMEZ-HÁMOZ : To palliate, to extenuare, to beat about the bush.
———	
HENA	Doubtless, more than likely, a moral certainty.
HÁN	Yes, surely.
———	
HENAT, HENAN	To impress one. (E.g. in : " I partly believed it.") (See also HITU.)
HIN, HEN	Credo, puto = to trust, to rely on a person, to believe.
———	
HENDE PENDE	Putting off time. (E.g. in : " He is putting off his time and not working.")–HENDO : Lounging about.–HEŃJLAN : Slovenly.
HENYE	Torpidus, deses = inactive, lazy.–HENYÉN : Slovenly.

HENDOR HENDOR	Sound produced by spinning wheel.
HENTEREG, HENDEREG, HENDERED	Volutor = to revolve.

HENJET HENJET	Numerous, in crowds. (E.g. in: "They are coming in crowds.")
HEMZSEG	To swarm, to come in crowds.

HENSTA, HEMOSTA	To rail at, to despise, to contemn, to scout, to scoff at. (E.g. in: "He speaks contemptuously.")
HENCEG	To rail at, to scout, to speak contemptuously.

HEPER HENDE	To hang about.–EHER: To sit on the ground with the knees up to the breast. (E.g. in: "Why are you sitting? Go to your work.")
HEVER	Cubito, desideo = to hang about.–HÉVIZÁL: Otior = to idle.

HERAK	Brown, applied to fowls only.
HERJO	A partridge.

HEREL HOPON	A male. (HOPON: A child.)–HEREL: A man, a husband.
HERE	Virilia, testiculi = testicles. – HERÉCEL, HERGEL; To beget.

HESA HISI	Each telling the other to do something.
HISZEN	Well, but!–At least.

HEWA	To accustom, to practise, to break in cattle, to inure, to habituate, to season, to familiarize. (E.g. in: "By continued stealing he has become a confirmed thief." Or in: "He is a man accustomed to fast.")
HIVATAL	Vocatio = vocation.–Officium = profession, business.

HIDHIDI	To stand with the feet wide apart.–HUDRA: Steps on a ladder.
HÍD	Tons = bridge.–Board, plank, shelf.

HIJUK	To come, to approach. (E.g. in : " Come quickly.")
IGYEKVÖ	Endeavouring, making efforts.–To come. (?)

HILAU	To move, to shake, to tremble, to sway.
HÜL	Perterreor, obstupesco = to move, to be astonished, taken aback.

HIN	Low, deficient, weak, abated, decreased.
HINGA	Weak, feeble, unsteady.

HIN, HAN, HANI	Loss, deficiency.–HIDAN THAPAN : Thin, sparse, as badly germinated seed.
HIJÁN, HIÁN	Hoc defectu = loss by.–HIÁNY : Loss, deficiency.

HIŃHAU, HINHINAU	To neigh, as a horse.
HINNYOG	Hinnio = to neigh, as a horse.

HIRIC	A spasm of pain.
HIRICSEL	To languish.–To be parched with thirst.

HITU, HETO	Familiar, acquainted, known. (E.g. in : " You are a known person, get a loan for me.")–HETAO : To heed, to regard, to pay attention to. (E.g. in : "Pay attention to our prayer.")–(See also HENA.)
HIT, HÜT	Fides = faith.–HISZ : Credo = to believe.–HIHETŐ : Versibilis, credibilis, probabilis, authenticus = credible, authentic, well known.–HITEL : Credit.

HO	Used in calling attention.
HÓ	Used in calling attention.

HO	Also, even, too, besides.
HA	Etsi = even.–HOGY, HO : Quam, quantopere = also, too.

HOBON HOBON	Going here and there aimlessly.
HÉBEN	Frustra, inianiter = aimless, to no purpose.

HODO DODO	Quickly and indistinctly, applied to speech.
HADAR	Quickly and indistinctly, applied to speech.

HOE	Wind, air, climate.–HOYON: Breeze, wind, air, draught. (E.g. in: "There is much wind there—we will take shelter.")
HŐ, HEU, HOU	Aestus, calor, tepor = warmth, heat.–HŐ JŐN: There is much warmth there; a warm breeze is coming.

HOE HOE	Immodestly, without training. (E.g. in: "He does not know how to work, he has grown up untrained.")
HIUN	Otiore = slothful, idle.–HIU, HIV, HEI, HY: Vanus = vain, to no purposes.

HOETO . . . HOETO	Either . . . or; perhaps.
HÁTHA . . . HÁTHA	Either . . . or; perhaps.

HOHO	To call. (E.g. in "He called them near." Or in: "Call him to come.")
HÍ, HÉ, HIO	Voco, calo, incalo = to call.

HOLE, HALE	In this state, under the circumstances, thus.
HOL	Ubi (as a conjunction) = thus.

HON	A rat.
HONCSIK	A mole-hill. (CSIK: Stria = strip.)

HONAN, HONEC, HUTKAM	Used in conditional sentences in which the protasis (condition) is supposed not to have been realized, and, therefore, the apodosis (consequent) has not taken place.
HONNAN, HONNÉT	Therefore.

HOR	A path, a way, a road.
HORH	Pass, defile. (Ascendit per hurh.)–HOROL: To root out, to grub up.

HORA	A section, a line.
HÚR	Corda = segment of a circle.

HORO HORO	To carry food, etc.–HORO : To put on the person, as a coat, ring, ear-rings, a hat, etc. (E.g. in : " Santal girls wear anklets.")–HORA : To finish, to make a clean sweep. (E.g. in : " Do not allow it to accumulate, throw it all away.")
HORD	Porto, gero, degero, aggero, devecto = to carry, to wear, to bear, to transport, to throw away.

HOROK	To sink or become hollow, as the eyes.
HORPAD	To become hollow, as the eyes.

HORSEC	Obliquely, to one side, sideways.
HARÁNTOS	Obliquus = obliquely.–Sideways.

HOT	To strip off by running the hand up the stalk.
HÁNT, HÁMT	Excortico, decortico, glubo = to peel, to bark.

HOTERE, HOTETE	By means of, through. (ETE CETE : To attempt to do one's best.)–HATEA : Piteously, pitifully. (E.g. in : " Give him, he pleads so pitifully.")–(See also HAT CUT.)
HAT	To effect, to operate, to act upon.–To affect.–(MEG)HATÓAN : Piteously.

HOTO BUDHI	Foolish, senseless.
HIT, HEJT, HEUT	Stultus = foolish. (BUTA : Foolish, senseless.)

HOYO, HOYON	To shave.–HOPYO : The hair on the portion of the head which some men shave regularly.
HAJ	Crinis, capillus = hair.

HOYAN	Off the straight, at an angle, glancing off, twirling in the air as a falling leaf.
HAJOL, HAJT	Inclino, flecto = to incline, to twirl.

HUẠK	To eat.
HÚS	Carnis = flesh, meat.

HUBẠG, HUBẠK	To slash. (E.g. in : " They slashed and killed him.")
HUPÁL	To slash.–HUPPOL : To beat, to clap.

HUCẠK, HUCEC	To break off, to snip off.
HASASZT	Findo, diffindo = to split, to crack, to break off.

HUCHUCU	Lofty, high. (E.g. in: " The hill appears high.")
HEGY	Mons = mountain.

HUC	Quickly.–(GI: Incomp. emphatic.)
HUCSKI	Out! Quickly! (" Marsch hinaus!"– KI: Out!)

HUCAK, HUCEC	To break off, as an engagement; to be disappointed, as a hope or expectation.
HUCSOR	To take possession of something in an unrighteous manner.

HUDUL RAJ, HUDUR RAJ	The angel of death, the governor of the nether world. (RAJ: A king, a governor.)
HOLT, HÓT	Mors = dead.

HUGUI	Light, gentle, as wind.
HÍG	Uvidus = thin, tender.–Vitilis = flexible, supple.– HÍGUL: Eliquesco, emolior = to be cleared, to become thin, fine.

HUHU	An imitative word: weeping.
HUHOGAT	To weep continuously.

HUHU	The hooting of the owl.
HUHOKOL, HUHOL, HUHOG	To hoot as an owl.

HUJUK HUJUK, HUJTUK	In crowds, in swarms, from all sides.
HÚGY	Stella = star.

HUJU DURIẠ	An ornament worn by women and girls, attached to the coiled hair at the back of the head. (DURIA: A tassel, a fringe.)
HÍGY	Inauris = ornament for the ears.

HUJUR	To trickle.
HÚGY	Urina = urine.

HUL	To riot, to rebel, to mutiny.–HULAS BHANGA : To be dejected.–HULAK HULEC : To break off, to snipp off, with the fingers. (E.g. in : " They pluck off the buds of the tea bushes.") (BHANGA : To break.)
HULL, HÚL	Cado, caso, decido = to fall off, to revolt.–HULLAT: Dejecto = to deject.–HULLADÉK : Ramentum, scobs, fragmen = shreds, scraps, fragments.

HULAR, HULAR	To lay waste, to destroy. (E.g. in : " They laid waste the whole country.")
HULLONG	Erro = to live the life of adventurers.–HULLONGÓ : A tramp.

HULUK HULUK	Often, time after time.–(See also HANA NHA.)
HOL-HOL, HUL-HUL, HUN-HUN	Tum = time after time.

HUMTAK, HUNTAK	To splash up.–To raise or agitate water from underneath as a fish.–HUNDA, HUNDAK : To knock down. (E.g. in : " Reach and knock it down with a stick.")
HINT, HIMT	Spargo = to disseminate, to sprinkle.–Sterno = to let down, to knock, to cast down.–HÁNY, HÁN : Emolior, jacto, succutio = to throw, to cast.

HUNDAR	The Indian wolf.
HUSZTÁJ	The wolf.

HURA	Damaged, injured.–HURA : Having any deformity of the nose, whether natural or artificial.–HURJA : Having a stiff knee joint. – HURWAN : To injure, to damage.
HORGOS, HORGAS	Menda = a fault, a defect.–HURBANCS : Injured, torn, ragged, shabby.

HURA HURI	Pushing and pulling.
HURCZOL, HURCSOL (?)	Distraho, traho, tracto, vexo, rapto = to drag, to trail, to push and pull.

HURET	To give to the ankle a twist.–HURBAN: Curled up.–HARET PATET: Crossing the feet when walking. (PATET: To cross the legs, to plait.)
HORHAD (?)	Incurvesco = to become crooked.–HORGASZT: To give a twist.

HURU HURU	To doze.
HERE	An idler, a slothful person.

HURUM DURUM	To dragoon, to bluster, to hound, worry by bluster and threats.
HÚROL	Opprobro = to scold, to chide.–HURCOL: Vexo = to dragoon.–HURÉSZ: Domineering, imperious, playing the master.

HURUR	To strip off, as flesh from bone.–HURIT: To scrape off.
HURNYA	Flesh stripped off from bone.–HURNYAGYAPJU: Scraped off wool. (GYAPJU: Wool.)

HUSIẠR	Intelligent, prudent, cautious, smart, sly.
HUSZÁR	The special kind of Magyar soldier, the "hussar".

HUSUC	Hiding, keeping out of sight.–BOLO HUSUCAKANAE: He is hiding inside.–HOSEC: To get out of the way, to move, to sift. (E.g. in: "Move a little out of the way.")–HOSOT: To move while sitting on the ground without rising up.–HẠSUR: To set, as the heavenly bodies.
HÚZ	Traho = to draw, to pull, to haul.–BELEHUZÓD-IK Ő: He is hiding inside.–HUZÓD-IK: To move while sitting on the ground without rising up.–To set, as the heavenly bodies.

HUT HUTU	Lofty, high, tall.–HUTUK: Huge, large, very big, a very large rock.
HUTYOROD-IK	Cresco, incresco, surgo in altum = to grow in height, to crawl up.

HUIYẠ, HUIYẠTE	Being, an unexpected occurrence. (E.g. in: "Being such a man as you are could you do this work?")
HELYES, HEJES	Opportunus = opportune.

I

IẠ	What do you call it, so and so, you know ; to do. Used when the speaker does not remember the proper word or through delicacy omits to use it. -(See also IYO.)
ILY, IJ	Talis, eiusmodi = so and so, such.
IẠTE	Through, by means of, owing to. (E.g. in : " It is through you I am suffering too much.")
MIATT, MIÁT	Ob, propter, prae = by means of, owing to.-Per = through.
IBIL	Thick, dense, close together.-IBIL PAÑJAR : Stout, sturdy. (PAÑJAR : The part of the body in which the ribs are.)
IPERED	To grow strong, to augment.
IDI	The heel.
IDEG	Nerve, sinew, tendon.
IDHOC ODHOC CALAKKANA	He waddles.-(See also CALA.)
IDE-ODA	There and back.
IDU	Possibly, gives the idea of uncertainty.-IDI : To continue. (E.g. in : " He ate as he went." Or in : " This has been our unbroken custom.")-ẠDI, UDI, UTẠR : Much, many, very, a long time. (E.g. in : " Only after a very long time.")-ADHER : Past prime, getting old.-ẠDIN : Out of season, out of date, late.-ẠT : Opportunity, suitable time.-ẠTRE : After a lapse of, periodically.
IDŐ, EDE, ÜDE	The course of time.-Age.-IDŐVEL : With the time, possibly. IDŐZ : To remain, to continue, to sojourn.-IDŐS : Past prime, getting old.-IDÉTLEN : Out of season.-ITT : Here. (Suitable time.)-IDŐRE : After a lapse of, periodically.-IDGYOL : Forsan = perhaps.

IKOC SOKOC	To shake, to sway up and down, to joggle. (SOKOC: To shake up, to toss, to heave, to hitch up. E.g. in: "He shogged because he was mounted on a horse.")
ÜGET, IGET	Trotto = to trot, to jog. (SZÖK-IK: Salio, salto = to spring, to hitch up, to gallop.–ZÖKÖG: To shake up, to toss.)

IKOT	To be assured, to be relieved from doubt, fear or suspicion.
IGOD, IGYOLD	Satis bonus, sic satis bene = that is right.

IKOT	To decide, to settle, to sum up.
IKTAT	Deduco = to transmit, to settle, to decide.

IKRUM	To kneel.–THITRAK: The calf of the leg, the leg between the calf and the heel, the shin.
IKRA	Sura = the calf of the leg.–IKRÁLLÓ: Part of the shin.

ILENAE	He has decamped.–IL: A feather.
(EL)ILLAN	To decamp.–ILLA: Fuga, discessusu clancularius = flight, escape, run away.–ILLANA Ő: He has decamped.

ILET	To apply an ointment to a sore.
ILLET	Applico = to apply (as an ointment to a sore).

IŃ	The first personal pronoun I, also me.–IŃẠK, IŃ REAN, IŃAN: Mine.
ÉN, ÍN	The first personal pronoun I.–ENYÉM: Mine.

IN GAN, IN GANTE, IN GONTE	Reasonable, judicious, moderately, within compass.
IGAZ	Verus, verax, justus, equus = right, true, just.–IGAZÁN: Recte, directe rite, juste = truly, righteously, fairly.

INẠTE	Therefore, for that reason.
INNÉNT, INNÉT, YNÉTEN	Therefore, for that reason.

INDE	Here.–ITI : This, this present. (E.g. in : " Go this minute." Or in : " Do the work this minute.")
ITT, IDE	Here, on the spot, immediately.

INDIT	To blame.–ENDAK : To cross in front of (which is considered under certain circumstances as an omen presaging evil).–ENDE : Then.–ENDRE : To be angry.–EAD : To remember, to commit to memory.
INT, ENT	Moneo, commoneo = to admonish, to blame.–INDUL : Animo, moveor = to become excited, agitated.

INGUT	To stoop.
ING, INOG	Moveor = to be moved, to be shaken, to stoop (in walking).–INGAT : To agitate, to shake.

INKA	Like this, a little, not too much.–(See also UNKẠ.)
IGY	Sic = like this, a little, not too much.–INKÁBB : Rather, like this (?).

IR, IROK	To reap.–(See also ARAK.)
ÉR-IK, ÍR-IK	To ṛeap.

IRIC	To extinguish, to go out, as fire.
IRT, IROT	Runco, exputo, extirpo = to extirpate, to exterminate.–To extinguish.

IRẠ IRI, ERA IRI	Sulky, ill-natured, be at enmity.–IRẠ : Spiteful.
ÍRIGY, ÍRÉGY	Invidus, malevolus = envious, malicious, jealous.

IRIC CIKIC	Fond of jollity, junketing, revelry, amusement.
ÖRÜL, ERIL, ÜRÜL	Gaudeo, laetor, jubilo = to rejoice, to find pleasure in, to amuse.

ISẠRA	A sign, a hint, to make a sign, to give a hint.–ISTIHAR : Notice, proclamation.
IZEN	Nuncio = to give notice, to proclaim, to give a hint.–IZENET : Advice, notice.

ISBIS	Irritating, annoying, provoking, galling, aggravating.–ISBIS GODOKAE: He will at once become irritated.
IZGAT	To irritate, to annoy, to provoke, „to aggravate.–IZGUL: To become irritated. (BÖSZ: Furious.)–IZELKED-IK: To provoke.
ISI	A score, twenty.–(In Mundari: HISI.)–HIS, HISA: Share, portion, part, division.[1]
HÚSZ	Twenty.–KÉTHUSZ: Forty.–(KÉT: Two.)
ISI	The plough beam, to which the yoke is attached.
ÍZ	Articulus, pars = member, joint, part.
ISIN	To cook, to be inflamed, completion of fermentation.
IZZ	The glow.–IZZÓ: Fervens, fervidus = red-hot, boiling hot.
ISIR	To grin, to show the teeth as a dog when snarling, to sniggle, to joke, to be humorous, to make fun.
ÍZ-IK	To yawn, to gape.–IZÉL: To make fun.
ISKO	So, this.
EZ	So, this.
ISOT	To waddle.
IZOG	To waddle.
ISTOK	All, every. (E.g. in: "All the people have gone.")
ÖSSZES, ÖSSZ	All, every.
ITẠ	Seed.
ÜLTET, ŰTET, ÍTET	To sow.
ITẠT	Food left over on a plate.–ET ETE, TOM ET ETE: Uncomfortable feeling in stomach after having eaten to much.–UDKHUD: Food.–(See also ATA SATA and AHALAHAL.)
ÉT, ÉTEL	Cibus = food. (GYOMOR: Stomach.)
IYO	So, this, as . . . as. (E.g. in: "As large as this.") (See also IẠ.)
ILY, IJ, IJEN	Talis, eiusmodi = so, this, as . . . as.

[1] The Santal counted in twenties.

J

JA — Used when addressing a boy, or one's younger brother.

ÖCS — Frater germanus minor natu = one's younger brother.–A younger person in general.–CSÁCSÓ : A humorous apostrophe for men.–CSÁB, CSÁK, CSÁL : Nomen viri = a name for men.

JA — To fix, to settle, to fix certain areas by estimation. (See also BACA.)

BÖCS, BECS — Aestimatio, census = estimation.

JABRE — Thickly, close together, blotted.

CSOPORT, CSAPORT, CSIPORT, CSOPRON — Copiose congregatus = group, cluster.

JABDAO — To set down, to snub, to overpower.–JẠBUN : To overcome.–JẠBRI : Seriously ill.

GYÁPOL — To knock down.–ZSÁBA, SABA : Ischias = Sciatica.

JADA — More, much, too much.

SŐT — Immo = much more.

JADAM JADAM — Night-long, all night.

SÖTÉT — Tenebrae = darkness.

JAE — Victory.–JOS : To succeed.

GYŐZ — Vinco : to succeed, to triumph, to gain victory.

JAHAJ — A ship.

SAJKA — A ship, a little boat.–(The suffix KA is a Magyar diminutive.)

JAHIT — To exert oneself, to spare no efforts, to bestir, to take trouble.

CSAHIN — Alacer, vivax = lively, vivid, strong, vigorous, forcible.

JAKHAM	To wound, a wound.
GYAK	Pungo, figo = to pierce, to bore.
JAKIR, JAKIRA	To be assiduous, to persevere.
CSÖKÖNYÖS	To be assiduous, to persevere.
JAL	A net.-JHALI : A snare, trap, net to snare, trap, net.
GYALOM	Vericulum, sagena = a net (fishing tackle, drag-net.)-CSÁL : Decipula = a trap, a snare.
JALAI	To darn, to sew slightly and with long stitches.-JELJELIA : Not closely woven, as in coarse cloth.
SELEJT	Bad merchandise, bad, useless.
JALO	A species of hawk.
SÓLYOM	Falco, haliaetus = falcon.
JAM	A fixture.-JAMKA JUMKI : In knots, in a party, in a group.-JUMA JUMI : Together, united.-(See also CAMPTA.)
CSOMÓ, CSOM	A fixture.-A knot.-A group.-Conglobatim = assembled.-CSONK : A party, a group.
JAM BATI	A large brass drinking vessel. (BATI : A metal cup or basin.)
CSANAK, CSANYAK	Scyphus = a drinking vessel.
JAMANI, JAMIN	To become surety, á surety.
GYÁM	Trustee, surety, support.
JAMAO	To congeal, to coagulate, to curdle, applied to milk.
CSÁMPOROD-IK	Acesco = to curdle.
JAMBAK JOMBOK	Staggering.
CSÁMPÁS, CSÁMBÁS	Curvipes = bandy-legged. - CSÁMPÁSKOD-IK : Lento gradu incedo = to walk in a staggering manner.

JAMBHUẠ	Ignorant, foolish.
CSÁMBURDI	Half a fool.–CSÁMPÁS : Ignorant.

JAÑ JẠPI, JHAÑ JHẠPI, JHAÑ JHẠTI	Emaciated.–JONJROC : Slim, thin, poor.–JAÑJAL, JOÑJAL : Anxiety, trouble, embarrassment, difficulty. (E.g. in : " We are in great anxiety through poverty.")
CSONTORGÓ	Emaciated.–CSONKA : Poor, slim.

JANGA	The foot, the leg.
CSÁNK	The foot, the leg.–CSONGÁR (?) : A small leg.

JAORE JAORE	Imploring, earnestly, urgently.–DELA : To invite, to accompany, come.–DO : An emphatic or persuasive particle used with the imperative. (E.g. in : " Come in a little.")
GYERE GYERE, DELE DELE (?)	Come along !–GYÖN, JÖN, DÖN (?) : To come.

JAPA JOPO	Slow, as if benumbed with cold ; weak.
SÁPADT	Pale.

JAPAN JUPUN	Tottering, slowly and painfully, as an old person.–JAPAK JERET : To lounge here and there.–(See also CAPAT.)
CSAPONG	Fluctuo = to totter.–Oberro = to lounge here and there.–(MEG)CSAPPAN : Macescere, deficiere = to become lean, emaciated.

JARAC JURUC, JHARAC JHURUC	Small and ill-looking, as starved children.–JARO : Worn out, weakened, reduced.–JARAO : To become weak or helpless by hunger.
GYARLÓ	Debilis, infirmus, invalidus = weak, infirm, invalid. - GYARLÓD-IK : Labefactor = to become effete.–SARTÓD-IK : In miserum statum redigor = to stunt away.

JARAL JARAL	Flashing, shimmering.–JARI JARAO : To be burned up, to burn.–JOROK : To warm oneself over a fire.
ZSARÁT, ZSARÁTNOK, SARATNAK	Glow, embers.–SOROL : To burn up (?).

JARAPI, JARAPIẠ — Applied to property inherited from a wife's relative.

GYARAP-IK — Augeor = to augment, to increase (in property).

JARDE JARDE — Large clot of earth. (E.g. in: " Large clots of earth are turned up by the plough.")–JẠRHI: Marsh, swamp.

SÁR — Limus = mud, marsh.

JẠRI — To importune, to beg hard.–JẠRIBANA, JURIBANA: To impose, to fine.

ZSAROL — To extort.–ZSARTOS: Violent, outrageous.–CSARABUL: To obtain by begging hard.–SARC: Census, tributum, exatio = ransom, duty, penalty.

JẠRI BUTI — Medicinal roots, simples. (BUTẠ: Root.)

SARJU — Aftermath.

JARO — Line, race, ancestry.

SOR — Line.–Aetas = age.

JẠRUMDAK — Tears. (DAK: Water.)–SURUC SURUC: To sob.

SIRAM — Flatus, luctus = weeping, tears.–SIR: To sob.

JATAN — Adhesive, as clay. (E.g. in: " That soil is very sticky.")

CSÁTOS — Sticky.

JẠUSẠ JẠUSI — Quickly.–(See also DACAN DACAN.)

GYORS, GYARS — Quick, swift, prompt.

JE — Whatever, what; that, in introducing oblique narration.–JE JEMON: As, in conformity with.–JEMNE, JEMON: In order that, so that. (E.g. in: " Be careful so that he may not run away.")–JEMNEC: So that, in order that.–JENO: So that, in order that. (E.g. in: " So that it may not thus happen.)–(See also SE.)

SE, SEM — Nec, neque = " also not ".–It is used in Magyar with imperative and optative, as well as with indicative and conditional.–(HOGY) SEM, (MINT) SEM: Quam = as.

JEDER — Sunshine, to sun oneself.–SETON: Direct rays of the sun.

SÜTKÉREZ — To sun oneself in the sun.–SÜT: To shine.

JEKRE — As if rooted or anchored, said only when finding fault, adhesive, sticky. (E.g. in: "You went and anchored there.")

CSEKÉLY, SEKÉLY — Vadosus, exiguus, modicus = small, insignificant, insipid, shallow.–A ford.

JEL — A deer.–MEROM JEL, GOTHRA JEL: The hind of the ravine deer.

SÜLDŐ — Porcella, porculus = young pig.–Any young game in general.

JEL — Flesh, flesh meat.

SÜL — Torresco = to be grilled, roasted.–SÜLT: Flesh meat.

JENGET JENGET — Bright red, pleasing to the senses.–JENKETE: Virginity.–JANAM: To originate, to spring, to be born.–JANMAL: Offspring. (E.g. in: "He is my offspring.")

ZSENGE, SENGE — Primitiae = first fruits, tender, not ripe.–(KI)-ZSENDÜL: Egermino = to spring out.

JENTHE — Sticky, adhesive.

GYANTA, GYENTÉR, GYENTÁR — Resin, varnish.

JER — Gum, exudation of certain trees. – JERJER: Sticky, as bird lime.

ZSÍR — Fructus, humor = production, moisture.–(FENYŐFA)ZSÍR: Resina pini = resin of pine-trees.

JEREJERE — To be stunted as a plant growing under unfavourable conditions, unpropitious.–JERBAR: Reduced, wearied.–JERE BEDHE: Stunted, dwarfed.

GYÉR — Scanty, thin, scarce, few.

JERKEC — To copulate.

CSÖRSZÖL — To copulate.

JHABAR JHUBAR	Drenched, dripping, as the clothes of one who has just waded through a river.–JIPIR JIPIR: Drizzling.–(See also CABCAB CẠBUK and CHEPKO..)
CSEPEG, CSUPOG-CSEPEG	Stillo = dripping.

JHAJHARIC	A charm doctor, one who cures snake bite, etc.
GYÓGYIT, GYÓGIT	Curo = to cure.

JHẠKHẠND	Past its best, as a tree showing signs of decay.–JHAKAO: To subside, as water.
CSÖKKENT	Diminished.–CSÖKKEN: To subside, as water.

JHALKA	Flirtation, gallantry, coquetry.
CSALFA	Coquet, flirting.

JHANGA JHUTA	Broken, in holes, torn, dilapidated.
CSONKA	Mutilus, truncatus = mutilated, maimed, broken.–Defectivus, mancus, imperfectus = defective, imperfect.

JHAO JHAO	Applied to the continued barking of dogs.–JHẠU JHẠU: To bow-wow, to bark.
CSAHOL, CSAVOL	Nictare, gannire, latrare feram insequendo = to bark, to yelp.

JHAP	A challenge.–JHAP EM: To give a challenge, to brave.–JOBORI: Violent.
GYAPON	To get angry, to fall into a passion.

JHAR	Liquor which oozes out of the malted grain during fermentation; deposits of urates or phosphates in urine.
SER, SÖR	Beer.–SÁR: Filth, mire, mud, slime.

JHAR	A bush, clump, tuft, thicket.–JHAR, JHUR: A thicket, tangled branches.
SÓR	Lucus, baltus = a grove.–CSERJE, CSERNYE: Silva, virgultum frutex = bush, shrub.–CSERCS: (?) Thicket.–SÜRÜ: Condensa arborum = thicket.

JHARAK JHURUK	In a band, in a crowd.
SEREG	Turba, furma, agmen, caterva, exercitus, classis, cohors = hoard, mass, army, crowd.

JHARKAND	Full-grown.
SERKENT	Full-grown.–SERDÜL : Adolesco, cresco = to grow, having attained to (wo-)manhood.–SERDÜLT : Adult.

JHARNA	A spring of water.
CSERMELY	A spring of water.

JHIK	The Indian porcupine.
SÜL, SÜN	A porcupine.

JHIL JHILIA	Not closely woven, having intervals between the threads.
SILÁNY	Wretched.

JHILON JHOLON	Hanging down.
CSÜLLÖNG, CSELLENG	Pendeo = hanging down.

JHOPO TORO	Scrub, jungle. (THORO THOPO : Stunted, as trees and field crops.) JHOPRO BIR : Dense scrub, jungle. (BIR : Jungle.)–(See also CEPA.)
GYEP, GYEPÜ	Herbetum = grass.–Ager incultus = jungle (?)–GYOPÁR : Wild majoram and other similar plants.

JHOROE JHOROE	Sound of wind and rain.
CSERDÜL, CSÖRDÜL	Strepere = to rustle.

JHUNKẠ	Hollow bell-shaped ornaments of bell-metal having small stones or pellets of iron inside, which rattle when the wearer walks.
CSÖNGŐ	A small bell, a rattle.

JHURU JHURU	Polished, smooth, sleek.
SÚROL	Frio, frico, tero, attero = to rub, to clean by rubbing.

JI	To smell, to sniff.–JIBKẠ: To keep back part of an accusation, or of evidence, so that the culprit may not be utterly undone.
SZÍ	Sugo, attroho = to suck.–To sniff.–CSIBELLÉREZ: To sniff more and more.–(VISSZA)-SZÍV: To keep back.

JIẠR, JIOL	Always moist, as soil.
CSIATAG	Novellus = a water plant.–CSIBOR: Dysticus hydrophilus = aquatic beetles.

JID	To struggle, endeavour, to exert oneself, make effort, use diligence, be careful, apply oneself, be assiduous, persistent, persevere.–JIDẠHI: Persistent, persevering, vigorous, assiduous.–JIWER JEWER: Of viscous consistency, persistent under difficulties.
SITÁR	Cattle-driver.–SZIVÓS: Persistent, assiduous, perseverent.–Flexilis=supple, steadfast.

JIHU	Two species of birds bear this name, the Bengal babbler and the bush chat.
CSUHESZ	Passer = sparrow.

JILA	A district, a division of a country, for administrative purposes.
GYILÁSZ	A traditional high official (governor ?) of the Magyar.

JILIP JILIP	Showing off, flashing.—JHILE MILE, JHILMEL, JHALMAL: Shining, resplendent, clean and bright.–JIKI MIKI: Resplendent, flashy.–CILAK: Here and there, in patches, not in a continuous stretch.
SILÁML-IK	To shine, to be resplendent, to glitter, to glisten.–CSILLOG: To glitter, to be resplendent.–CSILLAG, CSILAK: Stella, aster, constellatio = star, constellation.

JILIP JILIP	To blink, as one who has looked at the sun.–JILPIT: To blink with eyes, unable to open the eyes full.–JILU MILA: Blinking with the eyes, weak from hunger or fatigue so as to be unable to open the eyes to the full extent.
CSILA	Strabo = a squinting person. – CSILLÁMIT: Prestringo oculorum acies = to blind, to make one to blink.

JINGAṚ	Keeping in good condition, although sparingly fed.
CSINGA	Slim, slender.–CINGÁR = meagre, thin.

JOKHA	Time; to measure. (E.g. in: " Time of going.")–JUG: Time, age, ancient; an emphatic negative. (E.g. in: " I have long been in posession." Or in: " It never will give it up.")–JUG HO: Never.
SOKÁ	Diu tarde = long, age upon age.–SOKÁ LESZ: Time of going. (LESZ: It will be.)–SOK: Multus, multum = much.–SOKA: The great quantity.–SOHA, SEHA, SOMHA, SONHA: Nunquam = never.–SÉG, SÁG: Time.

JOL	To light, set fire to, to burn, to lust. (E.g. in: " To be envious." Or in: " He is burning with lust.")–JOLON: To be hot, inflamed, burning, pain, painful.–JALAO: To set fire to.–JHOLA: To burn with a burning piece of wood.–JHOLPHOL: The radiance emanating from the sun before he appears above the horizon.–JHALA: Hot, applied mainly to the heat of the sun.–SENGEL JHALA: Heat, from a conflagration.–JULUT JULUT: Twinkling, flashing, quivering.–JUND: To set fire.–JUNDIAKOA: They apply fire.
GYÚL, GYUL, GYÓL,	Ascendo, flammesco = to kindle, to set fire to.–GYUJT, GOIT, GYOT: To set fire, to inflame.–GYULADALOM: Concitation animi = to burn with lust, passion.–GYUJTJÁK: They apply fire. (SZÉN: Coal, fire.)

JOLONIẠ	Plucky, intrepid, mettlesome, having plenty of nerve. (E.g. in: " He is a plucky fellow.")
JELES, GYELES	Insignis, insignitus, praestans, praestabilis, exquisitus, egregius, excellens, eximius, singularis, inclytus = excellent, distinguished, illustrious.–JEL, GYEL: Signum, character, specimen = sign, character, specimen.

JOM	To eat, consume.–JOMER ANGRA: A person which is good for nothing save eating.–(ANGRA, ANRA: Use, service, utility.)
GYOMOR	Stomachus = stomach.

JOM HUDAR, JOM RAJA	Angels of the death, or regents of the nether world.
CSOMA	A sort of evil spirit (" fene "); pestilence.

JOMHEM	Applied to a man or woman, who has lost several wives or husbands by death.
CSOM	Nomen virorum, nomen feminarum = term for men or women.

JON	A person.
CSON	Nomen viri = a name for men.

JONGRAO	To wrinkle, to crease.
CSONKOLYKOD-IK	Convolvor = to wrinkle. - CSONGORODOTT : Wrinkled.

JONJE	Slim, thin, poor.-JUNKI : To become lean.
GYENGE, GYÖNGE	Tener, mollis, delicatus = tender, soft, delicate.-Thin, poor.-GYÖNGÜL : Infirmus fiio = to become lean. .-CSONGORA : Corn having a slim, poor straw.

JOPATIŃ	All kinds of edible jungle produce, such as fruit, roots, nuts, leaves, gums, etc.
GYAPOR, GYOPOR	Alibilis, nutribilis = edible.

JOPO JOPO	To move slowly, as an aged person.
COPOG, CSUPOG (?)	To move slowly, as an aged person.

JOREA PONDA, JOREA PONDNAN	Piss-bed.
CSORCSOG	Mingo = to urinate.

JORMA	Small of stature. (E.g. in : " It is a match of two little people.")-JIRO KOTO, JIRO TOKO : Laden with children and package, so as to be greatly hampered.
GYERMEK, GERMÖK	Puer = child.-Parvulus = young, small of stature.

JOROK	Oozing out of water, as through the embankment of a dam.-JHARAO : To trickle.-JHORO-JHOC : Dripping.-JIRO JORO : To trickle, flow as blood from a wound.-(See also CORAN.)
CSOROG	To drip through.-CSOROGÓS : Dripping.

JORPOC	Ragged, tattered, poor.
CSORVASZ	Bad (?).-SORVAD : To fade, to wither.

JOT	To plough.
SCÓTÁR	Culter precisorius in aratro = ploughshare.

JOTE	The rope by which animals are yoked by neck.
CSAT, CHOT	Hamus, fibula = a buckle, a latch.–CSATTOL: Confibulare, connectere = to yoke, to tie.

JUKNI, JUKNU, JUKNUC	Shrivelled, applied to old woman.
ZSUGOROD-IK, CSUKORGAT	Rigor, contrahor, coarctor = to contract, shrink up, shrivel. (Applied also to old woman.)

JULẠP	A purgative, castor oil.
GYÜLEP, JULEP	Syrupus = syrup.

JURẠ, JURGẠ	Small, stunted in growth, applied generally to a breed of diminutive cattle found in the Santal country. (E.g. in: "I will not remain with this diminutive husband." – CURCUTUC: Stunted, undersized.
CSURA	Hinnulus, pullus equinus = a foal, a filly.– CSURMÁNCS: Stunted in growth, small.

JURẠU	To gather, to prepare, to provide.
GYŰR	Masso, commisceo = to gather together, to mass, to mix.

JURU JURU	Greatly distended stomach.
CSURKA	Intestinum = bowel, intestine.

JUSI	Impropriety.
CSOZ-IK	To have sexual intercourse.–CSOSSZANT: To raise a matter in an improper manner.

JUTẠU	To get, to obtain, to find.–JUTIC, JUTUC: To add to, to give more, to increase.
JUT, GYUT	Obtingo, obvenio = to obtain, to fall in one's lot.–JUTTAT: Perduco = to add to.

K

KABA KOBO	To bend down.–KABEA KOBEA, KẠBUẠ: Crooked, bent.–GHAWAR: To fence, as crops.
KÁVA	Cinctura = ring, circle.–KÁVÁS: Crepidine instructus = fenced.

KABAK KABAK	To go here and there idling; to nod the head, as an elephant when walking.–KABKABAO, KAP KAP: To go here and there idling, used when scolding young people. (E.g. in: "She is running about idling, instead of attending to her work.")–KOBOEKOBOE, KOBON KOBON: To go here and there gossiping, applied to girls.
KAVAROG, KAVALYOG	Vagor, grassor, oberro = to go here and there.–KÁVILLÁL: To loaf about.–KÓBOR, KÓVÁL: Vagor, grassor = to go here and there, to roam.

KABAK	To touch or prick with a sharp point, as of a sword, a sickle, etc.–KOBAK: To notch, to cut, to hack.
KAPÁL	To hack.–KAPA: Ligo = a hoe, a mattock, a pickaxe.–KOPÁCS: The engraving chisel.–KOPÁCSOL: To notch, to cut, to hack.

KABAR	Spotted, variegated.–KABRAK KOBROK: Spotted, mixture of colours.–GABAR: Mixed.–GABAR GUNJ: Disturbance.
KAVAR, KEVER	Misceo = to mix.–KEVERT: Mixed, variegated.–KAVARODÁS: Disturbance.

KABJA, KOPJA, KABJAO	A hinge.
KAPCS, KAPOCS, KAJCS	Fibula, monile, armilla, uncinus, clavicula = clasp, buckle, hinge, collar-bone.

KABKUB, KABKUPI	A kind of musical stringed instrument.
KOBOZ, KOBZ	Pandura, lyra = lute, lyre.

KẠBUẠ	Bent, curved, arched.
KEBEL, KEBÉL, KÖBEL	Sinus.–KEBELES: Sinosus = sinuous.

KAC KAC — To whine as a dog, or a petulant child.

KÁCSOG — To utter a harsh, jarring sound.

KACA, KẠCI, KẠCNI — A piece of cloth worn round the loins as a skirt.

KECSE — Soldier's mantle.–KACAGÁNY : Pellis, ovila = an overall, a cloak (of leopard or tiger-skin) worn by the ancient Magyars.

KACAL — To hamper, impede, to be in distress. (E.g. in : " She is hampered by that child.")–GÖCHAT : To hold in the lap as a child carries flowers in the pinafore by making it a bag.

GÖCS — Hindrance.–A knot.–A tie.–A bundle.

KACAR, KACOR — Dirty, dirty and miry, as a Santal village street during the rains.–KAC KAC : Dirty, muddy, miry, difficult, troublesome, annoying.

KÁTYUS — Muddy, miry, difficult.–KÁTYU : Pool, marsh, swamp.–KÁTYUBA JUT : To be annoyed, to be in distress.–KÁSTOS : Dirty and miry.

KACAR — To be in distress or strait.–KẠCRI : Unripe, raw.–(See also GIJRI.)

KESERÍT — Contristor = to be distressed.–KESERŰ : Amarus acerbus = butter.

KẠCLAK — A kind of basket.

KAS — Corbis = basket.–KASORNYA : Corbis ciborum = food basket.

KACRAT — Shoots about 5 or 6 feet high from the stump of a tree that has been cut down.

GACSALY — A shoot.–KOCSORD : Plant.–KOCSÁN : A peduncle.

KẠCUR MẠCUR — Inefficiently, quickly, rapidly.–KOCE : Sideways, obliquely.–KACRA KẠCRI : To bend or twist in all directions.–(See also KẠCI.)

(KERESZTÜL) KASUL — In all directions, zigzag.–Inefficiently.

KẠD	Prison, to imprison, to deprive one of his liberty of action.–KAD ORAK: A prison house.–KẠIDẠU: To imprison, to keep in safe custody.
KATRÓC, KETREC, KATRAC	Avinarium, saginarium=a cage, a prison.
KADAE KADAE	Always on the move, going about continually.
KATANGOL, KÓTOLOG, KÓDOR	Erro, vago, divagor = to dawdle about, to move.
KADAM KADAM	In the dark.
KÖD, KED	Nebula = mist, haze, fog.
KAELE	Near, in the vicinity, neighbourhood.
KÖZEL	Near, in the vicinity, neighbourhood.
KẠI	To commit a fault, to sin; a fault, a sin.–KẠIẠ, KAYA, KẠYẠ: Hasty, quick-tempered, passionate.–KẠITUK: To work in a frivolous way.
KÉJ	Libentia = sensual pleasure, lasciviousness, debauchery, etc.–Caprice, arbitrariness.
KAJ	Work, business, use.
KÖLCSÖN, KŐCSÖN	Mutuus, mutue = borrowed, hired, lent.
KAJAK	Perhaps, it is doubtful, possibly. (E.g. in: "It is doubtful if this man will recover.")–KECET KECET: Doubtful, dubious, uncertain.
KÉTSÉG, KÉCSÉG	Dubium, ambiguum, dubitatio = doubtful, ambiguous.–KÉTES: Dubious, uncertain.
KAJRA, KẠJRI	Dark grey.
KESELY	Flammei coloris, medii inter album et mere flavum = fawn coloured.–Varii coloris, vulturneus = of various colours.
KẠJIẠ	To quarrel, to wrangle.–KOCKOCO: To altercate, to dispute, to wrangle.–KACTA KẠCTI: To set on or attack from all sides.–(See also GAJAR.)
KÉSÁL, KISÁL	Certo = to quarrel, to wrangle, to fight.–KÉSA: Seditio = revolt, mutiny.–KÉSNYÁS: Jurgiosus, rixosus = quarrelsome, irritable.

KAKER	A species of tall swamp grass.
KÁKA	Juncus, scirpus = rush, bent-grass.

KẠL	To convince, to subdue.-KULẠU : To provide, to be sufficient.-(EM)GELAK : To offer. (E.g. in : "To taste by eating.")-GELA : To try, to attempt.
KELE, KEEL	Debeo = must, to be bound. - Libet, lubet, oportet = to offer, to suit, to please.-KELLŐ : Necessarius = Necessary, sufficient.-KELLEMES : Pleasant, agreeable.

KAL, KOL	A machine, any mechanical contrivance, a trap, the spring of a pigeon trap.
KAL, KOL	In : KALLANTYU, KOLLANTYU : Crank (of an engine).-KALINCS : A wooden latch.-KALAPÁCS : Hammer.-KALLÓ : Fulling-machine.-KALODA, KALAFA : Stocks.-Etc.

KAL	Time.
KEL	Pergo, eo, teno = to go, to come (as time).-KELT : Date.

KAL	A snake.
KIGYÓ, KÉGYÓ, KILGYÓ	Serpens = snake.

KALAK	Suspicion, accusation, fear of accusation.
KALÁK	Taxa indici = the reward for the indication of a theft.

KALAPẠNI	To transport as a convict. (PẠNI : Water.)
KELEM, KELET	Vadium = a ford-(ÁLTAL)KEL : Trajicio = to cross, to pass over.

KẠLI	A verse.
KÖLT	To make verses.-KÖLTŐ : A poet.

KALKAL	Numerous, very many. (E.g. in : "Very many people are assembled.")-GHALOK : Including, enumerating.
KALÁKA	An assembly for the execution of a common work.--GÁL, -GAL, -GÉL, -GEL : A frequentative verbal suffix.

KALOBALO, KALOK BALOK	Intoxicated, showing the effects of intoxication. (E.g. in : " What will you say to a madman ? " Or in : " You speak as if you were intoxicated.") (BHALOK : Mad.)-(See also GALAK SALAK and GOJRA.)
KALÁNTOS	Intoxicated, drunk. (BALYÓK : Mad.)
KAMAI	Earnings.-KAMAO : To earn.
KAMAT	Interest.-Earnings.
KAMDA, KHAMDA	To copulate.
KAMATYOL	To copulate.
KANDO, KHANDO	Riot, disturbance, discord, brawl, commotion, contention.
KONTATÁS	Instigation to rebellion, agitation.-KONTOGATÓ : Agitator, instigator.
KANAS	Direction, aside, ambush. (E.g. in : " Go in this direction.")-The person who keeps out of sight near the net into which hares are driven, is said to be " *kanasre* ".
KENÉZ	A chief, a director.-KENDÉSZ : Exploro = to search out.
KANEKANE, GHANEGHANE	Earnestly, again and again. (E.g. in : " He is always asking for food." Or in : " I told him repeatedly.")
KÉNE, KÉNE KÉNE	It would be earnestly useful, it would be necessary.
KANKO	Cloth.
KANKÓ	Garment.
KAOARI	To implore, to beg earnestly, to entreat.-KOE : To beg, to ask for, to pray.
KÉR, KYER	Rogo, peto, pregor = to beg, to desire, to implore.
KAPAT	A wooden door.-KOPAT : The leaf of a door.
KAPU	Porta, pylae = door.

KAPTAO	To seize, to grab, to grasp.–KAPCAO : To seize by the hairs.–KHABLAO : To grab, clutch, grip.–KHABAL : A handful, as much as can be lifted in one handful.–GOP : To steal, to purloin, to put out of the way.–GOP, GOPAO : To hide, to keep back, to suppress, to keep secret.–KHAB : To plunge or thrust suddenly and with force into a fluid or any other penetrable substance.
KAP	Rapio = to catch, to seize.–KAPÁS : Prehensio = seizure, taking in hand.–KAPÓS, KAPZSI : Acceptus, desideratus = in demand.

KAR	Side.–KARKARI : A lever with which a rope is tightened.–KARU : Handles on a box or trunk by which to lift it.
KAR	Arm, lever.

KAR	Time.–GHẠRI : A space of time ; a time piece.–ITI GHARI : This moment, instantly.–GHORI : Time.–GHURI : Time. – GHURIẠ : Again, next. (E.g. in : "This time next year.")–GHURIẠ GHURIẠ, GHURI GHURI : Time after time.–KUR, KURTE : After, subsequent, succeeding, next in on, thereupon.
KOR	Tempus, spatium temporis, aetas = time, a space of time, age. (ITT : Here, in this moment.)–AKKOR : Thereupon.

KẠR	An eruption appearing on the legs, mainly of children.–KARON : Disease, malady. KARRA, KORRA : A renal disease. KARNI : A person suffering from some disease or malady.
KÓR	Morbus = illness, disease.

KAR, KOR	A cess levied by "zemindars".
KORMÁNYOZ	To govern, to steer.

KARA	A kind of anklet.
KARIKA	Annulus, discus, rotula = ring, small ring, anklet.

KARA HAKO	Species of fish.
KÁRÁSZ	Species of fish.–(HAL : Fish.)

KARAHI	A round flattish dish.–KARAO : To make a kind of bread.
KARÉ, KARÉJ, KARAJ	Circumferentia, ora = edge, curve, segment, bow.– A slice of bread.

KARAJ	The peculiar, hoarse call of a jackal. (It is a popular belief of the Santal that this peculiar call of the jackal portends the death of some one.)
KÁROG	To croak, to caw. (It is a popular belief of the Magyar that this peculiar call of the crow portends the death of some one.)

KARAN KARAN	Exceedingly, very, applied to darkness, pitch dark.
KOROM (SÖTÉT)	Pitch dark.

KARAP	Imitative of the sound of clicking, or tapping of hoofs.
KALAPÁL	To click, to hammer.

KARCUP	Curled.–KARCAN KURCAN : Shrivelled up, as a dry leaf.
KARCSOL	To gird round.–GÖRZSE : Shrivelled up (as a dry leaf).

KARJA, KẠRJI	Tall, high.–KHẠRKU, KHẠRUGU, KHARGO : High, tall.–KẠRUN KẠCUN : Very tall, very high.–KURI, KORI : Young girl.
KARCSU	Gracilis = tall and slim.–GARINCA : A tall and slim girl.

KARKA	A hunt, employed as a synonym for sendra. (SENDRA : A hunt, to hunt, to follow the chase.)
KERGET	Persequor, insequor, insecto, fugo, propello = to chase, to prosecute, to pursue, to hunt.

KASI, KHASI	To geld.
KASZABOL	To geld.–KASZÁL : To mow, to cut.

KASAO, KASKASAO	To pull tight, pull together, to pack.–KACAR : To hamper, impede, strait.–KHACAKHAC : Closely.–KHACAO : To pack close.–KESKESE : Tight, stiff, as the neck of one wearing a tight stock. (E.g. in : " This coat feels a little tight round the neck.")–KOSKOS : Tight, to tighten.
KESKEN, KESKENY	Angustus = tight, narrow, thin.–KASZADÉK : An entanglement.–KAZAL : Acervus cumulus = stack, rick, pile.

KAT TILMIN	A wild variety of Sesanum Indicum.
KATÁNG	The sunflower.

KATA	Leg and foot from the knee downwards.
KÉZ, KEDE	Manus = hand.

KATAP KATAP, KATAP KATUP	Sound produced by feet striking the ground, as when a horse gallops.
KATTOG	To clatter, to rattle.

KATE	In continuing a narrative, then, after this.–A participial and adverbial particle. It very often takes the place of *and* or *by* in English.–KHATAE : Employed to introduce a statement of which the speaker has no personal knowledge, I have heard, it has been said.
HÁT	In continuing a narrative, then, after this. Very often employed to introduce statements of which the speaker has no personal knowledge, I have heard, it has been said.

KATKATAO	To set and grind the teeth, as in convulsions.
KATTOG	To set and grind the teeth, as in convulsions.

KATKATAO	Applied to the feeling of want of elasticity in the muscles.
KATTYÓS	Weak.

KATPAT	Firewood and leaves.–KATAKUTA : Rubbish.
KETEPUTA	Lumber = rubbish.

KAWET	Indian or wild liquorice root.[1]
KÁBIT	To stupefy, to narcotize.-KÁPRÁZ : Dum oculis repente quasi nubeculae offunduntur = to be giddy. (RÁZ : To shake, to tremble.)
KE	Every, each, by. (E.g. in : " He visits us every year." Or in : " He is growing day by day.")-(See also KHAN.)
KÉNT, KINT	Every, each, by.
KEDRAO	To enquire, to consult.-KHURIAU : To question, to enquire.-KUDUM, KURIT : A riddle, a guess, to propound a riddle, to give a guess.
KÉRD	Interrogo, querito, quero, rogo = to ask, to question, to enquire.-KÉRDEM : "I ask (now)." -(To propound a riddle, to give a guess.)
KEHE	The red-backed vulture.
KESELYÜ, KESELYE	Vulture, hawk.
KELE	A variety of rice.
KÖLES	Milium = millet.
KENEKEC	Pretty, good looking.-KENEKOTE : To set the head conceitedly, to look round proudly or conceitedly, as e.g. a girl.
KÉNYES	Setting the head conceitedly, looking round proudly or conceitedly, e.g. as a girl.
KEON MEON	To whine.
KÖNY, KENY	Lacrima = tears.-KÖNNYEZ : To shed tears, to whine.
KENTED	Intensely, violently.
KÉNTET	Urgeo, sollicito = to urge, to hurry.
KERKER	Stiff, rigid, to become hard or stiff, as skin or leather.-KAR GHAO : A pustular skin disease. (GHAO : Sore, disease.)
KÉR, KÉREG	Rind, bark, crust.-KÉRGESSÉG : Callosity.-(HAS)KÉR : Peritoneum.

[1] See Maori "kawa".

KEROT	To turn half round.–(See also GHERAO.)
KERÜL	To turn half round.–Circum = round about.–KERÍT: Circumvenio = to encircle.

KHAD, KHAḌ	A pit, a mine.–KUND: A pit, a pitfall, a hot spring.–KUI: A well.
GADAJ	Cave, cavern.–KŰT: A pit, a mine.–A well.

KHADA BHUSA	Grain mixed with chaff. (BHUSA: Chaff.)
BŰZA	Frumentum, triticum = wheat, corn.

KHAJAṆTI	A treasury, a treasurer.
KINCS, KÉNCS	A treasury.

KHAJUK	If, if only, provided that.
HACSAK	If, if only, provided that.

KHAKHO	To hiss, to puff, as a cobra snake.
KÁKÓ	A water-snake, a ringed snake.

KHAḶIS	To be relieved of encumbrance in the stomach.–GILTHI: A swelling in the groin.–(See also GAL GALAO.)
KELÉS, KILÍS	Apostema, ulcus, tuber = ulcer, sore, abscess.

KHAMID, KHAMIND	Master, head of household; worthy, respectable. KA: Uncle. (E.g. in: "Ho, uncle! Is it correct or not?")
KEMED, KEND, KED	An appellation of respect, used in the sense of master.

KHAN	If, then, a point of time, when.–(See also KE.)
KÉN	Forsitan = eventually.–KÉNT: If, then, a point of time, when.

KHANAK KHONOK	To sulk.
KONOK	Obstinate, stubborn, capricious.

KHAṆDI	A sari, a full dress for women, a piece of cloth twelve cubits long and two in width.–KANSO, KANASO: A pleat, frill, tuck, gathering.–

Cloth drawn into folds round the waist.–KANTHA, KHANTHA: Patch-work, pieces of old cloth sewn together and above each, so as to make a piece without holes in it.–GANDREC: A rag, a piece of old cloth.

KENDŐ — Mantellum, mappa, mantile, linteum, manuarium = an overcoat, a shawl, a towel.–KÖNTÖS, KANDISZ: A coat.–KÊNTULA: A kind of cloth.–KANICSA: Texti genus (?) = a kind of material.

KHAPRI, KAPAR — The skull.

KOPONYA, KAPONYA — Cranium = skull.

KHAR — Sharp, keen, to swish as when cutting with any sharp weapon.–KHARKHAR: An imitative sound of cutting.–GADIAU: To carry a sword, to be armed with a sword.–KAIDA: A kind of knife with a curved blade.–KATAHA: Fierce, ravening; applied to any cutting instrument, used to kill an animal with.

KARD — Gladius = a sword.–KARDOS: To be armed with a sword.–Quarrelsome, contentious (said of women).

KHARA — To establish, ready, prepare.

KAR, KOR — Status = state.–KARBA (HOZ): To establish, to prepare.

KHARAN — A common grass, the culms of which are used make brooms. Aristida depressa.

KARAKÁNY — A sedge.

KHARAN KHARAN — Excitable, fiery, quick tempered; energetic, quick, active.–KHARAN KHURUN: Angrily, roughly.

KARAKÁN — Wanton, petulant, spiteful.

KHARAO — Bad.–KHARAP: Bad, ruined.–GHAR: At a disadvantage; strait, difficult, a vital spot.–GHARA GHARI: Sickening, strong and offensive, used only of smells.

KÁROS — Bad, injurious, sickening.–KÁROL: To consider as harmful.–KÁR: Detrimentum, perdition = damage; disadvantage, loss. – GERÊB: Hindrance.

KHARBARAO — To be restless, fidgety.

KORICA — To roam.

KHARCARI	A rammer, applied principally to the stick with which "dhan" is rammed down.–KOROT: A pit-saw.
KARÓ	A rammer, a pile, a stick, a rod, a vine-stock.
KHARKARAO	An imitative sound, as shaving with a thin razor, etc. – KHAROK KHAROK, KHOROK KHOROK: Sound of scratching or scraping.
KARCZOL	Scabo, frico = to scratch.–KORHOL: To rub, to graze.
KHARHIAU	To quarrel.–KHARBARAO: To be restless, to be fidgety, excited.
GARÁZ	Rixosus = quarrelsome person, squibbler.–GARBONCÁS: Quarrelsome.
KHARKHA	Adept, skilled.–KHẠRKHẠRI: Clever, expert, energetic, keen, adept, skilled.
KHARKÁSZ	A kind of tribal chief of the ancient Magyars.
KHẠRID	To buy, to purchase.
KERIT	Facio ut deveniat = to let come, bring, order.
KHAS	Private, own, proper, peculiar, in revenue language the term is applied to lands the rent of which are not leased out, but collected directly by the owner or his agent.
GAZDA, KASDA, KAZDA	Possessor = owner, proprietor. – Oeconomus = intendant, agent of the owner.
KHASA	Bright and cheerful looking, open countenance.
KACÉR	Coquettish.
KHẠSIA	Humorous, funny.
KACAJ	Laughter.
KHẠTI	To be certain.–KHATOR: A debtor.–KHẠTIR: On account of, owing to.
KÖTELES	Obligate.–KÖTÉLY: The debt.
KHATPAT, KHATPẠTI, KHATPẠTIẠ	To be at variance, to be hostile to each other, to be restive, restless, fickle.
KÖTEKED-IK	To be at variance, to pick a quarrel.

KHẠUẠ, KHẠWẠIẠ An eater.–KHẠUẠ KHẠWI : Greedy, gluttonous.

KAJTÁR Voracious.

KHEAS Intelligent, wise, expert, to learn.

KÉSZ Promptus = expert.–KÉSZÜL : Parare se = to prepare oneself.–KÉSZÜLET : Instructio = instruction.

KHEL To play, to dance, to flirt.

KELL, KEEL Libet, lubet, placet = to like, to love, to please.

KHELAO To spend. (E.g. in : "He spent much money on the marriage.")

KÖLT Expendo = to spend.–KEL : Pretium habeo = to be of value.–KELENGYE : Dowry.

KHEN Impending calamity.–KHANKHAN : Uncomfortable feeling of an empty stomach, the sensation produced by taking liquor on an empty stomach.–GHIN, GHIN GHIN : Disgust, disgusting.–KHENHAO : To beat, to subdue, to injure, to strike.

KÍN, KÉN Tortura = pain, ache, torture.–KINLÓDÁS : Pain, agony.–KÍNOZ : To torment, to torture.

KHERE KHERE Crooked, bent.

KEREK Rotundus = round.–KEREKDED : Orbicus = roundish.

KHERWEC Little, a term of endearment.–DELA KHERWEC, DELAŇ HEOMEA : Come little dear, come I will take you in my arms.

KEDVES Dear, a term of endearment.–(GYERE, DELE : Come.)

KHIJẠU, KHIJLẠU To nag, to torment by constant fault-finding.–KHIJLA, KHIJLI : To torment by constant nagging, to worry, to pester.–KICKIC, KICKICẠU : To be annoyed, to be pestered.

KEGYETLEN, KIJETLEN Inclemens, implacidus, tyrannicus = unkind, cruel, tyrannical.

KHIL	A nail of wood, to nail with a wooden nail or pin.
KÜLLŐ, KELŐ, KELŰ	Radius rotae = a spoke.

KHINUR	Mild, gentle.
KÉNYES	Delicatus = mild, gentle. - KÉNY, KÍNY: Delicium = deliciousness.–KIES : Mild, gentle.

KHIS, KHẠISA KHẠISI	To be irritated, to be piqued, to take offence.–KẠISẠU, KHẠISẠU : To be annoyed, to be vexed, troubled, worried, angry. (E.g. in: "I am worried with continuous work.")–KHESKHES: To breath with difficulty.–KUSKUSAU: Angry or offended and waiting for an opportunity to be revenged, vengeful.–(See also KOSTO.)
KÜSZKÖDI-IK	Luctor = to struggle, to strive after.

KHOCA	To come in contact with anything sharp.–KHES : To cut through with a swish.–KHACAK: To pierce, as a thorn, needle, sword, spear, etc., to prick as with a goad.–KHACAK MENTE: To pierce suddenly and deeply as a knife, etc.
KÉS	Culter, cultellus = a knife. (MENTEN : Suddenly, at once.)

KHODAO	To ask for importunately, to dun. (E.g. in: "He got it by persistent begging.")
KÓDUL, KOLDUL	To beg persistently.–KÓDUS : A beggar.

KHOJ	To seek.–KHOJ PAÑJ : To search for here and there, to go here and there in quest of.
KACSONT, KACSINT	Specto = ? to seek.

KHOK	To cough.–(See also GẸHET GEHET.)
KÖHÖG	To cough.

KHONOS	Ill-will, hatred, vengeance.–(See also GAÑJON.)
GONOSZ	Ualus, miseria, aeger, damnum, improbus = bad, wicked, malignant, misery, distress, disease, the evil, the foe, ill-will, hatred.

KHOR	An imitative word, a heavy grugg sigh.
KORNYIKOL, KORNYÉKOL	To grunt.

KHORA	The vessel which receives the juice of sugar cane when being pressed.–A kind of large brass bowl.
KOROGLYA	A bowl, used by the chemists.

KHORET	Limping, owing to one leg being short.
KORCS	Hibris, hibrida = degenerate.–KORCSFEJ : Misshapen, deformity.

KHORO	The teeth to be set on edge.
KORCOG	Rodo = to gnaw, to nibble.

KHORO	To find, to locate, to know one's whereabouts.
KORÉSZ	Scrutor = to seek, to scrutinize, to search.

KHORO KHORO	Applied to the noise made by a hubble-bubble.–KARKUR : sound of rumbling in the stomach.
KOROG	Crepitare = to growl, to snarl, to purr.–Sound of rumbling in the stomach.–KOROGTAT : Gargariso = to gargle.

KHOS	Freely, willingly, with pleasure.
KÉSZ	Promptus = willing, ready.

KHOS, KHAS, KASRA, KHASRA	Itch, scabies.–GOSEC : To prick vermin from the head.–GOSOC : Of dirty habits, dirty.
KOSZ	Scabies.–KOSZOS : Of dirty habits, dirty, scabby.

KHOTRAO, KHODRAO, KHADRAO	To scrape, to cut by a scraping action, to scrape out of a hollow, to gouge.–KHOTA, KHATAO : To rake up old stories.
KOTOR	Effrico, effodio = to scrape out, to scrape out of a hollow.–KOTRÓ : Scraping.–KATRAT : To scrape, to gouge out.

KHOTKHOTAO	To cackle, as a hen.–KOT : To cackle.
KODKODÁCSOL	Gracillo = to cackle. – KOTYOL, KOTYOG : Glocio, glocito = to cluck.

KHUCI	To accuse falsely, to be at variance.
GUCSMOL	To calumniate, to abuse.

KHUPẠ	Hollow, as opposed to straight, slightly concave.–KHUPI : The end portion of a pavilion roof.
KÚP	Cone, thorn, pin.–KÚPOS : Conical, dome-shaped.–KÉPP (?) : Crater.

KHUPA KẠPI	A special kind of battle-axe.–KẠPI : A battle-axe in general.
KOPIA, KUPYA	Hasta, framea, curis = lance, spear, dart.–KÉP : Venabulum, telum, jaculum = spit, pike, spear, peg.

KHUPUDẠU	To chase each other.
KOPÓ	Vestigator canis, indagator = sporting dog, hound.

KHURẠ, KHURE	A hoof.–KERKHOC : A whitlow.
KÖRÖM, KEREM, KÖREM, KAROM	Unguis = finger-nail, hoof, claw.–GÓR : Featherless.

KI	An interrogative.
KI	Quis, quae, qui, quae, quod = who, which (interrogatively).

KICHU, KICHU KICHU	Some, a little.–KIṄCIT : A little.–KICIN BIDRIC : To make or to tear in fragments. (BITHRI : Small, little.)
KICSI, KICSIN	Parvus = small.–KICSIT : A little.

KIKIẠU	To scream.
KIÁL	Clamo, vocifero, inclamo = to scream, to yell.–KIKIÁLT : Proclamo = to proclaim, to publish.

KIRIR	Loudly, to shout.–KIRIT KIRIT : Excessively painful.
KIRÍ	To shout loudly.–KIRÍVÓ : Excessively striking.

KO	Sign of the plural.
K	Sign of the plural.

KOCA, KONAC	A corner.
KOCIK, KUCIK, KUCKÓ	A corner.-The corner at the oven.

KOCE	Oblique.-KACA KUCA : Bent.-KACRA KẠCRI : Bent or twisted to one side or another, to bend or twist in all directions, as men struggling together.-KOJO : To stoop, to bend the back, round shouldered.-(See also KUKURBAN.)
KACS, GÁCS	Bent, crooked.-KACSIBA : Varus = bent, rounded.-KACSKA : Bandy-armed, crooked-armed. - GACSIBA : Bandy-legged, crooked-legged.

KOCKOCO	To altercate, to dispute, to wrangle.
KOCÓD-IK	Altercor, verbis contendo = to altercate, to dispute.

KOCOR	To hop.
KOCOG, KOSZOG	Offendo, impengo = to hop.-To trot, to jog.

KOENDA GAR	Fort mentioned in the traditions of the Santals.-KOENDA RAPAJ : The race of kings who reigned at the traditional fort of Koendagar. (GẠR : A fort.)
KENDE, KÜNDÜ	The traditional chief-king of the Magyar. (VÁR : a fort.)

KOELA, KUILẠ	Charcoal, coal.-KOYO : The kernel of a mangoe-stone.-KHAYUK : Deep, a pit, a pitfall.-GẠTI : Nodular limestone.
KŐ	Lapis, saxum, lithos = stone, rock.-KŐSZÉN : Coal, pit-coal.-KOLYUK : Specus, cavitas = hole, cavern.

KOKA, KUKI	Foolish, idiotic.
KÁKÓ	Homo plumbeus = blockhead, clumsy.

KOKUDO	Exhausted.
KÓKATT	Siccus, omni virore ac vigore exhaustus = exhausted.-KÓKADÓ : Exhausted.

KOL	To send.-KOLKEDEAŇ : I sent him.-KOLADEAŇ : I sent to him.-GODET : One

	of the officials of a Santal village, the headman's messenger.
KÜLD, KILD	Mittọ = to send.–KÜLDÖTT, KÜLDÖNC, KÜDÖTT: Messenger.

KOLO	Shaved bare, as the head.
GULACS	Depilis = baldheaded.

KOLON DOBON, KULUN DULUN	Distracted. (DOBON, DOB: To prohibit, to lay an embargo on, interdict; "*tabu*.")
KÜLÖN, KÖLÖN	Distinctus, separatus = distinct, separate.–KÜLÖNÖS: Special, singular.

KOMKOM	To be sullen, to sulk.–GAMPATAO: To sulk.
KOMOR	Gloomy, sullen, sulky.–KOMPOLOD-IK: To be grievous, to be easily offended.

KOMKOM	Swollen under the jaws, puffed or swollen face.
GAMBÁS	Swollen under the jaws, having puffed lips.

KOMOR	The loins.
KOMORKÓR	Disorder of the spleen. (KÓR: Sickness; bodily disorder.)

KOMOR BHANGA	To be weak. (E.g. in: "There is a weak place here, it will not do as beam, etc.")–KOMJOR: Weak, to become weak.
GÁMOR	The weak fence.–GÁNYOL: To fence weakly.–To build in a bad manner.

KONDHA	Crippled, maimed in the feet.–KONDE, KONDEA, KONDEC: Crooked, bent.
KONTA	Maimed.–KONYA, KUNYA: Crooked, bent.

KOP	Phlegm.
KÖP	Phlegm, spittle.

KORA	A boy, a young man.
KORACS	The youth.

KORBET, KURBAN	Crooked, bent.–KOBRE: Crooked.–KIRBON KORBON: Crooked, serpentine.
GÖRBE, GERBE	Girvus, curvus = crooked, bent, curved.–GIRBE-GÖRBE: Crooked, serpentine.
KORDHOC	Blind, used when scolding one who has overlooked something or has failed to find something he was sent for.–KORWAK: Staring.
KORDÉBAN	Inutilis, temere = useless, rash, thoughtless.–KORDÉRA: In vain, fruitless.–KÖR: Direction. (VAK: Blind.)–KORHOL: To scold.
KOROK, KOROT, KORKOR	Cackling of hens.
KÁRÁL	To cackle.
KORPA ARPA	To gather together by littles, perquisites received by yearly servants when harvesting crops, also by daughters previous to marriage.–KURPA, KORPA, KENHA: Perquisites collected by daughters before their marriage. These perquisites form the main part of a daughter's dowry.–KHANA PINA: Food, food and drink, the necessaries of life.–(See also ARPA DAHNA.)
KORPA	Furfur = bran.–ÁRPA: Hordeum = barley.–KENYÉR, KÖNÉR: Panis = bread. (PINA: The female genitals, sometimes used for women in general.)
KORRA, KARRA	To scourge, something of the nature of a riding switch, but much heavier.
KORBÁCS	Mastix, scutica = whip, lash, scourge.
KORO, KORO	Stooping, as when carrying a heavy load.
KORHOG	To shuffle, to walk slipshod.
KOS	To tan leather.
KÉSZÍT	Preparo, praemolior, apparo, accingo = to prepare, to adjust, to fit, to dress, to cook.
KOSA	Applied to the seeds of the palmyra palm, the plantain and the jack fruit.–KASKOM: Cotton before separated from the seed.
KOSZORU	Cotton of the fruits. (" Fruchtwolle.")

KOSLAENI	A midwife.–(See also KUSYẠ.)
KOSLAT, KOSLATAG	To be in heat, lecherous. (NŐ : A woman.)–KOSBOR, KOSZBOLY : Satyrion.

KOSOEYA, KASOEYA	The name of an insect to which decay in the front teeth of cattle is attributed.
KOSZOL	To decay.

KOSOT	To sulk, to gloom.–KOSOLA : To cause suffering, trouble, difficulty.–KASUR : The degrees of disease.
KÁSZOLÓD-IK	To get through painfully, to drag on (as a sick person).–KOČEGA : Wretched, miserable.

KOSTO	Distress, suffering. (E.g. in : " We are suffering from want of sufficient food.")–KOSTO MOSTO: With great difficulty, with great hardship, with much suffering.–KUSTI : A boxing or wrestling bout.–(See also KHIS.)
KÜZDÉS	To struggle, to combat.–KÜZDŐ : Pugil = an athlete, a boxer.

KOTAP	To rap, to make a rapping or a tapping sound.
KÓTOG	To rap, to knock.

KUẠRI	Unmarried.
KÉRŐ	Procus = one of the look-out for a wife.

KUCẠ	To bend.
GUZSADT	Bent.

KUDẠ	To walk as if the soles of the feet were tender.
KUTTOG	To move gently, to slink.

KUDẠM	The rear, behind, at the back, used mainly with reference to a house. (E.g. in : " Spread it out to dry behind the fireplace.")
KUDAR	The inner-room of the fireplace.

KUHẠU	To strike with the heel of the doubled fist.
KUJAK, KULYAK	The fist.

KUKURBAN, KUKURCAN, KURBAN — Crooked, twisted, curved, crumpled.-KUKUC: Crooked, bent.-KUKU: To raise one corner of a mat to cover anything drying on it.-KUKUC: To double up, to draw up as the legs, to bend, to reduce one to submission.-(See also KOCE.)

KUKORA, GURBANCSOS — Crooked, bent.-KUKORÉK: A fold, a plait.-The curvature.-KUKORODIK, KUTYORODIK: To squat, to crouch.-KUTYORÉKOS: Crooked, serpentine. - GUGSOL, KUKSOL, GUGGOD: To double up, to draw up the legs.

KUMẠ — Father's sister's husband.

KOMA — Compater = godfather, sponsor.

KUMAYA — Cruel, relentless, merciless.

KEMÉNY — Inmitis, repugnax = cruel, relentless, merciless.

KUCẠ — To be flexed, as a limb, to be injured.

KUSA — Maimed, mutilated.

KUHRẠU — To groan, to moan.

KUHINT — To groan.

KULẠM SIM — A species of fowls of large size. (SIM: A fowl.)

GULA — A species of fowl. ("Steisshuhn"?)

KUNDI — A recess in a wall to hold small articles, a corner.-KHUNDRI: A small room made by partitioning off a part of the verandah of the house.

KUNYHÓ, GUNYHÓ — A hut.

KUPẠ — A skin vessel for holding oil.-KUPI: A bottle-like vessel of earthern-ware for holding oil.

KUPA — Cuppa, crater = cup, bowl, green shell.-KUF: A little vessel.

KURAU — To provide.-KUPURAU: The reciprocal form of KURAU.

KURHÁSZ — To go in quest of, to provide.-KUPORGAT: To provide gradually, by degrees.

KURHIẠ	Lazy, idle.
KORHELY	Lazy, idle.–KORHANTÓ : Lout, ruffian.–(BESTE) KURA, (ETTE) KURA : Depreciatory term, said from men.
KURIẠ	A small hut.
KUCHYA, KUTYA	Peasant's hut.–GÓRÉ : Casa, tugurium = cot, hut.–GURGYAL : A hut.–GUGYALÓ : A small hut.
KURKUR	To show anger, as a cat.
KURRAN	To purr, as a cat.
KURKURẠU	To be enraged.
KORKOJÓ	Crazy.
KURTẠ	A jacket, a coat.
KURTKA, KURKA	Jacket, little coat, skirt.
KURYUT	To swallow whole, to bolt without chewing.
KORTYOG	To swallow.–KORTY : Haustus, stoppus = sip, gulp, mouthful.
KUSI, KHUSI	To be pleased, to rejoice.
KUSZOG	To look pleasant, to rejoice.
KUSTA	Refuse after threshing leguminous crops.
KACAT	Refuse.
KUSYẠ	An adverb possessing intensifying force. (E.g. in : "He beat him severely." Or in : "He ate amazingly.")–(See also KOSLAENI.)
KOSLATÁS	Discursitatio, grassatio = impetuosity, violence.–To be in heat, lecherous.–(NŐ : Wife).
KUT	To estimate, to measure.
KUTAT	To search.
KUTU	A dog, a puppy.–KUYA : A wild dog.
KUTYA	Canis, caniculus = a dog, a puppy.–KUTAK : Pumilio = dwarf. - KUASZ, KUVASZ : Molossus = a big dog.

L

LA	To dig.
LAPÁT	Pala = a shovel. - LAPICKA, LAPOCKA : A shovel.
LABAK	Green and luxuriant, succulent.-LEGEC LABAK : Fresh, green and tender, beautiful, as young, fresh leaves.-LEGEC LEGEC : Luxuriant and tender as grass.
LEVÉL	Folium, pampinus = leaves, foliage.-LEGELŐ : Pascum = willow.
LABAN LUBUN	Leisurely, slowly, applied mainly to the leisurely movements of wild animals when undisturbed. (E.g. in : "The tiger went away leisurely.")-LAMBHAC LUMBŰC : Leisurely.
LAPPAN, LABBAN LAPPAG, LAPPANG	To move leisurely.-LAMPAN, LAMPANG : To hide, to conceal oneself.
LABAS LUBUS	Applied to the walking of animals, mainly dogs and cats, just beginning to use their legs; flabby, weak on legs.-LAPAT LUPUT : To lift the feet slowly as old people.
LÁBAS	Pedatus, pedes habens = possessing legs, feet.-LÁB : Pes = foot.
LABDA, LABDAO, LEBDA	To throw at, as a stick, to hit or knock down anything.-LAP, LAPLAP : To catch with both hands, as a ball thrown.
LABDA, LAPTA, LOPTA	Pila = a ball.-LAPTÁS : Pila, lusio, pilaris = any game at ball.-LAPTÁZ : Pila palmaria ludo = to play with balls.
LABLAB, LABLABA, LAPLAPA	Broad, wide applied to anything very broad, or wide, to flap the wings, to expand.-LAPLAPA : Broad and horizontal, to extend horizontally.-LAPONDAN : Flat and extended, covering a large area, occupying much space.-LEPLEPE : Large in area, as a field.-LEP LEPE : Broad, flat.
LAPÁLY, LAPADÉK	Planities depressior = a plain, a flat country.-LAPÁC : Planities = a plain.-LAP : Planum = a plane.-LAPONYA : The plain.-LEPEDŐ : Bed-cover.

LABLABI, LABLABIA	Soft. (E.g. in: "The soil is so soft.")-LABAR LOBUR: Squashy, sloppy, uliginous, oozy, pulpy, pappy.
LÁP	Lacuna, uligo = swamp, marsh.-LEVES: Juicy.

LABUI	The pot which is hung on the palm-tree to receive the liquid from which "tari" is manufactured.
LÁBAS	Tripus, frictorium, sartago, lebes = a pan.

LAC	The belly, the stomach, the abdomen, inmost parts, the womb.-LAC LIC: The entrails.
LÁGYÉK	Groin.-Flank.-LÁGY: Mollis = soft.-(HAS)-LÁGYA: Viscera = entrails.

LACAK PACAK	Large drops of rain falling from the leaves of trees, etc.
LOCSOG	To splash (water).-LOCSOL: To water, to sprinkle.-LOCS-POCS: Eluvies, eluvio = running down of water.

LACAK LUCUK	Not to put the ball of the foot to the ground when walking owing to the presence of a sore, thorn, etc.-LECOK: To limp on one foot.
LOTYOG, LÖTYÖG	Fluito = to dangle, to totter.

LACAN LOCON, LOCAN LUCUN	Greedy, hankering after. (E.g. in: "He is always on the look out for something to eat.")
LES, LÉS, LESEG	Expecto, insidiose, insidior = to wait, to lurk, to look out for.-LECSETEL: To eat greedily.

LACAR, LACRA	Talkative, always chattering.-LAPCO: Loquacious, talkative.-LOCOR POCOR: Unreliable, not to be depended on. (E.g. in: "He is talking rubbish.")
LOCSKA	Talkative, gabbling, gossiping.-LOTYOGTAT: Carrio, blatero = to chatter, to babble, to tattle, to gossip.

LACHAN, LOCHAN	Bad habit, evil courses, bad behaviour.
LOTYÓ	Scortum, prostibulum = a whore, a harlot.

LẠDE	To load, to put one thing on another.
LÁDA	Arca, scrinium, cista = box, chest, coffer, trunk.

LADE	Slanting, off the perpendicular, leaning to one side.
LEJTŐ	Declivis, descensus, salebra = slanting.–A slope.
LẠUẠ	A dish made of the hard shell of pumpkin.–LẠDU : A kind of sweetmeat.
LŐNYE	A kind of cake, with poppy and honey.
LAGA	To occupy. (E.g. in : " A spirit possessed him.")–LAKER, LAKIR : Habit.
LAKÁS	Mansio, nicolatus = dwelling, habitat, haunt.
LAGAN LOGON	Preparations for a marriage.
LAK	To hold a marriage.–LAKZI, LAGZI : A wedding.
LAHAS	A corpse, a dead body.
LÉHA	The bag, the husk.
LAHKAO	To do anything with enthusiasm, with heart and soul, with great zest.–LALE : To force oneself in or forward, impelled by a strong desire.
LELKES	To do anything with enthusiasm, with heart and soul, with great zest.–Animatus = animate, having a soul.–LÉLEK : Soul, spirit.
LAJ, LAJA LUKA	Shame.
LÁSA	Horrible, terrible.
LẠJUN LẠJUN, LUJUN LUJUN	Slow-paced.–LAJHAK LUJHUK : Slow-paced, lazy, opposite of nimble.
LASSÚ, LOSA	Lentus, tardus = slow-paced.
LAKAR LAKAR	To protrude the tongue with thirst, as a dog.–LAKAR LUKUR, LUKUR LUKUR : To tremble owing to nervousness, to shake.
LÓG	Pendeo = to hang (as the tongue of a dog).–Agitor = to agitate.
LAKHAO	To be apparent, to be visible, to be known.
LÁTHATÓ	To be apparent, to be visible, to be known.–LÁT : Video, cerno, specio, conspicio, tueor = to see.

LẠKUC LẠKUC	To jerk, short sudden movement.–LUKUT MARTE, LUKUT MENTE : To give a sudden start.–(See also LEKE PHEKE.)
LÖKÉS	Tactus, missus = a jerk, a throw.–To give a sudden start.

LẠKUK PHẠKUK	Toothless, as having no teeth.
LYUK	A hole.–FOGAK :° Teeth.

LALAO LOLAO	To be tantalized, to long for.
LELÉS	Affectis = to be taken ill.–LEL, LÉL, LÖL : Afficio, offendo = to tantalize, to plague, to torment.

LAMAK	To cut deeply.
LEMEZ, LEMES (VAS)	Culter precisorius in aratro = culter. (VAS : Iron.)

LAMJAK	Insipid, savourless.–LAMBAO : To go bad, to begin to rot.
LAMOS	Insipid.

LAMOT, LAMPOT, LOMPOTIA	Lazy and dissolute, lewd.
LEMUS	Vox contumeliosa = an invective.–LOMPOS : Sloppy.

LAND	A defiance used in answer to threats. (E.g. in : " Did you press me down ? ")
LÁM	A defiance, " look here."

LẠNDHIẠ, LẠNDHUẠ, LONDHIẠ	Lazy, sluggish, inactive.
LANYHA	Lazy, sluggish, inactive.

LẠNDUR, LENDUR, LẠNDUP	To fall down, to collapse as a wall, house, etc.–(See also LELE.)
LEDŐL, LEDŰL	To fall down, to collapse as a wall, house, etc.

LANGA	To be tired, to be fatigued, to be worn out, as an old person, to be very ill.
LANKAD	Languesco, fragesco, lassesco, torpeo, torpesco = to be tired, to be fatigued, to be very ill.

LAPAK LAPAK, LAPAK LOPOG	A thudding or flopping sound, produced by something soft falling.
LAFOG	To rustle (as clothes, when walking).

LAPET	To put into the mouth, as natives of India do food. (E.g. in: "Eat it up quickly.")
LAFOL	To eat greedily.

LAPICKAK, LAPOCKAK	Corpulent, broad and flat.–LAPOT: Dewlap of a bullock.–(See also LABLABA.)
LAPOCKA, LAPICKA	Scapulae, armus = shoulder-blade.–LAPOSSÁG: Broad and flatness.

LAPLOPO	To crouch or sit huddled up as one very cold.
LAPÚL	Se demittare = to stoop, to knuckle under.

LASAK PASAK	Uncomfortable feeling of the skin, mainly in hot weather. (E.g. in: "The body feels sticky.")
LÁZ	Fever.

LASAK PASAK	Overcooked, or overripe, so as to be insipid.–LASKAL: To mate without the usual properties.
LAZA	Exilis, vilis = inferior, bad, deficient.

LASKAO	To be entangled, to be caught as a stick that has been stuck in some branches.
LÉSZKA, LÉSZA	A hurdle, a plashing fence.–Perticula, palus, palanga = a long wooden stick.

LASAN, LASANGA, LOSON	On account of.–LESRAO: To be unfinished, incomplete, to be to do.
LESZEN	Verbum supplendi = auxiliary word. – LESZ, LESZEN: It will be.

LASLASA	Occupying much space, spread out.
LAZUL	Dispergor = to be spread out.

LAT, LATLAT	To stick, sticky.
LOTTYADÉK	Any filthy fluid.[1]

[1] Santal DAK: water, fluid.

LAṬIC LADAR	To move the body, to posture, to wobble.
LADÁZ	To stretch oneself, to posture.

LAỤẠ	Ill-feeling, quarrel, dispute.
LEU	Offensive, indecent (?).–LEUZAT : Scandalum = scandal.

LAWAO, LAOWAO	To share, to divide. (E.g. in : " They have divided the carcass of the goat in shares.")
LEVÁG	Deseco, rescindo = to cut off, to share.

LE	To melt, to dissolve.–LE, LEI : Paste.–LEPEC : Of the consistency of curdled milk or soft paste.–LẠBUS : Soft, as a ripe fruit.
LÉ	Succus, liquor, jus = juice, liquor.–LEVES : Soup.–Juicy (as a ripe fruit).–LEPÉNY : Polenta, laganum, artolaganus = cake, lozenge, tablet.

LEBET	To tread, to trample. (E.g. in : " To step short." Or in : " Do not transgress this order.")
LÉP	To tread, to trample, to step.

LECER PECER, LECE PECE	Tired, fatigued.
LEGYHEDT	Feeble, weak, fatigued.

LECRE	To squash, as a hat by being sat on, to put out of shape.
LESKEDT	Squashed, as a hat by being sat on.

LEDE LEDE	To walk falteringly, as a child just beginning to walk, to move slowly.–LEDHA : To limp.
LÉDZEN	To move slowly, to walk falteringly, to move weakly.

LEDER BEDER	To scamp.–LẠDUR BẠDUR : Carelessly, thoughtlessly, negligently, perfunctorily. (E.g. in : " He is going about, neglecting his work.")
LEDÉR, LŐDŐR	Careless, frivolous, disorderly.–LŐDÖRÖG : To go about as a vagrant.

LEK	Capable, fit, worthy, fitting, becoming.–NUI HORE LEKENA: This man has become capable or able bodied.–LEKMAN: Full grown, able bodied.
LEGÉNY	Juvenis, adolescens, caelebs = youth, an adolescent, a bachelor.–Officinae administer = helpmate, assistant.–Servant.–Soldier.

LEKAN, LEKA	Like, such.–LEKATE: Like, by way of.–LOGBHOG: Almost.–LẠG: Sharp, pungent, acute, hot, strong, potent, fertile.–LOGNO: Strong.
LEG	Like, such. (As a suffix.)–LEG: The sign of the superlative. (As a prefix.)–LEG: An emphatic particle.–LEGALÁBB: Almost.

LEKE PHEKE	To bubble, as anything stiff when boiling.–LIKIC LIKIC: To shake, to vibrate.–LOKOT LOKOT: The throat move with each respiration, as a hen panting.–(See also LẠKUC LẠKUC.)
LÜKTET, LÖKTET	To shake, to vibrate (as veins).–LÜK, LÖK: To shake, to throb.

LELE LELE	Said to a dog when setting it on.–LẠNDHU: To lay low.–(See also LẠNDUR.)
LE, LENT, LÖNT	De, deorsum = down.

LEŃ	To creep, to crawl, applied mainly to the mode of propension of snakes, earthworms, etc.–LEŃCOK: To limp, limping owing to one leg being injured.
LENG	To vaccilate, to oscillate.–LENGES: Oscillation.

LEORA	The male organ.–LAT: The male organ.–LAT GHAT: Fornication.
LŐDÖR, LÓDING	The male organ.

LEPE PEJE	Soft and sticky, viscous, gummy.
LÉP	Viscus = bird-lime.

LEPE LEPE	To flap the wings slowly.–(See also LEWAK and LO.)
LEBEG	Fluito, volito = to flap the wings slowly, to soar, to float in the air.

LEREC PETEC	Of inferior quality, as flesh meat; poor.
LŐRE	Wine of inferior quality.
LESORIĄ	Lazy, feeble, weak.
LÉZEREG, LÉZENG	Oberro, fluito = to wander in a weak, feeble state.
LETEC	To be able, to succeed, to overcome. (E.g. in: "With men it is impossible, but with God all things are possible.")
LÉTES	Real.–LÉTESÍT: To effect, to overcome.–LEHET: It is possible.
LEWAK	To shake, to hang dangling, to vibrate.–LEWE: To tremble, to shake.–LAWAK; To dangle, to spring up and down, to jerk up and down, to hang loosely.–LAWAR LAWAR, LĄWIC LĄWIC: To bob up and down.–LAWER: To hang over or down.–(See also LO and LEPE LEPE.)
LEBEG, LEVEG	Palpito = to vibrate, to bob up and down.–Vacillo = to shakę.–Fluito, volito = to hang, dangling.–LEVEGŐ: Pensile=pendants, anything what hangs.–Vexillum (?) = a flag.
LIBOC, LOBOC, LIBA, LABE, LIBO, LOBO	Slow, sluggish in movement. (E.g. in: "She is going slowly.")–(See also LIBOC.)
LIBA	A goose.
LIBRUK	To become weak, feeble.
LIBÁR	Lean, thin, meagre.–Haggard.
LIHA LAHE, LIHA LIHI	Very little remaining.
LIHA	Little, trifling.
LINDHI	The anus.
LINDIK	The clitoris.
LINGIT	To be startled or frightened.
LINKÁBA	A nightmare.
LIPLIP	To tremble, to shake.
LÖBÖG	To tremble, to shake.

LIPOC	To walk slowly as one tired and foot-sore.–LIPẠ LAPE: To fly slowly.–LIPẠT LAPAT: Lagging behind.–(See also LIBOC.)
LIPEC, LIPHEC	Slow, sluggish.–LIPICKEL: To limp along.–LIPINKA: A hobbler, a bungler.

LIPUK, LIBUK	To deceive, to wheedle. (E.g. in: "He wheedled him into working and paid him nothing.")
LIFET-LAFET	Calliditas, astutia = subtlety, cunning.–LICIS: Wheedling.

LIRON LORON,	Slack, aimlessly.
LÍROM-LÁROM	(Stuff and) nonsense.

LIT	Now.
LÉT	Esse = existence, being (actual).

LITI	Gone bad, soured, mouldy, decomposition set in, used with regard to food.
LỊTY-LOTY	Squash, useless (used with regard to food).

LO	To burn, scold.–LẠPUR LẠPUR: To hang down, or over the edge. (E.g. in: "The cloth is hanging down over the edge.")–LOBOE: Long and dangling. (E.g. in: "We will dance with long dangling or waving skirts.")–(See also LEWAK and LEPE LEPE.)
LOBB, LOB	Flamma = flame.–LOBOG: Flagro = to glow, to blaze.–Vibro, fluito, tremo = to dangle, to wave, to jerk up and down.–LOBOGÓ: A large and dangling Magyar skirt.–Vexillum = a flag.

LO	To draw water, to lift water by dipping a vessel into it.–LOSOT: Mud, to become mud, to be spattered with mud.
LOBB	Fluito = to swim, to float.–LOCS: Illuvies, lacuna = puddle, pool.–LOCSADÉK: Colluvies = medley.–LOCSOS: Coenosus = muddy.

LOC	Membrum virile.
LŐC	Membrum virile (?).

LODO DHORO	Shaking as a very nervous person, anxious to get something, shaking with excitement.
LIDÉRCZ, LODOVÉRCZ	Ephialtus, incubus = nightmare.

LODOP	Shaking, swaying.–LODOP MENTE: To flop down, to fall with a slop, as anything heavy and soft.
LÓDUL	To move on.–(MEG)LÓDIT: To shake, to swing.

LOHOM	To die, used by women when scolding. (E.g. in: "Die, and rid me of yourself.")
LOHOG	To stow away oneself, to get away.

LOHOR	To dry.
LOHOSOD	To loose the feathers, to moult.

LOP	To elide, to be elided, to be lost.–LOT, LOT PAÑJ: A clew, part or whole of stolen property.
LOP	Furor, clepo, subripio = to steal, to purloin secretly.–LOPADÉK: Stolen property.

LOPAK, LOPHAK	A hollow, hole or cavity of no great depth in a bank, hill, hedge or other upright object.
LOPOR	A pyramid.

LUCẠ	Vicious, immoral, profligate, disreputable.
LUSTA, LUSNYA	Dissolutus, vilis = sloppy, lazy, idle.–LUSTOS: Nasty, a beastly person.

LUR, LURBHAS, LOR	Sense, skill, ability.
LURKÓ	Homo callidus, petulans = rogue, rascal, tricky.

LUTIA	Given to pillaging, plundering or robbing.–LATAK: A fault, crime.
LATOR, LUTOR	Latro, sceleratus = bandit, robber, outrageous.

M

MA	A particle used regularly with the optative of the verb ; frequently with the imperative, which it softens to an optative sense ; in speaking of future events, .to indicate the confidence of the speaker ; and even in principal sentences which state facts, to turn them into or imply that they are statements of reason or cause. (E.g. in : " Do come." Or " Then go."–" At that time."–" May he become fat.")
MAJD, MAJ	A particle used with the optative of the verb or in speaking of future events.–Mox, statim = soon, shortly.–MAJDAN : Jamjam, protinus, evestigio, extemplo, paene, fere = immediately, instantly, nearly.

MACHA	Approximately, resembling, like (used in composition).–MẠPHIK, MẠPIK, MẠPIT : Like, resembling.
MÁSA	Approximately, resembling, like (used in composition).–MÁS : Par, similis = resembling, like.–MÁSIK : Alter, alius = the other.

MACHE	The edge, lengthwise.–MACHE MACHE : Along the edge or border. (E.g. in : " Go along the border.")
MESGYE, MEZSGYE	Limes = border.

MACKUNDẠ	A large forest tree, Pterospernum acerifolium. (KUNDA : Bole of a tree.)–MAKARKENDA : A large forest tree (Diospyros embryopteris.) MAJ : Hard heart-wood, central wood of some kind of tree.
MAGYAL	A large forest tree, esculus, ilex aquifolium, arbor ulmi = holm, ilex, elm.–MAKK : Glans, balanus = oak.–MAG : Heart-wood, centre, kernel.

MẠCUK	To eat up, to gobble.–MẠCUR : To eat all, to finish.–MASRAO : To stuff food into the mouth. To crunch, as a horse eating grain.
MAHOL, MÁHOL	To eat up, to gobble.–MAJSZOG, MAJSZOL : To eat, to chew, to bite.

MAG	The tenth Hindu month, the end of the agricultural year.
MAG	Granum = grain.–MAGZ-IK : Semento = seed, bearing.

MAHNGA	High, high priced.
MAGAS	High, high priced.

MẠGDUR, MẠKDUR	Power, strength.–(See also MẠKUP.)
MEG, MÖG	A very common and mostly intensifying prefix of the Magyar verbs.

MẠGNI, MẠNGNI	Without payment, gratis, for the asking.–(See also MẠKU.)
MAGÁÉ	It is yours.–MAGA : Egomet = myself.–You.–MAGA KÉNYÉN : Sponte sua = of its (his) own.

MAHA	A day.
MA, MO, MAH	Hodie = to-day.

MAHARA, MAHRA	The Goalla or cow-keeping Hindu cast.
MARHA	Cattle. (GULYÁS : A cow-keeper.)

MAHAROG, MAHROG	Dear, high-priced, scarce and dear.
MARHA, MORHA	Wealth, goods, property.–EZÜST-MARHA : Silver objects.–(EZÜST : Silver.)

MAHEA	Palus-cat.–MAHLA, MAHALA : The Palm-cat.
MACSKA	Felix, catus = cat.

MAHRE	After. (E.g. in : "After he left, you came.")
MIRE	After.

MẠI	Used in addressing a daughter, younger sister, younger female cousin, niece and a female younger than the speaker ; a daughter, a female, the female organ.–MAEJIU : A woman.
MENY	Mulier juvenis, sponsa, nurus = a young woman, a bride, a daughter-in-law.

MAJAO, MAŇJAO — To scour.

MOS — Lavo = to scour.

MAK — To slash, hack, chop, or hew with any cutting instrument such as a sword, axe, etc. (E.g. in: " Cut off his head.")

NYAKAZ — Decollo = to cut off the head.–Colaphizo = to box a person's ears.

MAKMAK, MAKMAKAO — To frolic, to romp, to lark.

MÓKÁZ — To frolic, to romp.

MAKARGA̦TI — To cross over, to link; a method of wearing the upper loose garment when extra exertion is required.

MAK — The loop or mesh (on one end of a rope for the purpose of passing through the other end.) (KÖT: To bind, to link.)

MA̦KU — A term of endearment employed when according to Santal custom the speaker may not use the name of the person (female) addressed. (See also MA̦GNI.)

MAGA — You.

MA̦KUP, MA̦HKUP, MUKUP, MUKUPH — To be deferred, postponed, relinquished, delayed.–(See also MA̦GDUR.)

MÖGÉ — Backward, behindhand, after.–MEG: A frequent Magyar verbal prefix.–MEGTÉR: To return. (TÉR: To go, to walk.)

MA̦KUR — Sound of crunching, as when eating a raw carrot.

MAKOG — To croak.

MAL — Goods, effects, merchandise.

MÁLHA — Luggage, baggage.

MALAN, MALAO — To rub the body or limbs, massage.–MAL: An athlete, a wrestler.

MELLENT — Massage.–MÁL: Pars corporis infra pectus = the chest.

MALOT	Barren, unproductive, as soil.–MALKATA: A coal miner. (KATA: A pit-saw.)
MALÁSZ	Alluvial soil.–MÁL: Mountain-slope. (?)–MÁL: A pit excavated from the flank.

MẠLUN	To cause to wonder, or be astonished, to wonder, to be bewitched; to fascinate.
MÉLA	Pensive, melancholic, low-spirited.

MANDA, MANDHIVẠ	A temporary shed or box, erected on the occasion of the marriage.–MANDER: In a wide circle, a wide area.
MENYEZET	Lacunar, contabulatura = ceiling.–MENY: The Heaven.

MANDER	A multitude.–MONDAM, MODAM: Continually, always, every day.–MOT: Total, to total.–(See also MIT.)
MINDEN, MENDEN	Omnis, cunctus = all, all together, collective.–MINDIG: Continually, always, every day.–MIND, MEND: Total, to total.

MẠNDIAU, MANDAO	To take shelter, as a wild animal in a thicket, etc., when run to ground.
MENEDÉK	Shelter, protection.–MENT: Evasio, liberatio = rescue, protection.

MAŃJ	Hart-wood, core of certain trees.
MANCS	A wooden ball.

MẠŃJHI	A Santal male.–MẠŃJHIAN: A Santal female.–GICHO MẠŃJIAN: A Santal female named Gicho.
MAGYAR, MAGYARI[1]	A Magyar. (NŐ: Female.)

MẠNJUR GUDA	To tie the hands together. (GUTU: To string.)
MANCS	Extremities (hooves) of beasts. (KÖT: To tie.)

MAO	The mew or call of a cat.
MÁVOG	The mew or call of a cat.

[1] See page 167, foot-note 2.

MARA	A depreciatory term used mainly when finding fault, scolding or abusing, scoundrel, rascal, miscreant, jade, witch, etc., in contempt or irony. (E.g. in: "This stammering fool is unintelligible." Or in: "A little imp of a child.")–MORDHA: A depreciatory term.
MARHA	A depreciatory form, used mainly when finding fault, scolding or abusing. "Stupid creature!" (Duffer).

MARAK MOROK	To stare wonderingly, to stare vacantly, as one half-witted when spoken to, to be sad, to be depressed. (E.g. in: "He is staring in wonder.")–MOROL MOROL: Fixed stare, eyes riveted on, intently.
MERED	Subrigor, erigor = fixed stare, eyes riveted on.–MERŐEN, MEREVEN: Intently.–MERENG: To meditate, to be lost or absorbed in thought.

MARAN	Great, large, big, huge, to become great, large, big, huge; first-born, principal, head, chief. (E.g. in: "He is a great man.")–MAR: Game killed at a hunt.
BAROM, MAROM (?)	Ingens, rudis = huge, great.–Bestia = beast.

MARAO	To become extinct, to become exterminated, to die, to put an end to, when used with another verb it is intensive.–MARUR: To decay, just beginning.–MEREC: Just appearing.
MERÜL	Submergor, immergor = to sink.–(FEL)MERÜL: To appear.–MERŐ: Prorsus, plane, penitus, merus = entirely, complete, whole, all.–MER: Haurio = to bail.–(KI)MERÜLT: Exhausted.

MAR, MARMAR	Quickly, instantly, rapidly, hastily.–MARA: On the point of, about to. (E.g. in: "He is almost dead.")–MARGE: Now, now and quickly, without delay.–MARAN: Before, first, in time or place.–MARTE: Affixed to certain roots it forms adverbs implying sudden and single actions.
MÁR	Jam = already, yet.–MÁR, MÁR: Jam-jam = almost.–MÁRAN, MÁRON: (?) Jamque = before.–DE MÁR: Now and quickly.

MARCA	To lose vigour, deteriorate physically.
MARCONA, MARCHANA	Nequam = valueless, good for nothing.–MARCONASÁG: A trifle, a small matter.–MARÁZ: Pusillanimous.

MARE	Old, ancient, original, surplus over requirements for year, savings over year.–MARA : To allow a corpse to remain in the house.–MARHATHA : To persist in spite of discomfort and difficulty.–DABA MARA : To halt, to rest, to encamp. (E.g. in : "We will halt for a little at the village.")
MARAD	Maneo = to be left, to remain, to persist.–MARADÉK : Posteritas = posterity.–Refuse.–MARADI : Old, ancient. (TÁBOROZ : To encamp.)

MARGOT, MARGHẠITẠ	Dirty, soiled.–MẠHUR : Poison.–(See also MÉRELˌ.)
MÉREG	Venenum = poison.

MARKAT	To fight, to fight and slay each other, to persevere.–MARUK : To eat.–MARJAD, MARJAT : A present, mainly of a small piece of flesh meat.–MAR : Calamity.–MAR MUHIM : Distress, suffering, affliction.–MEROM GHAO : Sore at angle of the mouth.–(GHAO : Sore.)
MARAKODÁS	Rixa = a quarrel, a fight.–MAR : Mordeo = to beat.–To burn.–To itch.–MARÁS : Morsio = A bit.–MARIN : A sore, especially on the ear.

MẠRKHU MARAO	To extract the broken grain from the refuse of the husking machine.
MARKOL	To grasp (with the hand).–MARADÉK : Refuse.

MAROM	A raised platform or scaffold.–A platform, used to keep straw on, or from which to watch crops.–MARKOCA : The ridge of a roof.–(KOCA : A corner.)
MAR	The ridge (of a hill or of a roof.)–Wrist.–Neck-piece.–(KOCA : A corner.)

MAT	A bamboo.
NÁD	A bamboo.

MATBOR	Well-to-do and honourable, independent, proud.–MADHAS : Respectable.–METAHA : The face, countenance. (E.g. in : "He is not a respecter of persons.")–MOL : To price.–MẠNUS MAN : To become well-to-do, to become respectable.
MÉLTO, MÉLTA, MÉTO(?), MÉTA(?)	Dignus, condignus, meritus = honourable, well-to-do, proud.–Worthy, estimable.–MÉLTOSÁG : Countenance.–MÉLTAT : To price, to respect.

ME	Come! (E.g. in: "Let us go!")–(See also MEN.)
MÉN, MÉD, MEN	Eo, mo, pergo = to go, walk.–MENJ: Go!

ME	The form taken by the 2nd personal pronoun in inflections.–(See also TAM.)
TE	2nd personal pronoun.

MEHNOT	Labour, trouble, exertion; to exert oneself.–MEHNOTIẠ: Industrious, hard working, painstaking.
MŰ, MÉH	Opus, artificium = labour, work, production.–MŰVEL, MYHEL: Laboro, facio, excolo = to work, to till, to treat, to make, to exert oneself.

MEJAS, MEŇJAS	To consult together, to consider.
"MEGY AZ?"	"Is that possible?", "Is it advisable?"

MEK MEK	To bleat as a goat.
MEKEG	To bleat as a goat.

MELA	Without particularizing, general.
MÈLY, MEEḶ	Indefinitum. (Qui, quae, quod, qualis, quam) = indefinite. (Which, what.)

MELA, MELAN	Wide, large.
MÉLY, MÉLYEN	Profundus, altus = profound, low, far, high.

MELA ORAK	An empty house, used as a guest house, etc.
MELLÉK(HÁZ)	An adjoining (house).

MELOT	To protrude the tongue, to moisten the lips with the tongue, to lick the lips, to dart out the tongue.–MELOT CETOT: Always eating, keeping the lips moving, as when eating.–MẠLI: To cup; the surgical process of cupping.
NYELV	Lingua = tongue.–NYEL: Glutio = to swallow.–NYELDEKLÉS: Haustus = the chirurgical process of cupping.

MEN, MET	To say, to tell, to wish, to call.-MANTAR : An incantation.-MANAN : To vow.
MOND, MODJA	Dicit, indicit, ait inquit = to say, to tell, to call.-MENDE MONDA : Rumour.-MONDÁS : An incantation, a spell.

MEN, MENYA	An exclamation of warning, caution, admonition or alarm ; beware, take care, mind what you are about, look out. (E.g. in : " Clear out of the way ! " Or in : " Flee, there is a tiger." Or in : " Beware father ! " Or in : " Look out father ! ", etc., etc. ; respectful form used to elderly people.)-MENA : To exist.-(See also ME.)
MENJ	An exclamation of warning, caution, admonition or alarm.-" Go on ! "-MEN : Eo, meo, pergo = to go.-MÉN : locum habeo = to have place.-(ÁLTAL-)MÉN : permutor, vertor = change into, to become.

MENA	Probably, belike, most likely.
MONNAL	Quasi, paena = likely, almost.

MENKHAN	A particle which, when standing at the beginning of its clause, is a co-ordinating conjunction, signifying " but ", and, when occurring at the end, a subordinating conjunction or conjunctive adverb, signifying " if " or " when ".
MIKOR, MIKORON	Quum = but, when.-Quando = when.

MENTE	Affixed to certain roots to form adverbs, implying sudden or single actions. (E.g. in : " He came at once.")
MENTEN	Statim, protinus, continuo, illicet = instantly, at once.-" MENTEN MEGYEK " : Pergo = I go without delay.

MEREC	Just appearing, just beginning. (E.g. in : " His moustache is only now beginning to sprout.")
MERED	To raise up, to appear all at once.

MEREL	Eagerly, cravingly.-(See also MARGOT.)
MÉREG	Furor, ira = anger, annoyance.

MER SITRUC	Small, insignificant, petty, paltry, trivial, unimportant.–(SITRUC, SITUR : Unimportant, paltry, trivial, vain.)–MERAIC : An insignificant person.
MÉRA	Exiguus, vilis = small, trivial. – (SZITTY-SZOTTY : Unimportant, trivial, paltry.)

MESAL	To mix, to adulterate.–MESA MISI : To mix, to mingle, to confuse.–MESAO : To mix.
MESZEL	To mix with lime.–MÉSZ : Calx, coementum = lime.

MIẠD, MEAD	Term, period.–MIẠDI, MEADI : Terminable.
MEDDIG	Donec, dum = as long.–For a term, for a period.–(IG : To, up to.)

MISRI	Sugar-candy.
MÍZ, MÉZ	Honey.

MIT	A (the indefinite article), one single, to unite, to join, to mix. (E.g. in : " They have all gone.")–MIT, MIMIT : Each, singly. (E.g. in : " Give each of them.")–MIT : To unite, to join, to mix. (E.g. in : " We are working in partnership.")–(See also MANDER.)
MIND	Omnis, totum, simul, et quoque, etiam = every, all, at the same time, together, both, as well as. MINDEGYIK : Each of them.

MOAO	To damp, to moisten. (E.g. in : " They moisten it and eat it." Or in : " They damp the cotton seed and then sow it.")
MELEG	Caldus = warm, tepid.–MELEGET : Tepefacio, focillo = to warm, to dry.–To damp, to moisten.

MOCMOC, MOCMOCO	To pout, to push out the lips when sullen or displeased. – MALAC MULUC, MULUC MULUC : To smile.–MOCA : The mouth.
MOSOL, MOSOLY	Smile.–MOSOLYOG, SOMOLYOG : Subrideo, rideo = to smile.–MOCOG : To smile.

MODHOM	Middle, intermediate. (E.g. in : " How big is the bride ? Of nice middle size.")
MÓDOS	Moderatus = moderate, middling.–Ornatus = nice.

MOGON	The brain. (E.g. in: "His brain is injured, i.e. he is angry or insane.")–MOGON: To be careless, as one intoxicated.–MOKMOKOR: To sulk, to be sullen, to scowl.
MOGORVA	Tetricus, impolitus, inurbanus = surly, morose, sullen, angry.

MOGRA	A drain pipe, the ridge tiles of a roof.
MAKRA	Possessing a special form: downwards tight, upwards large.

MOH	Pity, compassion. (E.g. in: "Giving distress him, i.e. he is niggardly.")
MOH	Avidus, cupidus = eager, greedy, covetous.

MOHAN BẠSI	A variety of the plantain. (BẠSI: Fusty.)
MOH, MUHA	Muscus = moss.–MOHAE: Atractylis cartamus = miliary grass.

MOKA	The elbow.
BOKA	The elbow.

MOKON	To tire, to finish, to lose the relish for, to be done. (E.g. in: "I am tired sitting." Or in: "I am tired speaking, he will not listen.")
MEGÚN	Taedet, fastidio = to tire, to lose relish for.

MOLAO, MALAO	To polish, to burnish.–MOLAT: To sharpen, to give an edge to, as a razor on a strop. MÓLOK: To appear for the first time.
MILLING	A shining blade.–Lightning.

MON	Mind, spirit.
MANÓ	Malus genius, daemonus = evil spirit, demon.

MOROC, JOJO MOROC	Acid, acidulous.
MAR, MỌRYON	Mordeo = to bite, to burn.–MARÓ: Corrosive, caustic. (SÓS: Acidulous.–SÓ: Salt.)

MORGOT, MURGUC	Dirty and ill-conditioned.–MOROT: Stinking, fetid.–MURCẠ, MURCHẠ: To corrode, to rust, to wear or to be eaten away gradually.
MORTYOS	Dirty.–MURVA, MORVA, MURUGY, MURUGYA: Putrid chaff.

MOSAO	Silent and dejected.–MUSAK : Melancholy.
MAZUR	Misery, distress.

MOSOKUSI	To compel, to force, against one's will, to persuade, to coax. (E.g. in : " They compelled him to go.")–MUSAPHIR : A traveller. (PHIRPHIR : Restlessly.)
MOZOG	Palpito, moveor = to move.–MOZGAT : Moto, moveo, agito = to move, to persuade.

MOSTORAM	Careless of what may happen.–MOSTE, MOSTETE, MOSOKOT : Difficult, difficulty.
MOSTOHÁN	Careless of what may happen.–MOSTOHA, MOSTANHA : Step.–MOSTOHASÁG : Adversitas = trouble, difficulty, unkindness.

MOT	A bundle, to tie or make up into a bundle.
MOTYÓ	Baggage.

MOT	Method, way, mode.–MOTO : Only, like.–MOTON : Like.
MÓD	Modus, modalitas = kind, mode, way.–MÓDON : Like.

MOT	To tie or make up into a bundle.
MADZAG	A tie.

MUDGUC, MUIGUC	A depreciatory term, dirty.
MOCSKOS	A depreciatory term, dirty.–MOCSOK : Sordes, squalor = dirt, filth.

MULEHABAD	To destroy, to ruin. (E.g. in : " It all died.")
MÚL	Evanesco = to perish, to pass away.–MÚKÁS : Disappearance.–(KI)MÚL : To die.

MUN	A mythical semi-divine being.
MÉN	Equus admissarius = a stallion.–MÉN MARÓT : A traditional Magyar chieftain.

MUND MORON	A great hardship.–MUNIS : A male farm servant.–MUKAU, MUKER : To strike, to hit. (E.g. in : " They beat him soundly.")
MUNKA	Labor, tormentum = a great hardship.–MUNKÁS : A workman.

MUNDU	A fowl.–MUNDHAT CITRI : The black partridge. (CITRI : The grey partridge.)
MADÁR	Avis, volucris, volatilis = bird. (CSITLIKOL : Fritinnio = to twitter, to chirp.)

MUNGA MUTẠK	A thick club or stick of some light wood.
MANGA	Oar, rudder.–MANKÓ : Crutch.

MURẠI ARAK, MULẠ ARAK	The radish. (ARAK : Pot herbs, vegetables.)
MUROK	Napus = carrot.

MURHUC JOM	Leprosy.–MẠRI : The plague.
MIRIGY, MEREGY, MÉRIGY	Abscessus, apostema = ulcer, sore.–Pestis = the plague. (CSOMA : Plague.–Something ugly, frightful.)

MURUK	Physical or mental energy, vigour, strength, determination, perseverance, constancy, tenacity of purpose ; to energize, to be resolved, steadfast.
MER	Audeo = to dare.–MERÉSZ, MERŐ : Audax, intrepidus, cordatus, confidens = daring, intrepid, energetic, steady.–(VAK)MERŐSÉG : Temeritas, pertinacia = boldness, tenacity.–MORC, MORD, MORGYAS : Obstinate.–Wild.

MURUT HENDE HASA	A kind of black stiff soil. (HENDE : Black.–HASA : Soil.)
MURVA	Gravel, river sand-bank, boulder, rubble-stone.

MUSIN	A day or two, a short time.
MOST, MAST	Nunc, modo = now, presently.–MOSTAN : In presentarium = actually, presently.

MUSNẠ	Fine cloth.
MUSZULY	Clothing.

MUTHẠN	Form, likeness, resemblance.–HOR MUTHẠNANAE : He has the form of a man, or the likeness of a man. (HOR : A man.)
MUTAT	Monstro, ostendo, exhibeo = to show, to have the form, the appearance of.–MUT (?) : Monstro = to show.

N

NA	A particle signifying doubt or uncertainty.
NA	A particle (suffix) signifying doubt or uncertainty.
NẠBHUẠ	Funny, jocular; buffoonery, tomfoolery.
NYABÁLOD-IK	To be funny, jocular, buffoon.
NẠDI NALADIN	The rainy season, when the rivers are full.–(NALA: A stream.)
NEDŰ, NEDV	Humor, liquor = moisture, wet.
NAKẠTIẠ, NAKATIO	Rascally, mischievous, naughty.
NYAGGAT	To harass, to torture, to tease, to vex.
NAKHA	Direction.
NAK	A particle (suffix) signifying to, in the direction of.
ŃAM, ŃA	To seek, to find, to obtain, to get, to wish for.
NYOMOZ	To search into, to explore.
NAMJẠDI, NAMDAK	To be famous, notorious.
NEMES, NEMZETES	Eximius, clarus = famous, noble, gentle.
NANA	Aunt.–NA: Used by males addressing females, and by females unless the age is very disproportional. (E.g. in: "Oh, my elder sister, come this way.")
NÉNE	Aunt.
NAP	To measure.–NAPRAK: Great, large, big. (RẠKDUN: Height, tall, very, exceedingly, applied to height.)–NABAB: A great man, a prince. (BABA: Father.)
NAGY	Magnus, ingens, grandis, vastus = great, large, big.–NÁPIC, NÁPÉSZ: Little, small, thin, meagre. (ICI, PICI: Little, small.)

NARJOR	To marry.–NAIHAR: Applied to the parent's house after marriage.–NATAT ERA: The wives of brothers.–NATEA, ŃATEA: The relationship between wives of brothers or cousins.–NATA: Temporary relationship, to assume relationship for the purpose of addressing each other.
NÁSZ	Nuptial festivity, marriage.–NÁSZ: Relationship between the parents of the married couple.
NASE	A little, very little.
NESZ	A very little noise.
NASE	Untrue, false.
NESZ	A pretext, a subterfuge.
NAṬHU	The septum of nose.–NAṬHU PHORAO: To snort, to make a noise through the nostrils.
NÁTHA	Catarrh of the nose.
NE	A particle which signifies that something inanimate is being offered for acceptance; "take."
NE	Eu tibi = here it is for you, "take."
NE	Presently, in no long time, very recently.
NI	Presently, here presently.
NE	A particle signifying like the speaker, like myself, like ourselves.
NYI	A comparative particle.
NEHAE	An anvil.–NEHAḶI: Of no use, unable to work, not able to earn anything.–NEJHAR: To impede, to hinder. (E.g. in: "There is an impediment.")
NEHEZÉK	Pondus = weight.–NEHÉZ: Ponderosus, clivius = weighty, heavy.–Difficilis = difficult.–NEHÉZKES: heavy, clumsy.–NEHÉZSÉG: Impediment.
NEHAL	To do, to accomplish, used most frequently in sarcasm.
NOHÁT, NOH, NO	Agedum, age, agite = come on! now then! (Used most frequently in sarcasm.)

ŃEL	To see, to look, to appear, to seem. (E.g. in: " Fire is seen at a great distance at night." Or in: " The place where a festival is observed.")–NOJOR, NANJER: To look, to gaze; faculty of seeing.
NYÍL	To open, to appear.–NÉZ: Cerno, video = to see, to look, to gaze.–NÉZÉS: Faculty of seeing.
———	
ŃEREK ŃEREK, ŃERE ŃERE	Whiningly, pitifully, sorrowfully.–ŃERE ŃERE: In an undertone, scarcely audible.
NYIRBÁL	Pipulo postulo, peto applorando = to beg whiningly.–(EL)NYIRBÁL: Reticeo = to conceal, to pass over in silence (?).
———	
NI	This particular one (of animate objects).
(EZ)NI	This particular one (of animate objects).
———	
NI	A female.–SANTAL: A Santal; SANTALNI: A Santal female.
NŐ	A female, a woman.–MAGYAR NŐ: A Magyar female.
———	
NIC	Low, mean, small.
NYIZA	Meagre.
———	
ŃIR	To run, to flee, to disappear as the moon.
NYARGAL	Grassor, curso = to gallop.
———	
NIRBAH	Fare, daily fare.–NIRHI, NIRIK, NIRUKH: Price current, allotted task, to fix rate.
NYER, NYEER	Lucrifacio, lucror, demereo = to win. –NYERESÉG: The profit.
———	
NIRBOS	Weak, without strength or vigour.
NYIRKAD	Torpesco = to grow slack, to relax, to languish.
———	
NIRON	The hot weather.
NYÁRON	In summer time.–NYÁR: Summer.
———	
NIURI	A small forest tree, Eleodendron Roxburghii.
NYÍR	Birch-tree.

ŃO	A little, used only in composition.
NYI	A little, used only in composition.

NOMAN, NEMAN	About here, here about, here and there, in this direction.
NEMMEN	Instar, adinstar, propemodum, satis, utcunque = almost, closely, nearby.

NOMONA, NẠMUNA	Example, pattern
NEM	Genus, species = kind, species, sort.

ŃU	To drink.–ẠŃU : To cause to drink, to give to drink, to water cattle.
IN	To drink.

NUI	This, this one, applied to animate objects.–(See also NI.)
NI	This, this one, applied to animate objects.

ŃUMBẠK, AYUP ŃUMBẠK	A little after nightfall.–NOMAN : A little way off, here about.
NYOMBAN	A little after.–NYOMÁN : A little way off, here about.–NYOM : A spur. (ÉJ : Night.)

ŃURUC	Lean, emaciated.
NYURGA	Lean, emaciated.

ŃUTAT	The time between nightfall and the rising of the moon, applied only to the wane of the moon.
NYUGAT	Occasus = setting (of the moon).

O

O	An exclamation of defiance, not.
A	Negatio pervicax = not.

OAR	To take or pull out of, as out of water, a pit, etc., to skim, as cream off milk, to rescue, to deliver.–(See also ẠURI.)
ÜRÍT	Inanio, evacuo, casso = to empty, to drain, to clear out.–ÜRÜL : To be delivered.

OBOSO	Certainly, necessarily.
(A)BIZONY, BIZO, BEZE	Certainly, necessarily.

OCHA	Straw from which grain has been trodden out by cattle.
OCSU	Cus, palea, excretum = remainder (as of grain), rubbish.

OCO	Causative inflexion. (With dative giving sense of " allow ", with accusative giving sense of " cause ".)–AKHA MAKHA : Without reason, causelessly.
-ASS, -ESS	Causative suffix of verbs.–OK, OOK, OCC : Causa = a cause.–OKOZ : To cause.–(?) UK MUK FUK : (?) Without reason, causelessly (?).

OCOK	To remove.–OSOC OSOC, OSOS OSOS : Heavy, deep, as sleep.
OCSÚL, OCSÓD-IK	Expergiscor, evigilo = to awake.

OD, AD	To give shelter, protection, to take refuge, to hide.
ODU, ODOR	Shelter (of animals).–ÓV, OJ, OH, ÓTALMAZ : Tueor = to give shelter, protection.

ODHRAO, ODRAO	To remove, to become detached, to carry away parts as of the ridges of rice fields, by water.
OLD, ÓD	Solvo = to untie, to let loose, to solve.

ODROK — Fat, corpulent.

ODROS — Voracious, glutton.

OHMAN — To infer, to deduce, to derive as a consequence.

ONNAN — Inde = thus.

OHOWA — No ! An emphatic nagative. (E.g. in : " Can you give me ten rupees ? No ! ")

Ó HOVA — No ! What do you suppose !

OJ — Reasonable amount.

ÓCSÓ, OLCSÓ — Facilis pretii = reasonable, cheap.

OJA — Substitute, exchange. (E.g. in : " I will give you an exchange for this.")

AJÁNL, AGYÁLL — Deferre, offerre = to give, to offer.–AJÁNDÉK : A gift.

OK HULUN — Ugly, unprepossessing.

ÉKTELEN — Indecorus, turpis, infamis = ugly, repulsive, harmful.–ÉK : Decor, venustas, elegantia = decoration, ornament, elegance.

OK KISKU — A sub-sept of the Santals, the sept Kisku.–(OK MIRMU : The sept Mirmu, etc., etc.)

ÁG — Genus, tribus = sept, branch, tribe.

OKA BHAG — By what chance. (E.g. in : " By what chance have we met ? "). (BHAG : Chance, fortune.)–OKA BATE : How is it ?–OKOC, OKOCTE : In comp. with a limited number of adjectives and adverbs signifies very, in a high or eminent degree. (E.g. in : " Live in harmony." Or in : " Do not eat a great quantity.")

OK, OKA — Causa, ratio = cause, motive, ground, occasion.–OKOS : Reasonable, wise, judicious.

OKOK — Imitative of the sound produced when one is sick and about to vomit.

OKÁD — Vomo = to vomit.

OKROT — Short-necked, bull-necked.

ÖKÖR, EKR — Bos = ox, bull.

OL	To lie down.–OGRAO, ODAO: To lie in an ambush, to lie in wait.–(See also ULẠ.)
ÜL	Persedeo, situs est = to lie down, to be situated.–ÓLÁL, ORÁL: Insidior = to lie in an ambush, to lie in wait.

OLKOBAHA	Foolish, ignorant, imbecile.
OSTOBA	Inconis, rudus, stolidus = stupid, rude, stolid.

OLOM JHOLOM	Lounging idly.
ALAMÁR	Ignavus, deses = idle, lazy.

OLON	To be disconsolate, sad, depressed.–ALATOKA: Poor, to become reduced in circumstances.
ALANGYÁR	Devotus, humilis=devoted, humble.–ALACSONY: Depressus, humilis, submissus = depressed, humble, submitted.

OMBAK	To bend the body forwards from a kneeling position.–OBOR: To collapse, to lie down, to fall down. (E.g. in: "The house has collapsed with the wind." Or in: "To lie down through fatigue.")
OMOL	To collapse, to fall down.

ON, AN	Grain, food. (E.g. in: "He is unable to digest his food.")
EN	To eat.–ENNI-VALÓ: Food.

ONDGA	One who kills human beings for the purpose of offering the blood to a malignant spirit.
ONT	Fundo, dissipo = to pour, to waste.–VÉRT ONT: to bleed. (VÉR: Blood.)

ONEAO	Unjustly, unrighteously. (E.g. in: "Do not act unjustly.")
ÖNZŐ	Selfish.

ONE DHONE	Wealthy.
ÖNÖTT	(?) Beatus = fortunate, lucky, happy.

ONA	That.-ONE : That there.-ONKA, ONKAN : Like that.
AMA	That.-EME : That there.-OLYAN : Like that.

ONTEN	Yonder, that place.-(See also OTO.)
OTTAN, OTTON	Inibi, ibidem = there, yonder, on that place.

OR	To punish, to chastise, to get the better of one.
ORCÁZ	To reprimand severely, to scold.

OR ẠSIT	To pull or draw in or together, as a noose, a running knot, a snore, etc. (E.g. in : " We will tie it with a running knot.")-ORSEC : To draw in or contract the stomach, with all one's might.
ERŐSIT	Firmo, fortifio, muniọ, roboro = to fasten, to tack, to fortify.-ERŐ : Might.

ORAD	To infer, to guess, to estimate.
ÉR	Valeo = to be worth.

ORAK	House, dwelling place, home.-KAD ORAK : A prison.
ERESZ	Porticula, porticus, rustica, praestega = home in general, vestibule, gutter. - KETREC, KETEREC (?) : A prison, a cage.

ORAT	Beginning, original.-OR ORPAD : Beginning, inception.-ORAM : To begin.
ERED	Orior, incipio = to begin, to be inceptive.-EREDETI : Original.

ORE	Old, worn out.
ÖREG	Senex = old, aged.-Ó : Vetustus, obsolete = worn out, obsolete.

ORLOPORLO	Dusty, white dust. (E.g. in : " Having dulled in the dust.")
POR	Dust, white dust.

ORMOC	A bug.
OR MÉH	An insect (?).

ORTHO — Meaning.–OROM : To recognize, to know.

ÉRTELEM — Meaning.–ÉRT : Intelligo, persentisco = to understand, to recognize, to learn, to know.

OROP — To pile on fuel.

OROM — Pinna, fastigium = gable, summit.–ORMOZ : To elevate, raise aloft in a pointed manner.

ORWAL — To curtail, a curtain.

ORMÁN — Pinafore.

OSAR — To make broad, to widen.–ASEN TASEN : Spread out, scattered here and there.–ASES TASEC : To scatter, to squander. (E.g. in : " He has squandered his wealth.")–OSTE : Gradually.

OSZOL — Dispergor, dividor = to be spread out, to be squandered.–OSZT : To divide, to scatter.

OSOK — To become emaciated, to become lean.

ÖSZTÖR — Macer, marcidus, strigosus = thin, meagre, emaciated.

OSOR — To feel a call of nature.

ÖSZTÖN — Instinctus = instinct.

OTO — Only used in conjunctives with other verbs and conveys the idea of the actor departing after having performed the action. (E.g. in : " He left him altogether." Or in : " He gave it up to him." Or : " Leave him and come away.") –(See also ONTEN.)

OTT, OOTH, OTTON — Inibi, ibidem = there, on the spot.–ODA : Isthuc, eo isthuc = to, there.–ODAADTA : He gave it up to him.–HAGYD OTT : Leave him.–(HAGY : To leave.)

OYO — To put on, as a shawl, plaid.

ÖV, Ő — Cingulum, balteus, zona = belt.

OYON, UYUN — To look down, to look into, to look out. (E.g. in : " He is looking out of the house.")

AJ — A slit, a fissure.–AJTÓ : Os, apertura, janua, ostium, fores = an opening, an aperture, a door.

P

PACAK, PACAK PACAK	To spread out as anything soft falling on the ground.-PACSANGOL : To splash.
POTYOG	Assidue cado = continually falling.

PAÇLA, PAÇHLA PAÇHUAU, PAÇ	To give way, to draw back, to shrink. (E.g. in : " He is wriggling out of it.")
FESL-IK, FESEL	Rumpor, dissolvor = to detach oneself, to separate, to develop.

PADRA	A wooden cage with bars in front.
PADOL	Tabulo, coasso = to wainscot.

PAERA	To swim.-PAERE : An overflow channel of a tank, etc.
FÜRD-IK, FERŐT, FERŐDÉS	Lavare = to bathe.

PAETHAN, PAETHANI	A sore which affects the soles of feet.
PATTANÁS	Pustule, cutaneous eruption (as on the soles).

PAETAR	To foretell or prognosticate by divination or omens, to augur.
FÖLTÁR, FŐTÁR	To foretell the future. (TÁR : Aperio = to open wide.)

PAGUR	To chew the cud.-PACAH, PACHA : To prosecute research, to persue an inquiry.
FAGGAT	Macero, divexo = to tear, to lacerate.-Interrogando extorqueo = to inquire, to investigate, to reconnoitre.

PAINGAN	A hollow anklet of bell metal having shot or small stones inside which rattle as the wearer moves.-(See also BHANKUR.)
PENG, PÖNG	To rattle (as a spur).

PAJHRAO	To lose flesh, to become lean.
FOGY	Decresco, consumor = to decrease, to become meagre.

PAJET	Bother, wretchedness, distress, affliction.
FÁSULT	Apathetic.

PA̦JI	A scoundrel, scoundrelly, base, mean.–PA̦JI HOR: A mean rascal.
BETYÁR	Scoundrel.

PA̦K, PA̦K DON, PA̦K ENEC	The sword and shield dance. (ENEC: Dance.)
BAKOS (?)	Gladius, pugio = sword.–PAJZS: Clipeus, scutum = shield.

PAKAR, PAKOR	To seize, to take hold, to catch.–(IŇKO PAKARKEDIŇA: They apprehended me.–PAKORANAE, SE BAN? Has he caught any or not?)
FOG, FAG	Capio, prehendo = to seize, to take hold, to catch.

PAKAR, PAKOR	Wood and brake, bush and brake.
BOKOR	Dumus = bush, shrub, thicket.

PAKAS PUKUS	To be restless as an infant when hungry.
PÁKÁSZ, PÁKOSZ, PÁKOSZTOS	Given to eating, lickerish, loving dainties.

PALA	Leaves of trees which cattle will eat.
FALAT	Bucella, frustrum, offa, bolus = a mouthful, a fit.–Food.–FAL: Voro = to eat greedily.

PAL	A herd, a flock.–PAL BHIŇJAN: Together, in a body, in a company, to combine, as a herd of cattle. (E.g. in: "Supposing him to be in the company they went a day's journey.") (BHEŇJAN: To mix, to adulterate, to mingle.)
FALKA	A herd, a flock.–VAL (VEL): A suffix denoting "together," "in a body," "in a company."–(The English "with".)

PALA	Frost, snow.
FAGY	Algor, gelicidum, gelu, gelasco = frost, to get frozen.

PALAO	To nourish, to bring up as a child.
PALÓ	Fascia infantilis = swaddling clothes.

PALAT	A change of raiment, to change one garment for another.
VÁLT	Muto = to change something for another.

PALEK	Almost, peradventure.
VÉLETLEN	Inopinus, improvisus = unexpected, casual.

PALI	Turn, shift.
PALOL, PALLOL	Ventilo, dispergo = to aerate, to dismount.–PALLÉR: Conductor, prefectus operarum = foreman.

PẠLKU	Mixed with grey, as hair.–PẠLKU: To change colour from bright green to yellow, as grain, etc. when ripe.–PẠNDU: to become grey haired, to become yellow as leaves in autumn.–PẠNDUẠ: Greyish coloured, applied to buffaloes.
FAKUL	To become discoloured.–Mixed with grey, as hair.–FAKÓ: Equus flavus = light bay horse.

PALO	To be too old or too mature and unsuitable for food, as leaves, herbs, etc.
POLYVA, PELYVA, POLUA	Palea, gluma, acer, acus = chaff, husks.

PAŃC, POŃC, PANCẠHIT	A council, an assembly, a meeting, applied generally to an assembly of five men, convened to act as arbitrators, or to settle matters of dispute in an informal way. (From Hindi PANCH: Five.)
PANASZ, PANANSZ, PANOZ	Querimonia, querela = complaint.

PẠŃCI	A piece of cloth of less than the usual width.
FÁNCSIKA	A rag.

PAṆICHA	A bamboo bowstring.
PÁNYVA	Capistrum = halter, frontlet.–(KI)PÁNYVÁZ : Illigo = to put on the halter.

PANTE BELE	The testicles.
FAN	The penis. (BELE : The inner part.)

PAṚ	The beam or beams supporting the roof of a house.–MUTUL PAṚ : The ridge beam or pole of a house. (MUTUL : Gable of a house.)
PÁRKÁNY	Cornice, moulding, sill.

PAṚ	A coloured border on a cloth.
PEREM, PRÉM	Border on a cloth.–PÁRTA : Anadema=head-gear.

PARAK	To split, to crack.
FARAG	Sculpo, fabrico = to carve, to cut, to chisel, to split.

PARAK	The first ploughing of a field for the season.–PAṚTI, PORTI : Fallow, uncultivated, unfertile. (E.g. in : "This year field remained uncultivated.")
PARLAG, PARRAG	Ager desolatus, solum derelictum = heath, uncultivated soil.

PARAO	Weak, feeble.
FÁRADT	Lassus, fessus, defessus = tired.

PARAS, PARAS PARAS	Sounding of a slap ; succession of slapping sounds.
POROSZKA	The ambling pace of a horse.

PAṚCHA	To settle, as disputed matter.–PHIRIAḌI, PHURIAḌI : An accuser, a plaintiff.
PER, PÖR	Lis = dispute, quarrel, process.–PERLŐ : Petitor = plaintiff.

PARDAK	To bound, as a deer, to move by successions of bounds or leaps.–POTEA TAṚUP : A leopard.–(TAṚUP : The big felines, as tiger, panther, leopard in general.)
PÁRDUC	Leopard.

PARO	A plant so named.–PAROR JHINGẠ: A cultivated vegetable, Luffa acutangula. (JHINGẠ: A cultivated food plant.)–PALAK ARAK: A kind of spinach.–(ARAK: Potherbs, vegetables.)
PARÊ	Cabbage.–PARÉJ, PARAJ: Spinach.

PAROM	Across, beyond, far side. (E.g. "On the other side of the river." Or in: "Two villages beyond.")–PARA: A part of a town or village, a near village, vicinity.
PART	Ripa, litus = border, coast.–(MÁSIK) PARTON: Across, beyond, on the other side of the river.–PART: Ground, eminence, hill.

PAROSI	Neighbours.–PALTON: A soldier, an army.
PARASZT, PALASZT	Rusticus = peasant, cultivator.–Laicus = worldly, lay.

PARPAO, PẠRPẠU	To burn clearly and brightly as fire.
PERMED	To burn clearly and brightly as fire.–PERS, PERZS, PORS, POROS: Flame, fire.

PARTAP	Potency, splendour, courage, prosperity. (E.g. in: "I am delivered by your potency.")
PÁRTOL	To patronize.

PAS, PASE	Neighbourhood, vicinity.
PÁZTA, PÁZNÁT	A small part of an estate, a "line of the soil".

PASAR, PISAR PASAR	To be out of order, to be in disorder, to be disarranged, to be topsy-turvy, to be dislocated.
PACUHA	To be in disorder, to be disarranged.

PASAR	To spread out, to expand, to increase. (E.g. in: "He is stingy.")
PAZAL, PAZAROL	To waste, to squander, to be prodigal.

PẠSI	An iron staple fastening share to plough.–PẠSI: PHẠSI: A running knot, a noose, to snare by a noose, to hang by a noose; ensnared, involved. (E.g. in: "They hang murderers." Or in: "They have set a snare.")
FESZÍT	To stiffen, to prop, to span.–FESZES: Straight-laced, firm.–VÉSZ: A weir-basket.

PẠSIND, POSIND	To select, to choose, to estimate. (A word used in testing luck.)–(See also BESAHA.)
VESZ	To buy, to select, to choose.

PASRA	A smith, place where a blacksmith works, to work as a blacksmith.
VAS	Ferrum = iron.–VASAL : To shoe, to sheath.

PASU, POSU	An animal, cattle.
PESZÉR, PECÉR	Servant in care of animals.

PẠSUR	To miss, to lose, to fail in purpose.–PHES PHAS : To no purpose, vainly.
VESZT	Perdo = to miss, to lose, to fail in purpose.

PATAN	Irrigated, that requires irrigation.–PATAO : To irrigate.
PATAK	Brook, rivulet, rill.

PATAN BATAN	To snap at, to reply testily.–PATAS : Sounding of a slap.–PATPATOK : To crack, to patter.–PATA PUTU : To sound, or crack as grain when being roasted.
PATTAN, (FEL)-PATTAN	To snap at, to reply testily.–PATÉL : Percution, verbero = to slap, to thrash, to hit.–PATTOG : To crack, to patter.–To sound as grain when being roasted.

PATAR SATAE	Thin, sparse.
POTOM	Sparse.

PATARAK	Split up the middle.
PATA	A hoof.

PATET	To interlace.
PATICS	An interlaced work, a hurdle.

PICHA, PECHA	To follow up, to prosecute, a search as for one lost, to trace, to track.
VIZSGÁL, VISGÁL	Emendo, censeo = to search, to trace, to investigate.–VIZSLA, VISLA : Oculorum acie valens, canis sager = sharp-sighted, pointer, setter.

PELPEL, PELPELAO	To go bad, as cooked food, flesh, etc. (E.g. in: "The boiled rice has soured.")–(See also BASAN.)
FŐL, FŐ	Coquor = to cook, to boil.

PENDA	The bottom, base, foot, underpart. (E.g. "The water-pot has a hole in the bottom.")
FENÉK	Bottom, base, foot, underpart.

PEPERKAT	To brim with tears, to be suffused with tears, as eyes.
PETYEREG, PITYEREG	Lacrimo quirito, ploro = to be suffused with tears.

PERA	A kinsman, a relative.–(Bodding, in *Santal Folk Tales*, Vol. I, P. 296, remarks, that this word may be used also as "our friend". Ibid. BHARATA is often quoted as: the bride-groom's friends.)–BARIATKO: Those who compose the marriage procession.
BARÁT	Friend.

PERESAN, PERSAN	To jump or bound, as creatures without feet, to fall, to roll.–PHER: Turn, circumference.–PẠRI, PẠRI PẠRI, PẠRI PẠRITE: Turn, by turns, turn about, alternately, by shifts.–PẠRIẠ: Time.
PEREG, PÖRÖG	Volvor, rotor, volutor = to rotate, to turn, to roll.–PERGŐ: A spinning-wheel.–PERC: A minute.

PESGI, PESKI	An advance of pay.–PAE: A copper or bronze coin.
PÉNZ, PÉZ	Nummus, moneta = money, coin.

PESET PESET	Unpalatable, insipid, unappetizing, unrelishable.
PESZMET	Unpalatable, insipid, unappetizing, dishes.

PETER	To twist, to screw, to writhe.
PEDER, PÖDÖR	To twist, to screw, to writhe.

PHADDẠRI	Criminal, as opposed to civil courts, suits, etc.
FÖD, FEDD	Culpo, castigo = to reprimand, to chastise, to correct.

PHAELA, PHAELAO	To broaden, to widen, to extend.
FEJLŐD-IK	To develop, to widen, to extend.

PHAKAK PHUKUK	To mumble when eating or speaking.–PHOGRA: Having lost the front teeth.–PHOK: The notch of an arrow, the notch on the end of an arrow, where the string fits in.–PHAK: Open space, free space, an opening, an interstice, an interval, an interspace, a gap, a rift, opportunity.
FOG, FOK	Dens = tooth.–Gradus = pin.–The notch on the end of something (as of an arrow).–The eye of a needle.

PHẠKUA	Deceitful, tricky.–PHẠKI: To deceive, to trick.
FOGAS, FOGÁRD	Deceitful, tricky.

PHALNA	A certain, a particular, used when the speaker wishes to avoid particularizing.
FÉLE	Ex tali, eiusmodi = of that kind.

PHẠLTI, PHẠLTU	Supernumerary, superfluous, overplus, surplus.–PHẠJIL: Over and above what is necessary. PHẠUTI: Extra, over and above requirements, surplus.
FÖLÖS	Supernumerary, superfluous, overplus, surplus.

PHANGA	Deceitful, tricky, sophistical, exaggerated. (E.g. in: "It is an exaggerated statement, do not listen to him.")
PÖNYE	Deceitful, tricky.–FANTI: Crazy.

PHEC	To drop, to drip, to fall in spray.–PHICKẠRI: A syringe.–PHOCOR: A squirt, a syringe.–(See also BEC.)
FECSKEND, FÖCSKEND	Aspergo = to spray.–FECSKENDŐ: A syringe.

PHECAN	To backbite.
FECSEG, FÖCSÖG	Effutio, fritino, blatero = to babble, to tattle.–FECSE-LOCSA = Garrulus = chattering.

PHED	The bottom or lowest part of anything, base, foot.–PHEDREN HOR: A neighbour. (HOR:

	A man.)-PHEDAT : Root, base, birthplace.-PAO : The foot.
FÖLD, FED, FŐD	Terra, tellus, solum, regio = earth, soil.-FÖLDI : Neighbour, kinsman.-(SZÜLŐ)FÖLD : The native place.

PHEN, PHENDE	A parable, a metaphor.
PEDIG, PENIG, PENEG	Autem, vero, et quidem, fauste, prospero = although, luckily.

PHENTOR	To fly as sparks.
FÉNY, FÉN	Fulgor, nitor, splendor = the shine, glamour.

PHERE PHERE	To gush, to issue with violence and rapidity, as anything semi-liquid from confinement.
FERCSEN	Effervesco, excandesco = to gush, to issue with violence and rapidity.

PHESAD, PHASAD	Difficulty, violence, wickedness, false accusation; mutiny, sedition.
VESZT	Periculum = danger.-Tempestas = storm.-VÉSZ, VESZ : Perdo, dispero = to sink, to perish.-(IZ)VÉSZ : Tumultus = mutiny, sedition.

PHIDLI	To tease, to card, to open anything that adheres together, or is compact, to disarrange, to disorder, to rumble.
FEJT	Explico, enodo, resolvo = to unroll, to untie, to disjoin.-FINGELEDIK, FINYELEDIK, FINYEL : To involve.-FINYORÁN : Teasing.

PHIKIR	Thought, reflection, consideration, solicitude, contrivance.
FIGYEL	To be mindful, to consider, to observe.

PHINI PHINIẠ	Fine, thin, semi-transparent, as cloth, paper, etc.-PHINI PHIK : Clear, pure, as water; bright, cloudless.-PHINI-PHIK : Smooth, glassy, as a sheet of clear, still water.-(See also PHIRIPHIC.)
FINOM, FINUM	Clarum, purum = clear, pure.-FÉNY, FEN, FÍNI : Splendor, fulgor, nitor = shine, gleam, lustre.

PHIRẠU	To go to steal.-PHIRKẠ : A stratagem.
FÜRKÉSZ-IK	Investigo = to root about, to approach stealthily.-Perquiro, inquiro = to search, to spy out.

PHIRIPHIC	Clear, pure.-PHIRIPHAU : Clear, bright.-PHINẠU : To become clear, as water, the impurities of which have settled at the bottom, to rise to the surface, as the serum or watery part of milk.-(See also PHINI PHINIẠ.)
FEJÉR, FEHÉR, FEIR	Albus, candidus = white.-FEJÉR-IK : Albesco = to become white or clear.

PHIRKI	A door, a window, opening.
FÉRKEZ-IK	Accedo = to penetrate, to get in.

PHIRPHIR	To be restless, skittish, to start suddenly, to turn round, sullenly, restlessly.-PHURTI : Quickly, rapidly, to be quick.
FÜRGE, FIRGE	Agilis, celer, vividus=agile, rapid, vivid, skittish.-FIRKOL : Salito = to bustle about.

PHIT	To reject, defective, imperfect, spurious.-PISIR : To turn back the foreskin.
VISSZA, VISZ	Re, retro = back. - VISSZÁS : Perversus, pravus, distortus = wrong, defective, unsuitable.-VISSZADOB : To reject. (DOB : To reject.)

PHITẠ	Tape, braid, a band of plaited hair used by women to tie up the hair.-PHITI : A skein of thread.-PITET : To card or tease cotton with a bow.-PITI : To curl up, to coil.-PITUẠ PẠTWE : Crooked, serpentine, winding. - (See also PHODLO.)
FINTORÍT, FITORÍT	Curvo, flecto, inflecto = to bend, to twist.-FIKARC : Thread.-FIDEL : A shawl for the head, white.-VITLA : A whim, a winding-engine.-VITLÁZ : To curl up, to coil.

PHODLO	To be frayed, to open or untwist, as the end of a rope, etc. ; not sufficiently twisted, as twine, thread, rope, etc.-(See also PHITẠ.)
FODOR	Crispo = to curl, crisp, fold, plait, twist, twine.-FODROS : Crispans = Curled.

PHOKA	To blister, to rise in blister. (E.g. " His foot is blistered.")
FAKAD, FOKAD	Cutaneous, eruption (as on a foot), sprouting of trees.

PHOLAO	To suffer the pains and penalties of wrong doing, nemesis. (E.g. in: " He suffered for his misdeeds.")
FELEL	Respondeo = to answer for, to account for.

PHOLOK	To clear away, as mist.-PALAK POLOK: Blurred vision, dimly, the grey dawn before anything can be distinctly seen.
FELLEG, FÖLLEG	Nubes = clouds.

PHOR	To cut a dam to allow water to run out, to be breached as an embankment of a dam, etc.-PHUKẠR: An opening, an aperture, a hole through and through, as in a wall, a chimney opening.
FÚR	Foro, terebro = to pierce, to bore, to cut a hole.-FÚRADÉK: Foramen = an aperture.

PHORAO	To change, to turn.
FOROG	Rotor = to turn.

PHORMAN, PHORMAS	To give an order.-PARAMẠNIK, PARẠNIK: Assistant of the headman of a village.
PARANCS	Mandatum, imperatum = an order. - PARANCSNOK: The commandant. - PARANCSŐR. An orderly.

PHORPHOR	Imitative of the sound produced by a strong flame.-PHER: To blaze, to roar, as flames, to foam, to froth.
FORR, FOOR FORRÓ	Strepens, ferver, aestus = to boil, effervescent, hot, burning.

PHUCKẠ, PHUCKUC	Too low down, too short, projection too small, too small.-PHUCIẠ: Small. (E.g. in: " A bullock narrow in the hind quarters.")-PHUCKẠ: Thicker at one end than the other.
FOGY	Decresco = too low down.-FOGYAT: Minuo, debilito = to diminish, too low down. - FOGYATÉKOS: Defective.

PHULẠI	To jest, joke, make fun.–PHULẠNIẠ: A humorist a funny fellow; funny, humorous.
FURA, FURCSA	Funny, jesting, joking.

PHUPHUẠU, PHUPUẠ	To blow, to hiss, as a snake.–PHULẠU: To swell, to distend, to be proud, overweening, vaïn.–PHUR: To blow out of the mouth, to snort.–PUIPUI: To bulge, protrude, swell, as the stomach.
FÚ, FÚJ, FÚV	Flo, spiro, afflo = to blow.–To hiss (as a snake.)–To snort.–FUVALKOD-IK: Turgeo, turgesco = to be proud, to boast.–(FEL)FUJT: Protruding, swelling (as the stomach).

PHUS CATAO	To do one out of anything, not to give, not to receive.
FOSZT	Nudo, orbo, spolio, deglubo = to rob, to denude, to snatch away.

PHUSALẠU, PHUSLẠU	To cajole, to flatter.
HIZELKED-IK	Adulor, blạndior = to cajole, to flatter. HIZELGŐ: A flatterer.

PHUT	To separate, to break from.
FEJT	Explico, enodo, resolvo = to loosen, to untie, to resolve.–Diffundo = to draw, to pull, to take off.–Caedo = to break.

PHUT PHAT	To disperse, each to go his own way.–PHUTẠU: To spring, to begin, to start.
FUT	Fugio, curro = to run, to flee.

PIẠ, PIẠU	To fit closely, as a joint in woodwork.
FŰZ	Plecto, scirpo, vieo, texo = to twist, to joint, to bind together.

PIẠN PAYAN	The first blush of morning, break of day.–(See also BER.)
PIRKAN, PITYMALLÁS, PITYMALLAT	The first blush of morning, break of day.

PICẠ	The buttock.
PICSA	Vulva = genital part (region) of females.

PICLẠU, PICRẠU — To slip, to take a false step.

BICSAKLÁS — Luxatio = sprain.

PIDGẠK, PIDGẠU — To frisk, to gambol, as lambs, kids, etc.; to gallop, as a runaway horse, to twitch as the eyelids, etc., to throb, as an artery.

FICKÁNDOZIK, FICSKÁNDOZIK — Saltilo, petulcio, lascivio = to frisk, to gambol.–FINCOS: Gamboling.

PILCU, PILCUN — Little.–PICOPOCO: Weak, inferior, below par, not up to the mark. (E.g. in: "My bullocks are inferior.")–PIDGI, PEDGO: Short, dwarfish.–(See also PITIC.)

PICZI, PICZIN, PITI — Parvus, pusillus, minutus = small, tiny, dwarfish.

PILHOE — High, higher than the remainder.–PELAO: To trample over, to overcome. (E.g. in: "He threw the (responsibility) on the panchayat.")–PIND: A small raised platform.–PINDẠ: A raised platform round the house.

FÖL, FEL — Pars superior = the upper part.–FELJEBB: Altius = higher.–FÖNT, FENT: Aloft, on high.

PILKI, PELKA — Short-sighted, having a squint, oblique eye.

PILLANT — Nicto, soecto, aspicio = to blink, to twinkle. to glance.–PILLA, PILE: Cilicium = eyelid

---

PILPILẠU — To quake, as with fear.–BHILKI: To be startled, afraid.–PUYUL PUYUL: Very greatly, extremely, applied to fear.

FÉL, FÍL — Timeo, metuo, trepido, paveo = to have fear, to be afraid of something.

PIRIT — Friendly.

FRIGY, FIRIGY — Armistice.–"Entente"; union.

PISKẠ — A common climbing plant, Dioscorea oppositofolia.

PISZKE — Gooseberry.

PISKIC	To part with the tips of the fingers, as the hair; to remove with the thumbs.-(See also PASKA.)
PISZKÁL	Fodico, voluto = to agitate, to stir up, to run one's hand through.

PITHA	Bread, to make bread.-JHINUK PITHA: A kind of biscuit made by sticking two flat cakes of dough together with sweets, etc., between and then baking.-PIKTHAIC: A baker. (JHINUK: A bivalve.)
PITA, PITE	Laganum = a sort of cake.-PÉK: A baker.

PITHIẠ	A market.
PIAC, PIARC	A market.

PITIC	Small, as a child.-PITU: Small, as the ears. (E.g. in: " Some sheep have very small ears.")-(See also PILCU.)
PICI, PITI	Small, as a child, as the ears, etc.

PITIRI	A swelling of the glands, as in mumps.
PITRINGES	Sickly, unhealthy.

PO	To hoe.
POGONYÁZ	To hoe.

POCA, POCLA	Rotten, decayed, unserviceable, feckless. (E.g. in: "What will this feckless fellow do to me?" Or in: "A rascally weakling.")-POC: Imitative of a creaking, or nipping sound.
POCSÉK, POCSOK	Rottenness, dirt, filth, excrement.-FOS: To void excrement.-FOSOS: A feckless fellow.

POD	To build a second house at a distance from the first and to occupy both.-(See also BODLA.)
PÓT	Addimentum, appendix, supplementum = annex, supplement.

PODINA	Mint.
FODOR(MENTHA)	Mint.

PODRA, PODRAHA	Decayed.
PUDRA, PODVA	Rotten wood.

POJO	A large forest tree, Jetranthera monopetala.
FAGYAL	Ligustrun.

POKOT	A frog of the species which appears on the arrival of rains.
BÉKA	Rana = frog.

POKOT POKOT	To scold.
PÓKÁZ	To hackle, to censure severely.

POLOC	To issue in small quantities, to flee.–PUYU PUYU : To issue steadily from a small opening. (E.g. in : " The water is running out.") (See also BHODOR BHODOR.)
FOLY, FOJ, FOLYÁS	Curro, fluo, perlabor, decurro = to run, rush, flow.

POLOK, POLOKH	An instant.
PILLANAT	An instant.

PONEA	Four.–PONEATAK : The fourth.
NÉGY	Four.–NEGYEDIK : The fourth.

PORANI	A living creature.
PORONT	Numerosa proles, servulus = childhood, brood, brat.

PORJA	A tenant, a ryot.–POR JẠTIẠ : One of another cast. (JẠTIẠ : Of or belonging to the cast.)
PÓR	Rusticus, paganus = peasant.

POROE	Fine, as rain drizzling.
PEREG	Drizzling (of rain).

PORSAD	A small piece of flesh meat, food that has been offered to the deities.
PORC, PORCIKA	Membrum, artus = a small part, a little joint.–A small piece of flesh meat.

POSAO	To nourish, to rear, to fatten. (E.g. in : " I have reared that child.")
POSZÁKOL	To eat greedily.-PASZITA : Repast, feast.
POSET	To burst.-POSON : To leak, as bellows.
POSZ	Crepitus = a crack.-POSZOG : To let out belly wind.
POSKA, PHOSKA	Particles not cohesive, rotten, decayed.
POSZKONCA, PASKONCA	Rotten, decayed.-POSZKA : Miserable, decayed.-PISZKOS : Rotten, dirty. - FOSZLÁNY, FOSZTÁNY, FOSZTIKA : Rag, shred.
POSTA	Red thread employed to make the borders of cloth.
FOSZLÁNY, FOSZTÁN	Rag, shred.
POTHA HAKO	A species of fish.-(HAKO : Fish.)
POTYKA, PONTY, PONYTÓ	Carpio, carpus = carp.-(HAL : Fish.)
POTOM	To wrap up, to wrap round as a parcel in paper ; to cover, as a book.-PATHE : To bind round the loins.
PATYOL	To wrap up, to wrap round (as a parcel in a paper).
PUCHLẠU	To twist the tail.
FACSAR	Obtorqueo = to twist.-FACSINTOS : Bandy-legged.
PUCUC, PHUCUC PHUCUC	Quickly, without delay.
FUSS	Be quick ! hurry on ! (FUT : Fugio, curro = to run.)
PUHI	To rain gently.
PUHA	Mollis = soft.
PUKUPUKU	To swell, to be blown or puffed out, to be swollen, to be bulky. (E.g. in : " Frogs puff themselves out.")
PUKKAD	To swell, to be blown or puffed out, as frogs.

PURMU	Damp, wet, to wet.
PERMET	Drizzling rain.–PERMETEZ : To irrigate.

PUSI PAN	A moderately sized forest tree, Ehretia levis.
FŰZ, FYZU	Salix = the willow-tree.–PUSZPÁNG : The box-tree.

PUSI TOA	A small, wild milky plant. (Euphorbia pilulifera.) (TOA : Milk.)
FŰTEJ	The Euphorbia plant. (TEJ : Milk.)

PUSTI, PUSTIĄ	Addicted to smoking.
FÜST, FYZT	Smoke.

PUSTI, PUSTIĄ	A generation.
PUSZDARÉK	Genethlia, natalitia = birthday-celebration.

PUSUR PUSUR	To speak in a low tone, to whisper.
PUSZMOG	To speak in a low tone, to whisper.

PUTĄ, DHIĄ PUTĄ	The whole family.
PEREPUTY, PEREPUTYA	The whole family.

PUTRIT	To become big or swollen, as the belly.–POTPOTO, PUTPUTU : Prominent, swollen, as the belly when full, full stomach.–POTA : Stomach.–PETPOSA : The stomach, the belly.
POTROH, PATROH	A fat paunch, a big belly.–POCOS : Ventrosus, pinguis = paunchy.–POCAK : The belly.

R

RABAC RUBUC	Heavily, without elasticity, without spring, as a heavy creature walking.
ROBOG	Crepo, fremo = to rush, to rustle.–(MEG)-ROBBAN: Cum strepitu adsum = to arrive with noise.
———	
RẠBHUẠ	Ugly and lumpish, ugly and inactive, used by women when scolding men.
RAFONYA	Lumpish.
———	
RABOR	To claw, to scratch with nails or claws.–(See also RAWA.)
RAVASZ	Vulpes = fox.
———	
RACA	Courtyard of a house.
RÁCS	Fence, trellis, grating.–Stable-rack for fodder.–RIGYA: Concaedes = barrier of trees.
———	
RACAP RUCUP	Sound as of anything crisp being crushed.
RASTAG	To crush.
———	
RACATE	To urinate, used only of adult human beings.–(See also: RAJAK RAJAK.)
ROTYÓ	Voiding of excrement.–ROTYOG: To rustle.–RÖSGYE: Ordure, excrement.
———	
RAD, RADA	Scoundrelly, base, disobedient.
ROSSZ, RASZ	Scoundrelly, base, disobedient.
———	
RẠDHUẠ	Shapeless, dry.
REDVES	Decaying, rotten.
———	
RAGAE	Gritty, rough.–RAGAR, ROGOR, ROGOR ROGOR: Stony, gravelly, rough and stony as the bed of a river.–RADGA, RODGA: Stony, gravelly. (E.g. in: "My garden is stony.")
RÖGÖS	Rough and stony, bumpy.–RÖG: Globula, glarea = clod.

RAGAT	Rough, as speech.
REKEDT	Raucus = hoarse (as speech).

RẠGI	Spirited, active. (E.g. in: " It is a spirited horse.")
RAGAD	Rapio = to sweep away.-(EL)RAGADTATÁS: Extase.-RAGADÓS(LÓ): Spirited (horse).-RAGYIVA: Gnavus, solers = spirited, lively.

RAGRAGA	In position, undetached.
RAGAD	To adhere.-RAG: A suffix.

RAJ	Phthisis, consumption.
ROSHAD, ROSSAD	Tabesco = to pine away, to vanish slowly. RAGYA, ROGYA: Blight.-Rust.

RAJAK RAJAK	Moderately heavy, as rain.-(See also RACATE.)
ROTYOG	To crack, to crackle, to nestle, to rattle down.

RAJAK RAJAK	Moderately heavy, as rain.
RAGYÁZ	To rain (in sunshine).

RAJT	Bridle.
ROST	Fibrae = fibre, filament.

RẠK	Cry or note of a beast, bird, or insect.
RÁKOG	Cry or note of a beast, bird or insect.-REK: Croak of frogs.

RAKAP	To rise, to ascend, to appear, to fall. (E.g. in: " The sun is risen.")
ROKKAN	Desideo = to go down, to fall.

RAKEAKA, ROKROKO	Sticking out, projecting, as the branches of a tree.-(See also RAPRAPA.)
(KI)RAK	Expono = to stick out, to expose. (ÁG: Branch of a tree.

RAKHA	To lay an embargo on, to preserve as a forest game.
REKESZ	Gadira, spetimentum, agger = enclosure, fence, preserve.

ṚAKUDAN, ṚAKDAN	Very, exceedingly, applied to height.
REKKENŐ, REKKENTŐ	Very, exceedingly.

RAMO	Carefully.–RAMBAR ROMBOR : Whole, unbroken.
REMEK	Opus magistrale = a masterpiece.–Pars, segmentum = a piece.

RANGA RANGI	Quarrelling or disputing fiercely.
RÁNGAT	Vexo, agito, traho = to drag, to haul, to tug, to pick.

RAOAO	The sound produced by a flawless vessel when struck, reverberent, long drawn, as sound.–RARAN, RARAN RARAN : To clang as a bell, with a shrill sound.–RANRAN : To sound empty.
RENG	To tremble.

RAODAO	To traverse. (E.g. in : " We traversed the whole of this jungle.")
RAJTA, RAJT	Through.

RAORAO	To hum, as a crowd, the hum produced by a large crowd of people.
RAJOZ	To hum, as a crowd.–RAJ : A swarm, a crowd.

RAPRAPA	Sticking out, protruding, as branches. (E.g. in : " They have placed them sticking out and have obstructed the way.")–(See also RAKEAKA.)
REBEG	(?) Impeditus sum = to be obstructed.

ṚAPUT	To break.
REPED	To break, to burst.

ṚASIẠ	Partner, sharer, partnership.–RES : Residuum = dregs, residue, remnants. (E.g. in : " The dregs of this matter remain.")
RÉSZES	Partner, sharer, partnership.–RÉSZ : Pars, portio = part, share, dreg.–(KI)RÉSZEL : To segregate.

RASAO	To solder.
RÉZ	Aes, cuprum = ore, copper.

RASRAS, RASRASAO	The feeling of indisposition at the beginning of an attack of fever.–RAS DHARIA : A dancing boy.
RÁZ	To shake, to jolt.–(HIDEG)RÁZÁS : Feverish ague.–RÁSZTA : Hypochondrie.

RAT	Ray of the sun.–RAJAS, RAJOS : Pupil of the eye.–RAJAN BAJAN, RAJAN BAJON : Pomp and music. (BAJONDAR : A musician.)–RAJ, RAJA : A king.
RAGYOG	Radio, irradio, refulgo = to shine, to glitter, to sparkle (as the sun).–RAGYOGÁS : Splendour, magnificence.–Illustriousness, glory.

RAWA	Temperament, disposition. (E.g. in : " We were delivered by his bravery." Or in : " His temperament is fearful, he is easily startled.")–RAWIC : In comp. implies stealthily, surreptitiously, without authority.–(See also RABOR.)
RAVASZ	Callidus, astutus = cunning, sly, adrift.

RE	In, on, after.
-RE, -RA	In, on.–(MIRE : After what.–MI : What.)

REC	Imitative of a slightly rustling sound, creaking as of boots, cracking as of dry leaves.
RECSEG	Crepo, strepo = to crack (as dry leaves, boots).

REGHA, REGHAO	To sing.
REGE	Vetus cantilena = old„ chant.–REGÉL : To sing an old chant.–REGÖS : The singers of olden days.

REGO PETO	To quarrel, dispute, wrangle, bicker.
RIGOLYA	Quarrel, dispute, wrangle, bicker.

REGREGE	In position, undetached, applied mainly to the teeth and to the flowers of the matkom, which

do not fall from the tree.-RAGRAGA : In position, undetached.

RÖGÖZ — Figo, constituo = to fasten, to fix.-(MEG)-RÖGZÖTT : Constitutus, stabilitus, obfirmatus = settled, fixed, placed, planted.-RAGAD : To stick, to adhere.

REKH — A glutton.

REKKEN — Suffocor = to suffocate.

REMA — Of, if so be, in case it be.

REMÉNY — Spes = hope.

REME TELE — Short, stunted, little, diminished, undersized.-REMBRE : Small.-RIMSIC : Small, little.

RENKESZ — Undersized, little and fat.

REMET — Third stomach of a ruminating animal.

REMESE — Intestinum, rectum = rectum.

REND BEND — Completely, entirely. (E.g. in : "They have fenced it completely.")-RAE, RẠI : Rule, order.-RANEBANE : Plenty, profusion, abundance. (E.g. in : "This man's house appears well provided for.")-RET RETE : In a line, in a row.-RADA : A row, a line.

REND — Ordo, series, regula, norma = rule, order, series, row, range, norm.-RENDBEN : Completely, entirely.

RENGET — Importunately, persistently. (E.g. in : "She is begging persistently.")

RÉNYÖD-IK — To beg persistently.

RENGOS — A long time.-(See also RAKUDAN.)

RENGETEG — Very, much (generally applied to time).

RENKHA — One addicted to liquor whose hand shakes when raising the glass of liquor to his lips.-RUN-RUNẠU : To tremble.-(See also ROHDHO and RUMUŃ.)

RENG — To shake, to tremble.

RET	To wrap up, as a small parcel.
RÉT	Plica, senes=fold, plait, layer.–REDES : Plaited.
RETA	To saw, as when cutting with a knife, sword, etc., to draw backwards and push forwards, as a fiddle bow.–RET : A file.–RUSUK RUSUK, RASAC RUSUK : Sound of cutting, cropping or grazing.
RESZEL	Limo = to file.
RETHA, RETHEA	Small, stunted, undersized.–RETHMA, RETHMI : Small, short in stature.–RUIẠ : Very small.
RÖVID, REUID, RIVID	Brevis, curtus, contractus, concisus = small, short, stunted, undersized.
RIBI RIBI	To wriggle, to shake as one shivering. (E.g. in : " The fishes are wriggling.")
RIBÁL	To wriggle, to shake.
RICOT	To break, to snip off.
RIGYÁZ	To cut off, to clean the trees.
RIKOC ROKOC	Singly, irregularly, unevenly. (E.g. in : " They are coming singly, not in a body.")
RIGÁS	Light, sparse (as a forest).–RITKA : Loose, disorderly, dissolute.–Seldom.
RIMIL SADE	To thunder. (SADE : Sound, to sound.)
RÉMÜL	Tremisco = to tremble, to shiver. (SZÓL : To sound.)
RINGAU	To move quickly or rapidly, with force. (E.g. in : " Make the horse move rapidly, make him gallop.")
RINGAT	To balance, to rock, to swing.
RIÑJHI	Slowly.–RINGAM CINGAM : Quietly, slowly.
RENYHE	Slow, lazy.
RIPIRIPI	To flap the wings as bird of prey hovering over its prey.
REPÜL	Volo = to fly.–REPDEZ : Volito = to fly about, to hover.

RIPRIPI	To stare, eyes wide open, staring.
RÉVEDEZ	To dream.–RÍVÜLÉS, RÍVÜLET : Prodigium = a wonderworking image.

RISĄ	Dysentery.
RISZA	Clunes = the posterior.

RITIĄ, RITI	Joyfully, gleefully, in high spirits.–RITIĄU : To be pleased, to be in high spirits.
RIT, RIÜT, RÜT	Mente corripio = to enchant, to be delighted.

RITIĄU	To be in season, to be in heat, to be sexually mature.
RITTYÓZ	To pollute.–RITTYÓ : Sperm.–RÜHETÉS : Rut.

RO	A fly.
ROVAR	An insect.

ROCOT	To crush to pieces.
RASTAG	To crush to pieces.

ROD	To infringe, to violate.
RONT	To infringe, to violate.–To bewitch.

ROBEA	Pot-bellied, big-bellied.
ROPPANT	Ingens, enprimis, vastus = enormous.

ROGA, RUGI	Diseased, afflicted with a disease, disorder or malady.
RÖG	Disease of cattle.

ROHDA	Lanky, lean.
RIDEG	Macer = lean, slim, thin.

ROJHA	A small earthenware dish.
RICSA	" A kind of mixed dish."

ROK	To pierce, to perforate, to sew, to pin, to butt, to gore.
RÓ	To cut into, to cut up, to notch.–(ÖSSZE)RÓ: To fasten together.

ROK	To prohibit, to hinder.
RÓ	To requite (a wrong).–To reprove.–To censure.

ROKA	The same day, to-day.–ROKA RUKI: On the same day, not deferred till another day.
REGG	Tempus matutinum, die mane = the morning.–RÖGTÖN, RÖGVEST: Instantly, at once.

ROKA	An acknowledgment, as of money.–ROGORIA: A cupidonous person.
ROG	The debt.–RÓ: Censeo, censum, exigo = to claim, to collect.–ROVÓ: Exactor = tax collector.

ROKAO	To stop.
RÖKÖNYÖD-IK	To stop.

ROKOC GHAO	A kind of sore. (GHAO: A sore.)
RÖGÉN	A sore.

ROKOM	Kind, manner, method, sort.
ROKON	Kindred, allied, analogous, like.

RONDHO	Fat, corpulent. (See also RENKHA and RUMUÑ.)
RONDA	Ugly, sordid.–Shaking, trembling.

RONJO	Emaciated.
RONCS	A wreck.

ROPOT	To creak, as shoes.
ROPOG	To creak, as shoes.

ROSAO	To be absorbed in, to be engrossed in, to have the mind taken up with.
RÉSZEG	Ebrius, ebriacus potis, temelentus = intoxicated, benumbed.

ROS AMOL	Derangement of the humours of the body.
RASZT	Splenis tumor = disorder of the spleen.

ROROT	To peel off, or become rough, as the skin.
RÖRŐD-IK	To blunt, to rub off, to rub through, to rub sore.

ROTHA, ROTHAHA	Black and dirty.–ROHOR: To dry, to become emaciated. (E.g. in: " A dry leaf.")–ROTHA: Very black.
ROTHAD, ROHAD, RUHAT	Putreo, putresco = to be rotten.–ROH: A black horse.–ROHFEKETE: Very black. (FEKETE: Black.)

ROTOK	A seam.
ROJT	A fringe.–A seam (?).

RUKU	To shake.
RÚG	Ferio, tundo = to knock, to lash out.

RUM, RUMOK	To be possessed with a spirit.
RÉM	A spirit, a phantom, a ghost.

RUMUŃ RUMUŃ	A sensation as of trembling in the flesh.–RUNRUNẠU: To tremble. (E.g. in: " He is shivering with cold.")–(See also RENKHA and RONDHO.)
RÉMŰL	Tremisco = to tremble.–REMEG: To tremble.

RUN	A method used to keep flesh meat from going bad by half-roasting, during which process its bulk is reduced, shrivelled.–RUN: To crease, to be creased, to shrivel.–RUN TUKUN: To shrivel.–RONGO: To be burnt, to be burnt in cooking.–RO: To singe. (E.g. in: " They singed the fowl.")
RÁNT	Frigo = to bake, to burn, to roast.–(BE)RÁNT: To burn in.–RÁNC: Plica, ruga = wrinkle, pucker, fold.

RUP	To fall down, to collapse.
ROPPAN	Cado, ruor, collabor = to collapse.

RUTRUTU	Puffed out, swollen.
RÚT	Turpis, informis = ugly, misshapen.

S

SABA	A small tributary of a river in which the water is dammed back when the river is full.
SZÁJ, SZÁ, SZÁV	Orificium, bucca = orifice, mouth.-SZÁVA: The Save, a tributary of the Danube.

SABA	Spur, as of a fowl; a dew claw on the hind legs of a dog.
SZABÁS	Forma = form, figure.

SẠBRI	A pole, on which anything is slung and carried on the shoulders of two or more men.-SOP: To hold, to catch.
CAFKA	"A thick and robust stick for the purpose of holding together something."

SABAD, SABOD, SOBOD	Sound, noise, voice.-SAWAL, SOWAL: A question, to cross question. (E.g. in: "I have a question to put.")-SAWALIA: A speaker, one able to address a court or panchayat. SAD, SADE: Sound.
SZÓ, SZAW	Vox, vocabulum, sermo, sonus = word, voice, speech, sound.-SZAVAL: Recital.-ZAJ, SZAJ: Noise, tune.

SABAK	Insipid, owing to the absence of salt or sweetness.-SẠBRẠ: Insipid, tasteless, applied to those things which should generally taste sweet.-(See also CAWAOK.)
COPÁKÁS	Not properly made, sodden, as bread.

SABOL	An iron crowbar.
ZABOLA, SZABOLA	Frenus, camus = bridle, the iron bar of the bridle.

SABSAB	Infiltrated moisture.-SABJA, SABJAO: To become moist by attracting moisture.-SAPSAP: Moisture.
ZÁP	Putridus = moist.

SAD	Authority, power to break in, reduce to subjection. (E.g. in: "I have broken in this bullock.")-SODHI: A preparation of opium.
SZÉDIT	To cause giddiness.

SADGAEAK, SADGALAK	In disorder, disorderly, out of its proper place.-SADGA BIDIR: Lying about, disarranged, out of place, anyway, in disorder, disorderly. (SANAM: All.)
SZÉT, SAZNASZÉT	In disorder, disarranged, anyway.

SADGAL	A moneylender.
SZATÓCS	Tabernarius = tradesman, shopkeeper.

SADOM	A horse.
CSŐDÖR, CŐDER, CEDER	A stallion.

SAE	A hundred.-(In the Korwa dialect: SAIS.)
SZÁZ	A hundred.

SAEDAN	Sandy.
ZÁTONY	A sandy bank in a river.

SAEGAT	Rough, harsh. (E.g. in: "It is rough, not smooth.")-SEGE RORE: Rough, owing to the presence of numerous small bodies, gritty.-SEKSEKE, SOKSOKO: Sticking out, projecting.
SZEGES	Angulatus = cornered, edged.-Rough, harsh.

SAE SUI	Imitative of the sound produced by expiration and inspiration of breath.
SZÉL	Spiritus = breath.-Ventus, flatus = wind, breeze.

SAGAI	Relationship, kinship.-ATO SAGAI: Assumed relationship by those who meet together frequently. (ATO: A village.)
SZEGŐD-IK	Depaciscor, transigo = to bind oneself, to hire out oneself.-SZEGROL ÁGRÓL: Relationship, distant kinship.

SAGAK	The awns of certain grasses which prick when they come in contact with the person ; spear grass, to prick as the awns of certain grasses.-SEGA JẠNUM : A thorny bush. (JẠNUM : A thorny tree or bush.)-SOGE : To insert, to push in, between or amongst.
CEKA, CIKA	Germen herbarum = sprouts, points of grass.-SZEG, SZÖG : A nail.-SZEGES : Thorny.

SAGAR	A cart having solid wheels.
SZEKÉR	Currus, vehes, plaustrum = A cart with solid wheels.

SẠGUN	Omen, applied to both good and bad, but mainly to a good omen.-SAKET : The patron divinity of the Santal doctors.-SẠHẠI : To favour, to aid.-SẠHẠITA : Help, assistance, aid.
SEGITÉS, SEGEDELEM, SEGEDEM	Opitulatio, auxilium, juvamen, praesidiura = help, aid, relief, assistance.-SEGIT, (MEG)-SEHENCZEN : To aid, to help.-CUHADOS, CIHOS : An aid, an assistant.

SAHAO	To suffer.
ZAHA	Heart-burn.

SAHET	To breathe.
SÓHAJT	Suspiro = to breathe.-ZIHÁL : To breathe heavily.

SẠITẠU, SẠINTẠU	To store away, to lay away, to hoard.
SZED, SZÉD	To collect, to treasure up.

SAJ	Dress, ornament, framework, game, to be detached out, to embellish, to decorate, adorn, ornament.-SADOM SAJ : Harness for horses. (SADOM : A horse.)-SAJAO : To adorn, to clothe. (E.g. in : " They put it into a basket.")
SZATYING	A band.-SZŰCS, SZŐCS : Pellio, pellifex = furrier.

SAJAN, SAJON	Watered, as liquor, mixed as oil.
SZOTYKOS	Insipid, soft.-SZOTYVA : Juice, sap, liquor.-ZAGYVÁL : Commisceo = to mix.

SAJAO	To put in, to fill in.
SZATYOR	A market-basket, a pannier, a bag.

SAK	A system of borrowing money under which the borrower himself or someone in his name works for the lender in lieu of paying interest.
SZAKMÁNY	Statute labour.–CÖK : "The conclusion when bargaining."–Muleta = forfeit.

SAK	A division of threads in the woven mattress of a bed.–SAK : A leaf of a tree, book, etc.
SZAK, SZAKA	Pars, frustrum = a part, a division.

SAKHO	A bridge.
SZÁK	(?) Canalis = a conduit.

SẠKHRI, SẠKRI	Dirty, used as a plate, cup, etc., bits of food, grains of rice, etc., that have fallen during a meal.
ZÁKÁNY	Fex, sordidus, squalor, impuritas = dirty, dregs, sediment. – SZAKMAT : A fragment.– SZAKMATOL : To crumble.

SẠKIT	To congeal, to become dense, to coagulate. (E.g. in : "Allow the boiled rice to dry a little.")
SZAK	(?) Pap, mush, puree.

SAKOC	To shake.–SAKSAK : Quiveringly, tremblingly, to shake.–SOKOC : To shog, to shake up, to toss.
ZÖKKEN, ZOKKAN	Contremisco = to bump, to toss.–ZÖKÖG : To be shaken.–ZOKON : Painful.

SAKOR, SOKOR	Sound produced by an obstruction in the wind pipe or nostrils, to gurgle, rattle in throat.
ZOKOG	Plango = to sob.

SAKRA	Narrow, strait, not being room enough.–SAKRA SẠKRI : Narrow, strait, to be in a strait or

	difficulty.-SOKOT : Tight.-SOKRA : A narrow sloping valley of rice fields, generally of second quality.
SZŰK	Angustus, arctus = narrow, strait.-SZŰKSÉG : Inopia, penuria = difficulty, penury.

SẠKUC	To bring into subjection.
ZAKLAT	Cogo, torqueo = to compel, to subdue.

SAKWA	The purple sun-bird, Arachnechtra asiatica.
ZÁKÁNY	A bird.

SAL	A gregarious forest tree, Shorea robusta.
SZIL	The elm-tree.

SAL	Wedges joining the parts of a solid cart wheel.
SZÁL	Pars, fragmentum = a part, a piece.-Stilus, columna = stem, trunk.

SAL	House, as in school house, shop; as in workshop, place, as in dancing place.
SZÁLLÁS	Mansio, statio = house, station.-SZÁLLODA : A hotel.-SZÁLL : Se conferre, se recipere, rivertor = to set out, to join, to alight.

SALA	To pitch out impurities.
SZALAK	Vilis, nauci = vile, worthless.-SALAK : Scoria = waste, dross.

SALAKA	A present of cloth given to certain relations of a bride by the bridegroom.
SZALAG	Vimen, vinculum = ribbon, roller.

SALMUNGẠR	A heavy mallet.
SZALU	A hatchet.

SALSAT, SALTAT, SALTANT	Complete absence of any disquieting or disturbing element.-SOL SULUT : Peace, harmony.
SZELID, SZELED	Mansuetus, mitis, cicur = tame, gentle, mild.

SAMAG
To go away, used only by women. (E.g. in: " Where has our, or my husband gone to ? ")- SANGAR: To go, to walk.

CAMMOG
Otiose procedere, lente quasi furtive progreditur uti ursus = to trip, to dawdle.-CANKOZ-IK, CAMPOZ-IK: To go, to walk.-To sling, to lounge about.

SAMAN
Equal, similar, alike.-SẠMẠNI, SOMẠNI: Many, much.-SAMTHAO: To amass, to collect together.-SAMTHUL: Full, complete.

SZÁM
Tamquam, quasi = similar, alike.-SZÁMOS: Many, much.-SZÁMLÁL: To enumerate.- SZÁM: Numerus = number.

SAMAN
Front, to front or face. (E.g. in: " The front teeth.")-SAMKASẠTI: Face to face, to confront.-SAMEK: A vision, representation of some person seen in dream.-SOMUK, SẠMUK, SẠNMUK: Opposite, confronting. - IN SOMUKIN NELKEDA: I myself saw it.- SẠMUKRE: In presence of, before one's face.-SAMA GHAS: An excellent fodder grass, Panicum colonum. - SAṂAGIRI, SAMAGRI: Materials, elements.-SAMEK: A vision.-(See also SOMOL.)

SZEM, SZÖM
Oculus = eye. - Granum = grain. - Element.- SZEMKÖZTI: Opposite, facing.-SZEMBESÍT: To confront. - SZEMFOG: Eye-tooth. SZEMÉLY: Imago = a vision.

SAMANOM
An obsolete name for gold.

ZOMÁNC, ZAMÁNC
Enamel.

SAMBRAO, SAMBHRAO
To sustain, to assist, to help, to protect.

COMPÓ
An assistant, a helper, a guide.

SANA
Wish, desire, lust. (E.g. in: " I have a desire to go.")

SZÁNDÉK
Propositum, intentio, animus = plan, desire, lust.-SZÁN: Destino, propono = to intend for, to make up one's mind.

SANAK
Instantly, at once.-SAÑJOK: Opportunity, proper time, time.

SZINTE
Commode, maxime, ipse = just.-Etiam, aeque, pariter = again, also, even.-SZÜN: Modus, ratio = manner, method, way.

SAND	A bull.
ZANÓT	Resta bovis = stall-food.

SAN GARHE	To support, aid, assist by taking hold of. (E.g. in : " They support sick people when they give them water to drink.")
SZÁN	To have pity, compassion.

SANSANAO	To be excited or frenzied, to move rapidly as when excited or in a frenzy.–SANSAN : Rustling.
ZÁNDOR	A hot-headed person.–ZENDÜL : Sono, persono, tinnio, commoveor, tumulturo = to sound, to be agitated, become riotous.

SANSUN, SUNSẠN	Silent, hushed, no sound audible. (E.g. in : " When all the people are asleep, there is silence.")–(See also SUNẠN.)
SZŰN	Cesso, desino = stand-still, silence, repose.

SANTAP	Affliction, distress, to cause sorrow or suffering. (E.g. in : "They cause me much suffering.")–SANTAO : To afflict, to cause sorrow, suffering or distress, to persecute.–(See also SONPAT.)
SZENVED, SZENDUED	Suffro = to suffer.–CONDOLL-IK, CANDALOD-IK, CONDOROL : To be afflicted.

SAORA, SẠURI	Dark grey colour.
SZÜRKE	Fuscus = grey, dark coloured.

SAP	To seize, to take hold of, to hold, to catch.–SABOL : An iron crowbar.
ZABOLA, ZABLA, SZABOLA	Bridle, rein.–ZABOLÁZ : To break in, to master.–SZEPET : Cista = trunk, box, bag.

SẠPRUD, SAPROT SOPROT, SUPRUD	To entrust, to deliver over to, to give or put in charge.
SÁFÁR, SÁPÁR	Dispensator, diocetes, promus, condus, obsonator, cellarius, oeconomus = an " official ".–SÁFÁROL : To administer, to manage, to conduct, to hold the duties of an office.

SAPTA	To put close together, to stick together, to join closely.
SZAB	Apto, concinno = to join, to put together.

SAR	A tall grass.-SARHAR : Long, straight and with few knots as timber.-SẠRI : The sheath-like leaves of certain plants, as Indian corn.
SZÁR	Scapus, culmus=stalk, stem, trunk.—The sheath-like leaves of maize.

SAR	To open, as a flower, the eyes of a kitten, puppy. (E.g. in : " If the young men find him they bind him.")
ZÁR	Occludo = to close, to shut.-(FEL)ZÁR : to open.

SẠR	Smooth, level.
SZÁR	Calvus = bald.-SZER : Plica = layer, bed, stratum.

SARA	To turn over on the back, to tumble about like a horse on the ground.-SARHAD, SORHOD : A boundary.-SARBHARAO OCO : To give an impulse, to stimulate, to inspire, to put up to, to prompt, to encourage. (BHARAO : To be frightened, startled.-OCO : A causative inflection.)
SARKAL	Tergum do = to turn over on the back.-SARKALA : Meta finis, margo = a boundary.-SARK : Finis = the end.-SARKALÁS : Incitatio, impetus = an impulse, a stimulation.-SERKENT : Incito = to incite, to stimulate.

SARAJAN, SARAŃJAN, SOROJON, SOROMJOM	Materials, elements, used mainly with regard to marriages, offerings, and sacrifices to a deity.-SIRI : Luck.
SZERENCSE	Sors, fors, fortuna = fate, luck.

SARAO	To complete. (E.g. in : " If you have completed your work.")-SEROM : To assist, to help.-SORO : To constitute, to ordain.-SEREŃ : A song, to sing.-SORON SORON : In unison.-

SOROS: To be superior in size, skill, wisdom, strength, speed, etc., etc., with negative to be inferior to.

SZEREL — To fit, to adjust.–To construct.–To collect.–Constitus, ordino = to constitute, to ordain.–Versifico = to sing.–EGYSZERRE: In unison.–SZOROS, SZERES: Limes.

SARAM — The Sambar stag, Rusa aristotelis.–(See also SELEP.)

SZARVAS — Cervus = stag.–SZARV, SZARU: Cornu = horn.–ZERNA: Fallow deer.

SARẠSI, SẠRSI — Tongs, pincers.

SZER — Instrumentum = instrument.

SẠRDI — To be at the maximum, utmost height, highest pitch or culminating point, to be in full swing. (E.g. in: " The matkom season is not yet at its height.")

SZÜRET — Harvest, vintage.

SARGHẠRIẠ — Expert, clever, handy, adroit.–SARPHẠRIẠ: Clever, quick-witted, handy, adroit, applied to young persons.

SERÉNY — Alacer, expeditus, incitus, industrius, sagax, strenuus, celer = expert, handy, adroit, clever, quick.

SARHAO — To praise.

SZERET — Amor, dilectio = love, affection.

SẠRI — True. (E.g. in: " A true statement.")–SẠRINAK: True, truly, certainly.

SZERÉRÖL — Juste, vere = truly, certainly.

SẠRIẠT — The males of a bride's village, who go out to meet the bridegroom's party.–SẠRẠI: A caravanserai.

ZARÁNDOK, ZARAADNAK — Peregrinabundus, peregrinator = pilgrim, traveller.

SẠRIM — A roof, to roof.–(See also SIRHI.)

SZARUFA — Spars of the roof. (FA: Wood.)

SARKẠRI, SORKẠRI	Belonging to the state or government, etc., common to all partners in the estate.
SZERZET	Praeda = booty, loot.

SARNGAO, SARNGA SARNGI	To be excited, as with anger, to be inflamed, to be in frenzy.–SUṚMA, SURMẠN: To be excited, to be frenzied, to suffer from a paroxism of anger, fury, desperation, impatience.
SZÖRNYŰ, ZERNE	Teter, trux, atrox, dirus, immanus, terrificus = fierce, terrible, cruel, abominable, horrible.–Valde = much, greatly.

SAROTA	A knife used to cut the areca nut.
SARLÓ, SARRÓ	Falx messoria, sicilicula, falcula = a sickle-shaped knife, a pruning knife.

SASTOR	Sacred books, scriptures.
ZÁSZLÓ, ZAAZTO	Vexillum, signum = flag, token, sign.

SASU	To breathe heavily.
SZUSZOG	To breathe heavily.

SATRU	An enemy.
ZÁDOR	A quarrelsome person, preyer, ferreter.

SAYAN SOYON	Rushing, as a stiff breeze. (E.g. in: "Wind is rushing in at an open door.")–SAYAR: To blow hard, strong, as wind. (E.g. in: "The wind came with a rush.")
ZAJONG	Obstrepo = to rush, to bluster, to howl, to sough (as wind).–ZAJ, SZAJ: Fragor, crepitus = rushing, rustling.

SE	To boil over, to well up. (E.g. in: "The water welled up fifteen cubits above the mountains.")
SZÖK-IK, SZEK-IK	Salio = to spring up, to well up (as water).

SE	Or.–SEM: The abbreviated form of SE AM. (E.g. in: "Will you go or not.")–SE BHAL: Rather than, in preference to. (E.g. in: "I work so much and the wages you give me are

small, rather than that I will not work.")-SE GETHO : That at any rate. (E.g. in : " That at any rate it will not be.")-(See also JE.)

SE, SEM	Or.-Or . . . or not.-SEBAJ : Never mind ! That does not matter.-SEHOGY : At any rate not.

SE	Used to encourage or incite.
SZE	Particula adhortandi, age = particle used to encourage or incite.

SEC	Direction, side, quarter, forwards. (E.g. in : " Partisan of his." Or in " He also went with it.")
SZECSKEVÉS	A deserter.

SEKAO	To apply heat, to foment. (E.g. in : " They dry it at fire.")
CIKKEL	Ignem elicere = to light a fire.-CIKÓ : Furnus, caminus = a herd, a stove.-SZIKKASZT : Sicco = to dry.-SZIKRA : A sparkle.

SEKESEKE	To rage, to fume.
ZEKERNYE	Rage, impetuosity, violence.

SEKESEKE	A kind of amulet of bell metal.-SEKE DORE, SEKE MEKE : Covered with ornaments.
CIKORNYA, (?) CIKORÁZ	Ornamentum = ornament.

SEKREC	To clink, applied to metallic objects coming into contact with each other.
ZENG	Insono, crepo, sono, resono, bombillo = to sound, to clink, to buzz.

SELEP	The buck of the Ravine deer of sportsmen in Bengal, Gazella Bennetti.-(See also SARAM.)
ZERGE, ZERI, ZERNA	Chamois.

SELEP SAMANOM	A gorgeous flowering climbing plant, Gloriosa superba L. (SAMANOM : An obsolete name for gold.)-SINIC SAMANOM BAHA : A gorgeous flowering wild plant, Gloriosa superba L. (BAHA : Flower.)
SZŐLLŐ	Vitis, palmes = vine.-CINIFAJ : "A kind of vine." (FAJ : Kind, sort.)

SELSEL	Very fair, applied to fairness of complexion.
SZŐKE, (?) SZÖLKE	Blond, fair.–SELLŐ: A fairy.

SEMEC	Small. (E.g. in : " A small stone.")
SZEMECS	Small.–A little grain.–A small stone.

SENER	A sappling used as a rafter.–ENGA SENER: Thick rafters on which a framework is laid to support the lighter rafter above.
SZIN, ZEEN, ZEIN	Auguriolum, scena, nubilarium = a hut, a barn, a shed.

SENGEL	Fire.
SZÉN	Ignis = fire.

SENGEL ERE	A small species of woodpecker.–SENGEL TITI: The Guinea fowl.
CENEGE, CINEGE	Parus, meancha, seix = a tomtit.–CINKOTA: Aves mixtas de minoribus = different birds of smaller kind.

SERALI	A species of waterfowl.
SZÁRCSA	Fulica, larus, phalocrocorax, uria, querquedula = a coot.

SERE	A kind of bamboo basket used to raise water for irrigating purposes.–(See also SURKAU.)
SZŰR	Percolo, vindemio = to strain, to filter.–(FFL)SZÜR: To raise water.

SERER	To feel as if one were about to be sick, to feel the premonition of sickness.
SÉR	Doles, laedor = to have pains.

SERE SERE, SORO SORO	Fizzing sound, as that produced by fresh firewood when burning.
SERCEG	To crackle, to crepitate (as firewood when burning). –SZÉR: The fire-place.

SERMA	The sky, the firmament, the upper atmosphere, heaven.
SZÉRÜ	Area glabrescit = halo of the sun and of the moon.

SETA — A dog.–SETA ENGA: A slut, a bitch.–SUTUR NA GATAR: The opposite of what is fit and proper. (GUTRUT: A deer who has lost his horn.)–JHUTẠ: False, falsified.

SZATTIN — A little dog.–SUTA: Cornibus minutus = without horns.–A bitch.–Mutilus = mutilated.–A left-handed person.

SETE, SETE SETE — Imitative of a suppressed bubbling sound.–SATA PATA: A slight sound. (E.g. in: " They are searching and making a slight noise.") JHUTUK JHUTUK: Drizzling rain, to drizzle. Applied to rain which though not heavy is continuous.

SETTEG — Murmuro = to murmur.–(SUTTOG: Susurro, musso = to mutter.

SETEŃ — To ooze out. (E.g. in: " Water is oozing from the sand.")–SEDE BEDE: Sound produced by anything moving, floundering or squirming in small quantities, as water.

SÉD, SÉT — Brook, rivulet, rill.

SIBOR — To strip, to take off or out, to take away. (E.g. in: " They stripped him of his clothes.")

CIBAB — Nudus = naked.–CIBIKEL: Sursum traho = to take off.

SIGI — To make a deep incision with an ax.

CIKK — Sectio alicuius rei = an incision.

SIKIL — To polish, to burnish, to make bright.–(See also CIKAN.)

SIKÁL — To polish.–SIK: Aluta inaurata = leather plated with gold.

SIKIR, SIKIH — Dislike, antipathy, hatred.–SIKISIKI: To be restless.

SZIGORÚ — Strict, severe.–Afflicted, troubled.

SIKOL — A chain.–Thin straw rope.

SZÍJ — Corium, lorum, ligula = strap, belt, string, rope.

SIL	Nature, quality, civility, benevolence, humanity, politeness, generosity. - SOBHAB, SOBHAW: Nature, disposition, temperament.
SZELÍD, SZILÍD	Kind, mild, generous.-SZÍV, SZŰ: Cor, çordia, animus = heart, feeling, spirit, mind.-SZIVES: Benevolent, polite, generous.
———	
SIM OT	A form of edible mushroom of a red colour. (OT: Mushroom.)
SZIMÓC, SAMÓCA	Strawberry.-SZÖMÖRCSÖK: Species fungi = an edible mushroom, the German "Maurach".
———	
SIMẠ	To set a boundary or limit.-SOMAN, SOMASOM: Level, equal, alike.
SIMA	Glaber, = bare.-Planum = a plane, levelness.-SIMIT: Levigo, deplano = to smooth, to bare.
———	
SIMBRẠ	Polypus of the nose, a disease of cattle in which the septum of the nose is injured.
CIMPA	Cartilago nasi = septum of the nose.
———	
SIMPARE, SIMPASARE	To be at variance.
ZIMPORÁLATLAN	Cui effigie deest = without likeness.-ZSEMB, SIMB: Jurgium, litigium = dispute, variance.
———	
SIŃ	A day from sunrise to sunset.-SINẠM: Exactly, precisely. (E.g. in: "He looks exactly like him." Or in: "He is precisely like him.")-SIŃ SẠTUP: Often, continually, all day.-SIKTE: Analogously.
(NAP)SZÍN	Lux = daylight.-SZÍN: Color, imago = colour, image.-Forma, figura, species externa = form, figure, external aspect.-Modus, ratio = mode, way, method.-(NAP)SZIN: Lux = daylight.-SZÜNTELEN: Often, continually, all day long.-SZINTE: Etiam, eque, pariter = analogously, as it were, likewise!
———	
SIND KẠTHI	The implement by which thieves make a hole in the wall of a house.
CINKUS	A pointed forcing-implement made of wood or iron; a wedge for forcing.
———	
SINDIR	Edge, ridge.
CIN	A small plank in the middle of the shipboard.

SINGAR	To develop and become rigid.
CINGA	A hanging icicle.

SINIC, SINIT	Opportunity, chance, excuse, pretence. (E.g. in: " He is on the look out for an opportunity to do some one injury.")
SZÍN	Prextextus, prextextum = pretence, excuse.–CINCI: Cunning, insidious, artful, wily.

SIPI	To consult, to conspire, to agree, to elope.
SÜFÜTÖL	To make great preliminaries for something.–To lounge about.

SIPI	To knead, to knead while moist. (E.g. in: " They moistened and kneaded the flour.")
CIPÓ	A small loaf of bread (generally white bread).

SIR	Edge.–SIRA: In the front rank, principal. (E.g. in: " A cow in the first rank of excellence.")–SIRA: A stripe.–SIRA: Edge, corner.–PON SIRA: Four cornered, four square. (PON: Four).–SILI: A rope made of hair.–SILODHA: Huge.–SELE TOKE: Big and little. (E.g. in: " He has a large small family.")–SA: Side, edge, to go or put aside. (E.g. in: " The bullock on one side was wetted and not that on the other side.")
SZÉL, SZÍL	Extremitas, margo, ora = edge.–Confinium = boundary.–SZÉLES: Latus, prolixus = large, prolix.–(?) SZELE: (?) Huge.–SZÁL: Filum = rope.–CÍR: Thread-worm.

SIR	A nerve, a vein.
SZIROM, SZIRMA	Membrana colorata, pellis levigata = coloured membrane, light skin.

SIRHI	Branches laid on rafters underneath thatch.–A ladder, a stair.
CIRE	Dry branches, dry twigs.–Pole, beam, rafter.

SIRI	To inquire, to search for, to look out for. (E.g. in: " We are looking out for brides.")
CIRKÁL, SZIRKÁL	To inquire.—To search for, to look out.

D d

SIRJON SIRIJON, SIRIJOL, SIRIJALA	A creature. (E.g. in: "Who's creature is it? To whom does it owe its existence?")
CIRÁK, CIRÉK	Offspring, scion, descendant, creature.

SIROC SOROC, SIROT SOROT	Slight and frequent, applied to diarrhœa. (E.g. in: "This child has slight but frequent diarrhœa.") -SARLAHA: Rotten, used sometimes in abuse.
SZIRT	Dirt. - SZAR: Merda, excrementum = excrement.-SZAROS = applied to the slight and frequent diarrhœa of children; used sometimes in abuse.

SIROG	To mock, to taunt, to speak harshly.
SIRKA	Protervus = pert, saucy, forward, impudent.

SIROM, SIROM GHAS	A tall grass. (GHAS: Grass.)
SZIROMPÁR	Enchanter's nightshade. (GAZ: Grass.)

SIROPA	A piece of cloth.-SIRPA: A cloth given as a present.
SZŰR	A rough cloak, rough piece of cloth.

SISI SISI	To whistle through the teeth.
SZISZEG	To hiss, to whiz.

SISIRẠN	To quake with fear.
SZISZEREG	Prae timore mussito = to quake with fear.

SISIR, SISIR DAK	Dew. (DAK: Water.)-SISIR HẠNDI: Liquor given at the Sohrae festival.
SZESZ	Vapor, spiritus = vapour, misty exhalation, fume.

SITẠN	A kind of grass.
SZITTYÓ	Juncus, donax, cyperos = rush, bentgrass, sedge.

SIT BHAND, SITH BHAND	Foul, vile, as abuse. (E.g. in: "That woman gives foul abuse when scolding.")-SIDWAK

	BADWAK : Harshly, angrily. (E.g. in : "He scolded me angrily.")
SZID	Maledico, vitupero = to scold, to abuse, to rebuke.-SZIDÁS : A slate, a school slate.-(BÁNT : To offend. - VÁD : To accuse.)-SZITOK : Maledictum, vituperium = abuse, invective.

SITIC SITIC, SITIR SITIR	Gently, as rain.
SZITÁL	Drizzling of rain, to trickle, to purl, as rain.

SITKOC	Unprepossessing. (E.g. in : "He looks unprepossessing.")
SZITKOS	Wicked, abandoned.

SITO SOTO	Not close, having spaces.
SZÉT	Separated, having spaces.

SIWIŃ SIWIŃ	Thin, slender. (E.g. in "He is thin as a lath.")
SOVÁN, SOVÁNY	Macer = thin, meagre.

SO	Smell, odour, scent.
SZAG	Odor, odoramentum = smell, odour, scent.

SOBA	A handful, as much as can be lifted with the fingers spread. (E.g. in : "They gave me a handful of flesh meat.")
ZABÁL	To eat in an unmoderate manner, to cram.

SOBA	To pierce by something thicker than a needle or thorn.-SOBOK : To stab, to push or thrust the end or point of anything with force.
SZABLLYA	Pugio, ensis, gladius, frames, acinaces, sica = sword, pike, spire, lance.

SOBHA	To adorn, pleasant, beautiful.-SUPTẠU : To be good, as a crop; to grow or yield well, to cause to be excellent.-SAPOT, SOPOT, SUPOT : Good, excellent.-SUPUD : Gentle, quiet, peaceable. (E.g. in : "She is a very

	gentle bride.")-SEBEL : Sweet, good to take to, to appreciate.-SEBEL HASA : Good soil.-JOBOR : Great, rich.
SZÉP	Pulcher, formosus, venustus, elegant = beautiful, well formed, graceful, elegant.-Maris = agreeable.-Selectus = select, excellent.-Magnus = great.

SOC SOC	To go out, as fire; to burn feebly, without flame.
SZOTYOG	To totter, to dangle, to be loose.

SODOR SODOR, SODOR BODOR	Sound produced by pouring water.-SUTUK SUTUK : Sound produced by water falling on the ground.-SUT DAK : Water that has percolated into a cavity hollowed out of sand.-(DAK : Water.)-SUT : To dress or tie up the hair.-SUTẠM : Thread, yarn, any filmy substance produced by insects, such as spiders, silkworms, etc.-(See also CODO CODO.)
SODOR, SADAR	To sweep away, like wind, water.-(VIZ)SODRA : The current of a stream.-SODOR : Torqueo = to turn, to twist, to wrest.-SODRÁS : Filum = thread, yarn.

SOHGA	To assist, to help, to accompany.-SOL GOL : Together, in company.
SZOLGÁL, SZÓGÁL	To serve, help, aid.-SZOLGA, SZÓGA : Slave, servant, assistant.

SOHGA, SOHAGA	Borax.-SỌRA : Saltpetre.-JOJO : Acid.
SÓ	Salt.-SÓS : Salted, acid.

SOHOE SOHOE	Sound produced by a large body of running water, as a river in flood.-SOHOR : To thrust, forward, to throw, as a javelin, to hurl, as a dart; to throw as a shuttle.
ZUHOG	Ruendo stremo, fremo = to water, to storm.-SUHAD, SUHAN : Cado, labor, prolabor cum strepitu = to fall with a noise (as water).-SUHADALOM : Ictus, plaga = blow, stroke.-SUHINT, SUJT : Caedo, percutio = to blow, to thrust.

SOK — To carry a plough suspended on the yoke while still on the cattle's neck.

CAKÓ — A burden, a charge, a load.–CÓK, CÓK-MÓK : A burden (?).

SOKHAO, SOKHAT — To dry up, to become parched, to make empty of liquid. (E.g. in : " The water of the fields has all dried up.")

SZIKKAD — To dry up, to become parched.

SOLOK BOKOK — Confused, in disorder, disorderly.–(E.g. in : " Do not disorder the things.")–PURTHI : Quickly.

SZILÁL ZILÁL — Spargo, dispergo = to disorder, to disarrange, to dishevel.–SZELES, SZELEBURDI : Thoughtless, confused, a wind-bag.

SOM, SUM — Miserly, niggardly.

SZOMOR — Affliction, sorrow, sadness.

SOMBOND — Connection, affinity, relation.–SOMBONDRE : In connection with.–SOMPOK : Relationship.–ATO SOMPOK : Assumed relationship by people of a village. (ATO : Village.)–(See also SON, SONGE.)

SZOMBORA, CIMBORA — Consortium, pactio, partitio = connection, community, association, company.

SOMOL — To prepare, to get in readiness, to prepare and take on a journey.–(See also SAMAN.)

SZEMEL, SZEMLÉL — Eligo = to choose out, to select out, to fix on.–Aspecto = to survey.

SON — To measure.–OTKO SONGA : They measure land. (OT : Land.)

CANKOL — To measure.

SON, SONGE — A companion, a partisan, an attendant.–(See also SOMBOND.)

CINCIUS,(?) CINCIOS — Administer, satelles facioris = an attendant.–CINGARA : Consors, socius = a companion.

SONPAT	Fistula = due to a decayed tooth or teeth, any swelling of the lower jaw, due to cancer, etc.–(See also SANTAP.)
SENYV	Tabes, putror, rancor, putredo = rottenness, putrefaction, decay.–SENYVED : To become decayed.

SOP	To be breathless as one out of breath through continual exertion.
SZOP	Sugo, lacto, fellico = to suck.

SOPOR	Near or close to each other, very near or close to each other. (E.g. in : " They are villages very near to each other.")–SOPTÓK : Immediately preceding and following each other in birth.
SZAPORA	Plentiful, abundant.–Rapid.–Fertile, prolific.

SOPOT	To wash cloth by dumping it down on a board or a stone, applied mainly to cloth that has been boiled with ashes to wash fibre by striking in water.
SZAPUL	To soak in lye, to buck, to soak out, to wash.

SOPOT	To be in great fear, to be put out of breath and heart beating through fear.
SZEPEG	Timeo, paveo, trepido = to fear.

SORA	To divide, to split.
SZÓR	Vanno = to disperse.

SORAN	A cart track, an unmade cart road.–SOROK SOROP : A road, a made road, the opposite of a cart track.–(See also SARAO.)
SZER	Plated, vicus, via = street, road.

SOROM	Delicious, good, savory.–(See also SOROR.)
SZERELEM, SZEREM	Dilectio = to be fond of.

SOROM	Modest.
SZERÉNY	Modest.

SORON POTON	Plastered. (E.g. in: " His mouth is plastered with food.")
SZUROK	Resina, pix = pitch, cobbler's wax.-SZURKOS: Sordidus, squalidus = sordid, defiled.

SOROR	To shoot forward as one unable to stop short owing to impetus.-(See also SOROM.)
SZERELEM, SZEREM	Zelus = ardour, impetus.

SOSROC	A grasshopper.
SZÖCSKE	A grasshopper.

SUDRO BUDRO SODRO BODRO, SODO SODO, SODO BODO	Rough, shaggy, hairy, hirsute.-SONDRE, SODRE: To enter without being invited, applied mainly to woman's entering a man's house to live with him as his wife.-SANDGAR, SANDGUR: A shameless, lustful person.
CUNDRA, CONDRA, CONDORA, CODORA, CANDRA	Saga, lanea = a kind of rough cloth.-Having dirty and shaggy hairs.-Meretrix = courtesan, kept mistress.-CANGÓ, CANGA: A woman squandered in debauchery.-CÓDLI: A hussy.

SUGHOR	Good, beautiful, excellent, grand, often used in fault-finding and sarcasm. (E.g. in: " She is a beautiful bride.")-SUTHẠR: Fine, grand, beautiful, used mainly in sarcasm. (E.g. in: " You appear very grand.")
SUGÁR, SUDÁR	Procerus, gracilis = grand, fine.

SUGUI SUGUI	Gently, as wind.-SUGUM SUGUM: Stealthily, without making noise, noiselessly.-SUGU-BUGU: To be cowed and speechless.-SUG BATRA: News, intelligence.-SUGUBUGU: To move or struggle, as a swarm of ants.
ZÚG	Murmuro, spiro, anhelo = to murmur, to blow along.-SÚG: Susurro musso = to whisper. -SUGOGAT: Clam refero = to report secretly. -(BE)SÚG: To denunciate.

SUKHLE	Empty-handed. (E.g. in: " We are empty-handed to-day, we have nothing.")
SZŰKÖL	To miss, to be empty-handed, to be in want of.

SUKWẠR	Sedentary, accustomed to ease.
SZÉK	Sella, sedes, habitation = seat, chair, dwelling.
SUL	Dysentery.
SÜLY, SÜL, SUL	Marisca, mariscus, fungus, scorbutus = scurvy.
SULẠ	The part of a piece of wood reduced in dimensions to fit another, a tenon.
CULÁK	Stipes, palus, paxillus = pile, pier, peg.
SULẠK	A long thatching needle.
SZULÁK	Spina = spine, thorn.
SULGẠU	To kindle, to light, to cause to burn, to inflame, to be at its height, as harvest, or a fruit season.–JELEP JELEP: Showing off, flashing, as lightning.
SÜL	Torresco = to be baked, roasted.–SÜTŐS: Calidus, fervidus = warm, burning.–(EL)SÜL: To explode.
SULI	A kind of raft generally made of " sol " (a small bush frequenting marshes), used to cross rivers when in flood.
SZÁL	Trabica, rates = rafter.–SZELEMEN: Trabs, transtra, tignum = rafter, beam.
SULI	A measure of ten seers. (A seer: about 2 lb.)
SŰLY, SULLY	Pondus, onus = charge, weight.
SULON	Friendship.–SULUK, SULOK: Peace, harmony, to be in harmony.–SULẠN: To deport oneself properly.
SŰLÖLKÖD-IK	Capto, blande insequor = to pursue in a friendly manner.
SUMẠN	To become quiet, to desist, to come out and leave, as a spirit which had possessed one.
SZUNNYAD, ELSZUNNYAD	Dormito = to become quiet.–To desist.
SUNẠN SUNẠNI	To have effect as medicine.–(See also SANSUN.)
SZŰN-IK	Cesso, desino = to cease, stop, end, give over.

SUNDUC	To go or push oneself in head foremost, as an animal to hide among leaves, straw, grass, etc. (E.g. in: " The fowl has hidden herself somewhere.")
SUNYOGÓ, SUNYI	Clancularius, sublestus = hiding, cunning.

SUNUM	Oil.
CINED	Genus olei = a kind of oil.

SUPTIC	The instep, the dorsal of the foot, as opposed to the " talka ", the planter surface or sole.
CUPÁK	A muscular part of the lower end of the leg. (TALP: Sole.)

SUPTIC	A small fan.
SZUPOLYKA	Small.

SUR	To insert, to go into or among. (E.g. in: " This bird is very given to boring its way through the grass.")–SURUN: To bore a hole in a rock for blasting.–SURSA: A disease affecting cattle, perforation of palate.
SZÚR	Pungo, jaculo = to pierce, to pinch, to perforate.

SUR	Excitation of feeling.
ZÚR	To trouble.

SURIK	Manner, mode, like, calculation. (E.g. on: " Give him according to his calculation.")
SZERINT	Like.–According to the calculation.

SURKAU	To sniff, to suck up, to draw up as by a syringe or pump. (E.g. in: " They sniff oil to test it.")–SORKOT: Imitative of the sound produced by an animal sucking liquid.–SIRUP: To nip, to suck in.–(See also SERE.)
SZUR	To strain.–SZURCSOL, SZIRICSÖL: Sorbeo, petisso = to sniff, to suck up.–SZÖRTYÖGET: To sniff repeatedly.

SURUC	Narrow.–(E.g. in: "A narrow path.")–SOR: close, near, nigh, in time or space; to make close, to come near, nigh, close.–SORGA, SORONGA: Big but slim, without rotundity

	of body, applied mainly to goats and swine.–SORO: To take shelter.–SURIAU: To go or push oneself in head foremost, as an animal to hide among leaves, straw, grass, etc.–SURUSUC: To huddle up oneself, as for cold.–SORLOK: To enter craftily. (E.g. in: " That Hindu forced himself in the village.")–SOR MARTE, SOR MENTE: With one rapid impetuous movement.
SZOROS	Angustus = close, narrow, tight.–Paltry, mean.–(MEG)SZORÚL: To take shelter.–SZURDÉK: A narrow path.–Angulus, latebra = a secret corner, a hiding place.–SZORUL: To huddle up oneself.–SZORGOZ: To force.–SZORÍT: Stringo, premo, arcto = to throng, to penetrate.–SZORGOST: At once.

SURUI BẠI	Sunstroke. (BẠI: Evil, disease.)–SURẠJ: The sun.
(NAP) SZÚRÁS	Sunstroke. (BAJ: Evil, disease.)

SUSẠRI, SUSẠRIA	The appellation of the priest who officiates at the Jatra festival. (Jatra = a good omen, a sign, an omen.)
CUC, CUCORMÁNY	Magic, sorcery, spell, enchantment.

SUSTI	Slow, lazy, idle.
SZUSZMA, SZUSZMATA	Lentus, tardus cunctator = slow, lazy, a temporizer.

SUSTOK	Good, well, absence of defect.–SUSULTAK: In good condition physically, to be bright as the countenance.
SZŰZ	Virgo, purus, vacuus = virgin, pure, not mixed.

SUSUẠ, SUSWẠU, SUSṄẠU	To shiver.
ZŰZ	To shiver.

SUTUK	Sound produced by water falling. (E.g. in: " It rained the whole night.")
ZÚDUL	To fall, as rain.

SUTUR	The opposite of what is fit and proper. (E.g. in: " You look untidy or slovenly." Or in: " You are speaking improperly."—" You have done the work badly.")
CUDAR, CUDOR, CODAR (?)	Laciniosus, improbus, turpis, deformis, sordidus, miserabilis = ragged, abject, unpleasant, despicable, miserable.

T

TABA TUBU — Imitative of the sound produced by striking the water with the feet when swimming.–TAPTAP: Imitative of a sound of tapping. (E.g. in: " This horse makes a sound resembling taptap when walking.")–TABUK TABUK: Sound of water agitated in a hole, cavern, or water pot.

TAPOD — Calco, occulco = to tread with the feet.–TAPOG TOPOG: Tundo = to strike with the feet.–TAPOS: Calco, conculco = to stamp with the feet.–TAPOR, TIPOR: To stamp with the feet. - TAPOT, TAPAT: Pulso = to throb.–TAPODAT: A step.

TAGAR — A trough.–TAKNAK, TOKNAK: A small earthenware vessel.–(See also DAKA DAK.)

TEKNŐ, TEKENŐ — Alveus = a trough.–TEKE: Globus, discus, sphaera = a globe, a sphere.

TAGOJ — Strength.

TAGOS — Membrosus = strong.

TẠGUTẠSU — Disorderly, littered. (TASRA: Scattered about.)

TÊKOZOL — Dissipo = to litter.

TAHA — Certainly, without doubt. (E.g. in: " You were certainly there till dawn and you say: I came home during the night.")

TEHÁT, TAHÁT — Igitur, quapropter, ergo = thus, therefore.–Without doubt.

TAHAKA — Without hindrance, easily.–TAHA TẠHI: Quickly, industriously, at high pressure.

TEHET — Possum efficere = possible, without hindrance.

TAHAO — Feeling the way, groping as with a stick to try the depth of water, or in darkness.–TAHAP TẠTUP, TẠHUP TẠTUP: Stumbling, floundering, as one walking in the dark; to go slap dash.–THAPA: To slap, to hit, to beat slightly.–THAPO THAPO, THAPRE: To pat.–THAPA: To come slightly in contact with.

TAPOGAT — Palpo, manu investigo, scrutor, inquiro, experior, certior, fio = feeling the way, to grope in the dark, to investigate.-TAPOG : Nuto, vacillo = to go slap dash.-TAPOD, TAPAD : Pulso = to knock.-TAPASZTAL : Tango = to come slightly in contact with.-DOBOLÓD-IK : To pat.

TAK	Time, season, opportunity, proper time, nick of time, crisis.-TAP : Time.
TÁJ, TÁLY, TÁJÉK	Tempus = time.-TÁJÁN : Circa, circiter = about.-TÁJBAN : At that time, at that season.

TAK	Stock still.
TÖKRÉSZEG	Stock drunk. (RÉSZEG : Drunk.)

TAK	In composition one. (E.g. in : " Which one will you take.")-(PONEA : Four.-PONEATAK : The fourth.)
-DIK	In compositions an affix.-NÉGY : Four.-NEGYEDIK : The fourth.

TAKAO	To look at, to watch, to look intently.-TAKONIA : Staring, starer.-DEKHIT : Deliberately, with eyes open.-TẠHKIẠT : To take oversight of.-(See also DEKHENSE.)
TEKINT, TEKENT	Conspicior, aspicio = to look at, to regard, to watch, to look intently.

TALAO	To spend or pass, as time.-TALAO, TALETAL : Without intermission, continually. (E.g. in : " It rained without change." Or in : " People are coming continually.")-TAL : Equal, without change.
TEL-IK	To spend or pass, as time.- -TALAN, -TELEN : Without (as suffix).

TALEBOR	Rich, gre[illegible]
TALABOR	Large, extended.

TẠLI, TOLI, TULI	Underneath, root, fundament.-TULI : Foundation, as of a wall.
TALAJ	The soil, ground floor.-TALP : Basis = foundation.

TẠLIM	To teach, to instruct, to impart knowledge.
TANIT	To teach, to instruct, to impart knowledge.

TALA	The sole of a boot or shoe.
TALP	The sole of the foot, of a boot or shoe.

TAḶUK	A base in perpetuity, a subdivision of a zila or country, the latter consisting of several taluks.–TAḶUKDAR: A landlord, the holder or proprietor of a taluk.
TELEK	Praedium = real estate, piece of ground.

TAM	In comp. thine.–(See also ME.)
TEN	Tuus = thine. (In comp.)

TAMASA	An entertainment.
TOM	An entertainment.

TANA BHANA	To make preparations to begin a work.–(See also THANAO.)
TANA	Deliberation.

TANAK, TANIC	Or such like, or some one or something similar; perhaps, when used with a verb.–DHANI = An interjection of surprise. (E.g. in: "What! can he go?)–DANDHA MANDHA: Uncertain, vaguely, doubtfully.
TÁN	Forsan, forte = vaguely, doubtfully, perhaps.–An interjection of surprise.

TANDA	To straddle, to keep the legs far apart from each other.–TANGAR MATUA: Lightly intoxicated. (MATUA: Intoxicated.)
TÁNTOROG	Lapso, titubo, vacillo = to stagger, to vacillate. (As one intoxicated.)

TAO	To heat, to be heated, to be excited.–DHAU: Blazing, flaming.–TINGI: To light a fire, to put fuel on a fire. (E.g. in: "They used up all the firewood, burnt it all.")
TÜZEL	To heat, to be heated, to be excited.–TŰZ, TÍZ: Ignis = fire.–TŰZHELY: A hearth.–TŐHELY: A hearth.

TAP	To pass through. (E.g. in: "He dug through.")
TÖP	To pierce, to perforate.

TAPOK	A kind of bird trap.
TAPOGATÓ	A kind of fish trap.
——	
TAPOS	To care for, to nurse.
TÁPLÁL	Sustento, foveo, focillo = to nourish, to support, to care for.–TÁP : Food.
——	
TAPRA TOPRA, TOPRA TUPRI	Very small, as field.–THOPRO BIR : A jungle in which there are no large trees. (BIR : Jungle.)–TOPRA : A small lot of rice land.–TEPRA TIPRI : Small, short of stature.
TOPORA, TÖRPE	Dwarfish, very small, as fields.–TÖRPE BIRTOK : A very small estate. (BIRTOK : Estate.–BÍR : To possess.)–TÖPRÖ : Pusillus = small, short of stature.
——	
TAPTAPA	Wide apart, wide spread, sprawling.
TABÉRTOS	Wide, largely extended.
——	
TARA TORO	In company.
TÁRS, TARÁS	Socius, coamicus, sodalis = a partner, an associé, a compagnon.
——	
TARAR	To creak, to rend, to crack, to split.–TOR : Force, velocity, as of a current, energetically.–THORAO : To clear away by breaking.–TARAO : To dig out, to tear up by roots.–DHARA DHẠRI : To pull, to offer violence. (E.g. in : "The money-lender knocked me about.")–DẠR : To run, to flee, to change residence.–THẠHRI, THẠHRI THẠHRI : Disjointedly. (E.g. in : "He speaks disjointedly.") –(See also : DHOROT DHOROT.)
TÖR	Confingo, subtundo, frio, frango, fero = to break, smash, to crack, to split, to burst, to rush as current.–(KI)TÖR : To break out, to tear up.–TÖRÉS : Callis = a drift.–TÖRT : A fraction. – TÖRI(BESZÉDÉT) : He speaks disjointedly.
——	
TAREN	The shoulder of a human being, the neck of an animal on which the yoke rests.
TARKÓ	Neck, back of the neck.
——	
TARGHA	Method, proper times, proper way, customs, ins and outs. (E g. in : " I have not yet mastered

the ins and outs of this village.")-DHARA: Section. (E.g. in: "Under what section was he tried.")

TÖRVÉNY, TERUIN Lex, jus, ritus = law, custom, ins and outs.

TARGUM To scold, to speak harshly.

DORGÁL To scold, to blame.

TARHAO, TAHRAO To fix, to settle, to come to a decision or determination, to stop, to rest, to remain, to be determined, to be established. (E.g. in: "He made the dam stable." Or in: "He seized it by the ear with his teeth and held it fast.")-THATHAO: To spend time, to remain, to live. (E.g. in: "They could not remain in this village.")-TATLE: Continually.-TATBIR: To take care of.-TATKA: To be alarmed

TART Teneo = to hold, to retain.-Sustineo = to support.-Duro = to remain.-Asservo=to take care of.-Nutrior = to nourish.-Timeo = to be alarmed.-Puto, censeo = to be of opinion, to believe, to think.-TARTÓS: Durable, stable, valid, permanent.

TARKAO To relish, to enjoy food.

TORKOS Glutton, voracious.-Lickerish; given to eating.

TA̤RKHA TA̤RKHI To be seized with spasms, spasmodic twitching of the muscles.

(NYAVALYA)TÖRÉS Epilepsy. (NYAVALYA: Sickness, in general.)

TARSE To be scattered by falling.-TARAL BASAL: Scattered, dispersed, here and there, sparse.

TARASZOL To scatter, to disperse.

TA̤RU The hard palate.

TOROK Jaws, throat.

TARWA̤ To pain, to become tender. (E.g. in: "The feet have become tender through travelling the whole day.")

TÖRVE Wounded by walking, as feet.-TÁRAGY: A sore.

TASAK, THASAK, TASKAO	To move, to shake, to cause to stir, to affect, to overcome.
TASZÍT	To move, to shake, to cause to stir.–TUSZKOL: To push on.

TATA	Grandfather.–TATAEA: The relationship between grandfather and grandson.
TÉTA	Avia = grandmother.–DÉD: Proavus, atavus = = great-grandfather, great-grandmother. – (?) Grandfather.

TATAK	Suddenly.–TATKA MAR: Suddenly, quickly, at once. (E.g. in: " He suddenly arrived.")
TET-IK	Appareo, emico = to appear, to shine.–Adsum = to arrive suddenly.

TATOK, TATAK, TOTOK	A sorcerer.–A juggler.
TÁTOS, TÁLTOS	Magus = sorcerer.–(Name of the priests of the ancient Magyar.)

TAWAK TẠTUK	Stumblingly, flounderingly.–TAWAR TAWAR: To shake, to move, to dangle, to hang and swing, to vibrate.–TIWAR TAWAR: Dangling.
TÉVELYEG	Pererro, divagor = to lounge about.

TE	Into, in, by, with, because, as; used also to form adverbs. (E.g. in: " He died by his own hand.")
TŐL	By, because, as.–ÖNKEZÉTŐL: By his own hand. (ÖN: Own.–KÉZ: Hand.)

TEBEC TEBEC	Quickly, with short quick steps, said of small males.–TIBIC TIBIC, TIBIK TIBIK: Quickly trippingly, said of small females.
TEPECKEL, TIPPEC, TIPEG	To tripple, to mince one's steps.

TEGETEGE, TEGTEGE	To stretch, to pull out as a piece of elastic.–TOC TOC: Stretched out.–(See also DHẠBIC.)
TÁGIT	To stretch.–TÁG: Laxus, latus, relaxus = wide, extended.

TEGHAN, TEGHEN	A prop, anything placed so as to keep an object from falling or changing its direction.
TEGEZ	Pharetra, corytus = quiver.

TEHEŃ, TEHEŇOK To-day. (E.g. in: ' He will come to-day and presently.")

TÉNY, TÉNYLEG An actual fact, a positive happening, positively.

TEJO A maggot.–A creeping insect.

TÜCSÖK A cricket.–A maggot.

TEK To live, to survive.

TENG Victito, dego, vivo utcunque = to live in penury.

TELE Young lice of the species Pediculus capitis.

TETÜ, TETÖ, TETWE Pediculus = lice, especially of the species Pediculus capitis.

TEMBROT Small, little.–TEMEL: Little, dwarfish.–TEMRET: Small, little.

TEMPE Little, dwarfish.

TENGEN To kill for sacrifice.–THANGAR, THUNGUR: Big and little.

TENGERI Summus = highest (with respect to God).–TENGER: The sea.

TERE To anoint with oil and fumeric. (Bodding, in *Santal Folk Tales*, Vol. I, P. 327, quotes for " tere ": to rub.)

DÖRGÖL, DERGEL To rub.

TERE TERE To vaunt or boast, applied to insignificant persons.

TERE-FERE To chatter, to gossip (applied to insignificant persons).

TEREC TEREC Shrilly, in a high key.

TERGELYE Asper = shrilly, rough.

TEREJHAK Big, huge, applied to huge objects lying on the ground. (E.g. in: " The tree has fallen with its huge length on the ground.")

TÉRES Laxus, amplus = roomy, spacious.–TERÜL: To fall with its length.

TEREM TEREM	Quite, applied to fullness.
TEREM	Procreo, profero = to bring, bear, produce.–TERMÉS: Crop, harvest.

TESNEK	As it was, in its first state, without change or detriment.
TISZTA	Purus, merus, non mixtus = clear, pure, unmixed.

TESTA	To endeavour, to apply one's mind to, to exert oneself.
TISZT	Officium, functio = function, duty, office.

TET	A particle affixed to nouns adds emphasis or definiteness, also employed to form abstract nouns. (E.g. in: "The greater part is finished.") -GETTET: The cut.–ACTET: Himself.
TET, TAT	A particle employed for the formation of nouns.–MET: To cut and METTET: Scissura = a cut.–AZTAT: Itself.–ÖTET: Himself. (Ő: He.)

TEWELGAT	Faint, unconscious.
TÉVELYGŐ	Confused, troubled, errant.

TEWET	To confute, to silence, with negative to obey, to move.
TÉVED	Erro = to be confused, to be in error.–TÉVŐ, TEVÉKENY: Active, mobile.

THẠBU	Large, big, very large, very big. (E.g. in: "They have cut the meat into very big pieces.")
TEBE	Thick, misshapen, clumsy.

THAG	To deceive, to oppose, to swindle.
TAGAD	Nego, infitior = to deny, to disavow.

THẠI	A place, to place.–THẠI THẠI: Close together, near to each other.
TÁJ	Vicinity.–A place.

THẠICA	A quarrel, a wrangle, a dispute.
TORZSALGÁS TORZSA (?)	A quarrel, a wrangle, a dispute.

THAK THUK	Imitative of the sound produced by hammering, or one object coming into contact violently with another. (E.g. in: "They hammered each other.")–DHAKA, DHẠKLAU: To push, to thrust.–DHAKA DHẠKI: To push each other again and again during a quarrel.
TAGOL	To beat, to cudgel (soundly).–TAGLÓ: The butcher's hatchet.–DÖGÖNYÖZ: To beat, to strike, to dash, to puff.

THAK, THOK	A division, a pile, a company, a band, a lot, a heap, a party.–(See also DẠHGI.)
TAGOL	To divide.–TAG: Membrum, corpus = limbs, member.–A lot of ground.–A heap.

THAKAMEAN	Well-to-do, rich.
TAKAR	Lego, congero = to collect.

THAKAR BAKAR, THOKOR BOKOR	Greasy, dirty owing to grease, etc., etc., adhering to the person.–TIKOR TOKOR: Hanging down, as mucus from the nose or viscid saliva from the mouth.
TAKÁR	Slime, phlegm.–Blennorhoe.–TAKONY: Mucus, phlegma, mucus narium = mucus from the nose, slime, phlegm.

THAKROK	Applied to the sound produced by driving the thread home when weaving.–THAKRAO, THOKRAO: To threaten, to upbraid, to twit, to bring up old matters.
TEKER	To wind, to wind off, to turn.–TEKETÓRIÁS: To make many formalities, to make a big affair from a trifle.

THẠKUẠ	To deceive, to cheat.
TÖKÍT	To defraud, to purloin.

THAN	Place, the place where a deity is supposed to reside.–THANIT: Residence, place, camping ground.
TANYA	Sedes, villa = abode, farm, camp, hamlet.–TANYÁZ: To reside.

THAN THUN	Imitative of the sound produced when iron is struck by iron.–THANKA THORAN: Loud rapping sound.
DÖNG	To resound (like when iron is struck by iron).

THANAO	To determine, to resolve, to settle. (E.g. in: "He determined in his mind.")
TANÁCS	Consilium, sententia, propositum = determination, resolve, resolution.

THANKAO	To cease, to become less, to decrease.
TÖNK	Ruin.–TÖNKRE MÉN: To cease, to decrease, to be ruined.

THẠR, THOR	There, on the spot. (E.g. in: "I kept him on the spot."–(See also DAR.)
TÉR	Spot.–Place.

THASAK, TASAK	To move, to cause to stir.
TASZÍT	To move, to cause to stir.

THASAO	To mix by kneading.
TÉSZTA	Massa = dough, paste.

THASAO	To do for, used in threats. (E.g. in: "We will take you in court and do for you.")–DHEJ: To succeed, to accomplish, to be able to do.–DEC: To mount, climb, embark. (E.g. in: "He put me up.")
TESZ, TESZEN	Facio = To make.–Creo = to accomplish.–Pono = to execute.–TESZEK RÓLA: To manage (in a threatening sense.)–(FEL)TESZ: To put up.

THẠUKA	The whole piece, as opposed to a part, total, a large quantity.
TŐKE	The capital.

THELA	To push, shove.–TUL: To lift, to raise. (E.g. in: "He raised it up.")–THELA GẠDI: A carriage pushed by a man. (GẠDI: A carriage.)–

	THELA JAL : A fish net fixed on a handle and worked by being pushed through the water.
TÓL, TOLY, TOY, TÚL	Trudo = to push.–TOLÓ : Trusatilis = to be pushed.–TALIGA : Biga, cisium, carruca = vehicle with one or two wheels, generally pushed by a man.–TALICSKA : Pabo = wheelbarrow. (GYALOM : Sagena = fish net.)

THELE THELE	Ample, more than sufficient.–DOROBOTOLO : Full to overflowing.–TILTILAU TOLTOLAO : To be superabundant. (E.g. in : " The cow's udder is congested with milk.")
TELE	Plenus = full up.–TOROKIGTELE : Full to overflowing.–TELESTELE : To be superabundant.

THEMA	To stick in. (E.g. in : " He gave him lime and tobacco, he stuck it in his waist cloth.")–THAMKAO : To cease flowing, to be stanched. –TOMBA : Full. – TOMBRE : To gather together, to assemble.–TOMTOMBAO : Full to the brim.
TÖM, TEM	Stipo = to stick in, to choke, to obstruct, to stanch.–TÖMVE : Stipatus = crammed fully ; full.–TÖMB : A group.–TÖMBEZ : To group.

THENGA	A staff, a club, a cudgel.
TÖNKŐ	A club, a trunk, a stump.

THETHEA, TETHA	To ask a question a second time or repeatedly.
TEDDEGÉL	Factito, frequenter pono = to do repeatedly.

THIK, THIK THAK	Right, correct, exact, accurate.–TAK ROKOM : Method, mode, in and outs, habits and ways. (ROKOM : Kind, manner, method, sort.)
TŐKÉLY	Rightness, perfection, correctness, exactness, accurateness. (ROKON : Kindred.)

THISI	A guard to prevent a ring or other ornament coming off.
TŰZ	To fasten on with a pin.–TŰZŐ : The fastener.–TŰ : Needle, pin.

THIT	Security for a loan.
TÍT, TÉT	A deposit.–A fact.

THOL	Place, abode, to abide, to repose.–TOLA: An outlying hamlet as a part of a village.
TELEP	A near colony, an outlying hamlet as a part of a village.–TELEPED-IK, TELEPSZ-IK: Recumbo, considео, subsideo = to abide.

THOMSOK, THEMSOK	Short in stature, squat, applied to females.–TEMSO, TEMSOK: Short in stature.
TÖMZSI	Squat.

THOPNAK	The hand from the wrist, branched as a tree.
TOP	Ila = hip, leg.

THOPRAM	To plaster, to smear. (E.g. in: "They have plastered it with mud." Or in: "They plaster medicine on them.")
TAPASZT	To plaster.–TAPASZ: Lutamentum = lute, paste-work.–Plaster.

THORE JAN	The ankle bone, shin bone, elbow bone.
TÉRD	The knee. (CSONT: Bone.)

THORO TOTO	Imitative of tooting sound. (E.g. in: "They are tooting on a horn.")–TORRE: Trumpet.
TÁROGATÓ	Buccinator = horn-blower, bugle-player.

THOROT THOROT	To limp, to walk feebly, as from fatigue or age.–THORIO: Feeble.
TÖRŐD-IK	Defatigor, laboribus conficior = to drudge, weary, weaken.–TÖRŐDÖTT: Feeble, weary.

THOSOT MORGOT	Pithless and slovenly. (MORGOT: A depreciatory term.)
TOSZONKOS	Awkward, clumsy, heavy.

THOTKAO, THOTRAO, TUDA	To touch with the point of anything, to employ the point of anything to remove, extract, etc. (E.g. in: "He touched me with the point of his finger.")–TODA: The sharp point of a wooden plough in which the share is fixed.–TUTURI: To cover the head.
TETŐ, TETÉ	Culmen, cacumen, columen, fastigium, apex, summitas, pinna, etc. = a point, a summit.–Caput = head.

THOTMA	Very fat and dumpy.-THOTOMTOROK: Very, extremely, applied to obesity.
TETEMES	Vastus, ingens = very, extremely.-HOLT-TETEM: Panus, atheroma, steatoma = an ulcer, abscess on the throat. (TOROK: The throat.)
THOYO	Hollowed out to a shell. (E.g. in: "They have eaten it into a shell, have eaten all the inside of the fruit, and left only a shell.")
TOJÁS	Ovum = egg.-Shell. (?)
THUBE, THOBLA, THABA THUBE	In a cluster, in clusters, closed or crowded together. (E.g. in: "They have knotted it many times, i.e. made a cluster of knots.")-TOBRE: To gather together, to assemble.
TÖBBSZÖR	Many times.-TÖBB, TEB, THEB: Plus = more.-TÖBB-TÖBB: More and more.-TÖBBIT: Angeo, multiplico, augmento = to multiplicate, to augment, to gather together.
THUTHI	Memory. (E.g. in: "The memory is superior to a book."-This shows the estimate in which oral tradition is held by the Santal.-(See also TODAROT.)
TUD	To know. - To think. - To be able. - TUDÁS: Knowledge.
TI	The hand.-TI BẠISẠU: To be accomplished, to become expert. (BẠISẠU: To be accustomed to.)
TŐ	A stump.-Pars ima, pes = foot.-TÖKÉLETES: To be accomplished.
TIẠK	A sacrificial fowl.
TÍK, TYÚK	A fowl.
TIHKAU	To be hot and painful, throbbing, applied to the sensation which accompanies inflammation.-TIHKẠ TIHKI: Hot and painful.
TIKKAD	Langueo = to weary, to exhaust (by heat).
TIJ	A thing, an article, property, goods.
TŐZSÉR, TÜSÉR	Mercator = merchant.

TIKIN	The meridian, midday, noon.-DHINAN : After-part of the day, afternoon.
DÉL, TÉL, DÍL, DIÉ	Tempus meridianum, meridies = midday, noon.-DÉLUTÁN : Afternoon.
TIRIOT TORIOT	Cry of small parrot.-TIRIO : A flute.
TIRICSEL	To sing as birds.
TOJAHI	Lazy, stingy, niggardly.
DŐZSÖL, DÉZSÜN	To be lazy, to idle.
TOA	Milk, the female breast.-TOA BAHA : The milk flower. (BAHA : Flower.)
TEJ, TÉJ	Milk.
TOA	A part of the female organ.
TŐGY	Udder.
TOBO, TOBO TOBO	To be cloyed, to be surfeited, to be filled to satiety and loathing, to glut, to be exhausted.
TOBZÓDÁS	Intemperance, gluttony.-To feast, to live in debauchery.
TODAROT, TODONTO	To investigate, to inquire.-(See also TUTHI.)
(KI)TUD	Indago = to investigate.-(MEG)TUD : Exploro = to explore.-TUD : Puto, arbitror = to mean.
TOJAHI	Stingy, niggardly, lazy.
TOHONYA	Lazy, sluggish.
TOLOKE	Proud flesh, large granulations.
TÁLÉ, TÁLGYU	Vomica, struma = wen, goitre.
TOLGOYAM IL	Down, soft hair on body of feathered creatures when hatched. (IL : A feather.)
TOLL, TOLÚ	Penna, pluma = feather, down.

TON DEHI, TONDOHI, TONDORI	To investigate, to inquire into.
TANU, TANÓ	Testis = witness.

TOPOT	Reciprocal form of TOT, to peck at each, as fowls, to pull each other's hair when quarrelling.–TOT : To pull out, to extract.
TÉP	Vellico, lanciro = to pull, to pick.–(MEG)-TÉPET : Lint.

TOR	Food and liquor given to the bridegroom's party.
TOR	Feast, banquet, meal, funeral repast.

TOR, TORTOR, TORTORAO	To croak, to croak incessantly, to give no peace.
TORNYIKOL	Blatero, crocito = to babble, to croak.

TORAO	To repay, as a debt.
TÖRLESZT	To pay off a debt.

TORMAR OT	A form of edible mushroom. (OT : Applied to mushrooms almost without exception, and to several forms of fungi.)
TORMA	Nasturtium, cardanum = horse radish. (ÉT : Cibus = foot, dish.–EHETŐ : Edible.)

TORODAN	A kind of fish trap.
TŐR	Laqueus, tenus, decipula, tendicula = loop, tendril, snare, fish trap.

TORTOR	Viscous, tenacious, glutinous.
TORHA	Pituita, mucus = phlegm.

TOTHA	Having a defect in speech.
DADOG, DODOG, DADÁG	Balbutio, blatero, obstrepo, blactero = to stammer, to babble, to stutter.

TUBET	To stuff, to plug, to cram in.
TÖPÖTT	Crowded, compact, crammed.

TUC	To pull out the ear of a straw or grass.
TÜSKE	Thorn, fish-bone.–Straw, grass. (?)
TUHET	To fill full, to cram full, as a store.–DAHALAO: To saturate, to become waterlogged.
TUHASZT	To fill full, to cram full as a store.–DUHAD: Aggregation.–TUHUL (?) = to dam up.
TULẠ	Scales, a balance.
TEL-TŰL	To and fro.
TULAU	To collect.–TULANI: Market dues, claimed by the official who measures and weighs.–TULNI: A partisan.
DÚL	Multam irrogare = to fine.–DULOU, DULLÓ: Official claiming the taxes.–A partisan.
TULIẠU, TULI	Rich, well-to-do, to rise in social position. DẠULAT: Wealth, property.–DẠULATAN: Wealthy, possessed of property.
TULAJ	Solus, peculum, proprium = sole, propriety, wealth.–TULAJDON: Proprius = possessed of property.
TURTA	To invent, to fabricate. (E.g. in: "It is a fabricated statement.")–TORAHET: To embellish, expand or exaggerate a statement or history.
TÖRTÉNET	A history.
TUSẠ	A bud, a leaf bud, a shoot, the tip.
TÜSZŐ	A follicle.–The husk of a fruit.–A bud (?).

U

UẠI	Another, a stranger.
ÚJ, UJU	Novus = new.
UCIT	To be intelligent, to be attentive, mindful, observant, regardful, wise.–UẠKEP, UẠKHEP: Experienced, intelligent, knowing, sensible.–UCRAU: To be seized by a fit of insanity.
ÜGYEKEZ-IK, IGYEKEZ-IK	Attendo, intendo = to be attentive, mindful, observant.–ÜGYES: Experienced, intelligent.–ÜGYEFOGYOTT, EGYÜGYÜ: Dull, stupid.–ÜGY, ÍGY: Causa, negotium, res = concern, affair, cause, transaction.–(?) Res = thing.–Jus = right.
UDI	Petulant, sulky.
ÜDE	Gay, lively, bright, fresh.
UDRẠ UDRI	To go off in companies on the impulse of the moment on seeing, or hearing of others going. (E.g. in: "One year the people through fear were flying.")–UDRẠU: To go off on the impulse of the moment.
ÚTRA (KÉL)	To go off.–UTAZ: Peregrinor, itineror = to travel.–ÚT: Via, iter = way, road.
UH	Cry of pain or sorrow.
UHUGAT	Cucubo = to cry.
UJẠR	To lay waste, deserted, desolated. (E.g. in: "This is the time when the fields are bare.")
UGAR	Arvum novalis, vervactum = fallow land, bare field.
UJOK, UC	To jump about.
USSANT	To run away, to jump away, to escape.–USDI: Stow away !–UGR-IK: Tripudio, salto = to jump about.–ÁSKA: Locust, grasshopper.

UJU UJU	True, accurate. (E.g. in : "Speak truthfully.")
ÚGY	Ita, sic = so, thus.–ÚGY BESZÉLJ : Speak truthfully ! (BESZÉLJ : Speak !)
UJUK	To fall from a standing position. (E.g. in : "He has fallen." Or in : "It fell on him.")
ES-IK, ES, ÉS	Cado, ruor, labo = to fall.
UKHRAU	To pluck up, to eradicate, to be rooted up, to raise up, to stamp, to be imprinted. (E.g. in : "The feet marks are imprinted on the damp soil." Or in : "The marks of the bed are imprinted on his back.")–AK : A figure, a numeral.
ÉK	Cuneus = a wedge-shaped piece, a point.–EKE : Aratrum = plough.–(BE)ÉKEL : To imprint (as feet marks, etc.).–ÉKIRÁS : The cuneiform script.–(IRÁS : Script.)
UKHUR	A spring of water.–UJHLAU : To pour out.
UGRÓGY	Flumen = a river (?).–ÜGY : A spring of water.
UKUT	Burning to tell, to know, to see, etc., unable to keep a secret.–OK : To smoke, to be burned as food when being cooked.
ÉGET	Burning.–ÉG, ÍG : Ardeo, flagro, uror = to glow, to burn.
ULA	Metal bush fixed into the nave of a wheel, on which the axle rests.–(See also OL.)
ÜLÉS	A seat.–ÜL, IL : Sedeo = to sit, to rest.–ÜLLŐ : Incus = an anvil.
ULI DAK	Saliva.–(DAK : Water, liquid.)
ÜLEDÉK	Sediment (of any liquid substance).
UMAR	To fill as full as it will hold, as a measure heaped full of grain, to give liberally. (E.g. in : "If he recovers I will give you as much as you can take.")–(See also AMAR OMOR, ELEM CELEM, EPEL and UPEL.)
EMEL	Aufero = to take.–Levo = to lift.
UM AREC	Pouring, as if one were pouring water on himself for a bath. (AREC : To throw water at.)–

	UM: To immerse, to bathe, to baptize.–UNẠN: To spread as a report, a rumour.
ÖMLESZT	Pouring water on himself.–ÖML-IK: To pour.–ÖNT: Fundo = to pour, to sprinkle, to water, to discharge itself, to overflow. (ÁRASZT: To throw water at.)

UMDHI	To be drowsy, to be very sleepy.
ÉMÜL	Expergiscor = (?) to awake.

UMUK	A certain (person). (E.g. in: " He blamed many, this one and that one and the other.")
AMA, AMAZ	A certain (generally a person).–That one.–EME: This one.

UŃ	To twist, as strands into a thread.–(See also BUNCAMPA.)
FON, FONY	Neo, filo, texto = to twist.

UNKẠ	A little over and above the exact weight, given to the purchaser.–(See also INKA.)
INKÁBB, ENKAB	Magis potius = rather, besides, more.

UNU UNU, UNU ẠNU, ẠNU ẠNU	Of many kinds, various, of different degrees. (E.g. in: " Many kinds of stories are heard in the country.").–UNẠK: As much as that, so much. (E.g. in: " He did not give us so much as that.")–UN KHON: Since then.–UN ANEC: Not till then, only then.–UN DHẠBIC, UN DHẠRIC: Up till then, up till that, up there.–UN: Then, at that time. (E.g. in: " I was not there then.")
ANNYI, ANNA, ANN-J-AN	Tot, tanti = of many kind, various.–Tantus = as much as that.–ANNYEG, ANNYI-IG: Tamdiu = not till then.–ANNYIRAG: Tam, adeo = up till then, up till there.–ON: An affix with a locative sense.

UPEL	To arise, to come into existence, to appear, as an apparition or a ghostly visitant.–(See also EPEL.)
EMELKED-IK	Levor, elevor, erigor = to arise, to come into existence, to appear.–EMEL: Levo = to lift.

URẠLIA	One who incites, induces, allures.–URẠL: To persuade, to induce, to incite, to instigate, allure.–URIẠU: To have presence of mind, to occur to one on the spur of the moment, to feel an impulse to, to suggest itself to. (E.g. in: "I lost all presence of mind.")
URALJA	One who dominates the others.–URALKOD-IK: Regno, domino, imperor = to govern, to, dominate.–(ÖN)URALOM: Presence of mind, self-control.–ÚR: Dominus = master, Sir.

URIC	Firm, steadfast, tight. (E.g. in: "Hold tightly, hold fast.")
ERŐS	Firmus, robustus = firm, steadfast.

URIC HON	A species of large rat. (HON: Rat.)–(See also ERGO.)
ÜRGE, ÜRÖG	Cuniculus, curculio = a species of rat.

URU SURU	Out of sorts, indisposed owing to a catarrh (cold). (SURSUR: To dart.)
HURUT	Catarrh. (SZÚR: To dart.)

URUT	To cause to spin round by pulling a string first one end and then the other, to rub on a stone as when sharpening a knife, axe, etc.
ŐRÖL	Molo, pinso = to grind, to mill.–KÖSZÖRÜL: To rub on a stone. (KŐ: Stone.)

USAS	To help, to assist, to minister, to give respite or relief.
ÓSZ, ÓZ	Tueor, caveo = to watch, to guard, to help, to give relief.

USẠT	To be exhausted, as soil; insipid as food; faded as a flower, to lose strength.–USTẠHA: Exhausted, faded.–ẠSIT: To die down, as plants in winter, to be exhausted.
ASZOTT	To be exhausted, as soil; faded, as a flower.–ASZÚ, OSZÉ: Siccus, aridus = dry, arid, withered.–Macer, macilentus = lean, meagre.

USKUR	To rouse, incite, excite, stir up, to energize, to stimulate.
USZÍT	To incite, to excite, to energize.–UZÉS: Incitatio = incitation.

USLẠT — Acknowledgment of payment, to give credit to in an account, a receipt, from usual to repay.–USRAU : To hasten, to succeed, effective, ready, active.

ÜZLET — A business.–ÜZ, ÍZ : Pello, fugo = to hasten.–ÜZ : Exerceo = to exerce, to be active.

USNA — Having inoculation or vaccination marks on the person : rice which has been boiled before being husked.

ÜSZÖK, ÜSZÖG — Titio, torris, serugo, myagrum, rubigo = brand, scald, embers, mildew.

USUK PUSUK, USKUPUSKU — To move about.–USKẠU : To raise up, to move.–(PHUSPHAS, PHASPHUS : Slightly, very small in quantity.)

IZEG-MOZOG — To move often, but slightly.–UCCU : A word of tempes. – (?) " Rush ! " – (The German " Heissa ! ")

UTẠ — To turn up or lift up with the snout or head ; to root, as swine. (E.g. in : " The bullock hit me with his head.")–UTIC : To horn, to hit with the horns.–UTKẠ : To turn up. (E.g. in : " He is hoeing and turning over the soil.")–UTKAU : To prize, to raise or force with a lever.–UTHUL UTHUL : Throbbing in the head when in pain.–OTOR : To pull down, to dismantle, to demolish. (E.g. in : " They pulled down the walls.")

ÜT, IT, ÖT — Cudo, figo, infligo, tundo, pavio, quatio, tango, percutio, ferio = to hit, to toss.

UTAHULI, OTAHOLE, OTAHULI — One after another, before and after with an interval of a day or two.–UTHUM : Owing to, in consequence of. (HOLO : Every day, repeatedly.)–OTON TAENOM, OTON TAEOM, OTOR GOTOR : One after the other, in Indian file.

UTÁN, UTON — Pone, post = after.–In consequence of. (HOL-HOL : Tum-tum = first one then another.)

UTET — To obtain a living.

ÉLTET, (?) ÉTET — To obtain a living.

UTKUT — To nudge.

ÜTKÖZ-IK — Impingo = to nudge.

UTLAU	To raise anew, to raise to the surface, to become known, to make known, to boil up or over.–UT UTU: Rising above the surrounding surface, bossed, bumpy.–UT: A camel, a dromedary.
ÖTL-IK	Mano, penetro, injicior, invado = to press in, to press.–To appear.–(KI)ÖTLIK: Ebullo, ejaculor, exundo = to burst out quickly, to boil up or over.

UTU	Relish.–JEL UTU: Flesh meat.–HAKO UTU: A fish relish.–UDKHUD: Food.
ÉT, ÉTEL, ÉTEK	Esca, cibus = relish, food.–SÜLT ÉTEL: Flesh meat.–HAL ÉTEL: A fish relish.

UTU PUTU	To be anxious, to fret.
ÁLALL, ÁTU	To be anxious, to fret.

UYUK	To bring down the hand, or the hand grasping anything.
UJJAK	The fingers.–UJJ: Digitus, dactylus = finger, toe.

APPENDIX II

SANTAL TUNES

SANTAL TUNES[1]

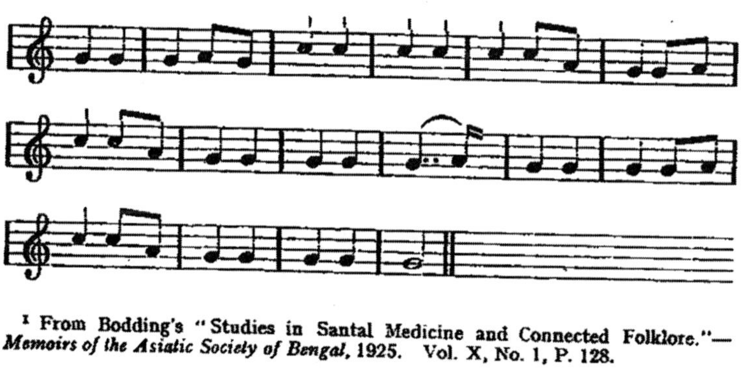

[1] From Bodding's "Studies in Santal Medicine and Connected Folklore."—*Memoirs of the Asiatic Society of Bengal*, 1925. Vol. X, No. 1, P. 128.